Fractional Freedoms

Fractional Freedoms explores how thousands of slaves in colonial Peru were able to secure their freedom, keep their families intact, negotiate lower self-purchase prices, and arrange transfers of ownership by filing legal claims. Through extensive archival research, Michelle McKinley excavates the experiences of enslaved women whose historical footprint is barely visible in the official record. She complicates the way we think about life under slavery and demonstrates the degree to which slaves were able to exercise their own agency, despite being caught up in the Atlantic slave trade. Enslaved women are situated as legal actors who had overlapping identities as wives, mothers, mistresses, wet-nurses and day-wage domestics, and these experiences within the urban working environment are shown to condition their identities as slaves. Although the outcomes of their lawsuits varied, *Fractional Freedoms* demonstrates how enslaved women used channels of affection and intimacy to press for liberty and prevent the generational transmission of enslavement to their children.

Michelle A. McKinley is the Bernard B. Kliks Professor of Law at the University of Oregon Law School. She has published extensively on public international law, globalization, and legal history, particularly the law of slavery. McKinley has received fellowships from the American Council of Learned Societies, the National Science Foundation, the National Endowment for the Humanities, the American Philosophical Society, the Newberry Library, and was fellow in residence at Princeton University's Law and Public Affairs program. She was awarded the Surrency Prize by the American Society for Legal History, and the Lidia Parra Jahn award for her article "Illicit Intimacies."

STUDIES IN LEGAL HISTORY

Editors

Sarah Barringer Gordon, University of Pennsylvania
Holly Brewer, University of Maryland, College Park
Michael Lobban, London School of Economics and Political Science

Felice Batlan, *Women and Justice for the Poor: A History of Legal Aid, 1863–1945*
Stefan Jurasinski, *The Old English Penitentials and Anglo-Saxon Law*
Sophia Z. Lee, *The Workplace Constitution from the New Deal to the New Right*
Michael A. Livingston, *The Fascists and the Jews of Italy: Mussolini's Race Laws, 1938–1943*
Michelle A. McKinley, *Fractional Freedoms: Slavery, Intimacy, and Legal Mobilization in Colonial Lima, 1600–1700*
Karen M. Tani, *States of Dependency: Welfare, Rights, and American Governance, 1935–1972*
Mitra Sharafi, *Law and Identity in Colonial South Asia: Parsi Legal Culture, 1772–1947*

Fractional Freedoms

Slavery, Intimacy, and Legal Mobilization in Colonial Lima, 1600–1700

MICHELLE A. MCKINLEY
University of Oregon

CAMBRIDGE
UNIVERSITY PRESS

CAMBRIDGE
UNIVERSITY PRESS

University Printing House, Cambridge CB2 8BS, United Kingdom

One Liberty Plaza, 20th Floor, New York, NY 10006, USA

477 Williamstown Road, Port Melbourne, VIC 3207, Australia

314-321, 3rd Floor, Plot 3, Splendor Forum, Jasola District Centre, New Delhi-110025, India

79 Anson Road, #06-04/06, Singapore 079906

Cambridge University Press is part of the University of Cambridge.

It furthers the University's mission by disseminating knowledge in the pursuit of education, learning and research at the highest international levels of excellence.

www.cambridge.org
Information on this title: www.cambridge.org/9781316620106

First published 2016
First paperback edition 2018

A catalogue record for this publication is available from the British Library

Library of Congress Cataloging in Publication data
Names: McKinley, Michelle A.
Title: Fractional freedoms : slavery, intimacy, and legal mobilization in colonial Lima, 1600–1700 / Michelle A. McKinley, University of Oregon
Description: New York, NY : Cambridge University Press, 2016. |
Series: Studies in legal history | Includes bibliographical references and index.
Identifiers: LCCN 2016026761 | ISBN 9781107168985 (hardback)
Subjects: LCSH: Slavery–Law and legislation–Peru–Lima–History–17th century. |
Women slaves–Legal status, laws, etc.–Peru–Lima–History–17th century. |
Marriage law–Peru–Lima–History–17th century.
Classification: LCC KHQ2920. P44 M35 2016 | DDC 342.8508/7–dc23
LC record available at https://lccn.loc.gov/2016026761

ISBN 978-1-107-16898-5 Hardback
ISBN 978-1-316-62010-6 Paperback

Contents

Figures

Tables

Maps

Acknowledgments

Over the course of writing this book, I have received generous and insightful comments from numerous colleagues and friends. I thank Carlos Aguirre, Maribel Arrelucea, Susana Baca, Steve Bender, Herman Bennett, Larissa Brewer-García, James Brundage, Sherwin Bryant, Antoinette Burton, Hugh Cagle, Jesús Cosamalón, Sueann Caulfield, Mariana Dantas, Laura Edwards, Brodie Fischer, Katharine Gerbner, Malick Ghachem, Pablo Gómez, Bob Gordon, Janet Halley, Michael Hoeflich, Betsy Kuznesof, Jane Landers, Sophia Lee, Sonia Lipsett-Rivera, Renisa Mawani, Sally Merry, Bernie Meyler, Nara Milanich, Joane Nagel, Rachel O'Toole, Kunal Parker, Sue Peabody, Ricardo Pereira, Aziz Rana, Karen Spalding, Amy Dru Stanley, Tamara Walker, Barbara Welke, David Wheat, and Alex Wisnoski. Renzo Honores – a walking encyclopedia of all things legal procedure – saved me from committing egregious errors and saying foolish things. Kris Lane and Karen Graubart later revealed themselves as reviewers for Cambridge, and their perceptive and generous critiques have made this an infinitely better book.

At the University of Oregon, I am profoundly grateful to Erin Beck, Liz Bohls, Michael Hames-Garcia, April Haynes, Lamia Karim, Daniel Martinez-Hosang, Carol Stabile, Lynn Stephen, and Courtney Thorsson for providing a stimulating feminist intellectual community at the Center for the Study of Women in Society. My colleagues at the law school, Adell Amos, Stuart Chinn, Michael Fakhri, Susan Gary, and Ibrahim Gassama deserve special thanks for tolerating my endless prattle about legal cultures and histories that were far removed in space and time from the verdant Pacific Northwest. I appreciate those who make the University of Oregon a wonderful place to teach, learn, and serve – Isla Dane, Jill Elizabeth, Polly Habliston, Sabrina Leathers, Terri Libert, Robert Long, Stephanie Midkiff, Tonya Perkins, Kelly Sparks, and Debbie Thurman.

The origin of this book dates back to animated conversations during misty winter walks along the Malecón in Miraflores with María Emma Mannarelli, and I am indebted to her for inspiring me to continue along the research path she forged with *Pecados públicos*. Special thanks are due to my indefatigable and meticulous research assistant, Raúl Jimmy Martínez Cespedes, and to the dedicated archivists at the Archivo Arzobispal de Lima, Laura Gutiérrez and Melecio Tineo.

Portions of this book have been presented at several annual meetings of the Law and Society Association, the Rocky Mountain Council on Latin American Studies, and the American Society for Legal History. This research has also been discussed at the University of Michigan's inaugural program in Race, Law and History, the Law and Humanities Colloquium at Cornell Law School, the TePaske seminar in colonial Latin American History at Georgetown University, the Berkshire Conference of Women's Historians (the "big Berks"), and the interdisciplinary "Law As" *tertulia* at the University of California-Irvine School of Law. Friends and colleagues have graciously invited me to present at Stanford Law School, UC-Davis Law School, University of Minnesota, University of Pennsylvania Law School, the Newberry Library, and Vanderbilt University. Portions of Chapters 3 and 5 were published previously in the *Yale Journal of Law and the Humanities* and *Slavery and Abolition*.

As a feminist writing about care work and domestic servitude in the past, I am reminded constantly of the ways that I depend on a vast web of care work that sociologists have cleverly dubbed the "global nanny chain." This book would never have come to fruition without the affection and support of Juan Guevara, Elizabeth LaMar Sanner, Brett Raney, Beatriz Solorio, and Marilu Shupigahua. Norma, Maruja, Fernando, Mama Meche, and the entire Rodríguez clan deserve my deepest appreciation.

I have also accrued financial debts to many who took interest in this project and supported it with kind curiosity. Thanks to Linda Musumeci at the American Philosophical Society for repeatedly imparting good news to me about the Society's support for archival research. I received grants and fellowships from the National Endowment for the Humanities, the American Council of Learned Societies, the National Science Foundation's Law and Social Science Program, and the Newberry Library. A year at Princeton as a Law and Public Affairs Fellow provided the respite to finish the book, and was a perfect environment to write, reflect, and engage. The Deans of the School of Law, Margie Paris and Michael Moffitt, Rich Linton and Moira Kiltie at the Office of the Vice President for Research, the Oregon Humanities Center, and the Center for the Study of Women in Society provided repeated funding for my archival research, and only politely asked (like my children) when I thought the project would be done.

My intellectual debts extend to those who are no longer with us in body, but always in spirit. Peggy Pascoe – peerless historian, mentor, colleague, and friend – reminded me the summer that she died, how important this work was, and not to rush. Icylin McKinley insisted that I combine anthropology with law, and taught me firsthand about the politics of the domestic sphere. Kerry Liewicki reminded me why I love to teach. Alex Rodriguez and Keith Aoki left us too soon. I learned from my father, Ray, the love of narrative and the delight in telling a good story, and I am grateful to him for sharing his lifelong passion for oral history with me.

My greatest debt goes to my children, Max, Isadora (Izzy), and Gideon. They were always upbeat and cheerful about embarking on yet another summer in Lima and patient with their mother's erratic disappearances for hours on end to that mysterious place called the archive. They were good humored when their mother absentmindedly attended to their needs while being immersed and haunted by the subjects of the past. They accompanied me on many walks in rather dodgy sections of downtown Lima as I searched for old convents and churches, despite their lack of interest in the historical wonders or dubious architectural charms of old decrepit buildings. On one memorable occasion, Izzy and I timed a walk between Barrios Altos (today's Santa Ana parish) and the Cathedral to see how long it would have taken María Josefa to get back and forth to give her statement of consent to marry Pedro. (Walking quickly that day, I felt the perils and pitfalls of the historian who loved too much.) I thank them for their encouragement, unconditional love, and constant support.

I could not have asked for a better midwifery team for this book: Holly Brewer, Sally Gordon, Dirk Hartog, Sarah Levine-Gronningsater, and Chris Tomlins, intellectual doulas and midwives extraordinaire, patient with the long gestation, and supportive when it was time for the final push.

Gideon relocated with me to Princeton, and endured the eighth grade in the wilds of New Jersey. Because he has lived the longest with the idea of this book, Gideon asked me when I would be finished and how I would know when I was done. I replied that someday it hopefully would all make sense; that I would have figured it out only when I thought I knew what it was like to be a woman, enslaved, vindicating her grievances and fighting for her children in the seventeenth-century ecclesiastical courts of Lima. Hopefully, this book conveys some of the determination and tenacity that enabled the not infrequent victories of these litigants.

Introduction

On August 9, 1659, Ana María de Velasco filed a complaint in Lima's ecclesiastical court against her owner, the cleric Pedro de Velasco.[1] Ana asked the court to impose an obligatory transfer of ownership on the grounds that Pedro had deflowered her and punished her cruelly. In addition, Ana requested a new appraisal of her purchase price and restitution of back wages. Her complaint reveals a cleric obsessed with his young domestic slave, a man who stalked and beat her and forced her to live in isolation with their two young children to cover up their sinful cohabitation. When she tried to leave Pedro, he raised her purchase price so that her meager earnings as a laundress were inadequate to make the monthly payments toward her freedom. Then Pedro limited her day-wage earning potential by denying her any opportunity to seek live-in employment, which also had the effect of keeping his nocturnal access to her intact.

Desperately trying to avoid returning to Pedro, Ana filed a lawsuit. Fearing reprisal, Ana asked the court to protect her from the wrath that would surely be unleashed once he learned of her complaint to his religious superiors. Ana requested that she and the two children be placed in protective custody (*depósito*), which would prevent Pedro from locating them until the magistrate had a chance to investigate the charges and find her another owner. Ana further asked that the court grant her request for a new day-wage arrangement that would give her at least two hours a day to attend to her litigation, which was the amount of time customarily allotted to slaves who were pursuing legal claims. Despite Ana's enslaved status, she sought legal recourse against her master – a high-ranking cleric – and tried to control the terms of her enslavement by both changing owners and lowering her purchase price. Months later, Ana secured a partial victory in her case when the ecclesiastical court granted her many of the concessions she sought.

Cases like Ana's raise a set of questions that animate this book. How could a young enslaved woman assert claims to personhood, wages, and virtue when her legal status was that of mere property? How did the dynamics of gender, status, sexuality, and religious virtue shape the contours of Lima's slaveholding society? How did the civil law of slavery enable enslaved litigants to access justice from the same legal institutions that simultaneously enforced the laws of property, succession, and contract that legitimated their enslavement?

I situate enslaved women like Ana de Velasco as legal protagonists who occupied multiple identities as mistresses, street vendors, wives, mothers, wet nurses, religious servants, and domestics, and explore how these experiences within the urban labor market conditioned their identities as bondswomen. In addition to and often in tandem with legal action, enslaved women used channels of affect and intimacy to attain freedom and prevent the generational transmission of enslavement to their children. Although attentive to the overarching oppressive structures of slavery, this book reveals instances in the lives of enslaved women when they acted as subjects rather than human property. More broadly, a review of the voluminous amount of slave litigation demonstrates that access to courts and the power of the Catholic Church shaped early modern Iberoamerican slaveholding societies, constrained the repressive behavior of slave owners, and afforded the enslaved a measure of autonomy over their lives in bondage. A retrospective look at these proceedings tells us how litigants and their advocates strategically exploited the rhetorical power of liberty within the courts, even when their lived realities were decidedly *unfree* and *unequal*.

Readers may reasonably ask whether the appeal to law was not after all proof of Ana's ultimate disempowerment. Ana had no one else to turn to: she seemingly led an isolated and sequestered life in religious enclosure with her owner's co-conspirators or in servitude with Pedro. It is true that those who seek legal recourse are often among the most powerless and that they unwittingly reify patriarchal structures through their appeals rather than undermine them. Others may challenge the very words that struck me as I first read through Ana's folio nearly a decade ago. "He importuned me repeatedly to enter into illicit relations, persuading me to leave the convent. As a result of his tender caresses and entreaties, I gave myself to him."[2] The tenor of the words she uses to describe the persistence with which Pedro seduced her and convinced her to leave the convent where she was interned strikes us as chaste, circumspect, and confessional. Though Ana was not illiterate, her words were mediated through her notary's (and perhaps her confessor's) pen. As José Jouve Martín argues, these utterances were polyphonic, in that both litigants and notaries collectively shaped and produced the scripted narratives we read today.[3]

Ana de Velasco appears fleetingly in the archival record on three other occasions. Twice, we see her name in the parish sacramental ledgers as the enslaved mother of Juan Asunción and Petronila – who were freed at the font by Pedro de Velasco in 1653 and 1656 respectively.[4] The baptismal register is formulaic and discreet on the subject of the children's paternity, simply reciting that each child was born to Ana de Velasco, slave of Pedro de Velasco, and an unknown father. See Figure 4.5. Were it not for Ana's lawsuit in 1659 in which she named Pedro as the children's father, their paternity would have remained unrecorded like that of countless illegitimate children of Spanish fathers and enslaved mothers. We know that Pedro died in 1666 and that the following year Ana married Francisco Mexía.[5] The marriage of Ana de Velasco, *mulata libre*, and Francisco Mexía a free *cuarterón*, is recorded on August 3, 1667.[6] What transpired between Ana and Pedro in the seven years following her lawsuit is not clear, and unfortunately, Pedro de Velasco's last will and testament did not survive the passage of time. Given the proximity of Pedro's death and Ana's marriage, we surmise that Pedro either freed her by testament or that she negotiated a lowered purchase price prior to Pedro's death.

Fortunately for historians, Ana's archival footprint is felicitously large (though not oversized). Aspects of Ana's case are found in other change of ownership (*variación de dominio*) lawsuits, although some were unique to her situation.[7] Ana appealed to the judges to find a suitable owner for her whom they deemed moral and honorable. Ana denounced her owner's sexual improprieties to his superiors, using a judicial forum to expose their illicit relationship and Pedro's obsession with her. This was more powerful than parish gossip about a lascivious priest.[8] Her actions subjected Pedro to disciplinary sanctions by his superiors.[9] Pedro had to respond to the accusations in front of an ecclesiastical panel, even if all he did was refute the charges in a defensive manner. Given his family's prominence, Pedro's obsession with his young slave was socially indiscreet and imprudent. Though Ana was presumptively dishonorable as an enslaved young woman, Pedro's behavior transgressed the boundaries of prescriptive masculinity that derived from the honor of his office as well as the social expectation that he would behave as a respectable patriarch.

How could Ana convincingly allege that enslaved litigants were allotted two hours a day to devote to their legal matters? Were these arguments based on law or custom? Comparative law scholars typically address these questions under the rubric of legal transplants.[10] Undoubtedly, Ana reiterated what every aggrieved subject knew – litigation was slow and time consuming. Recalcitrant parties had to be personally served before they were legally required to respond to a complaint, interrogatories had to be drafted, witnesses had to be summoned and questioned, and judicial panels had to weigh evidence before ruling on even the most mundane issues before the court. Prosecutors, procurators, lawyers, judges, and notaries were occupied with high-volume caseloads; Iberoamerican litigation was characterized by heavy evidentiary burdens, prolonged delays, and uneven judicial representation. Thus, it seems reasonable that pursuing a case would take two hours a day. What is more remarkable, perhaps, is the expectation that Ana would be entitled to those two hours from her workday to seek a legal resolution to her situation.

Slaves' access to courts was primarily a continuation of legal practices developed on the Iberian Peninsula beginning in the High Middle Ages. Indeed, many arguments made in New World slave litigation echoed those made by enslaved litigants on the peninsula.[11] This represents the view of legal transplants from comparative legal scholars that a somewhat seamless transition of legal processes and institutional practices unfolded between Castile and the *ultramar* (Spain's overseas possessions). Lima was severed geographically but joined spiritually and administratively to Spain – undergirded by the crown's indefatigable efforts to maintain the illusion of spatio-legal contiguity within its realm.

In this book, I look broadly at the juridical and social currents that unfolded at the time of Spain's imperial expansion to the Americas to contextualize the normative legal tradition in which slaves litigated their claims. As scholars have repeatedly shown, colonial subjects quickly acquired an avid appetite for litigation. Iberian litigiousness – already notorious on the peninsula – became a constant feature of life in the New World.[12] Barriers to court entry for legal dependents (widows, slaves, children, unhappy wives, indigenous subjects) were low, replicating a peninsular pattern of expedited legal recourse through direct appeal to the crown from *desamparados* or *miserables*.[13] Court-appointed protectors assiduously took on the cases of *desamparados*. Instrumental motives undergirded this zealous representation – many aristocratic creoles (criollos) sought nomination to the ecclesiastical court as an accelerated step to securing a coveted administrative career.[14] Appointments to the ecclesiastical court were segues into the higher echelons of the viceregal or the Archbishopric administration that were limited exclusively to members of the peninsular nobility.

Careerist notions aside, the absolutist discourse of good government (*buen gobierno*) and the king's political authority enveloped the viceregal bureaucracy and those with aspirations to join it. This meant that judicial actors and institutions were invested in litigating on behalf of slaves and other legal dependents – even if the substance of their complaints was of less interest than upholding and exalting the king's authority. Justice – rooted in the idea of *buen gobierno* – provided Iberoamerican subjects with a vernacular with which to express their claims. The ideal of "good government" created an expectation that a remote and benevolent sovereign existed, "onto whom all manner of protective policies could be projected."[15]

Justice, legality, and law were articulated in early modern notions of loyalty and benevolence.[16] Archbishops and viceroys were appointed on the basis of their "wisdom, piety, and liberality"; they were counseled and exhorted to be men of justice and clemency.[17] Justice and legality were vigorously debated not only on the Iberian Peninsula but also in Lima's ecclesiastical and city councils by viceroys, judges, prelates, priests, and parishioners alike. The mutuality of justice and abjection created an expectation of intervention and, in some cases, resolution by a more powerful remote intercessor, who delegated his authority to locally appointed officials.

Here we have the essential scaffolding of the early modern Iberoamerican system of justice or what we might call the architecture of paternalism. This rendition is by no means a triumphal narrative of the civil law of slavery: this book describes modest demands for liberty decorously veiled in a paternalistic discourse of protection and abjection. Nevertheless, the demands resonated within a judicial system that operated on clientelism and personal patronage. Although we may quibble among ourselves as to how much agency slaves really exercised given these parameters, very few would argue that legal action was devoid of protagonism.

A further consideration that explains the volume of litigation among colonial subjects is related to the creolization of Iberian practices of law. Both civil and ecclesiastical courts encompassed a bifurcated system in which procurators and *letrados* (university-trained professionals) assumed various duties in litigation. Procurators had no formal legal training.[18] Like notaries, procurators could purchase their office, while others garnered their training through apprenticeships to more senior personnel. Procurators drafted briefs (*escritos*) and complaints, ushering necessary paperwork through the lower rungs of the legal ladder, and entered written pleas on behalf of the complainant. In essence, industries of procurators and notaries provided legal advice and representation to those who would not ordinarily have access to crown-appointed protectors and to litigants of modest means.[19]

How did slaves and other colonial subjects construct networks through which to transmit legal knowledge? How did Ana become a savvy legal actor? Ana's legal sophistication makes sense when we consider that she was enslaved within a distinguished ecclesiastical household and that she was raised for sixteen years in the Monasterio de la Encarnación, one of the largest and most prestigious convents in colonial Lima.[20] Many of the litigants whom I discuss were attached to prominent households of viceregal and ecclesiastical administrators, curates, judges, and magistrates. Others toiled as religious servants (*donadas*) in the elegant cloistered quarters of abbesses and elite laywomen, women who often mobilized their relationships with powerful magistrates, magnates, and notaries to minister their legal affairs.[21]

Slaves garnered reputational knowledge about the legal acumen of procurators, judges, and notaries and could learn about the outcome of pending cases by listening to professional gossip in their households.[22] Not infrequently, married slaves who belonged to different owners instrumentally used the professional relationships between their owners to shore up their conjugal rights. Many enslaved litigants within elite households besmirched their owner's reputation by airing their grievances in court. Slaves constructed and circulated legal knowledge among themselves, spreading the word of the protective powers of the church and its courts for plebeians, in the plazas as they ran errands, washed clothes, and sold foodstuffs and in the city's ubiquitous *pulperías* (small shops that sold food, wine, and dry goods), bakeries (*panaderías*), and religious spaces wherein they labored and worshipped. The records also show that litigants frequently borrowed arguments that were successful in similar cases (*pleitos*), importing them into their own legal repertoire.[23]

Slaves learned about protective legal provisions and mobilized them in court, preventing them from becoming dead letters. Legal mobilization was most pronounced in the area of family unification and conjugal rights. When an owner's travel plans threatened to separate a married couple, spouses quickly sought court intervention to prevent such separation by claiming their marital rights. Similarly, hundreds of male slaves raced to hallowed ground to protect themselves from secular prosecution by claiming sanctuary.[24] Other areas of legal action were pursued: divorce, annulment, inheritance, enforcement of self-purchase contracts, clarification of testamentary and baptismal bequests of manumission, and remedy for battery, assault, and extreme cruelty (*sevicia*). However, in none of these areas was success as pronounced as it was in cases pertaining to family unification and ecclesiastical immunity.

This raises the practical question why enslaved litigants pursuing claims other than spousal unification demonstrated such willingness to engage with the law when the chances of favorable outcomes were negligible. My sense from reading through these records is that a successful outcome was never foreclosed. From a top-down perspective, the crown and church devoted extensive resources to establishing a judicial system to adjudicate complaints of *miserables* and *desamparados* throughout the Americas. Most cases were resolved by split decisions, derived from the canon law's preference for conciliation between the parties.[25]

From the litigant's perspective, we need to expand our views of what constituted "success" or legal efficacy. An exclusive focus on the "law" or even the tribunal does not take into account the importance of early stages of claims making: seeking advice from a procurator, drafting a complaint before a notary, or coming to the notary armed with witnesses that enabled a litigant to draft an interrogatory. If success is viewed too narrowly, we lose sight of the power of *censuras hasta anatema* that were read by priests at high mass at the behest of enslaved litigants. These *censuras* threatened the malfeasant parties with excommunion. Errant parishioners would not be able to partake in the body and blood of Christ. Moreover, *censuras* were posted on the church doors (*tablillas*) for all to see, alerting everyone to a parishioner's iniquities and violation of the law.

Thousands of *censuras* were read in Lima's churches every year. *Censuras* were powerful shaming mechanisms with real consequences for recalcitrant parties in legal claims, especially when issued within the context of a religious society. *Censuras* were an equally compelling means of summoning witnesses, functioning as a sort of spiritual subpoena. These extralegal measures and pretrial motions may seem like petty wrangling on the lower end of the judicial scale, but they built up a powerful momentum that compelled courts to rectify wrongs and that recalibrated the equilibrium between enslaved peoples and their owners.

SLAVERY, COMPARATIVE SLAVERY STUDIES, AND THE LAW

Fractional Freedoms is part of a veritable boom in studies examining slaves' entanglement with the law in colonial Latin America.[26] Legal records provide the most complete picture of the daily life of urban Hispanic American enslaved peoples. North American scholars draw richly on slave narratives, letters, novels, and abolitionist treatises, but Iberoamerican scholars have comparatively little access to the voices and experiences of Latin American slaves, especially during this early period. There is, however, a prolific legal record at our disposal.

Slaves quickly assimilated their owners' litigiousness, zealously claiming rights and airing grievances that were read before magistrates in daily court sessions. Even incomplete or unresolved case records abound with interrogatories and witness statements. Exhorted by priests intoning *censuras* at mass and by public calls for witnesses (*publicación de testigos*) posted by judges, Limeños traipsed steadily into notaries' offices to relieve their consciences or attest to what they knew about a particular case. Though parties never faced their adversaries in courtrooms, their complaints were the grist for parish sermons, feast-day gossip, and hushed conversations in the city's numerous *pulperías*. Not infrequently, slave complaints were heard in the important sessions of Lima's city council (*cabildo*), diocesan synods, and in the high court (*Real Audiencia*).

Of course, legal records are not perfect sources. Neither are they unmediated texts. And they reflect an Iberian rather than an African sensibility.[27] Yet because of the pervasive tension between agency and structure in slavery studies, we are drawn to litigation as evidence of agency and resistance. Venturing away from the early legocentric/textualist examination of slave codes and royal decrees, scholars today pay close attention to court records in the hope of providing an intimate look at the individual experience of enslavement. This rich body of archival sources demonstrates how slaves actively created legal norms and customs and pressed for rights far beyond their legislative intent.

The law of slavery is undeniably about power. This stark realist view is readily apparent in laws that authorized and legitimated human ownership. Slaves did not possess conventional sources of political or economic power that would sway courts in their favor. But slaves repeatedly recruited courts to redress their grievances and, despite their situational disadvantage vis-à-vis their owners, often prevailed in their complaints. If we embrace only the realist or biopolitic vision of law, we overlook counterhegemonic processes of resistance and negotiation and minimize the power of early modern debates about justice. Our scholarly development in the law of slavery reflects realist sensibilities, as well as the enduring question of how the law can be simultaneously wielded in the name of liberty, salvation, and bondage.

MANUMISSION, QUASI EMANCIPATION, AND GENDERING
THE TANNENBAUM THESIS

Every two decades or so, the study of slavery and the law shuttles between agency and resistance, reflecting the trends in slavery scholarship more generally.[28] Early historians of the laws of slavery focused almost exclusively on the promulgation of written codes, royal decrees, and viceregal proclamations, and linked the redaction of ameliorative slave codes to theological and philosophical dilemmas of human bondage.[29] Earlier generations of Latin American historians studied the institutions of law, governance, and the church, and the men who were appointed to run them. Indeed, much of colonial Latin American historiography was synonymous with the history of legal institutions.[30] These studies were not focused on subaltern resistance or agency; rather they traced the transfer of legal and religious institutions, or the consolidation of economic and political systems. Slaves, Andeans, and subalterns only figured into such works as objects of studies of grand rebellions, uprisings, or acts of capitulation.

On the agency side of the pendulum, scholars were drawn to study those without history, shifting the focus away from celebrated revolutionaries or maligned traitors toward tool breakers and dilatory workgang members (hitherto denounced as lazy, shiftless, and undisciplined) as cultural and political agents. As scholars palpated the complex textures of resistance, they became more interested in cultural brokers: those comparatively obscure figures who converted, cooperated with, slept with, and negotiated with social superiors in order to secure better deals for themselves, their children, or communities within the structures of slavery, religious conversion, and colonialism.

Inevitably, a new generation of historians began to fret about the enchantment with resistance, exceptionalism, and the absence of attention to coercive state power. As the pendulum swung back toward structure, it collided spectacularly with the forceful thesis of slavery as social death and its axiomatic denial of personhood. However, there was too much empirical evidence of agency and resistance (particularly from Latin America and from gender history) to capitulate completely to the social death thesis. Instead, there was convergence around negotiation and accommodation. Latin Americanists who had been constrained by futile efforts to prove the mildness of slavery or to demonstrate disputed racial democracies found the resistance-accommodation continuum quite congenial. The continuum also paved the way for an incipient rapprochement between Latin American legal history of slavery and sociolegal history.[31]

By my own chronology, we should have headed back to structure (or at least gravitated ineluctably in that direction) a decade ago. However, this has not happened. Rather, recent accounts interrogate the often comfortable coexistence of accommodation and resistance in the lives of enslaved peoples. Many scholars attribute the current state of the field to the reliance on local records as historiographical tools, fueled by the cultural turn, the attention to gender and race, and the attraction to microhistorical and biographical methods.[32] Local records reveal a great deal more about daily contestations and pragmatic accommodations than royal proclamations and imperial decrees. The reliance on (or turn to) microhistories is not without its critics. The somewhat muted critique relates to the lack of an overarching comparative model or "big question." As one scholar commented, "We are left wondering how to generalize or integrate these cases into larger narratives about slavery ... beyond the [cumulative] examples of the diversity of each."[33]

With this grand theory desideratum, unsurprisingly, we have returned to the comparative questions posed by Frank Tannenbaum nearly fifty years ago in *Slave and Citizen*. Tannenbaum claimed that the influence of Roman law on Iberian slave laws, combined with the pervasive authority of the Catholic Church, endowed slaves with a legal and moral personality and created greater paths to manumission than the common law.[34] Alejandro de la Fuente led the charge in Latin American legal history, revisiting the Tannenbaum debate in a symposium during which he asked what Tannenbaum can still teach us about the law of slavery. Like de la Fuente, I find the first part of the Tannenbaum thesis useful for thinking through slave litigation and "claims making." Tannenbaum's faith in the Iberian laws of slavery has been the subject of deserved critique. As de la Fuente points out, Tannenbaum gave laws "a social agency that they did not have."[35] Indeed, it was litigants like Ana de Velasco who pressed their claims in courts and secured important gains against their owners. Nevertheless, it was significant that Ana litigated a claim against her master within a normative framework that denounced the condition of enslavement as contrary to natural law. Apertures – or fissures – in slavery's legal edifice could be wedged open when claims were brought within a jurisprudential framework that valued liberty.[36]

Alfonse the Wise, drafter of the *Siete Partidas*, pronounced slavery to be "the vilest and most contemptible thing in the world," in contrast with liberty, which was "honorable and precious."[37] Slaves were brought to the Iberian Peninsula through capture and trade throughout the High Middle Ages and the early modern period: historical epochs characterized by a militant Catholicism that framed the legal conditions for emancipation and bondage.[38] By the age of imperial expansion in the sixteenth century, Iberians had developed an expansive body of laws to regulate status and set conditions for ownership and emancipation. Borrowing heavily from the Justinian code, the *Siete Partidas* had extensive provisions for manumission compared to the British Atlantic common law tradition. Tannenbaum erroneously equates the *Partidas'* legal provision for manumission with its nearly automatic guarantee. Moreover, he controversially claims that the moral personality of slaves under the civil law created more harmonious postemancipation societies than chattel slavery systems that were marked by hostile racial segregation and rigid exclusion.

Critics dispute the relevance of either Justinian or Iberian legal codes in their appraisal of slave systems and slave experiences and the construction of

postemancipation societies in Latin America.[39] Royal edicts exhorting masters
to Christianize, feed, shelter, and clothe their slaves were largely ignored unless
masters were convinced that their enforcement would increase their slaves'
productivity or quash rebellion. Scholars of slavery in Louisiana query the
veracity of the claim that the civil law tradition was favorable for slaves.[40]
Empirical scholarship reveals that Louisiana's large population of free blacks
coexisted seamlessly with racial subordination and repressive master-slave
relations despite Louisiana's civil law tradition and its Latin heritage. Rejecting
both Tannenbaum's thesis and the "exceptionalism" of Louisiana within US
slavery, scholars have concluded that slavery continued to be harsh and brutal,
showing little preference for manumission or evidence of egalitarian race relations.[41] Consonant with arguments in legal realism and Critical Legal Studies,
Tannenbaum's critics deemphasize the importance of law, challenge the autonomy of the legal institution, and unmask its collusion in perpetuating socioracial hierarchies, and reiterated the racial subordination of Latin American
postemancipation societies.

These various scholarly approaches have had a chilling effect on the comparative conversations of slavery and the law in the Americas. Today, Tannenbaum
invariably surfaces in any discussion conducted by Latin American historians
of the law and slavery like the proverbial uninvited guest. Chastened by decades of skeptical materialist scholarship, we gingerly ask, what do we want to
do with Tannenbaum? Can we use him to support our case studies with (yet)
more empirical evidence that slaves made use of the law, or should we discredit
the thesis on the basis of its proven shortcomings and outdated assumptions?
Whether the Tannenbaum thesis is used as a signifier of agency or refuted on
materialist grounds depends on one's scholarly orientation in sociolegal history. In her work examining the legal maneuvers of the royal slaves of El Cobre
(Cuba), María Elena Díaz rejects the opportunity to use Tannenbaum's thesis, explaining that she worries that his "static, anachronistic, and even reduc-
tionistic approach to the realm of the law may obstruct the formulation of
more sophisticated and challenging questions along new lines in [the] field."[42]
Notwithstanding these valid reservations, it seems reasonable that we use
Tannenbaum's thesis to understand the legal framework adopted by subalterns
and situate it within broader sociolegal conversations about law, legality, and
legal mobilization.

Despite the controversy generated by the Tannenbaum debate (or perhaps
because of it), comparative approaches came to frame the historiography of
slavery and racial formations in the Americas during the 1980s and 1990s.
Much of the scholarship has been focused on Brazil and the United States,
with Cuba coming in as a third site of research.[43] Concurrently, parallel
developments in legal history and sociolegal studies converged to reinvigor-
ate the fields of comparative law and slavery studies and Latin American legal
studies. Moving away from formalist analyses of legal codes – or handwring-
ing over the inefficiency and tenuous reach of the law (the infamous breach

between *el hecho y el derecho*) – Latin American legal studies have been nourished by writings in gender and subaltern studies and political and legal anthropology that have increasingly insisted on the power of the law as an agent of both counterhegemonic and traditionalist forces.[44] Social scientists in Latin America – particularly those studying gender-based and *campesino*- or identity-based mobilizations – have decentered the state as the legitimate object of analysis in an effort to account for the complex negotiations that less powerfully situated actors engaged in through legal action. These studies specifically reject the narrow conflation of law with governance.[45] Cultural anthropologists urge us to focus on law as process rather than outcome. Perhaps the most significant impact has been felt in the shifting emphasis on sources that derive from the cultural turn in history. Local archival records revealed a wealth of primary data on gender and class relations, demographic and marital patterns, and intimate struggles between superiors and subordinates that reveal courts as vibrant outlets for settling disputes around rights to property, liberty, paternity, inheritance, and marriage.[46] This turn to local sources reflects a generational shift and a preference for interdisciplinary studies. The lively debate between ethnographers and historians about the writing of history and culture has stimulated greater attention to the sources we choose and the interpretive methods we adopt and has made us more aware of the privileging of certain histories in national narratives. Ethnographers who have devoted a longer period of time to reflecting on the writing of "culture" have contributed to the richness of this conversation.

Given the intense debates around the Tannenbaum thesis over the decades, it is surprising that his claims have not been considered from a gendered perspective. Indeed, *Slave and Citizen* has been underappreciated by historians of gender, despite its emphasis on the civil law's multiple avenues to manumission.[47] Slavery scholars have repeatedly demonstrated the unequivocal link between gender and manumission outcomes. Clearly, sexuality, affect, and gender shaped the avenues to quasi emancipation and liberty accessible to slaves. Higher rates of manumission among female domestic slaves and their offspring suggest that sexual and nonsexual intimacies forged in the household created paths to freedom.[48]

Most subjects studied in this book lived in a state of quasi emancipation or conditional liberty. Ana de Velasco's lawsuit is instructive here: she sought to change the terms of her ownership, not argue for her freedom. Even when legally free, formerly enslaved peoples did not enjoy complete autonomy over their labor or their bodies. I argue here that contingent liberty (or fractional freedom) was the reality that all – whether enslaved, freed, or free – accepted and to which they accommodated their lives. Neither total bodily autonomy nor absolute bondage was the norm for most enslaved peoples in Lima during this period.[49] Reenslavement was a constant threat for both men and women and particularly for children. Given the ubiquitous practice of slaves' self-purchase through installments, people lived in a protracted state of quasi emancipation: reenslavement could ensue from changes in an owner's economic circumstances or changes of heart.

The civil law's multiple and overlapping outlets for manumission were tempered by an owner's economic fortunes and exigencies (the raw pragmatics of human ownership) and religious sentiments. These factors converged to make quasi emancipation both an aspirational and lived reality. Small-scale, private emancipations accrued fractional freedoms: self-purchase through installments, freeing a child while remaining enslaved, and manumission after years of service were gendered processes, accessible to men and women in distinct ways.[50] As Camillia Cowling has written about women's legal activism in late-nineteenth-century Rio de Janeiro and Havana, "these individually small but cumulatively significant actions helped shape the course of emancipation and construct freedom's meaning in slaveholding territories."[51] Indeed, as Christine Hünefeldt reminds us, President Ramón Castilla's formal abolition of Peruvian slavery in 1854 was hardly momentous because slaves had constructed myriad and diverse avenues toward manumission in the preceding three centuries.[52]

Slave and Citizen exhaustively documents the numerous ways in which the *Partidas* qualified a slave for manumission, from gaining entry into a religious order to securing testamentary grants and denouncing a master's immorality.[53] Some conditions were clearly vestiges of the Roman law incorporated by Alfonse into the *Partidas* and had little relevance to Mediterranean slavery let alone Iberoamerican slavery. Tannenbaum mistakenly presumes that manumission was the terminus of the relationship – that slaves, once manumitted, made the transition into freedom and citizenship and were never subject to reenslavement. This is perhaps an unfair criticism of the book: Tannenbaum never set out to explore the afterlife of manumission. His purpose was to compare the multiple opportunities for manumission in the civil law, as opposed to its virtual foreclosure in the British West Indies and the United States.[54]

According to the *Partidas*, freedom was the greatest "gift" that a master could bestow on a slave. Therefore, the legal factors that governed its acquisition are critical to comprehending the lifelong relationship between owners and slaves.[55] Studies of manumission reveal that it was a protracted process, subject to negotiation, the possibility of retraction, change of heart and fortune. Perhaps more importantly, manumission was rarely a gift – "poisoned" or otherwise. Manumission was overwhelmingly achieved through self-purchase, both throughout the Americas and on the peninsula.[56]

Consequently, I use Tannenbaum's insights about the civil law's plurality of legal mechanisms for manumission as a springboard to examine and understand how enslaved persons adapted and even aspired to the condition of contingent liberty. How did liberty function in societies with slavery? In particular, since domestic slavery is the focus of this book, what did contingent liberty mean for domestic slaves? Here, I approach the domestic slaveholding household as a political space – no less riven by competing interest groups and factions, fault lines, and complex transactional costs than other public socioeconomic and political spaces.[57] Intimacies – sexual and domestic – were forged with soiled bed linens, fever-soaked rags, chamberpots, and breast milk. The detritus of care work nurtured thick relationships that factored into the calculus of liberty and bondage.[58] Manumission practices attendant to Iberoamerican urban domestic slavery were embedded in multigenerational relations of dependency and semiautonomy. Indeed, former owners continued to feel entitled to the intimate labors of their freed slaves under the powerful premise that enduring ties of loyalty, obligation, and affection rendered all members of a household one family. This sense of entitlement was reinforced by legal requirements of "reverence and obligation" that inhered in the grant of manumission.

The "boom" in the new social history of slavery studies has problematized our erstwhile views of domestic slavery: domestic slavery was neither singular nor hegemonic. The plethora of studies shows more exceptions, leaving open the question of what rules and cadences governed these relationships. Legal action invariably accompanied these contested and negotiated processes of self-purchase, quasi emancipation, and protracted manumission. This book addresses those instances of legal action.

LAW, CHRISTENDOM, AND SLAVERY

Law provided the basis for empire itself. Spain subjected its ability to trade, proselytize, and possess distant lands to exhaustive legal analysis and debate. In the sixteenth century, the Salamancan jurist-theologian Francisco de Vitoria deliberated on the rights and duties of the crown vis-à-vis the Indians, whom he conceded did have certain rights of dominion over their lands. Their sovereign rights were contingent, however, on the Spaniard's greater duty of Christian conversion. Although the natural law framework provided an overarching spiritual basis for conquest, it did little to resolve the question of the treatment of slaves, particularly those of African descent.

It is surprising that so much of the scholarship on the Salamancan school has been almost exclusively focused on indigenous affairs and imperial governance.[59] Historians have written much more about indigenous people's use of courts, and our understanding of New World litigiousness has been shaped by the seminal studies of indigenous legal dependents.[60] In fact, Las Casas's later treatise on wrongful enslavement of Africans is eclipsed by his infamous defense of the rights of Indians.[61] Yet the extensive discourse regarding the enslaveability of Indians undeniably affected the development of slave laws in the Americas.[62]

Sixteenth- and seventeenth-century Iberian slave law bore the unmistakable imprimatur of scholasticism. Unlike Muslims (*moriscos*) and Jews, indigenous peoples had not been tainted by their refusal to convert to Catholicism. Thus, although indigenous peoples were consigned to a state of permanent tutelage, slaves were alternately viewed as inheritors of innate Hamitic sin and patronless victims. The laws that were developed to discipline slaves and deal with their claims reflected this duality. This duality reinforced expectations of clemency and paternalism, key concepts in Iberian forms of imperial governance, from benevolent ecclesiastical and secular patrons.

This book examines the administration of justice and the jurisdictional tensions between church and crown in the baroque Spanish Empire. The baroque Spanish Empire has been described as a "composite monarchy": it was inclusive yet hierarchical and is best visualized as a baggy set of multiple corporate interests bound by religious beliefs and allegiances to the crown.[63] Spain was arguably the most important royal power in Christendom during the sixteenth century – the heralded Golden Age – and secular rule was legitimated only to the extent that it endorsed its spiritual mandate.[64]

Richard Ross and Philip Stern have recently drawn our attention to what they call the "messy pragmatics of rule" in early modern Europe, which necessitated a "generous legal pluralism" that emerged in response to imperial expansion.[65] As this generous legal pluralism took root in American soil, it reproduced a regime of jurisdictional flexibility and a competitive market in areas of legal competence that provided litigants with multiple outlets in which to air their grievances. Litigants thus logically sought the forum in which they believed they stood the best chance of prevailing in their complaint: a practice that lawyers refer to as forum shopping.

Legal scholars largely agree that Castilian private laws were successfully transplanted and reproduced in the Americas.[66] Other scholars have been more critical of the legal transplant thesis – largely because it presumes a linear process of adoption and awestruck reception of Roman-Iberian law that denies the creative capacities of criollo lawyers.[67] I avoid the extensive debate about legal transplants (which ranges over topics such as borrowing, diffusion, translation, imposition, verisimilitude, and customary or "folk" law) that at times has seemed larger than the phenomenon it seeks to describe. In my view, the debate about legal transplants works best in tandem with the framework of "generous legal pluralism." This framework inverts the familiar top-down narrative of leaders forming alliances with subordinate groups whom they wanted to dominate by showing how frequently the interests of plebeians and legal dependents aligned with the goals of multiple social superiors, who competed with each other to shore up their respective jurisdictions.[68]

SOURCES

Fractional Freedoms is principally based on archival research conducted at the Archbishopric Archive and the National Archive in Lima. My analysis draws on hundreds of suits brought by or involving slaves between 1593 and 1700. Like the reviled weevils that consume the furled pages of archived folios, I burrow into rich cases, following the protagonists in and out of court and in some instances until their death. This book mines these sources, using them to analyze how enslaved peoples availed themselves of legal forums and capitalized on jurisdictional tensions to press for fractions of freedom. Its focus on one city and archival site enables us to follow enslaved peoples as they navigated and experienced the law in contradictory ways.

As historical subjects, slaves look very different in criminal law or in property transactions than they do as agentive subjects in civil law. In notarial sources and parochial ledgers, slaves appear industrious, beatific, and enterprising. They drafted wills and contracts for self-purchase and apprenticeship; they transmitted and transferred property and at times accumulated modest wealth. They leased rooms and bargained for the fruits of their labor. In criminal sources and administrative decrees, slaves were denounced as dangerous, rootless, rebellious, and un-Christian. In ecclesiastical sources, slaves often were portrayed with a double image: as simultaneously Catholic and potentially treacherous.

BAROQUE LIMA: BETWEEN THE HAPSBURGS AND BEFORE THE BOURBONS

Focusing on the seventeenth century addresses important gaps in the historiography of the black Andean-Atlantic.[69] It fills the chronological vacuum left between Frederick Bowser's and Colin Palmer's masterful studies of the African slave experience in Peru and Mexico in the sixteenth century, James Lockhart's compendious rendition of colonial history in the first three decades of conquest, and the nineteenth-century works of Christine Hünefeldt and Carlos Aguirre.[70]

The cases I analyze were brought in the aftermath of the sixteenth-century Toledan reforms and before the eighteenth-century Bourbon reforms. Viceroy Francisco de Toledo instituted a series of reforms during his lengthy reign (1569–81) designed to centralize the indigenous tax and tribute structure according to residence (*reducciones*). Under the Toledan reforms, Andean communities were accorded limited self-governance and subjected to religious instruction.[71]

In addition to his fiscal activism, Toledo was equally energetic in the legal domain. He established Lima's Inquisition tribunal in 1570 and appointed a generously salaried official to serve as the legal protector of Indians (*protector de naturales*). What marked Toledo's regime was the thoroughgoing attempt to assert royal control over the Peruvian colonies through administrative reforms of a legalistic nature. Baroque governance was tethered to a pattern of local loyalties and periodic general inspections that were ideally executed by men of the highest ethical principles.[72]

The dynastic change from Hapsburg to Bourbon crowns in the late eighteenth century resulted in greater royal control over the church and administrative severity both on the peninsula and in the Americas. The impetus for the Bourbon reforms suggests a laissez-faire attitude on the part of the Hapsburg crown in imperial affairs. Iberoamerican governance appears less muscular in the seventeenth century than in either the sixteenth or the eighteenth, particularly in light of the characterization of the seventeenth century as one of decline and "general crisis" in Europe.[73] When compared to seventeenth-century Europe, which was plagued by numerous revolts and spiraling economic inflation, Peru appears surprisingly stable and, above all, internally prosperous.

Scholars of political, institutional, and economic history have prolifically studied Toledan and Bourbon reforms, demonstrating only a desultory interest in seventeenth-century imperial governance. However, judicial regulation in seventeenth-century Peru was not static. The historiography of the *Real Audiencia*, the *cabildo*, and the Archbishopric reveals intense jockeying among criollo elites for power and control over viceregal appointments. Building on the wealth of chronicles and voluminous administrative correspondence, as well as prosopographical studies, scholars of seventeenth-century Lima shed light on a thriving court society that emerged largely as a response to the sale of public administrative offices to generate income for the cash-strapped royal treasury.[74]

Although much of this work continues in the tradition of the Great Men strain of political history, thankfully for those interested in writing history from below, servants and slaves of Great Men also left paper trails. Although most African-descent peoples left small archival footprints, those like Ana de Velasco who were connected to prominent families are visible to us through the prolific documentary records left by their owners. Archbishops, extirpators, magistrates, viceroys, canonists, and priests reveal their secrets, promises, and betrayals in the lawsuits described herein, giving us a deeper appreciation of the "inextricably interwoven lives" in plebeian and patrician Lima.[75]

FREEDOM IN INSTALLMENTS

Following the pattern developed on the Iberian Peninsula, many modest Limeño households survived exclusively by subcontracting their slaves for daily wage labor. Slaves gave a fixed portion of their earnings (*jornales*) to their owners but could accumulate additional wages for personal use or pay toward their purchase price.[76] Ironically, the day-wage system (*trabajo a jornal*) rendered slaves partial owners of themselves. The day-wage system was slightly different from the Cuban version of *coartación*, although both functioned according to similar logic. Lima's slave owners rented out their slaves to another employer for a fee on a daily, weekly, or monthly basis. Small-scale artisanal workshops, bakeries, masons, carpenters, bricklayers, and ship captains could rent slave labor on a weekly or peak production basis without the significant cash outlay required to purchase a small team of enslaved workers. Owners recouped their investment by charging the rental fee. Whatever the enslaved person earned over and above the fee was hers to keep.

The evidence shows that women and men *jornaleros* experienced the urban labor market in different ways. Given the market logics of the day-wage system, urban slaves had to be mobile to maximize their earnings. They often lived in spaces separate from their owners. This semiautonomous existence potentially created confusion over identity, condition, and status. The ubiquity of slave labor in urban mercantilist, domestic, and artisanal sectors meant that freed and enslaved blacks, *castas*, less economically fortunate Spaniards, and Andean migrants worked in the same pursuits. The line between free and enslaved was amorphous, enabling men and women to keep one foot in the free world and one in the slave community. This was a transient, multiethnic space charged with calumnious intimations of dishonorable sexual liaisons and characterized by complex patron-client relationships. Extensive contact inevitably led to tensions and emotions that would divide and unite slave, poor, and free. When sexual or economic relationships deteriorated, slaves, plebeians, and Spaniards turned to the courts with decisive litigiousness to settle old scores and smoldering grudges. Their lawsuits comprise the remaining chapters of this book.

CHAPTER OUTLINES

Chapter 1 reviews legal actors, the jurisdictional history of the court, and the role of law. It employs the methodologies and tools of sociolegal history and legal anthropology to pose questions about both professionally trained personnel and the litigants who sought their services. Who used the court and for what purpose? How and where were professionals trained? What were their social backgrounds and career prospects and what kinds of professional networks did they have?

Using cases involving injunctions to prevent the separation of enslaved spouses, Chapter 2 explores how marriage and slavery in urban Iberoamerica were at times mutually constitutive and at other times incompatible. It also examines the ways in which slaves used their marital rights as an expedient mechanism to resist criminal sanctions.

Chapters 3 and 4 probe affective relationships between owners and slaves that were not based exclusively on sexual intimacy. The intimate presence of slaves in the household fostered relationships of co-dependency and racial hierarchy. These relationships normalized, tolerated, and promoted inequality to the extent that it was impossible to imagine life without domestic servitude and the embodied presence of slaves within the household. Drawing on the growing historical literature of emotions and intimacy, Chapter 3 examines cases of nonsexual intimacy to explore affective relationships between owners and their domestic slaves that resulted in contingent liberty.[77] Chapter 4 explores the status of quasi emancipation from the perspective of freed children of enslaved mothers. In keeping with the thesis that most Limeño slaves occupied an ambiguous terrain between slavery

and freedom, Chapter 4 focuses on the particular challenges that children
who were freed at the baptismal font presented in the protracted process of
manumission. In approaching children's condition as simultaneously freed
and dependent on their enslaved mothers, the chapter also illuminates the
impact of mixed status on social mobility.

Chapters 5 and 6 join a long-standing conversation among slavery scholars
regarding the tensions that emerged from the legal status of slaves as property
and as persons. In Anglo-American historiography, "double character" refers
to the slave's status as property and as person in criminal law.[78] These chapters
consider another angle of slavery's double character by exploring what hap-
pens when enslaved persons acted *as property* to regain their humanity and
a semblance of autonomy.[79] In Chapter 5, we see how an enslaved woman
positioned herself as property to be freed by testament in order to force her
owner's unwilling heirs to honor their mother's testamentary bequest of freedom. Chapter 6 looks at redhibition lawsuits: breach-of-contract disputes
against sellers for failing to disclose faulty merchandise, analogous to a breach
of implied warranty. What happened when slaves were defective merchandise –
not in the foot-dragging, tool-breaking way but literally defective: kleptoma-
niacal, immoral, or heretic? Or when a slave was weak or sickly? This chapter
highlights the working of Lima's resale market for domestic slaves.[80] A focus
on the transition from property to person challenges both the redemptive and
totalizing narratives of life in bondage and is a fitting place to end our reflections on urban Iberoamerican slavery.

Fractional Freedoms offers readers an opportunity to rethink the conventional
rendition of the lives of enslaved women and to consider the impact of slavery
on intimate life. The chapters move the reader through the life stages of birth,
childhood, marriage, and death, following the gradient from bondage to quasi
emancipation as enslaved people accrued fractions of freedom.

Courts provided an outlet through which to challenge and undermine the
pretensions of some patriarchs to power. *Fractional Freedoms* takes a comparative look at the differences between urban Hispanic slavery and the emerging British Atlantic slave system, showing more clearly the impact of religion,
gender, and domestic relations in the variations of slavery.

NOTES

1 AAL Causas de negros, leg. 13, exp. 16, año 1659.
2 "Me solicitó diversas veces para tener mi amistad ilícita persuadiéndome a que sali-
  esse de dicho monasterio y con efecto mediante las caricias que me hizo me reduje
  a ello."
3 Jouve Martín, *Esclavos de la ciudad letrada.* Jouve Martín also analyzes Ana de
  Velasco's case in his work. See *Esclavos de la ciudad letrada*, 105–8.
4 Libro de Bautismos, Esclavos, Negros, y Mulatos, Parroquia el Sagrario, año 1653
  and 1656 (see Figure 4.5).

5 In 1666, Inés de Velasco, Pedro's mother, as the trustee of his estate, petitioned for *censuras generales* to summon witnesses who knew of the misappropriation of funds that were owed to Pedro, who should have received payment in 1660 from a *diezmo* he held in Cañete in 1660. According to the records, Cañete was a profitable parish for those who collected the tenth (*diezmo*). In 1663, the amount collected was 9,220 *pesos ensayados*, and in 1664, the amount calculated was 7,620 pesos. See Albarrán and Pinto Huaracha, *Diezmos de Lima*, 28–30. Before Pedro died, he left an endowment (*capellanía*) of 20,000 pesos, which gives us an idea of his wealth and social stature. See Mendiburu, *Diccionario histórico-biográfico del Perú*, 6:284.

6 Libro de Matrimonios de Negros, El Sagrario, años 1660–1669.

7 At least in the extant seventeenth-century records, not many change of ownership lawsuits allege sexual impropriety. Christine Hünefeldt and Maribel Arrelucea document many more lawsuits alleging corrupted virginity and sexual impropriety in the eighteenth and nineteenth centuries than I found in the seventeenth century AAL lawsuits. Hünefeldt's fictional account of the Lasmanuelos family uses three cases of corrupted virginity to illustrate the story of Manuelita's rape by her owner's husband. See Hünefeldt, *Lasmanuelos*, 35–37. Arrelucea shows how *sevicia* encompassed sexual transgression through what enslaved complainants called "sevicia espiritual" (*Replanteando la esclavitud*, 31). This is not to imply that rape or sexual coercion were not features of slave ownership in the seventeenth century. However, extreme cruelty (*sevicia*) was much more commonly alleged during the late eighteenth century. Frank Proctor has recently reviewed a body of *sevicia* cases heard in the *Real Audiencia* that were increasingly brought by slaves after the Bourbons promulgated a series of ameliorative slave codes in the 1780s. See Proctor, "An 'Imponderable Servitude'."

8 María Emma Mannarelli devotes considerable attention to the accusations of priests who indulged in concubinary relationships. According to Mannarelli's survey of seventeenth-century denunciations of concubinage (*amancebamiento*) in Lima's parishes, 58 involved priests – which she surmises represented only a small fraction of all concubinary relationships that were punished (*Pecados públicos*, 108). Ana's recourse to the court does not detract from the power of community gossip. Her case was singular in that she had no witness testimony to substantiate her claim. On the power of community gossip, or what Minheiros alliteratively called *murmuracão*, see Ramos, "Gossip, Scandal, and Popular Culture in Golden Age Brazil."

9 We do not know how severe the sanctions were, or indeed if they were imposed – Pedro hailed from an established Limeño family that counted among their ranks an *oidor* (high court judge), and a prelate of the Archbishopric. Ana's owner inside the Monasterio de la Encarnación was doña Francisca de Ampuero, who was Inés de Velasco's sister. For a biography of the powerful Ampuero family, see Lohmann Villena, *Los regidores perpetuos del Cabildo de Lima*, 65–71.

10 Watson, *Legal Transplants*, and Cutter, *Legal Culture of New Spain*.

11 The fictional conversation between two Sevillano slaves in Cervantes' *Entremés de los mirones* depicts the pervasiveness of litigiousness and its constraints on slave owners' power. In this story, one slave asks another to confirm the rumor that his owner sold him for 120 *ducados*. The other replies affirmatively. When the interlocutor expresses surprise at the high price he fetched, the other retorts that he married a woman from the neighborhood against his owner's wishes. When his

owner resisted recognizing his conjugal rights, he threatened to go to the ecclesiastical judge. This threat apparently resolved the situation in his favor, as his owner sold him to another who did not interfere with the couple's exercise of their conjugal rights ("Oyó que uno preguntaba a otro si era verdad que su amo lo había vendido; replicó el interpelado que sí, en 120 ducados, y como el primero se extrañase porque, a su parecer no valía más de 80, le explicó que la causa de la venta fue que se había casado contra la voluntad de su amo con una negra del barrio, y que poniéndole impedimentos el dueño le había amenazado que recurriría al juez eclesiástico").

12   On Iberian litigiousness, see Kagan, *Lawsuits and Litigants in Castile.*

13   The consolidation of royal court power in the late medieval period created an expedited review process of complaints and grievances brought by *desamparados,* who could opt out of the jurisdiction of their local courts, or *fueros,* and seek recourse from crown-appointed ombudsmen in Castile. This system of multiple and overlapping jurisdiction led to a situation that provided dependents with a plethora of authorities to whom they could take their complaints. See Borah, *Justice by Insurance,* Dueñas, *Indians and Mestizos in the Lettered City*, and Meiklejohn, "The Implementation of Slave Legislation in Eighteenth-Century Nueva Granada." For medieval Iberia, see Vallejo, "Power Hierarchies in Medieval Juridical Thought," and Bermúdez Aznar, "La abogacía de pobres in Indias."

14   By the eighteenth century, the composition of Lima's ecclesiastical council was overwhelmingly creole. See Ganster, "Miembros de los cabildos eclesiásticos y sus familias."

15   Díaz, *The Virgin, the King, and the Royal Slaves of El Cobre,* 15–17, and Souloudre-La France, "Esclavos de su magestad."

16   As John Elliott reminds us, "The organic concept of kingship was deeply entrenched throughout the King of Spain's dominions. Loyalty was integral to such a concept: loyalty to a monarch who in turn cared benevolently for the wellbeing of his subjects" (*Spain, Europe and the Wider World,* 178).

17   Cañeque, *The King's Living Image.* See also Erasmus, "Education of a Christian Prince."

18   Brundage, *The Medieval Origins of the Legal Profession.*

19   Honores, "Litigation Masters in the Colonial Andes."

20   van Deusen, *Between the Sacred and the Worldly,* 169.

21   On the notion of the "spiritual economy," see Burns, *Colonial Habits.*

22   I think about the priestly household or conventual *celda* as domestic spaces with large numbers of dependents and slaves under one roof. I draw upon both Paul Ganster's description of "clerical patriarchs" and Kathryn Burns's portrayal of "religious maternity" in colonial Peru to envision how these households functioned. These spaces were not isolated from the secular world, and slaves in particular were intermediaries who circulated news and gossip to their owners. See Ganster, "Miembros de los cabildos eclesiásticos y sus familias."

23   We see this borrowing distinctly in the arguments raised in Andean litigation (*el pleitismo indígena*) and the cases brought by slaves. It is in the ecclesiastical forum that we can isolate common arguments and ways of articulating grievances among Andean and enslaved litigants, despite the differences in subject matter. For example, Andeans complained during ecclesiastical inspections about the laxity of the

priests assigned to their communities, just as slaves complained about owners who did not properly expose them to the Catholic doctrine. Similarly, Andeans' reports of immoral or abusive behavior of their priests or protectors also resonate with slaves' denunciations of their owners' moral turpitude. These likenesses in the way they framed their grievances do not imply that Andeans and slaves experienced the abuses they complained of in the same way. Rather, they point to a legal lexicon that was used by all involved in court complaints to articulate situations and predicaments that were commonly understood as unjust. The networks of professionals that served both Andean and enslaved litigants likewise borrowed extensively from this lexicon when representing their clients.

24 McKinley, "Standing on Shaky Ground."

25 Brundage, *Medieval Canon Law*, chapter 6.

26 For a representative (though by no means exhaustive) sample of important work on slaves and courts in Latin America, see Aguirre, "Working the System"; Arrelucea Barrantes, *Replanteando la esclavitud*; Barcia Paz, "Fighting with the Enemy's Weapons"; Bennett, *Africans in Colonial Mexico*; Bryant, "Enslaved Rebels, Fugitives, and Litigants" and *Rivers of Gold, Lives of Bondage*; Cowling, *Conceiving Freedom*; de la Fuente, "Slaves and the Creation of Legal Rights in Cuba"; Grinberg, "Freedom Suits and Civil Law in Brazil and the United States"; Landers, *Black Society in Spanish Florida*; Lane, "Captivity and Redemption"; O'Toole, *Bound Lives*; Owensby, "How Juan and Leonor Won Their Freedom"; Proctor, *Damned Notions of Liberty*; Premo, *Children of the Father King*; Scott and Hébrard, *Freedom Papers*; and Souloudre-La France, "Socially Not So Dead!"

27 The African experiences of *bozales* were virtually erased during their interface with legal and religious institutions, because it behooved them to express themselves in Catholic and Iberian idioms in any interaction with the Church, given the latent suspicion of African's Islamic beliefs and the pronounced hatred of Muslims (*moriscos*). On the difficulty of reading *bozal* identity within the text, see Bennett, *Africans in Colonial Mexico*.

28 Early studies of the slave trade treated slavery as an institution within the particular purview of economic, religious, military, labor, or social history. In addition to these comparative, macrolevel studies of the slave trade, there is a considerable body of scholarship devoted to country-specific histories of slavery within Latin America and the Caribbean. This list is representative of the country-specific works produced in the 1970s. See Hall, *Social Control in Slave Plantation Societies*; Knight, *Slave Society in Cuba during the Nineteenth Century*; Lombardi, *The Decline and Abolition of Negro Slavery in Venezuela*; Díaz Soler, *Historia de la esclavitud negra en Puerto Rico*; Sharp, *Slavery on the Spanish Frontier*, Aguirre Beltrán, *La población negra de México*; Palmer, *Slaves of the White God*; and Bowser, *The African Slave in Colonial Peru*.

29 Malagón Barceló, *Código negro carolino 1784*; Panzer, *The Popes and Slavery*. Cf. Avalos, "Pope Alexander VI, Slavery and Voluntary Subjection."

30 See, for example, Basadre Grohman, *El conde de Lemos y su tiempo*; Vargas Ugarte, *Historia del Perú, Virreinato siglo XVII*; Zavala, *Las instituciones jurídicas en la conquista de América*; and Altamira, *Técnica de investigación en la historia del derecho indiano*, all of which focused on the laws implemented in the Indies (*el derecho indiano*).

31 de la Fuente and Gross, "Comparative Studies of Law, Slavery, and Race in the Americas."

32 In *New Studies in the History of American Slavery* (2006), Edward Baptist and Stephanie Camp suggest that three factors account for the new directions in the field of slavery studies: "the influence of cultural history, the centrality of women and gender to our understanding of experience and identity, and new questions about the meaning and stability of the social category 'race' in the Americas" (3).

33 Jennings, "In the Language of the Criminal," 287.

34 Tannenbaum, *Slave and Citizen*.

35 de la Fuente, "Slave Law and Claims-Making in Cuba," 341.

36 A comparable argument could be made for the persuasive moral authority of abolitionist discourse in the nineteenth century. Frank Proctor examines the conundrum of Afro-Mexican slaves arguing for "liberty" in the absence of an Enlightenment sensibility of freedom. See his *Damned Notions of Liberty*. Although "libertad" in the early modern world did not connote the "freedom" that amounted to the autonomous rights-bearing subject of the Enlightenment, it did convey a sense of self-determination over the disposition of one's possessions and assets, body, and labor. Seventeenth-century manumission documents from the period formulaically pronounce the slave "free from captivity and subjection, with legal authority to contract, make wills, and dispose of their property as free persons." See Chapter 5.

37 Burns, *Las Siete Partidas*, 4, Title 5, 901, and Title 22, 981.

38 Verlinden, *The Beginnings of Modern Colonization*; Blumenthal, *Enemies and Familiars*. William Phillips also highlights the "striking elements of continuity in the legal sphere from ancient to modern slavery" and reminds us that Justinian's corpus provided Europe's jurists with an "easily available manual for the administration of a slave system [during the eleventh century that] significantly influenced the subsequent history of slavery" on the Iberian Peninsula and in its imperial possessions ("Manumission in Metropolitan Spain and the Canaries," 32–33).

39 For a materialist criticism of the Tannenbaum thesis, see Genovese, "Materialism and Idealism in the History of Negro Slavery in the Americas," and Sio, "Interpretations of Slavery: The Slave Status in the Americas." Marvin Harris querulously refutes Tannenbaum's thesis with demographic data that points ineluctably to the fact that economic imperatives determined slave policies and master-slave relations, not the slaveholder's legal tradition. Genovese notably chides Harris's critique of Tannenbaum's thesis, calling it an example of a "savage polemical excursion that confused ideological zeal with bad manners" ("Materialism and Idealism," 239).

40 For Louisiana's slave codes in the civil law tradition, see, for example, Ingersoll, *Mammon and Manon in Early New Orleans*, and Din, *Spaniards, Planters, and Slaves*.

41 Rankin, "The Tannenbaum Thesis Reconsidered"; cf. Landers, *Black Society in Spanish Florida*. Landers argues that the two legal systems coexisted in Florida. In the urban areas, the Spaniards respected slaves' legal rights and kept pathways open to manumission until they were expelled, while plantation owners and judges in rural circuits foreclosed manumission altogether.

42 Díaz, "Beyond Tannenbaum," 373. Díaz criticizes the use of Tannenbaum's thesis to "provide some theoretical justification for the study of slave law in slave

societies in the New World, and in particular, to legitimize the emerging specialized field of such legally oriented studies in Latin American societies" (373). For reasons pertaining to my own intellectual interests, I depart from this critique.

43 The comparison between Brazil and the United States is readily comprehensible. Both were large slaveholding societies with distinct regional variations. For an early study that includes Cuba within the comparative frame, see Klein, *Slavery in the Americas.*

44 Nader, *Law in Culture and Society*; Lazarus-Black and Hirsch, *Contested States*; Falk Moore, *Social Facts and Fabrications*; Starr and Collier, *History and Power in the Study of Law*; Merry, *Getting Justice and Getting Even*; and Sarat and Kearns, *Law in Everyday Life.*

45 See, for example, "Latin America at a Crossroads," the influential work of post-development scholar Arturo Escobar. On the tense relationship of Latin American scholars with subaltern studies, see Mignolo, "Afterword," and Mallon, "The Promise and Dilemma of Subaltern Studies."

46 For important works in colonial gender history using parish sources, see Arrom, *The Women of Mexico City*; Seed, *To Love, Honor, and Obey in Colonial Mexico*; Mannarelli, *Pecados Públicos*; Twinam, *Public Lives, Private Secrets*; Lavrin, *Sexuality and Marriage in Colonial Latin America*; Stern, *The Secret History of Gender*; and Hünefeldt, *Liberalism in the Bedroom.*

47 See, for example, Brana-Shute's critical assertion that "[as] historians have moved away from the juridical and cultural argument of Frank Tannembaum, they have come increasingly to minimize the importance of affection, humaneness, and gratitude as prime movers in facilitating manumissions" ("Sex and Gender in Surinamese Manumissions," 185).

48 The literature linking manumission outcomes to gender – and particularly to domestic service – is profuse. For representative texts, see Jouve Martín, *Esclavos de la ciudad letrada*; Cowling, *Conceiving Freedom*; Arrelucea Barrantes, *Replanteando la esclavitud*; Scully and Paton, *Gender and Slave Emancipation in the Atlantic World*; Higgins, *"Licentious Liberty" in a Brazilian Gold-Mining Region*; Proctor, "Gender and the Manumission of Slaves in New Spain"; and Johnson, "Manumission in Colonial Buenos Aires, 1776–1810."

49 Arguably this observation extends to all urban Iberoamerican centers. See Cañizares-Esguerra, Childs, and Sidbury, *The Black Urban Atlantic in the Age of the Slave Trade*, pt. 3. See also Welch, *Slave Society in the City*, for a British Caribbean example during a comparable time period.

50 See Scully and Paton, "Gender and Slave Emancipation in Comparative Perspective," 8.

51 Cowling, *Conceiving Freedom*, 2

52 Hünefeldt, *Paying the Price of Freedom*, 5.

53 Tannenbaum, *Slave and Citizen*, 50.

54 Ibid., 69.

55 Bradley's observations about the ancient world are relevant to medieval and early modern Mediterranean grants of manumission (*Slaves and Masters in the Roman Empire*, 84).

56 Blumenthal, "The Promise of Freedom in Late Medieval Valencia." Proctor documents an important exception to the pattern of self-purchase in late-seventeenth-century

Mexico. The records in New Spain indicate that only 1 in 675 manumissions arose out of circumstances resembling self-purchase (*Damned Notions of Liberty*, 161–62).

57 For a study of the labor logics and disciplinary regimes of the US plantation household, see Glymph, *Out of the House of Bondage*.

58 Lyman Johnson persuasively argues that, "historians should pay more attention to the emotional and not just evidentiary content of [slave] litigation" ("A Lack of Legitimate Obedience and Respect," 635).

59 Hanke, *The Spanish Struggle for Justice in the Conquest of America*.

60 See, for example, Borah, *Justice by Insurance*; Kellogg, *Law and the Transformation of Aztec Culture*; Hanke, *The Spanish Struggle for Justice*; Spalding, *Huarochiri*; and Charles, *Allies at Odds*. The historical interest in indigenous peoples' engagement with the *Audiencias* (both in the Andes and New Spain) has inspired scholars to examine courts as contested sites of authority. Woodrow Borah's early study of the General Indian Court in Mexico City spawned a number of studies of top-down legal reforms and their impact on indigenous claims for justice. The General Indian Court was funded by a special tax of a half-*real* allocated from indigenous tribute. The General Indian Court developed out of a longer peninsular tradition of royal appointees of advocates on behalf of the poor (*protector de pobres*), as well as the constant attempt to centralize and streamline legal processes and administrative practices that purportedly contributed to indigenous abuses. This innovative financing system emerged in response to the outrage from legal practitioners that indigenous petitioners were exempt from paying fees. See *Justice by Insurance*, 98.

61 Adorno, *Polemics of Possession in Spanish American Narrative*, chap. 3.

62 In a similar vein, Herman Bennett posits that the exemption of Indians from the jurisdiction of the Holy Tribunal rendered African slaves members of Christendom and hence subject to its rules.

63 Elliott, "A Europe of Composite Monarchies."

64 Muldoon, *The Americas in the Spanish World Order*; MacLachan, *Spain's Empire in the New World*.

65 Ross and Stern, "Reconstructing Early Modern Notions of Legal Pluralism," 111.

66 Writing in 1934, legal historian José María Ots Capdequí referred to Castile's colonial enterprise as a "verdadero trasplante de leyes e instituciones" (*Estudios de historia del derecho español en las Indias*, 137).

67 See Pérez Perdomo, *Latin American Lawyers*, 12–13.

68 On slaves' successful efforts using Dutch and Spanish imperial competitiveness to facilitate their own mobility, see Rupert, "Seeking the Waters of Baptism."

69 The important role of the Pacific in the slave experience and in diaspora studies more generally has been overlooked in studies that followed in the wake of Gilroy's *The Black Atlantic*.

70 For studies on Peruvian slavery during the seventeenth and eighteenth centuries, see the works of Rachel O'Toole, Maribel Arrelucea Barrantes, José Ramón Jouve Martín, and Bianca Premo.

71 *Reducciones* were sites of religious indoctrination where through proper exposure and education, indigenous peoples would learn the arts of enlightened government and Catholic morality.

72 As Kenneth Andrien points out in *Crisis and Decline*, the post-Toledo years did not unveil a professional civil service bureaucracy of a mature administrative state.

See also Cañeque's *The King's Living Image* where Cañeque argues for a study of baroque power grounded in and organized around networks of loyalty and patrimonial authority.

73 For a useful overview of the "seventeenth-century general crisis" thesis launched by Eric Hobsbawm and Hugh Trevor-Roper in 1954, see the American Historical Review Forum, "The General Crisis of the Seventeenth Century Revisited." With specific regard to Peru, see Andrien, *Crisis and Decline*; with regard to Spain, see Elliott, "Revolution and Continuity in Early Modern Europe."

74 See Torres Arancivia, *Corte de virreyes,* and Latasa Vassallo, *Administración virreinal en el Perú.*

75 On the dilemmas of writing within the Great Man genre, see Lucy Riall, "The Shallow End of History." On the interwoven lives of Great Men and enslaved women, see Gordon-Reed's reflections in "Writing Early American Lives as Biography."

76 *Coartación* appears to be a uniquely Cuban variant, where the *coartada* slave established her purchase price through a public assessment and then found her own employer to pay off her purchase price. The Brazilian practice known as "trabalhar a ganho" also resembled *coartación.*

77 On intimacy in indigenous slavery, see van Deusen, "The Intimacies of Bondage." On intimacy as a research project, see Steedman, "Intimacy in Research."

78 See, for example, Gross, *Double Character.*

79 Painter, *Southern History across the Color Line.*

80 See Johnson, *Soul by Soul.* On the internal slave trade, see Johnson, *The Chattel Principle.*

I

Litigating Liberty

> For pity is the virtue of the law
> And none but tyrants use it cruelly.
> *Timon of Athens*

On September 14, 1616, Anton Bran petitioned Lima's ecclesiastical court to compel Josef de Barcala to pay his wife for meals that she had cooked and delivered over the course of the preceding seven months.[1] Anton's wife, Ysabel, diligently prepared meals for Barcala as the parties had agreed. As the weeks progressed, Barcala apparently became more enamored with Ysabel's cooking. Barcala asked Ysabel to deliver his meals on the weekends and to increase the amount of food she provided so that he could share meals with a fellow priest. Barcala agreed to pay for the extra food by raising the monthly stipend to fourteen patacones (pieces of eight). However, Barcala did not honor the agreement. Instead, he continued to pay for his meals at the originally contracted price of twelve *patacones*. Ysabel did not discontinue her food deliveries, but all entreaties for increased payment were unsuccessful over the next two months. Consequently, Anton filed this petition.

This case involves a married couple claiming payment for breach of an oral contract. At first blush, Anton's complaint is the type of case that contemporary legal practitioners would classify as belonging to the subject matter jurisdiction of small claims courts – disparagingly categorized as "garbage cases."[2] Yet Anton's complaint was heard by Lima's most prominent jurist: the chief ecclesiastical judge (*provisor*) of the Archbishopric court, don Feliciano de Vega.[3] Of particular interest for the purposes of this chapter are Provisor Vega's thorough investigation and the ruling he subsequently issued in favor of Anton and Ysabel. The celerity with which Provisor Vega issued his ruling is also significant.

Provisor Vega's ruling was brief and does not offer much in the way of an explanation as to why he ruled in their favor, but it does suggest he was most persuaded by the couple's uninterrupted efforts to deliver Barcala's food, honoring their end of the bargain. Four witnesses gave testimony, including the priest, Luis Nieto Palomino, with whom Barcala shared Ysabel's cooking. It was a shrewd move on Anton's part to present Nieto as a witness, since Nieto's concurrence strengthened Anton's case. Two young apprentices living and working with Anton testified that they delivered the meals to Barcala's quarters. The apprentices were identified as belonging to the "tierra Bran, morenos ladinos en la lengua española," a hybrid status that signified their familiarity with the Spanish language though they were African born. There was no written contract between the parties, and no one alluded to any formal agreement beyond the oral promise of payment for services rendered.

On October 20, 1616 (twelve days after witness testimony was recorded and approximately five weeks after Anton's initial complaint), Provisor Vega ordered Barcala to pay Ysabel 20 pesos. This included the outstanding amount due to Ysabel plus legal costs incurred in the complaint.

It bears repeating that there was nothing particularly complicated about this case. Once the couple established a breach of promise, it was incumbent on Barcala to make restitution to the harmed parties. Yet Anton and Ysabel's experience with the law enables us to chart larger patterns with regard to enslaved complainants' expectations that they would be able to air grievances against their adversaries in the ecclesiastical court. Legal action was pursued without hesitation when negotiations between Anton and Barcala did not yield the desired result. Though they did not have extensive legal knowledge, Anton and Ysabel were undoubtedly mindful of the weight that a priest's testimony would carry in an ecclesiastical forum. Anton Bran's relatively insignificant case and others like it suggest that the urban enslaved and freed community constructed networks of shared legal knowledge: one successful outcome or strategy could convince others to use the courts to air (and perhaps resolve) their grievances.

This chapter examines litigation in societies with slavery.[4] It describes the kinds of litigation pursued by enslaved and freed peoples and gives an overview of the legal process, paying particular attention to the ecclesiastical court.

The first section retraces the steps of enslaved litigants who sought legal intervention. Although the idea of a continuum between accommodation and resistance has largely fallen into desuetude, the empirical impulse looms large in our historical accounts of litigation.[5] How many slaves went to court? Did they win or lose? Who were their advocates? How were they paid? The second section describes the professional judicial hierarchy of notaries, procurators, lawyers (*letrados*), prosecutors or solicitors (*fiscales*), and magistrates (*oidores*). In so doing, it looks in depth at the social background of legal practitioners and their professional networks, the jockeying for appointments to the *Audiencias* by peninsular courtiers and aristocratic criollos alike, and the contentious practice of the sale of judicial appointments. The third section focuses on the process of issuing *censuras generales* to address jurisdictional pluralism and the opportunities for forum shopping open to plebeians and enslaved complainants. In the last section, I discuss Anton and Ysabel Bran as legal protagonists and as historical and historiographical subjects, considering the ways they have been portrayed, enumerated, and studied by generations of historians, census takers, people in their community, and legal professionals.

THE LAW OF SLAVERY VIS-À-VIS ENSLAVED LITIGANTS

A study that takes as its subject slaves' use of courts implicitly differs from a study of the laws of slavery, although both approaches ultimately are shaped by the issue of agency and structure. As a qualitative study, my aim is to discover and explain how people like Anton and Ysabel located themselves in and experienced structural processes of enslavement rather than give the reader a macro-level analysis of Iberoamerican urban slavery. Generations of earlier scholars may have ignored Anton Bran's lawsuit as tangential to the laws and decrees that proclaimed Anton's rights, his legal personality, or the lack of both. Those adhering to Marxist or materialist approaches would probably not have regarded Anton as a legal protagonist at all. On the contrary, they might have seen Anton's victory as evidence that the court conceded individual gains to co-opted and compromised subjects: individual victories provided an escape valve from the seething cauldron of discontent whose eruption would have led to real revolution and social change.[6]

Undeniably, the material conditions of people's lives matter. Ysabel sued Barcala to force him to pay what amounted to the equivalent of a month's day wages for a *jornalera* slave in seventeenth-century Lima. This was not a negligible sum for someone trying to purchase her freedom. In focusing on moments of "resistance" or what I prefer to call "protagonism," I do not intend to detract from the important intellectual work performed by superstructural analyses of slavery. However, since I am urging readers to take contingent liberty (as opposed to abstract freedom or total bondage) seriously as an analytical construct, I look more closely at the instances when fractions of freedom may have been accrued through recourse to the law.

BAROQUE LIMA

The City of Kings (or la Ciudad de los Reyes), as Lima was known, was the capital of the viceroyalty of Peru. After its founding in 1535 and notable growth through the viceregal reforms in the 1570s, Lima blossomed into a bustling metropolitan center by the late sixteenth century. The city's population and commerce boomed. Lima and the entrepôt of Callao served as vital port cities importing people and goods from Central and Western Africa, the

FIGURE 1.1. Façade of the Church of San Francisco, Lima Peru.
Image credit: Kelly Donahue-Wallace.

Philippines, and Europe and exporting precious metals and other rich commodities from the Andes.[7]

In 1544 the crown established Lima's high court (*Real Audiencia*), with competency over regional *Audiencias* in Panama, Santa Fe de Bogotá (1554), Quito, Charcas, Buenos Aires, and Chile. (See Map 1.1). The *Audiencia* reviewed cases on appeal and also functioned as a court of first instance. Irresolvable cases were referred to the Council of the Indies, which met in sessions convened by the kings wherever they were in residence. Lima's tribunal of the Inquisition

MAP 1.1. Map of Peru with Audiencias.
Map by: David Cox.

began operations in 1570, exercising jurisdiction over the non-Andean population for crimes against the faith. The Inquisition tribunal was under the jurisdiction of the *Suprema*, located in Madrid.

In 1546, Pope Paul III elevated Lima to an Archbishopric, with authority over the bishoprics of Cuzco, Quito, Popayán, Panama City, and Léon
(Nicaragua). Religious orders flocked to Lima, constructing vast convents and
monasteries that essentially functioned as cities within the city. The crown also
authorized the establishment of colleges to educate Spaniards and the children
of Inca nobles in religious instruction and arts and letters. In 1551, Carlos V

issued the charter inaugurating the University of San Marcos, which was rati-
fied by the papacy in 1571, rendering it the first university in the Americas. (See
Figure 1.5). The Dominican order established the earliest college in 1548, and
the Augustinians, Mercedarians, and Franciscans quickly followed suit. The
Jesuits built the College of San Pablo in 1568, initiating a stormy relationship
with the crown that arose from the order's unyielding insistence on independence and autonomy that lasted until its expulsion 200 years later.[8] Between
1561 and 1624, five monasteries were created to minister to the spiritual needs
and education of Spanish women from well-known families.[9] Religious orders
and the city's philanthropic elite financed hospitals, orphanages, and other
charitable institutions for the less fortunate (*los desamparados*).

Some demographic data will be helpful to contextualize the commingled
lives of enslaved and free peoples within the dense urban spaces of colonial
Lima. A well-cited census conducted in 1613 estimated the city's population
at 25,167. Numerically, the largest group were blacks and *mulatos*, followed
closely by Spaniards.[10] Anton Bran was among the 10,000 plus *negros* visited

FIGURE 1.2. Main cloister of the Monastery of San Francisco, Lima 1557–1678.
Image credit: Kelly Donahue-Wallace.

by an indefatigable enumerator in the 1613 census. Also enumerated were small numbers of urbanized Andeans living within the city walls and others who were interned (*recogidos*) in religious institutions.[11]

By the beginning of the seventeenth century, the Spanish population included at least four groups: an established criollo community (*beneméritos* who traced their lineage back to the earliest conquistadors), peninsular nobles and functionaries serving in the viceregal bureaucracy, other migrants, artisans, and merchants seeking fortune and fame in the Americas, and members of religious orders or secular priests who spread the Catholic faith in the New World.[12]

1613 Lima Census

	Men	Women	%
Españoles	5,271	4,359	38.9
Religious personnel	894	826	6.9
Negros	4,529	5,857	41.9
Mulatos	326	418	3.0
Andeans (*indios*)	1,116	862	7.9
Mestizos	97	95	0.8
Interned population (orphans, divorcees, the infirm)	79	438	1.3

Source: Padrón de los Indios de Lima en 1613.

With the development of the Transatlantic Slave Trade Database, we know a great deal more about the African-descent population in the Americas. Questions invariably remain, but we know enough to make a set of educated guesses about the provenance of people enumerated as "*Negros*" in the 1613 census.[13] Most of the slaves destined for Lima disembarked in Cartagena de Indias, the Atlantic port city that furnished slaves for all of Spanish South America.[14] As Table 1.1 shows, Cartagena experienced a surge in slave imports between 1601 and 1625. Approximately half this number arrived in the preceding and subsequent decades. Most of the Cartagena-bound slaves in the late sixteenth and early seventeenth centuries came from the Upper Guinea Rivers, Senegambia (Cabo Verde), and West Central Africa.[15]

Throughout the sixteenth and early seventeenth centuries, the Spanish Crown relied exclusively on its Portuguese subjects for slave procurement. Spain made little effort to invest in the slave trade: it built no alliances with West and Central African kingdoms and established no maritime forts or trading posts on the Slave Coast or Gold Coast of Africa. Rather, Spain pursued alliances through imperial annexation and dynastic marriage, thereby exploiting the efforts of their subjects who had connections and commitments to the slave trade. Throughout the sixteenth century, the merchant guild and the royal house of trade (Casa de Contratación) complained

TABLE 1.1. *Provenance of Slaves Landing in Cartagena de Indias, 1576–1650*

Years	Port of origin	Cartagena
1576–1600	Senegambia, West Central Africa	37,819
1601–25	Bight of Benin, West Central Africa, Senegambia, Gulf of Guinea	79,332
1626–50	Gold Coast, Senegambia, Gulf of Guinea, West Central Africa	38,740

Source: Transatlantic Slave Trade Database

vociferously to the crown about unreported freight and lost income that resulted from the Portuguese monopoly over the slave trade. However, the *asiento* model (whereby the Spanish Crown granted royal licenses to certain commercial trading houses) was convenient as long as Portugal and its colonies were ruled by Spain. Moreover, the Portuguese *asiento* upheld the theological justification that undergirded the slave trade as the church and crown struggled with the thorny issue of indigenous slavery.[16] As George Fredrickson puts it succinctly, Spaniards were "more averse to making slaves than buying them."[17]

Concomitantly, the Dutch increasingly grew prominent in the slave trade after 1596, and the British solidified their presence in the Caribbean in the latter half of the seventeenth century.[18] The Dutch rivaled the Portuguese in the seventeenth century and even occupied parts of Brazil between 1630 and 1654.[19] After the separation of the crowns, the Spanish authorities were demonstrably reluctant to grant the *asiento* to the Dutch traders, whom they continued to regard as former vassals rather than global powerhouses in the slave trade. Spain's hostilities with the Netherlands would not end until the Peace of Westphalia in 1648. In sum, Spain's lack of maritime infrastructure, strained relationships with the powerful trading entities in Britain, the Netherlands, and Portugal, and a growing need for slave labor in the Americas created a trifecta that led the crown to grant the *asiento* to two Genoese trading houses between 1663 and 1674.[20]

In this tableau, slave procurement was marked by transimperial traffic and contraband.[21] Even with the Transatlantic Slave Trade database, we know comparatively little about the importation of Africans into Peru after 1640. Older scholarship on the slave trade identified Buenos Aires as an important secondary source of slaves for Lima, especially with regard to contraband trading.[22] The most current scholarship depicts a precipitous decline of slave importation into Spanish America after the separation of the Portuguese and Spanish crowns.[23] Thus, the increase in the African-descent population throughout the seventeenth century was due to a combination of "internal" trades, contraband, local reproduction, and the growing community of freed people and quasi-free *pardos* and *mulatos*.[24] Newly arrived *bozales* in the latter part of the seventeenth century were likely to be in the minority of the black population.[25]

Given the prolific investigation of slave importation associated with the Transatlantic database, today's slavery scholars are both blessed with an abundance of information about ports of provenance and cursed by the interpretive impulse of microhistory. On one hand, we have reliable information (subject to constant modification and updating) of the early waves of African arrivals. On the other hand, we have a legacy of qualitative scholarship that accepted African ethnonyms (within certain constraints) as evidence of ethnic affiliation.[26] Quantitative scholars answer with greater precision the questions of where (provenance), who (ethnic affiliation), and how many (unrecorded voyages, contraband, and surges related to raiding, political strife, dynastic decline). Social historians figure out who individuals were, how they forged new lives and families, and how they reconstituted new identities.

Let us presume that Anton Bran did, in fact, hail from "the rivers of Guinea" as we retrace his steps as a litigant in the early decades of the seventeenth century. By the time Anton Bran sought judicial recourse in 1616, he could rely on an elaborate set of ecclesiastical, administrative, and juridical structures. King Philip III had just appointed the Prince of Esquilache, don Francisco de Borja y Aragón, as viceroy in December 1615. The city was on edge, due to an attempted attack by Dutch pirates intent on diverting the galleons of the Armada. The viceroy's principal agenda was to secure the port of Callao, as well as fortify the defensive structures to guard against foreign attacks.

The resplendent viceregal couple entered Lima with an unprecedented number of courtiers and attendants, which caused both awe and resentment among the local criollo elite.[27] An aficionado of the arts and belle lettres, Esquilache expanded "court society" in Lima and relied heavily on legal and ecclesiastical advisers for daily affairs of governance. During Esquilache's six-year reign, governance was largely in the hands of learned advisors and magistrates (*letrados*). This greatly increased the power and influence of the men appointed to the bench. In fact, when Esquilache withdrew from his viceregal post in 1621, he left the chief judge at the time, don Juan Jiménez de Montalvo, in charge of governance in the viceroyalty until his successor arrived one year later to assume his post.[28]

MERCY IN THE MARKETPLACE

The sale of high-level judicial appointments was vigorously contested throughout the colonial period, but it became particularly heated during the sixteenth and seventeenth centuries.[29] Viceregal policies dictated that magistrates should not be citizens (*naturales*) of the locality or jurisdiction over which they presided, creating a preference for staffing judicial positions in the *Audiencias* with *peninsulares*. However, the fiscal crisis at the dawn of the seventeenth century unleashed by Philip II's exorbitant military expenses incurred in the Dutch wars and by his foreign policy commitments increasingly led to the (somewhat disingenuous) practice of creating supernumerary judicial offices and then selling them to generate revenue for the crown.[30] In tandem with the fiscal emergencies of the period, a considerable number of well-trained criollo jurists were willing to purchase judicial posts at significantly high prices.

Besides inveighing against the commodification of justice, royal advisers repeatedly cautioned against selling judicial appointments to wealthy local bidders, warning that criollos were so imbricated in economic, political, and social relationships that they could not possibly issue impartial judgments in cases brought before them. Perhaps more importantly from a monarchist perspective, the commodification of these positions imperiled the king's ability to reward his loyal subjects, whose families spent decades if not generations in his service. These advisers also warned of potential criollo insurgency, raising the prospect of the lack of fealty or allegiance to the monarch if offices were sold.[31]

However, even before the systematic sale of supernumerary offices was formally endorsed in 1687, the practice of selling judicial posts piecemeal did not lead to any discernible secessionist uprising or ardent criollo republicanism. By nominating criollos and those who claimed status as *beneméritos* as servants of the king, the viceroys strategically reinforced institutional and political loyalty to the crown.

Beneméritos were descendants of the conquistadors and early settlers who claimed the right to royal grants of encomiendas (tributary rights paid by indigenous subjects) and favors (*mercedes*) based on their long-standing service to the king in the Indies.[32] Disgruntled aristocrats vociferously complained to the king about viceroys who granted income-generating municipal appointments to their retainers, violating the king's explicit orders to set aside a number of positions for *beneméritos*. They were particularly outraged when the Prince of Esquilache granted his personal musician a lucrative *corregimiento* in flagrant disregard of the king's orders. This appointment prompted a furious flurry of correspondence to King Philip III, alerting him to the viceroy's infractions.[33] King Philip responded with a lengthy decree prohibiting his viceroys from nominating members of their entourage to positions in the Indies and limiting the number of retainers with whom viceroys could travel from Spain.[34]

Despite the *beneméritos'* bitter complaints, they did not reject the underlying regalist premise that authorized the king to name his courtiers as advisers.[35] Rather, *beneméritos* were angered by the unfair geographical advantage peninsular retainers enjoyed in securing the king's patronage and his *mercedes*.[36]

In the judicial realm, nominations unfolded differently than they did for the Treasury (Hacienda). *Beneméritos* who specialized in law used their position, legal training, and expertise to consolidate their social standing, precisely because of the career paths that a law degree facilitated. Viceroys often circumvented the king's orders by nominating criollo *letrados* to the *Real Audiencia*. Astute viceroys recognized the impracticality of the embargo on criollo appointments to the *Audiencias* and often intervened personally on behalf of a preferred nominee to the monarch for special dispensation.[37] As the president of the *Audiencia*, the viceroy was especially motivated to request these dispensations. A viceroy's tenure was relatively short – ranging between three and five years. As evidenced by Montalvo's transitional reign, magistrates with long-term appointments provided administrative stability. When faced with a criollo nominee who demonstrated moral rectitude and probity in his affairs or an inexperienced *peninsular*, viceroys did not hesitate to express their preferences for local appointees. Indeed, a careful review of administrative correspondence shows that viceroys were not above rigging elections to ensure that preferred *beneméritos* were appointed to the bench.[38]

Though the plebeian litigants who sought the would-be nominee's services had little influence over who was appointed, they were nevertheless significant for two reasons. First, the most important feature of Iberoamerican law was the magistrate's position as a delegate or instrument of the king's clemency and justice. A magistrate's professional reputation depended in large part on his fairness in the courtroom ruling over the cases plebeian litigants brought before him.[39] The appeals to justice were directed at the king, whose appointees were duty bound to execute his will with fidelity and rigor. The normative appeal and moral stature of this discourse was a powerful disincentive to challenging or undermining those ideals themselves. Nowhere or at any point did the discourse of mercy undermine social hierarchy.

Second, the closeness of the legal community itself also opened up the potential for scrutiny from intimates and confidantes. What this meant in practice was that a small legal community existed among Lima's elite with aspirations and the requisite connections to judicial appointments, but also whose private affairs were subject to scrutiny; in the event of egregious infractions, information leaked about such infractions could lead to magistrates being removed. Magistrates and their families were subjected to a strict body of rules intended to diminish the inevitable conflicts of interests that would emerge as they adjudicated legal affairs in the jurisdictions in which they wielded influence.[40] Practically, these rules were impossible to enforce, as magistrates were thoroughly connected through social ties of marriage, kinship, and servitude – networks that in effect determined their eligibility to serve in the positions they sought.[41]

Slaves lived in close proximity to their masters; they knew their secrets and could put their most intimate and embarrassing secrets on display. Allegations of scandalous behavior, vindictiveness toward one's neighbors, associates, and slaves, and financial irresponsibility were detrimental to one's public standing and honor. Sexuality was constantly subject to judicial review.[42] Slaves often occupied a supporting role onstage in colonial scandals – either as protagonists or as witnesses. The knowledge they held could be selectively wielded (or strategically disclosed) to secure individual victories.

The (OFTENTIMES) LENGTHY LIFE OF A LAWSUIT

If you need to slow down the timing of the lawsuit
Ask for three recesses during the time of harvest.
When harvest is over,
You need to present your proof,
(which is the stage for which you requested a recess). You should then request a fourth
extension of twenty days.

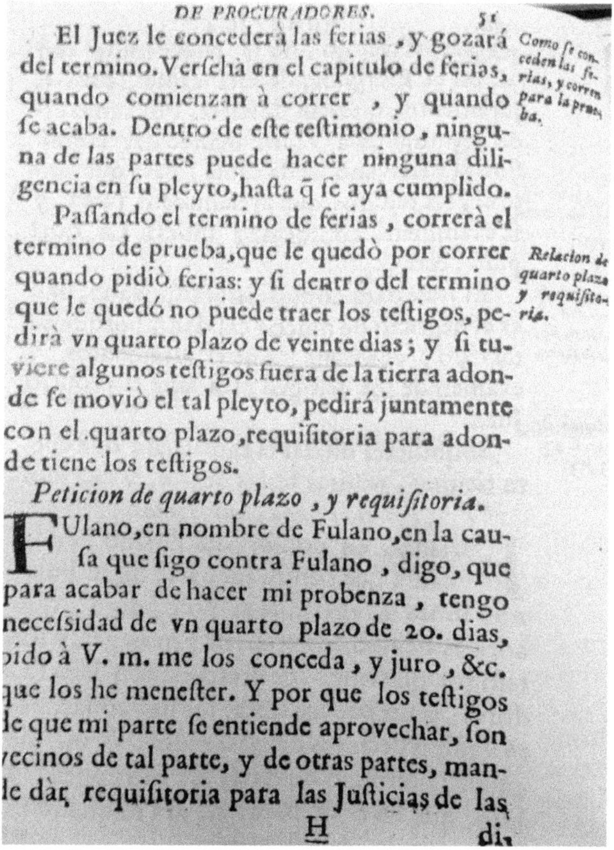

DE PROCURADORES.   51

El Juez le concederà las ferias , y gozarà *Como se con-*
del termino. Verselià en el capitulo de ferias, *ceden las fe-*
rias, y corren
quando comienzan à correr , y quando *para la prue-*
ba.
se acaba. Dentro de este testimonio , ninguna de las partes puede hacer ninguna diligencia en su pleyto, hasta q̃ se aya cumplido.

Passando el termino de ferias , correrà el
termino de prueba, que le quedò por correr *Relacion de*
quando pidiò ferias: y si dentro del termino *quarto plazo*
y requisito-
que le quedó no puede traer los testigos, pe- *ria.*
dirà vn quarto plazo de veinte dias; y si tu-
viere algunos testigos fuera de la tierra adon-
de se moviò el tal pleyto, pedirá juntamente
con el quarto plazo, requisitoria para adon-
de tiene los testigos.

Peticion de quarto plazo , y requisitoria.

Fulano, en nombre de Fulano, en la causa que sigo contra Fulano , digo, que
para acabar de hacer mi probenza , tengo
necesidad de vn quarto plazo de 20. dias,
pido à V. m. me los conceda , y juro , &c.
que los he menester. Y por que los testigos
de que mi parte se entiende aprovechar, son
vecinos de tal parte, y de otras partes, man-
le dar requisitoria para las Justicias de las
H   di-

FIGURE 1.3. Juan de Muñoz, *Práctica de Procuradores* (Madrid, 1596).

Because Lima was the site of the *Real Audiencia* and the Archbishopric
court, enslaved men and women there had relatively unimpeded access to
both tribunals to request injunctive relief, to air grievances, and to protest
breaches of oral and written contracts. No legislation prevented slaves or
other dependents from approaching a procurator about retaining their case.

Andeans had special procurators (*protectores de naturales*) appointed by the crown to adjudicate their complaints. Indigenous disputes were presided over by *alcaldes mayores* and *corregidores* at the district or municipal level.[43] This administrative structure was intended to consolidate the spatial/territorial arrangement of two separate republics – one for Spaniards and the other for Andeans who were brought under the protection of the crown.[44] Slaves, like other nonindigenous plebeians, were subjects of the jurisdiction of the *república de españoles*.

The steps taken by enslaved or freed peoples seeking legal representation reflected those of any potential litigant – notwithstanding their gender, status, or condition. It is true that Anton Bran brought a suit on behalf of his wife Ysabel, but the laws of coverture did not prevent Ysabel from retaining her own counsel. Indeed, enslaved married women litigated independently of or on behalf of their husbands.[45]

From the extant records, it is impossible to estimate Limeño slaves' litigiousness with any degree of precision. An impressionistic view of the traffic in the ecclesiastical and royal court does, however, lead to the unequivocal conclusion that slaves took legal action quickly, filing petitions and seeking protection. Some cases warranted rapid legal action. Petitions for injunctive relief were filed almost immediately when a spouse's owner threatened to separate the couple through travel or relocation. Similarly, slaves filed writs of *amparo*, requesting the royal court's protection against inflictions of physical harm, to stay the abusive actions of owners and aggressors.[46] Enslaved criminal fugitives swiftly sought protection against their arrest by secular lawmakers by claiming sanctuary on hallowed ground. These sanctuary cases were sites of vigorous contestation between church and crown over public order and ecclesiastical privilege.[47]

Other causes of action – divorce, breach of contract, annulment, probate, inheritance, and change of ownership – followed the more typical glacial pace of colonial litigation. *Causas de negros* were civil actions brought by enslaved and freed litigants, like the action Anton Bran brought against the gluttonous priest in the ecclesiastical court, which exercised jurisdiction over actions involving religious personnel and institutions. Enslaved parishioners could also bring accusations of concubinage and idolatry to the attention of church authorities, as these were deemed crimes against the faith. Divorce and annulment petitions, as well as enforcement of matrimonial promises, were also subject matter that fell within the ecclesiastical court's jurisdiction.

The first step in lodging a complaint was to approach a notary to record one's grievance. The initial complaint is often the least mediated part of the folio that constitutes the legal record. Although the complaint was highly stylized and formulaic in that the petitioner presented himself with the utmost respect for the law before the magistrate (*con la major forma que haya lugar en derecho parezco ante Vuestra merced*), this is where the person told his story and appealed for justice. It is perhaps more accurate to depict the person as a supplicant rather than as a complainant at this point.

Once recorded by the notary, the petition was read during one of the daily sessions in front of a panel of magistrates. The magisterial panel in the *Real Audiencia* was much larger than the panel in the ecclesiastical court. In the ecclesiastical panels, petitions were read to the provisor, the *promotor fiscal*, and two notaries assigned to the court. The Archbishopric employed its own sheriff (*alguacil eclesiástico*) and operated its own jail where it incarcerated ecclesiastical personnel and perpetrators of crimes against the faith.[48] If the Archbishop was present in the city, he made every effort to attend the sessions, and his presence was recorded. Many Archbishops had doctorates in canon law and played an active role in the ecclesiastical panels that were convened after daily mass.[49] If neither the provisor nor the Archbishop were available, the dean, archdeacon, or cantor would convene the sessions.

Lima's *Real Audiencia* had a staff of eight judges (*oidores*), four criminal prosecutors (*alcaldes del crimen*) and two civil prosecutors (*fiscales*) who represented the crown's interest, one sheriff or voluntary law enforcement officer (*alguacil mayor*), and a notary attached to the court (*escribano de cámara*) who recorded the proceedings.[50] The large number of criminal prosecutors was related to the crown's mandate to keep the peace, which had to be defended and upheld, even if the victim or the aggrieved parties chose not to press charges.[51] *Alcaldes del crimen* were responsible for the pretrial stages of detention and criminal adjudication. They conducted daily prison inspections – especially during an active investigation – apprehended suspects in tandem with the volunteer constabulary force (*cuadrilleros*) that patrolled the city at night, brought charges against the suspects in custody, and ordered interrogation and torture to obtain confessions.[52] Given the size of the *Audiencia*, it is unlikely that all personnel would have been present at the daily sessions. In addition, judicial offices often remained vacant if the post was up for sale or if bidding for the position was under way after a sitting magistrate died while holding a seat. However, a quorum of magistrates would convene to hear cases on the daily docket.

In both judicial forums, the magistrate would rule after oral presentation as to whether to admit or dismiss the complaint. If the complaint was deemed meritorious, the magistrate summoned the other party to appear before the court within a brief period. The notary or a member of his staff attached to the court who recorded the session served the defendant notice, usually that afternoon.

These initial proceedings did not take a particularly long time.[53] Hearings were convened almost every day of the calendar year except feast days, Sundays, and special occasions, such as the birth of a prince, the coronation of a monarch and entry of a new viceroy, or death of an important official.[54] The expedited nature of getting on the docket largely explains why the courts adjudicated so many complaints. Nevertheless, a notary still had to be found (and paid) to record the complaint. Furthermore, there were numerous points subsequent to the initial filing at which an enslaved litigant's complaint could be delayed.

The first potential delay occurred at the stage when the opposing party was notified about the action pending against him. Notice had to be personally served, and witnesses had to verify that the defendant understood the charges that were read to him. A defendant who wished to evade service could simply refuse to open his door, have a slave attest to his absence, or not leave his home. Pedro de Velasco – the lascivious priest denounced by Ana de Velasco – avoided service for five weeks with these tactics.[55]

Once the defendant was summoned to appear in court, he had to be notified three times before a default judgment could be entered for failure to appear. In practice, the court gave the defendant between two weeks and twenty days to appear after each citation for nonappearance, thus potentially extending the case for another six weeks.[56] After each consecutive failure to appear, the petitioner accused the defendant of violating a court order. Upon the third citation, the petitioner asked the court to issue condemnatory *censuras generales* with the threat of excommunion (*sopena de excomunión mayor*). These *censuras* were not taken lightly and had the pronounced effect of ensuring a court appearance from the opposing party if he was present in the city.

Defendants routinely deployed dilatory techniques before responding to the substance of the complaint alleged by the enslaved plaintiff. Magistrates would not expedite the proceedings unless the subject matter warranted prompt judicial intervention. Thus, in a suit where a parent contested the continued enslavement of a child on the basis of a testamentary grant of freedom or purchase, the judicial process was slow and weighted down by procedural impediments. Unless the parent could prove that the child was in danger of imminent physical removal from the city, the courts continued to demand formal adherence to procedure, notwithstanding a parent's anguish. This was the cumulative effect of having low barriers to court entry, administrative torpor, and labyrinthine procedures in place to deal with clogged dockets. There was also nothing that prevented petitioners from lodging complaints in multiple forums.

When a defendant finally appeared in court, invariably his response was to refute the charges alleged against him by the enslaved petitioner either on substantive or procedural grounds. Sometimes, defendants would allege that the property relationship negated the complaint altogether, that they could not be sued by their own slaves. However, this was a weak argument and never alleged as the sole basis for summary judgment or dismissal. The defendant's response was also subject to review by the magistrate, and the case could be dismissed for lack of merit.

Before a case could proceed further, both parties had to retain a procurator who was capable of representing their interests in court. The provisor ordered the plaintiff and the defendant to name procurators and to grant them powers of attorney. Retaining a procurator was another source of potential delay.

However, the process of gathering witness statements and admitting written evidence could not begin before both procurators entered their appearance into the written record. Some enslaved litigants took their cases to a special procurator for the poor (*procurador de pobres* or *procurador de menores*) who provided services free of charge.[57] However, in the majority of cases, litigants paid procurators – either on retainer or on a fee-per-service basis.[58] Though I have not seen official decrees setting prices for legal fees, I suspect that procurators adjusted their fees according to the petitioner's abilities to pay and used the notarial fee structure (*arançeles*) as a guide.[59]

The crown rigorously regulated notarial fees. Fees were authorized according to the kind of document being drafted and the amount of paper used for recording. The archived cases often include jotted calculations on loose papers or at the end of proceedings that tabulated their fees – calculations that depended on how the court allocated legal costs. (See Figure 1.4). In Anton Bran's case, for instance, Barcala was responsible for the costs of the proceeding.

In the incipient life of a lawsuit, notaries and procurators were vital to the litigation process. We deduce that notaries and procurators often worked together as a team, as the same names appear repeatedly as representatives and recorders of enslaved litigants' complaints. In addition, procurators worked

FIGURE 1.4. Papelito inserted into a case folio.
Image credit: Kathryn Burns.

for both enslaved litigants and for slave owners. In other words, they did not establish a professional reputation by aligning themselves with one or another side.[60] Rather, they were retained because of their punctiliousness or their infallible sense of when to intervene, when to switch tactics, and above all, how best to slow down or expedite the process depending on the interest of the party they represented.

Juan Muñóz's *Práctica para procuradores* excerpted earlier is filled with tips and strategies for delaying a lawsuit on procedural grounds. (See Figure 1.3). Because all procurators were well versed in these dilatory techniques, the opposing party had to be vigilant in order to ensure that the case moved forward. In his study of Lima's procurators, Renzo Honores calculates that there were at most twelve registered procurators in the *Real Audiencia* at any given time.[61] The evidence I have examined suggests that procurators served in both secular and ecclesiastical forums. Lima's professional community was similar to other close-knit legal systems, in that referrals and preferential networks existed between notaries and procurators. Accordingly, a well-prepared litigant initiated her lawsuit with the procurator-notary team in place.

The slow-grinding pace of justice was not always an enemy of the enslaved. Sometimes it could be to the litigant's advantage that a case moved slowly, particularly when slave owners used the courts to contest ownership over a slave's body, offspring, and labor. A few lawsuits show the court levying lowered day-wage payments due to owners while the lawsuits were ongoing – lower *jornales* were beneficial to enslaved litigants and enabled them to meet their legal costs. In lawsuits over disputed inheritance and ownership, the courts could allow petitioners a reprieve until the legal issues were settled.[62] Since this could potentially take years of litigation, this reprieve effectively removed the petitioner from the custody and supervision of her new owner. As we see in Chapter 5, this release does not mean that the petitioner gained her freedom. Rather, it gave her time to perhaps find another owner, cultivate more powerful patrons and allies, amass enough evidence to prove her case, or frustrate her opponents through persistent pleadings.[63]

Agitated or repeated pleadings in the record on the part of enslaved petitioners showed persistence and a determination to move their cases forward in the repetitive, back and forth, formal requirements that comprised the legal process. Cases were rarely resolved quickly – which is why the celerity with which Anton Bran's case was settled was so remarkable. Lawsuits against religious orders were always long, drawn-out affairs: with typical baroque irony, people commonly joked that those who sought immortality started an ecclesiastical suit.

Letrados, provisores, prosecutors, solicitors (*fiscales*), and judges were officials appointed to the upper branches of the judicial hierarchy. *Letrados* intervened when arguments had to be made before the magistrates or at decisive moments in the life of the lawsuit.[64] In contrast to procurators and notaries, *letrados* had university training. *Letrados* could be trained in either civilian or canon law, and most of Lima's *letrados* chose to specialize in both. Students who specialized in canon law required two more years of training beyond civil studies.[65] Criollos' embrace of a law degree reflected the immense popularity of legal studies in sixteenth-century Spain, where increased litigation created the need for practitioners and specially trained jurists.[66]

It took seven to eight years to earn a civil law doctorate, and a canon law doctorate was conferred after ten years of study.[67] The lengthy duration of study did not seem to deter erudite criollos from pursuing both civilian and ecclesiastical doctorates. The doctorate in law conferred tremendous prestige and created an expedited path to the corridors of justice as learned viceregal advisers. Biographies and prosopographical studies of Lima's magistrates highlight the allure of legal learning and the brilliance with which celebrated canonists and jurists articulated their subject in the classrooms and *tertulias* of the city.[68] Don Feliciano de Vega (the provisor who presided over Anton Bran's case) excelled in his qualifying exams at an astoundingly early age, after which he was unanimously appointed to hold an endowed chair and professorship in the University of San Marcos's law faculty.[69] In addition to serving as provisor of the ecclesiastical court, he served as the rector of the University of San Marcos on four occasions and was elected to prestigious bishopric appointments until his death in 1639.[70] Vega was an exemplary criollo jurist whose

FIGURE 1.5. Patio de los Naranjos, University of San Marcos. Author's photograph.

qualifications rivaled – if not exceeded – that of peninsular judicial appointees. Hence Vega played a particularly important role at a time when criollos and *beneméritos* sought to prove their stature and readiness for assuming judicial posts vis-à-vis *peninsulares*.

"ANTE MI" AND "EN NOMBRE DE": THE LOWER BRANCHES OF LIMA'S LEGAL PROFESSION

Recognizing the importance of those who worked at the lower rungs of the legal hierarchy, historians are paying closer attention to those who served as legal intermediaries and "fixers": Andean pettifoggers (*tinterillos*), public defenders (*síndicos procuradores*), and the epistolary teams of scribes, scriveners, and notaries.[71] Drawing on the insights of sociolegal scholarship, historians try to understand what these practitioners actually did, and what their clients expected them to do. The focus on the law's "lower branches" reflects a burgeoning interest not only in the documents as sources. It also reflects our interest in those who laboriously produced the "templates of truth" as Kathryn Burns so nicely puts it, and in the environments through which the documents circulated.[72] Despite the fact that they were professionally subordinate to *letrados* and magistrates, these intermediaries were the people who administered "justice by paperwork" to many of our petitioners.[73]

Civil cases involving enslaved litigants rarely employed *letrados*. Anton Bran's case did not proceed beyond the procuracy stage, suggesting that the two-person team of notary-procurator provided sufficient legal expertise to suit the petitioners' purposes. Some complaints did not even advance beyond the stage at which a notary recorded the substance of a petitioner's grievance. Notaries essentially wrote down the "facts" of the legal complaint – fulfilling a critical role in a "lettered city" with low literacy levels. Notaries were also recorders of the agreements that many enslaved litigants sought to enforce. They were present at deathbeds to draft codicils and revise wills, and they witnessed contracts of sale and *cartas de libertad* – crucial evidentiary documents that preceded the life of the lawsuit. Their presence literally transformed desire into legal action.

Notarial documents, however, were civil documents. The documents belonged to the notary and to the parties whose transactions he memorialized. Unless introduced into evidence (and most of the lawsuits I analyze were brought precisely because of the *lack of* written evidence), they are not found within the Archbishopric archive. By law, each notary had to organize his documents into a thick hidebound volume (*protocolos*) at the end of the year.[74] This archival practice reinforced the legal validity and public memory of the transaction.[75] Notaries also sold their practices with their documents, so the *protocolos* frequently changed hands. Although it is difficult to suture together these archival fragments, notarial documents provide us with a composite picture of slave life in baroque Lima. Indeed, what we know about of the lives of people like Anton and Ysabel Bran comes from the notarial records of their encounters with Spanish and ecclesiastical law.[76]

Not surprisingly for a regulated profession, notarial services were rigorously monitored. According to a 1617 fee chart, notaries could charge 4 *reales* for personal service, 3 *reales* for a complaint, 3 *reales* for the *autos de rebeldía*, 3 *reales* for drafting each interrogatory, and 2 *reales* for each witness examination (3 *reales* if the witness's testimony went on for more than a page).[77] A typical case with ten witnesses would encompass thirty pages at the very least. Calculations would run accordingly:

Complaint:	3 reales
10 Witness statements:	30 reales
3 × Personal service:	12 reales
3 × Autos de rebeldía:	9 reales
Interrogatories:	6 reales
Total	**70 reales**

Instigating a routine lawsuit could thus cost a litigant upward of 70 *reales* (or the equivalent of 9 pesos), if there were ten witnesses.[78] A *jornalera* slave earned between 10 and 12 pesos per month. More enterprising *jornaleras* could earn about 16 pesos monthly, but this was at the upper end of the day wage spectrum. Notarial fees thus represented a significant investment from the enslaved litigant.

Procuracy fees were also important to litigation.[79] Procurators were essential to the lower rungs of the legal process: they paid who needed to be paid, drafted interrogatories for witnesses, and were the liaison between *letrados* and notaries. Procurators did not make legal arguments in court, although many demonstrated a familiarity with legal arguments in the briefs and petitions that they drafted. James Brundage describes procurators as "useful all-purpose agents ... who had hands-on experience with the ways that lawsuits were actually conducted and familiarity with the habits and preferences of judges and other court officials with whom they worked."[80] This kind of practical experience was far more valuable in plebeian lawsuits than sophisticated mastery of canon or Roman law.

Many complaints that end abruptly in the archival record seemed to stall at the point in which a defendant had to name a procurator. This raises the question whether the procuracy stage was a way of distinguishing strong cases from weak ones. Unlike the fictional Sevillano slave owner in Cervantes's *Entremés de los mirones* who capitulated at the mere mention of going to court, we do not have evidence that the threat of a petition or the early stage of filing one was enough to cause an owner to accept the litigant's terms and settle out of court. Unless other archival evidence serendipitously appears, it is unclear whether the parties dropped the case or whether they settled out of court. Because of the expense involved, the procuracy stage also entailed additional cash outlays, although procurators may have taken cases on a contingency basis. Most procurators asked the court to assign costs to their client's opponent in their briefs.

PROCURATORS IN ACTION

Let us review two cases regarding the liberty of a child and a mother with similar outcomes that did not advance beyond the procuracy stage. In 1673, María de la Torre presented her notary with a bill of sale that included a clause for her self-purchase.[81] Her previous owner, Jesuit priest Josef de Alamo, sold her to Gaspar Román, a prebendary (*racionero*) of the Archbishopric, when he was departing for Chile.[82] In the sales contract, María's self-purchase price was set at 400 pesos. The contract included an explicit agreement that Román would free María once she had the money to purchase herself.[83]

Over the span of two years, María accumulated 400 pesos, but Román refused to accept the payment. When the court ordered Román to honor the agreement, Román claimed that María had given birth to a child in secret eight months earlier. Citing the law of the slave womb, Román denied his obligation to accept the money María offered in exchange for her freedom. Román then portrayed María as disingenuous in concealing her child and also alleged that she was attempting to despoil (*despojar*) his property. Román appealed to the court to annul the clause and order María to produce her child.

María, however, ignored Román's claim about her secret pregnancy and doggedly focused on the letter of the agreement. No calls for witnesses were issued, although Román alleged that he learned of María's pregnancy through others who "saw her give birth to a child" (*la vieron parir*). The case ends with Román accepting María's offer of 400 pesos and issuing her a *carta de libertad*.

In another case brought decades earlier in 1628, a husband sued his wife's owner to enforce a promise to accept payment for his child.[84] The wife's owner, the cleric Juan Pacheco, originally agreed to accept 150 pesos from the couple for their daughter's freedom. When the parents presented Pacheco with the payment, together with the notarized agreement, Pacheco refused to honor the agreement. The child's father asked the court to issue *censuras*, claiming breach of contract. Under threat of *censuras*, Pacheco acquiesced and granted Juanita (the child) her letter of freedom.

Neither of these cases proceeded very far up the judicial ladder. Both were resolved relatively quickly. Of course, this does not diminish the mounting frustration that the parties experienced before bringing their complaints to the court. However, both cases ended with a result favorable to the enslaved litigants. The written record is more generous in María's case, but we do not have a judicial ruling (*hallo* or *sentencia*) in either case issued from the court that provides clues about the outcome.[85]

Román's subsequent decision to accept María's offer may have been based on rational calculation. He had the opportunity to accept the 400 pesos that

María offered or fight her and assume the costs of feeding, clothing, and caring for her child, all in the hopes of increasing his estate by at most 100 pesos. Moreover, as clerics, the defendants were susceptible to institutional pressure and disapproval within the ecclesiastical forum. Román was particularly exposed because of his endowed position. The claimants also had written documents that promised the sought-after freedom.[86] Failure to live up to these promises would have been deemed callous and dishonorable by the religious community. That claimants were able to submit their owners' professional reputation to judgment by an ecclesiastical panel of peers and superiors largely explains the quick, out-of-court resolution.

In addition, both cases concerned the freedom of a child. If the parent had evidence that proved she had paid toward the child's freedom, having been assured of the owner's intent to free the child and the owner having received monies for this purpose (as in the case against Juan Pacheco), there was little room for the court to rule against the parent. In the best-case scenario, the parent could produce written proof: a clause in a sales contract with those terms recorded by a notary and a record of installment payments made for that purpose. The weight of such evidence left little room for the owner to invoke an argument based on property rights. Owners like Román may have attempted to posit their property rights as a defensive posture, but this was not enough to sway the court in light of prevailing evidence. The judicial posture here demonstrates quintessential casuistry: a combination of property, contract, and equity determined the outcome in these cases.

Of course, not all cases were as clear-cut or well endowed with irrefutable evidence. However, it bears mentioning that at least in the cases examined here, owners did not arrive in court with the upper hand nor prevail in their cases by asserting their property rights or an untrammeled right of possession. Not every enslaved litigant prevailed, nor were the courts impervious to the power of their owner's wealth or social position. However, the qualities of mercy were not strained by owners who flexed their privilege.

SPIRITUAL SUBPOENAS: *"CENSURAS HASTA ANATEMA"*

In all legal systems, particularly where there are multiple forums, litigants instrumentally bring cases in a court where they believe they will prevail. Enslaved litigants had a far greater chance of prevailing in the ecclesiastical courts than in the *Real Audiencia*. This does not mean that enslaved litigants refrained from using the *Real Audiencia* to lodge their complaints. However, the *Audiencia* heard numerous causes of action from slave *owners* – more so than from enslaved litigants themselves (see Table 1.2). Moreover, the *Audiencia* wielded jurisdiction over criminal matters and issued harsh disciplinary judgments to slaves, *mulatos*, and freed peoples of African descent whom they deemed responsible for the city's crime, brigandry (*bandolerismo*), and social unrest. Criminal sanctions were either public execution by garrote or hard labor in exile for a defined period (generally up to five years).[87] Other sanctions were nearly as gruesome as the garrote: these included whipping, ear excision, and castration. Even in noncriminal cases, enslaved litigants fared poorly in front of *Audiencia* panels. To circumvent negative rulings or to expedite drawn-out procedures, enslaved litigants appealed to the Archbishopric court to issue *censuras generales*.

According to a seventeenth-century treatise of ecclesiastical procedure, the Tridentine Council authorized priests to summon all parishioners to testify or aid in an active investigation that was either convened in church courts or in the secular forum. This was a singular instance of cooperation between forums that jealously guarded their respective jurisdictions. In fact, the treatise admits that *censuras* were the only means by which the ecclesiastical judge was allowed to assist his secular colleagues. *Censuras* were meant to exhort parishioners to help in recovering stolen goods of modest value and could be read and published during high mass up to three times.[88] They could also be issued to compel parishioners to disclose secret information or illicit affairs. Failure to respond to these *censuras* was a crime against God and the community of faith.

Priests were instructed by the ecclesiastical court to issue *censuras* each week at high mass (*misa mayor*), which ensured that they would be heard by the maximum number of parishioners.[89] Spiritual penalties increased with severity upon each exhortation. By the intonation of the third *censura*, those who failed to come forward were condemned to eternal damnation and excommunion. Their wives and children were similarly doomed:

And if three additional days have passed after the first and second threat of excommunion, you will declare the malfeasants permanently excommunicated because of their hardened souls. You will censure and condemn them because their guilt and contumacy has increased. Consequently, their punishment must increase in severity. We order all priests and their assistants to issue the following order at high mass, in all major cathedrals, on each Sunday and feast day. These words must be uttered with a black cloth covering the cross and burning candles held high. You will thus curse the malfeasants:

"Cursed are all who are excommunicated from the fellowship of God and his Holy Mother. Their children will become orphans and their wives widows. The sun will darken their days and the moon will not illuminate their nights. They will walk begging from door to door and find no one to take pity on them. The plagues sent by God to the kingdom of Egypt will strike them. The evil of Sodom and Gomorrah that consumed their people alive for their sins will afflict their families." Amen.[90]

The tenor of the *censuras* is steeped in the inquisitorial idioms of medieval and early modern Catholicism. Beleaguered souls could be redeemed only through confession and penitence.

Limeño litigants used *censuras* in two contexts. First, they posited the malfeasance of their opponent as a crime against the faith and a crime against the laws of the church. Almost every case brought in the ecclesiastical forum shows an irate petitioner urging the court to issue *censuras hasta anathema*

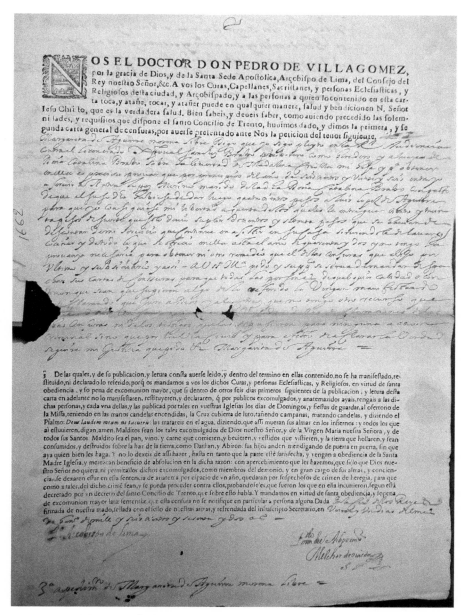

FIGURE 1.6. Margarita de Aguirre, Censura 1661.

that threatened the opposing party with excommunion for failure to respond to a court order. (Litigants in the *Real Audiencia* did not have recourse to *censuras*, as they were ecclesiastical tools of admonition.) Second, they used *censuras* after they had been disqualified in the secular forum to compel witnesses to come forward in church to relieve their consciences.

Archivists at Lima's Archbishopric archive led me to thirty folios of uncatalogued *censuras* that were issued between 1600 and 1699. I believe the practice of issuing *censuras* accelerated under Provisor Pedro de Villagómez's tenure at the court, when they became available in boilerplate. (See Figure 1.7). Each preprinted sheet corresponded to the forms used for the first, second, and third exhortation. On the basis of a rough calculation, we estimate that there are over 9,000 *censuras* at the archive. Each bound packet of single sheet folios (*legajo*) contains an average of 300 *censuras* each. Clearly, this was a widely used method of harnessing the power of the pulpit – together with the threat of bell, book, and candle – to get people to come forth and testify. But for this discovery, I would not have known how widespread the practice was. For years, I had been poring over case folios in which petitioners in active litigation appealed to the church to issue *censuras* without understanding that it was an independent legal procedure or cause of action.

Common sense suggests that when a procedure is so widespread it loses its effect. Because of the fragmentary nature of the evidence, determinations of efficacy depend on a longitudinal, outcome-driven study in which one matches the *censuras* to lawsuits, testaments, and notarial *cartas de libertad*. The evidence is simultaneously overabundant and dispersed. Nevertheless, we can still make reasonable assessments about the efficacy of *censuras* by examining how parishioners used them when stymied by recalcitrant or inadmissible witness testimonies in their cases. I now turn to three *censuras* that illustrate how the process worked. Given the nature of the evidence described and analyzed thus

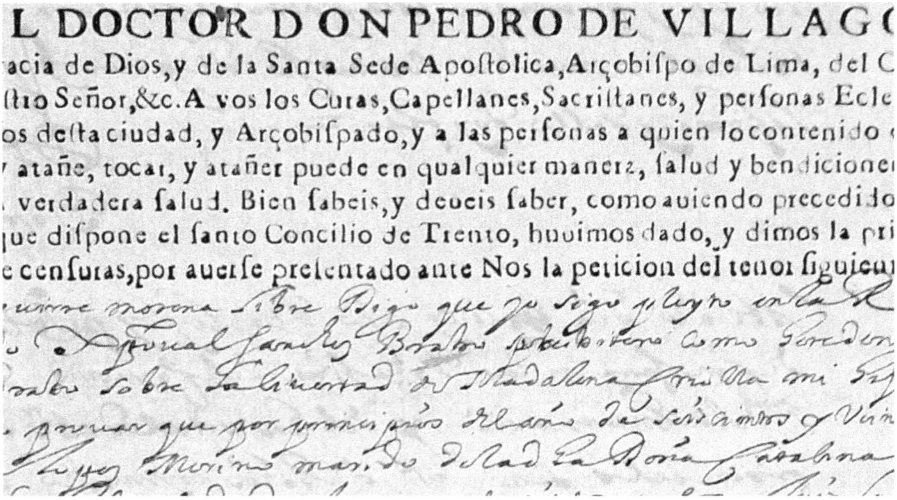
L DOCTOR DON PEDRO DE VILLAG
acia de Dios, y de la Santa Sede Apostolica, Arçobispo de Lima, del C
ltro Señor, &c. A vos los Curas, Capellanes, Sacristanes, y personas Ecle
os desta ciudad, y Arçobispado, y a las personas a quien lo contenido
atañe, tocar, y atañer puede en qualquier manera, salud y bendiciones
verdadera salud. Bien sabeis, y deveis saber, como auiendo precedido
que dispone el santo Concilio de Trento, huuimos dado, y dimos la pri
censuras, por auerse presentado ante Nos la peticion del tenor siguien

FIGURE 1.7. Boilerplate of censura with don Pedro de Villagomez's name in the template.

far, readers will anticipate that the cases are deficient in some aspects but meritorious and compelling in others. I recount three of these in detail not only to show the dynamics of legal and ecclesiastical institutions but also to underscore the power of *censuras* as spiritual subpoenas.

In 1661, Margarita de Aguirre brought a case against Cristóbal Sánchez Bravo in the *Real Audiencia*, but all the witnesses in her case were disqualified because of "tachas": relationships of blood or servitude that obligated a witness to lie in favor of a party to the litigation.[91] After sustaining this defeat in the *Real Audiencia*, Margarita went to the ecclesiastical court and appealed to Provisor Pedro de Villagómez to issue *censuras* to compel witnesses to testify about what they knew in that forum.

Cristóbal Sánchez Bravo was a priest and the trustee and heir to the estate of Margarita's former owners, Antonio López Medina and Catalina Bravo. According to Margarita and her witnesses, Margarita came to Lima from a northern province of Peru, pawned (*en empeño*) for 260 pesos. Margarita had owed her owner 260 pesos to settle the balance due on her purchase price. He in turn had an outstanding debt of that equivalent amount with Antonio López Medina, and so he sent her to Lima to satisfy that debt. Within two years of Margarita's arrival in Lima, Antonio sent money to her owner in the north to settle her purchase price. In Margarita's calculations – which were allegedly endorsed in public on numerous occasions by Antonio and Catalina – her services were valued at 200 pesos a year.

Although freed, Margarita continued to work for Antonio and Catalina for an additional seven years. Antonio and Catalina had no children of their own, but they adopted an orphaned baby (*un niño expósito*) who had been abandoned at the door of the Monasterio de la Santísima Trinidad. Margarita nursed this child, as she had milk of her own (Margarita was perhaps working as a wet nurse [*ama de leche*] or she might have been nursing her own child at the time). Many of the witnesses insisted that Margarita nursed the child (*lo crió de pecho*) as part of her unpaid domestic duties. Since Margarita was legally freed, she claimed that she continued to work for Antonio and Catalina for seven years in exchange for the freedom of her daughter and granddaughters. But there was no written proof of this compact. After Antonio died, Margarita continued to work in the household to care for Catalina. Upon Catalina's death, her nephew and heir Cristóbal refused to honor the oral agreement. Instead, Cristóbal laid claim to Margarita's daughter and granddaughters whom he inherited as part of his aunt's estate.

At least thirty witnesses testified in the *Real Audiencia* in Margarita's favor. The witnesses came from all ends of Lima's social spectrum. Genteel Spanish maidens (*doncellas*), *castas*, slaves, nuns, carpenters who formerly worked for Antonio, neighbors, friends, merchants, and priests all verified Margarita's story. One of Margarita's witnesses even included a *mulato sacristán* (the highest ecclesiastical position that could be held by a non-Spaniard). They unanimously verified that Margarita had indeed served Antonio and Catalina with diligence and care. They knew she worked exclusively for Antonio and Catalina and calculated that her excellent service was worth at least 200 pesos each year – which was the going rate for personal domestic services in the seventeenth century. Margarita's work as a wet nurse increased the calculation of wages for the personal services rendered.

After the first *censura* was issued at mass, the notarial record of witness testimonies was remitted to the ecclesiastical court from the *Real Audiencia* as if it were on appeal.[92] We do not have access to the full transcript of the case. Therefore, we are only privy to the witness statements that were sent over for Provisor Villagómez's review. Cristóbal Sánchez immediately filed a counterclaim resisting Margarita's call for *censuras* by noting that the case was being litigated in the *Real Audiencia*. Sánchez called Villagómez's attention to the fact that all of Margarita's witnesses had been disqualified because of *tachas*. However, technically, that was not the point. As parishioners, they were still obligated to bear witness to what they knew about the matter. Failure to do so would have resulted in their excommunion and eternal damnation. Within a month, Cristóbal capitulated and granted Margarita's daughter and granddaughter their *cartas de libertad*.

A similar outcome awaited Brídiga de Córdoba in her 1669 lawsuit against the heirs of her owner's estate.[93] Like Margarita, Brígida sued the trustees of her owner in the *Real Audiencia* for failure to honor a promise to free her and her son Alejandro. Unlike Margarita's opponent, these trustees were not clerics. There must therefore be another explanation besides vocational pressure from superiors that accounts for the efficacy of *censuras*.

Brígida also had a convoluted property history with her owner. Brígida was exchanged (*trocada*) between two sisters, Luisa and Francisca de Córdoba. According to Brígida, doña Francisca – her original owner – agreed to free her and her son after she died. This promise was conveyed to doña Luisa as part of the exchange, who agreed to honor it. Doña Francisca departed Lima for a *corregimiento* with her sister's slave Ynez, whom she exchanged for Brígida.[94] Again, there was no written document to prove the compact. By the time Brígida brought her lawsuit, doña Francisca was either dead or faraway in the *corregimiento*. So Brígida asked the church to summon witnesses through reading *censuras*.

Ynez de Córdoba, *morena libre*, responded to the *censuras*. Ynez testified to a priest from what appeared to be her deathbed. The tenor of her testimony was reminiscent of a confessional – no interrogatories were prepared.[95] Ynez happened to be the slave who went to the *corregimiento* with doña Francisca. Ynez's last act corroborated Brígida's version of events. Since Ynez had been freed by doña Francisca, it was clear that doña Luisa should have followed suit. Subsequently, Brígida also secured a *carta de libertad* for herself and her son.

When dictating the information to the ecclesiastical notaries or *relatores* who completed their paperwork, neither petitioner mentioned a procurator.[96] It is likely that the procurators retained by Brígida and Margarita recommended the women ask for *censuras* to be read when their witnesses were disqualified in the

Real Audiencia. Alternatively, the practice could have been so widespread that every litigant knew they should request *censuras* – in the same way that everyone who wanted to marry knew they had to file a marriage petition. Because each party to the lawsuit attempted to discredit the other, witness disqualifications were important to prevailing in one's case.[97] As Tamar Herzog explains, "Social networks between a wide range of people who were connected to one another by ties of family, friendship and personal dependence ... produced obligations which were sufficiently strong to justify lying in legal proceedings."[98] Sometimes witnesses were certified by virtue of their admission to *generales:* a legal obligation imposed on witnesses to disclose any relationships of blood, alliance, or godparenthood (*compadrazgo*) with the petitioner. If the opposing party did not object to the testimony of kinfolk or dependents, the testimony became admissible. Parties to a lawsuit shared the same notary, so both sides had ample notice about the individuals who testified in a given case.[99]

Margarita's and Brígida's cases share similar characteristics: a complicated property history, geographical relocation, and disputed promises of eventual manumission: "contexts pregnant with the potential for conflict and ambivalence."[100] Each factor individually could have created a cause of action: when combined, they were potentially devastating to the enslaved person's lawsuit. The lack of written proof also encumbered the claims. The petitioners attempted to compensate for each of these weaknesses by flooding the proceeding with the oral testimonies of witnesses who could corroborate their version of events. Bringing those witnesses into court through *censuras* was critical if they were to secure their liberty.

A third *censura* proceeding brought in 1685 illustrates the confluence of negligent notaries, geographical relocation, installment payments toward a family's freedom pocketed by an unscrupulous third party, and socially powerful defendants. As in Margarita's and Brígida's cases, the *censura* brought by Margarita Florindes in 1685 alleged conditions that were potentially disastrous to her claim. However, Margarita faced adversaries who were socially prominent and who chose to litigate in a special tribunal in which they were particularly favored. Perhaps because of the social position of her opponents, Margarita's procurator asked in her name for the *censuras* to be read during mass to summon witnesses.

Margarita's mother, Ysabel, was previously owned by a family whose patriarch was a member of the chivalric order of Alcántara. Ysabel asked one of her owner's friends, don Martín de Zavala, to purchase her and paid him 400 pesos as a down payment toward the purchase price of her daughter Margarita. This agreement was notarized on a blank sheet of paper (*en blanco*) two days after don Martín received the money from Ysabel. Ysabel worked off the remaining 650 pesos in don Martín's service. Over the span of two decades, Ysabel had paid over 1,000 pesos for her family's liberty.

Don Martín de Zavala was an accountant for the order of Santiago and a mayor (alcalde) of Lima. Given his powerful position, he undoubtedly had a number of notaries with whom he conducted business on a frequent basis.[101]

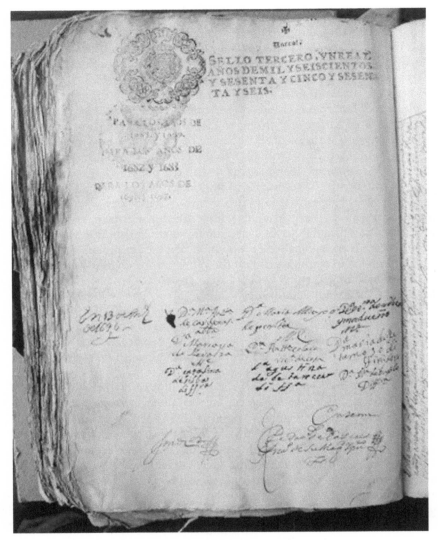

FIGURE 1.8. Blank notarial signed sheet in a Protocolo.
Image credit: Kathryn Burns.

That may have explained his willingness to entrust a notary with a blank signed sheet, which presumably the notary – or his copyist – would have filled out later in the notary's office. However, no details were ever recorded. Signing sheets in blank without the details of the transaction was a prohibited (and above all negligent) notarial practice. However, it was not uncommon in high-volume notarial offices. Kathryn Burns shows how many of Cuzco's notaries signed off on blank sheets, despite the royal pronouncements against the practice. (See Figure 1.8).

As she writes, "Clients perhaps found it convenient, since signing a blank page meant they did not have to wait around while copyists drafted each legalistic word of their business. More importantly for notaries, it was profitable: this practice enabled them to do more business in a given amount of time."[102]

In brief, Ysabel's agreement with don Martín, her down payment, and the entire contract went unrecorded by the notary. Whether this was negligence or deliberate oversight, we do not know. When Margarita went to find the paperwork, she not only discovered that the contract was blank, but also found that the notary who had supposedly recorded the original transaction had sold his practice to someone else. Margarita thus protested her sale and continued servitude without having plenary documentary proof that her mother had purchased her. While Ysabel went to work for don Martín twenty-five years earlier, Margarita stayed in the house of Ysabel's original owners. They either unscrupulously held her in servitude as a child, or don Martín never revealed the pact he made with Ysabel. Don Martín also never disclosed the payment that he received to Margarita's "owners." However, since Ysabel had paid 400 pesos in 1657 (twenty-five years previously), that should – at the very least – have satisfied Margarita's purchase price.

Margarita's case was litigated in the Tribunal de la Santa Cruzada, which exercised personal jurisdiction over members of the chivalric orders of Alcántara and Santiago.[103] To make matters more complicated, don Martín served a lifetime appointment as the tribunal's primary accountant. Margarita's "owners" were also members of the order of Santiago and subject to the jurisdiction of the Santa Cruzada. As Margarita put it, "I have no other recourse but to ask for *censuras*, since the persons against whom I am litigating are powerful."

The first witness who appeared after the *censuras* were read at high mass was doña Francisca de Coya. Doña Francisca was the widow of Ysabel's previous owner. Doña Francisca verified that don Martín had indeed received 400 pesos from Ysabel that was meant to pay for her child's freedom. She also verified that Ysabel had her husband's permission to change owners and transfer the payment arrangement to don Martín. The second witness, doña Francisca's slave Ignacia, also corroborated the account.

The outcome of Margarita's case is unknown. However, she showed that the payment that her mother made twenty-five years earlier was made at a time and in an amount intended to purchase her freedom. More importantly, the widow of her opponent's friend in court verified this payment and its purpose. It is not implausible to conclude that don Martín acquiesced to Margarita's demands to protect his friendship and professional reputation.

A LITIGIOUS SOCIETY?

The historical record has always led us to believe that colonial Iberoamerica experienced an explosion of litigation, or a "judicial awakening." These ideas of explosive litigiousness were largely formulated in response to Andean and Spanish patterns. The number of lawsuits brought by slaves in the *Real*

TABLE 1.2. *Litigation Brought by Enslaved Petitioners in the Ecclesiastical Forum, 1593–1699*

Type of litigation	Number of cases
Spousal unification	270
Divorce and annulment	20
Disputes over day wages, testamentary disposition, contracts	88
Cruelty, change of ownership	10
Ecclesiastical immunity	328
Redhibition	129
Censuras	1500

TABLE 1.3. *Litigation Pertaining to Enslaved People in the Real Audiencia, 1600–97*

Type of litigation	Number of cases
Testamentary manumission	4
Redhibition	8
Wrongful enslavement, property disputes	15
Liberty	5
Total	32

Audiencia pertaining to wrongful enslavement, for instance (fifteen), is quite modest considering the size of the enslaved population in baroque Lima. Most *causas de negros* were brought in the Archbishopric court. As reflected in Table 1.2, spousal unity injunctions and ecclesiastical immunity suits were the most numerous forms of legal action in the ecclesiastical forum.[104] Were it not for the discovery of *censuras,* the numbers would remain underwhelming. While all the caveats about archival loss and the fragmentary nature of the evidence are relevant here, the question nevertheless emerges: how litigious were Lima's slaves?

The view of litigiousness has also been accompanied by a negative portrayal of litigation and a general distaste for the legal process. Even contemporary scholars suggest that people resort to the courts when they have exhausted all other options.[105] Marc Galanter famously contends that people "lump" their situation because they would rather not go through the excruciating or arcane legal process.[106] Those who "lump it" are potential litigants with legitimate grievances but who lack both the sophistication and financial resources that repeat legal actors possess.

People in early modern Iberia expressed similar distaste for the legal process. Indeed, in an effort to preempt the transfer of Iberian litigiousness to the purity and innocence of the New World, lawyers were banned from sailing to

Peru by royal decree in 1529.[107] Richard Kagan acknowledges a conundrum in his study of sixteenth-century Iberian litigiousness: why would Iberians file so many lawsuits while denouncing legal action and lawyers with such fervor?[108] As Kagan writes, Castilian theologians inveighed against legal action, arguing that the "rancor and passion" of lawsuits were incompatible with the "love and concord amongst Christians."[109] However, despite the fact that lawsuits were unpleasant procedures, they were increasingly undertaken to resolve complex and minor issues alike.

Ultimately, it is immaterial whether lawsuits were as widely denounced in Lima as they were on the peninsula. Rather, we presume that throughout the centuries, powerless and aggrieved people were among those most motivated to use legal channels to rectify conditions of inequity and unfairness. The critique of "rancor and passion" largely reflected elite anxieties about plebeian litigiousness, false accusations, and commercial grudges, fed also by inquisitorial fear.

Conclusive accounts about rates of litigiousness are predicated on reliable access to litigation records that were filed in a fixed jurisdiction over a defined period of time. Kagan's much-cited study of Castilian litigation in the sixteenth-century *cancillería* of Valladolid examines annual caseloads that ranged between 6,000 and 7,000 lawsuits "on the books."[110] Kagan analyzes well-preserved archival sources, providing us with a history of the *cancillería*, the practitioners who worked in it, and those who sought its services. No historical study can be attempted without sources, and those lawsuits that survive in the archive (whether in detail or in fragments) are documented in this book. The idiosyncratic nature of each collection explains why this study is unsuited to statistical analytical methods.

What do we know about Lima's enslaved litigants? No doubt, the majority of Lima's slaves "lumped it." It is unthinkable that only ten people experienced cruelty at the hands of their owners in over a hundred years. We conclude that people used extralegal means to resolve their situation – they ran away from cruel masters and hapless marriages, or they changed owners without legal intervention. We presume that most of these personal arrangements went according to plan, since we have no record of them. So many lawsuits described here come before us because relationships and promises based on trust deteriorated or went unheeded by heirs.

Those who were most active in litigation were people who had a meritorious claim with varying levels of proof. Litigants buttressed the merits of their claim with testimonies of numerous reputable witnesses who were prepared to testify under solemn oath. Litigants also expressed confidence that the court could potentially resolve their grievance. As previously noted, most of Lima's enslaved litigants came from households where they could have had access to legal knowledge, and conveyed this knowledge to others. Moreover, those litigants in servitude of prominent households were most active in court. They did not cower before their owner's social power or prestige; rather they cleverly used the courts as a public forum to hold their owners accountable. Those who came to court had a decent chance of prevailing. Often, they in fact did prevail. But even those who lost their cases garnered important victories. For this reason, we need to reformulate how we think of legal efficacy. Moreover, if we posit claims making as a process, the act of asking the church to issue *censuras* in front of the community of faith is tantamount to a form of plebeian legal mobilization. The fact that these actions forced one's owners and opponents to defend themselves and their honor in a public forum is an important index of legal efficacy.

It is important to look at litigation from the point of view of enslaved litigants, thereby revisiting the question of legal efficacy from a plaintiff-centered perspective. Legal anthropologists have chided lawyers (and others) for focusing unduly on the "end result" of litigation. In other words, so much of what we deem to be reasonable motivation for embarking on litigation is related to favorable outcome. Social psychologists and anthropologists have given us a deeper appreciation for the noninstrumental, intangible, and emotional reasons why people turn to the law.

The entanglement of slaves and courts is generally viewed within a Gramscian optic of power, legitimacy, and hegemony. These are, of course, heavily freighted ideological terms in sociolegal studies. At some level, legitimacy involves a combination of acquiescence and resistance. Subaltern groups agree to be governed through legal rules that often constrain and place them at a disadvantage yet turn to the law when they believe their rights have been violated. This belief that the law is "just" (derogatorily labeled "false consciousness") naturalizes inequalities between classes, generations, genders, and castes. In baroque Iberoamerica, legitimacy became more complex when courts – which were themselves embedded in other forms of paternalistic social control and profoundly linked to structures of governance and power – dispensed "justice."[111] Yet plebeian and enslaved litigants who sought recourse in the ecclesiastical or secular courts must have believed it was possible that such appeals to the law could resolve their problem. In this way, the law served as both an instrument of domination and as a means of resistance to that domination.

Locating the fault lines and fissures of agency, cooptation, and resistance is difficult within this hegemonic frame. Furthermore, to peer into the dark thicket of the resistance-cooptation continuum in search of agency guided by three and a half centuries of hindsight is seldom a productive enterprise. As scholars increasingly argue, to posit legal action within the confines of this continuum is an impoverished way of looking at slave agency.[112]

It is never presumed – rightfully so – that slaves wield power. But it is not true that urban slaves possessed no ability to recruit the courts in their favor through an appeal to the king's clemency. This ability may have had more to do with larger political struggles between and among elites jockeying for power and using special constituencies to buttress their position. It may also have had to do with the workings of monarchical forms of governance that operated on personal patronage and with intermittent, spectral violence.[113] Enslaved litigants did not possess conventional sources of political or social power that would have swayed courts. Nonetheless, this book describes a good number of situations in which Limeño slaves were able to prevail against their owners. None of this detracts from the superstructural thesis advanced by Marxist historians of slavery. Neither does it undermine the realist observation that law can be simultaneously wielded as an instrument of liberty and bondage. At the very least, these cases present an opportunity for us to see how enslaved litigants could use laws for very different purposes than their legislators intended. With law's duality and indeterminacy in mind, and with the tenacity of the foot-dragging legal subject, let us conclude by returning to the case of Anton and Ysabel Bran.

ON BEING AND BECOMING BRAN

In the house of Anton Bran, licensed tailor, a young Indian man named Juan Lima was found working as an apprentice. He was from the pueblo of Santo Domingo, Yauyos.

Census of Lima's Indian population, 1613

We began this chapter with the case of Anton and Ysabel Bran pursuing legal action against a gluttonous priest who refused to pay an agreed price for his meals. In closing, I want to return to Anton Bran as a way to sketch a profile of a "repeat legal actor" within Lima's enslaved and freed community.

Anton Bran has been the subject of previous historical gazes. As seen from the excerpt, Anton was one of the more than 10,000 *negros* enumerated in the 1613 city-wide census. Frederick Bowser uses this census, together with notarial purchase documents, to reconstruct the African origins of Peruvian slaves. Anton, Ysabel, and their two apprentices from the *tierra Bran* would have been part of Bowser's quantitative study of Upper Guinean slaves who were imported to Peru.[114] Bowser also mentions Anton's purchase of his wife Ysabel in his chapter on manumission practices in Lima.

While we do not have enough for a biography of Anton and Ysabel, we can glean information about them from three local sources: a lawsuit, a census entry, and a notarial self-purchase agreement. When viewed holistically, they enable us to explore and imagine the ways that this couple and their contemporaries lived their lives in the City of Kings. Anton and Ysabel are not just historical subjects "from below"; they become historiographical subjects through our attention to legal mobilization, gender, diaspora, mixed status, and social identity.[115]

According to Bowser's calculations, 849 people imported to Lima between 1560 and 1650 were identified as "casta Bran." Though we are all indebted to Bowser's careful analysis of notarial slave purchase records, he relied on the ethnonym rather than interrogating the process of "being and becoming" a member of the Bran nation. The source of this reliance can be traced to how, as Rachel O'Toole notes, slaveholders "labeled captive Africans." It is also reflected in the categorization undertaken by the Cartagena-based Jesuit priest Alonso Sandoval, who "collapsed the multiplicity of diasporic identity and transatlantic allegiances from the Rivers of Guinea into the *casta* category of Bran... Bran was many of the *casta* terms of slave trading and would become an identity for Africans and their descendants in the Americas."[116]

Unlike many of the litigants examined herein, Anton Bran was not attached to a high-ranked household. On the contrary, Anton was a free African-born slave (*bozal*). Ysabel was also a *bozal* from the *tierra Bran*. At forty years of age, Anton had achieved his freedom relatively early – he seems to have possessed a degree of industriousness and enterprise that no doubt derived from his skills as a tailor. From the lawsuit and the census, we know that Anton had enough resources and work to employ four apprentices: one Andean apprentice, one mestizo, and two others from the *tierra Bran*. Ysabel was a likely candidate for lifetime manumission: the income she earned from cooking in addition to Anton's earnings would conceivably have been directed at purchasing her freedom.

Guided by Bowser's cryptic footnote 33, I retraced Anton's steps to his notary's records, which thankfully survived.[117] In 1615 (one year before Anton filed his complaint against Barcala), the couple arranged with Ysabel's owners to purchase her freedom for the astounding price of 1,000 pesos.[118] According to the notary who drafted Ysabel's manumission agreement, Anton Bran was a free bozal "ropero." One year later in his complaint to the ecclesiastical court, Anton would refer to himself as an *oficial de sastre*, suggesting upward occupational mobility in becoming a royally licensed tailor.[119] In the manumission agreement, Ysabel was referred to as Ysabel Bran, or Ysabel de Guadalupe. Anton paid Ysabel's owners 500 pesos in cash, and secured 300 pesos on credit, payments that he amortized over three years.[120] Ysabel's owners agreed to apply two years of her *jornales* (200 pesos) to her purchase price. When we calculate the timing of the couple's dispute with Barcala, it becomes evident that it unfolded in the midst of the installment plan with Ysabel's owners. It thus explains the strengthened resolve of the couple to make a claim for the breach of payment.

A nagging question remains: why would Anton pay so much for Ysabel's freedom? From the terms of the letter and his lawsuit, Ysabel already lived a semiautonomous life. It appeared that the couple lived together but that they had no children of their own. Ysabel's owners did not oppose her side ventures in cooking for others. Indeed, they profited from her labor in the form of the installment agreement and their application of her wages to an already inflated purchase price. Perhaps the answer lies in prestige. Purchasing Ysabel's freedom enabled Anton to become a prominent member of his ethnic community and serve as a benefactor of the city's enslaved population.[121] Marriage not only gave Anton and Ysabel the capacity to pool financial resources but also structurally enabled them to incorporate new enslaved arrivals from the *tierra Bran*. As apprentices, the new recruits then worked for and learned skills from Anton and Ysabel. Given Anton's refusal to "lump it," it is not implausible that litigiousness was among the skillset the new recruits acquired.

CONCLUSION

This chapter has painted a picture of legal practitioners, court society, and the litigants within to give readers a sense of the composition of the city, and highlight the importance of legal forums in baroque governance. My method here has been more ethnographic than historical because my aim is to provide the reader with a day-to-day account of the ecclesiastical legal system during the century of unparalleled church power. I have tried to situate readers within the entrails and sinews of a living organism rather than describe its incubation, maturation, or demise. That work has already been ably done by many other historians.

I have argued that enslaved litigants fared best in court when their case was fortified with irrefutable evidence, as that provided them with an equitable basis on which they could substantiate their claim to liberty, and accompanied by witnesses of social stature. This is by no means a grand claim about the civil law's commitment to upholding the slave's legal personality. It is rather a more contextual argument about equity in first instance courts that resulted in small or partial victories. Although these victories did not undermine prevailing power structures, they nonetheless represented accretions of custom that led to shifts in legal practice.

As we will see, cases were decided mostly by split decisions. Legal action was part of a lengthy, protracted process in the fight for liberty that was mostly waged outside of court. The next set of chapters chart the course of an enslaved person's life through the rites and stages of baptism, childhood, marriage, death, inheritance, and resale, as people struggled to accrue fractions of freedom in the Hispanic baroque.

NOTES

1   AAL, Causas de negros, leg. 3, exp. 4, año 1616.
2   On the small claims court "revolution" and working-class litigiousness, see Merry, *Getting Justice and Getting Even.*
3   On Vega's career as provisor, see Dammert, "Don Feliciano de Vega," 25, Gálvez Peña, "Obispo, financista y político," and Barrientos Grandon, "Un canonista peruano del siglo XVII."
4   The composition of baroque Lima's population complicates an already problematic distinction between a society with slaves and a slave society. The mathematic problem emerges because a slave society is one in which bonded labor is essential to the modes of production, typically those in plantation or mining societies. The original formulation outlined by Moses Finley estimates that a slave society was one in which more

than 30 percent of its population was enslaved. See Berlin, *Many Thousands Gone*, for the formulation in the United States. Baroque Lima had a 50 percent African presence. However, Lima's slaves were overwhelmingly urban and domestic, even though the ratio of its enslaved population to its free population puts it squarely within the classification as a slave society. The equation is cumbersome because the legal activism and customary practices that Lima's slaves developed were more commonly found in a less rigid "society with slaves." Alejandro de la Fuente makes this argument for Cuban slaves' court use in the nineteenth century. See his "*Coartación* and Papel." Though with reference to North America, Chris Tomlins has usefully proposed that we abandon the distinction in favor of "societies with slavery." Tomlins writes, "Virtually every mainland colony became a society with slaves; not all made the further and final move to become slave societies" (*Freedom Bound*, 417).

5   The dichotomy between resistance and accommodation became particularly salient in the 1980s and was strengthened by James Scott's work on everyday forms of resistance. Scott unmasks covert forms of resistance (pilfering, deliberate laziness, work slowdowns, and deliberate tool breaking), and his formulation was helpful to slavery scholars at the time who were struggling to find agency in what was seen as the totalizing institution of slavery. Earlier gender-focused studies examining enslaved women's experience of subordination and double exploitation were also enhanced by the concepts of everyday resistance and hidden transcripts. For a representative anthology, see Clark Hine, *Black Women in American History*. For an intriguing analysis of the dichotomy of accommodation/resistance in reference to a slave-authored peace treaty, see Schwartz, "Resistance and Accommodation in Eighteenth-Century Brazil."

6   "Cualquier litigio permite observar el comportamiento de las partes y los intereses en juego, siempre y cuando desechemos imágenes simplistas que piensan al derecho solo como una imposición de la clase dominante; se trata mas bien de un terreno de confrontación, donde por eso mismo tienen que salir a relucir los intereses y própositos de los sectores populares: aunque sean más frecuentes los fallos en contra, *el funcionamiento del sistema exige que ellos puedan obtener algunas victorias y alcanzar ciertas reivindicaciones*, a pesar de ser negros y esclavos" (Flores Galindo, *Aristocracia y plebe*, 18, my emphasis).

7   In an effort to centralize imports, collect tax and excise duties, and diminish contraband, the crown channeled all silver exports through the port of Callao. Biannual fairs (*ferias*) were held in Portobelo, Panama, where European commercial goods were traded for silver bullion as the Spanish Armada sailed from Callao to Seville. Despite the crown's centralizing efforts, contraband accounted for much of the trade in and out of the city.

8   Martín, *Intellectual Conquest of Peru*; Martínez-Serna, "Procurators and the Making of the Jesuits' Atlantic Network."

9   Van Deusen, *Between the Sacred and the Worldly*.

10 Peoples of Castilian descent and those born on the peninsula were referred to as Spaniards (*españoles*). Even though African-descent peoples were referred to as *negros*, white (*blanco*) was not a racial category of the period.

11 Recent scholarship disputes the low numbers of mestizos and Andeans in the 1613 census. See Graubart, "Hybrid Thinking," for a thorough discussion of the inability to enumerate or understand urban Andeans.

12 Altman, *Emigrants and Society*.

13 Eltis, "A Brief Overview of the Trans-Atlantic Slave Trade"; Voyages: The Trans-Atlantic Slave Trade Database, www.slavevoyages.org.

14 Slaves who disembarked in Brazilian ports, as well as those who were destined for Mexico, have been separately accounted for in the transatlantic database, giving us a clearer idea of the African-descent population in Peru. Cartagena was of course not the only port of origin for Peru, although it was the major transit point for Lima. See Newson and Minchin, *From Capture to Sale*, on early seventeenth-century slave transfers between Cartagena and Lima. Nicholas Cushner notes that Jesuits purchased slaves directly through their own agent in Panama. He also writes that Jesuits participated in the internal resale market through conventional sources: "through local slave markets offering blacks brought from Buenos Aires and Córdoba, the official *asentista* who unloaded his cargo in Callao, from adjacent haciendas which put up for sale slaves unwanted for one reason or another" ("Slave Mortality and Reproduction," 179). Jane Mangan notes that slaves destined for the mines of Potosí – though fewer in number than those headed for the coastal haciendas – came via Brazil through Buenos Aires and then overland to Potosí (*Trading Roles*, 41).

15 Wheat, "The First Great Waves"; Landers, "Cartagena"; Bühnen, "Ethnic Origins of Peruvian Slaves (1548–1650)"; Newson and Minchin, *From Capture to Sale*.

16 Sandoval, *Treatise on Slavery*. We should also remember that sixteenth-century theologians focused their debates on the illegitimacy of indigenous slavery, given that Iberian conquistadors believed they had a locally available – and free – labor pool of indigenous people.

17 Fredrickson, *Racism: A Short History*, 38.

18 Eltis and Richardson, *Atlas of the Transatlantic Slave Trade*, 30.

19 Ibid., 30. After 1630, the Dutch moved their operations to Pernambuco.

20 Vega Franco, *El tráfico de esclavos*. The crown viewed the Genoese as "royal subjects," on par with their erstwhile Portuguese and Dutch counterparts.

21 Rupert, *Creolization and Contraband*. As Rupert notes, Curaçao's strategic location, the long-standing patterns of smuggling unregistered slaves in as part of recorded and taxed voyages, and the increasing demand for slave labor rendered contraband feasible, pragmatic, and desirable.

22 Enriqueta Vila Villar ("Los asientos Portugueses y el contraband de negros") contends that the primary agents of contraband were the *asentistas* (royal license holders) themselves because they had both the incentive and the opportunity to underreport the human cargo they had aboard.

23 Borucki, Eltis, and Wheat, "Atlantic History and the Slave Trade to Spanish America," 442. On contraband, see Vila Vilar's early study, "Los asientos Portugueses."

24 Bowser, "Colonial Spanish America."

25 According to the recent survey by Borucki, Eltis, and Wheat, "Africans arriving in any Spanish colony [after the mid-seventeenth century] were surrounded by criollos, their mestizo progeny, and a growing creole population of full and mixed African ancestry" ("Atlantic History and the Slave Trade to Spanish America," 458).

26 Historians in the quantitative tradition have both attempted to situate the slave trade numerically (as exemplified by Philip Curtin and Herbert Klein) and also account for the undeniable presence of peoples of African descent in Latin America.

Those scholars have had to battle against the prevailing declaration that there were no blacks to be found here (*no hay negros aquí*), and at the same time substantiate their assertions and research claims with qualitative evidence.

27 Vargas Ugarte, *Historia del Perú, Virreinato siglo XVII*, 139–41. The viceroy concluded his reign with the death of King Philip in 1621. Ibid., 189–90.

28 Ibid., 197. Esquilache was succeeded by the marqués de Guadalcázar in 1620, who had held a previous appointment as viceroy of New Spain.

29 Although the sale of public offices was vigorously debated, the commodification of some posts did not generate much public uproar. Notaries, for instance, were obligated to purchase their office and would do so pending their qualification, since they would be able to recuperate much of their capital investment in purchasing their office through the fees they charged for their services. Indeed, the sale of notarial offices (*escribanías*) had been a feature of life in the New World since Columbus set sail from Seville. See Tomás y Valiente, *La venta de oficios en Indias*. Those responsible for public order and public services – bailiffs, sheriffs, postmaster generals, tax assessors – also purchased their office without much controversy. The sale of judicial offices, however, was extremely controversial, as it "violated the most firmly accepted principles of government." See Parry, *The Sale of Public Office in the Spanish Indies under the Hapsburgs*, 49.

30 Elliott, *Spain, Europe and the Wider World*, 280.

31 See, for example, the writings of the celebrated jurist Juan de Solórzano Pereira, who served as a long-standing *oidor* in Lima's *Real Audiencia* from 1609 to 1625. After Solórzano returned to Spain, he was appointed to the Council of the Indies, in which capacity he cautioned strongly against appointing native sons to the *Audiencia*: "Pero en las Audiencias de las Indias, como son menos y su poder se ejerce también entre menos súbditos y vecinos y el estrecharse con algunos de ellos, *ya por parentesco, ya por amistad* puede producir tan peligrosos efectos, se ha cuidado y se debe cuidar siempre mucho que ninguno vaya a ejercer semejantes cargos a su patria, ni aun a la Provincia de donde es natural" (*Política indiana*, bk. 5, ch. 4, no. 29, my emphasis).

32 See de la Puente Brunke, "Las estrellas solo lucen cuando en sol se pone." See also Burkholder and Chandler, *Biographical Dictionary of Audiencia Ministers in the Americas*, and Parry, *Sale of Public Office*.

33 Philip III's admonition of his viceroy for his dispensation of favors to his retainers and favored advisers must have fallen on deaf ears. By the time he wrote these cautionary missives, the weak and profligate king had fallen under the notorious influence of the Duke of Lerma, who was appointed as the first "minister-favorite" to the Spanish court. The duke used this position to amass spectacular personal wealth and to exercise royal powers of patronage. On the influence wielded by the Duke of Lerma and the office of "the minister-favourite," see Williams, *The Great Favourite*.

34 In 1618, King Philip wrote the following lengthy remonstration to Viceroy Borja: "El Rey Príncipe de Esquilache, primo, mi Virrey, por diversas relaciones que se me han enviado de esas provincias y por lo que algunas personas celosas de mi servicio me han escrito, he entendido el gran desconsuelo que hay en ellas entre las personas beneméritas y que me han servido por verse sin ninguna esperanza de premio de sus servicios respecto de que siendo el mas propio y ajustado a

ellos que los Virreyes que gobiernan en mi nombre les provean y ocupen los cargos militares, de gobierno y hacienda, no se hace así sino que los dan y proveen todos en sus criados, parientes y allegados de su casa y de los oidores y ministros de esa Audiencia, a que no se debería haber dado lugar así por los efectos referidos ... y que para remedio de todo convendría limitar el número de criados que los Virreyes de esas provincias han de ocupar en oficios ... dando los demás a gente benemérita de esa tierra ... por lo mucho que conviene que estas plazas se den a personas natu-rales... Y habiendo visto en mi Consejo Real de las Indias, he acordado ordenaros y mandaros, como lo hago, que en cuanto a los parientes, deudos o criados de los oidores y demás ministros de esa Audiencia hagáis averiguación citada la parte de mi fiscal, quiénes y cuántos son los que de ellos están proveídos en oficios contra lo dispuesto por cédulas y ordenanzas ... los removeréis y nombraréis en su lugar otras personas ... y de las que me han servido en esa tierra y tienen su origen de los pobladores y descubridores de ella ... y en lo que toca a los criados y allega-dos vuestros que tuviéredes ocupados, me avisaréis ... os encargo así lo hagáis inviolablemente, y por excusar la mala consecuencia y pernicioiso ejemplo que trae el nombrar semejantes oficios en deudos o criados vuestros" (cited in Konetzke, *Colección de documentos*, R.C. 133, 26 de abril de 1618, 198–99).

35 Eduardo Torres Arancivia, for instance, argues in his *Corte de virreyes* that criollo agitation against the viceregal practice of naming favorites and relatives repre-sented an incipient criollo republicanism. My sense is that it promoted factionalism and competition for the viceroy's bestowal of favors on *beneméritos* and aristo-cratic criollos, not an undermining of the system of dispensation.

36 Securing an appointment in the Indies involved waiting in the king's court for dec-ades or serving as a page or vassal in the household of one of the king's close advi-sors or family members. This was for the most part impossible for criollos located in the Americas. Criollos who did achieve a royal post spent considerable time on the peninsula advocating for their appointment. See Burkholder's description of don Alonso Bravo de Sarabia's appointment to the *Audiencia*, in *Spaniards in the Colonial Empire*, 79.

37 See de la Puente Brunke, "Los ministros de la Audiencia y la administración de justicia en Lima," describing the intervention of Viceroy Montesclaros on behalf of Alberto de Acuña to secure his appointment to the *Real Audiencia*.

38 Luis Martín details the Jesuits' disgust at the Viceroy Alba de Liste's machinations on behalf of his local favorites (*Intellectual Conquest of Peru*, 72).

39 Jorge Basadre Grohman's account of the magistrate Bernardo de Iturrizarra illus-trates how judicial fairness and treatment of others played into one's professional reputation: "Al oidor Iturrizarra murmuraba que le quitaba el agua a los vecinos, *que trataba mal a los litigantes*, mantenía trato indecente con algunas mujeres" (*El conde de Lemos y su tiempo*, 224, my emphasis).

40 "A los oidores, alcaldes, y fiscales, se les prohibía también que poseyeran casas, chacras, estancias, huertas ni tierras en las ciudades donde residieran, ni fueran del-las ni en otra parte en todo el distrito de la Audiencia. Estas prohibiciones se hacían extensivas a sus mujeres e hijos" (Ots Capdequí, *Estudios de historia del derecho español en las Indias*, 83). As José de la Puente points out repeatedly, these royal prohibitions aimed at preventing conflicts of interest were mostly aspirational and never applied in practice.

41 Both Tamar Herzog and José de la Puente encapsulate the essence of these judicial networks as *ius amicitiae:* networks that traversed the boundaries between friendship and politics. See Herzog, *Upholding Justice,* 146, for a detailed study of judicial social networks in Quito.

42 As Nicole von Germeten notes, "Private lives and colonial courts intersected via the rhetoric of honor and the hazy, disputed boundary between licit and illicit sex" (*Violent Delights,* 85).

43 The existence of these officials did not preclude Andeans from approaching the ecclesiastical court or the royal court to file a grievance. This did entail traveling into Lima, but historians of Andean litigation point out that such travel was frequently undertaken. See Charles, *Allies at Odds,* 52–53, and de la Puente Luna, "The Many Tongues of the King."

44 On the *protectores de naturales,* see Dueñas, *Indians and Mestizos in the "Lettered City."*

45 See, for example, AAL, Causas de negros, leg. 4, exp. 2, año 1619 ("Autos seguidos por María Zape, morena libre sobre que le restituya los 60 pesos por los jornales que le debe a su marido"). See also, *Partida* 3, Title 5, law 5, 587, "We declare that a woman can act as an attorney to liberate her relatives from slavery."

46 Lira González, *El amparo colonial.*

47 See McKinley, "Standing on Shaky Ground."

48 According to the Franciscan chronicler Córdoba y Salinas, "Tiene el Arzobispo un provisor, un promotor fiscal, y dos notarios públicos que acuden al expediente ordinario de las causas eclesiásticas, sus receptores y otros ministros menores. Tiene su cárcel con su alcalde, alguacil y ministros que sirve de casa de disciplina" (*Teatro de la Santa Iglesia Metropolitana,* 26). The *alguacil eclesiástico* investigated accusations of concubinage and arrested iniquitous couples while the charges against them were investigated. See Chapter 4 for the investigation of the cleric Sebastián de Loyola's nocturnal trysts.

49 See Córdoba y Salinas for biographies of Archbishops Arias de Ugarte, Villagómez, and Liñan Cisneros, who held doctorates from Salamanca, Alcalá, and Seville, respectively (*Teatro de la Santa Iglesia Metropolitana,* 61–74). Lima's third Archbishop, Bartolomé Lobo Guerrero (1609–22), studied canon law at the University of Salamanca and the University of Seville, where he earned his doctorate and held a chaired position. During his lengthy tenure as Archbishop, Lobo Guerrero was present at almost all ecclesiastical panels and cosigned many *autos* with Provisor Vega.

50 Burkholder and Chandler, *Biographical Dictionary of Audiencia Ministers in the Americas,* xii.

51 Herzog, *Upholding Justice,* 29.

52 *Alcaldes del crimen* were *letrados* who presided over criminal cases of first instance. They often used the appointment as a stepping stone to the post of magistrate (which was also purchased) or *corregidor.* Ernesto Schäfer's catalog of ninety-seven *oidores* who served on the *Real Audiencia* from 1600 to 1700 shows that one-third of those were promoted from *alcaldes* to *oidores.* Many *alcaldes* were also appointed to official posts within the viceregal administration in other sites in the Americas. See Schäfer, *El consejo real y supremo de las Indias,* 2:418–21.

53   In Charles Cutter's account of judicial hearings in northern New Spain, *oidores* convened daily sessions that lasted for three hours and delivered their judgments that same afternoon (*Legal Culture of Northern New Spain*, 52).

54   Seventeenth-century chronicles show the pervasiveness of ceremonial life in Lima's religious processions, liturgical rituals, inaugurations, weddings, entries into religious orders, and funerals. For a daily listing of ceremonial events, see Suardo, *Diario de Lima, 1629–1639*, Mugaburu, *Chronicle of Colonial Lima*, and Cobo, *Historia de la fundación de Lima*.

55   AAL, Causas de negros, leg. 13, exp. 16, año 1659. It took nearly seven weeks from Ana's initial complaint for Pedro to be personally served. According to the notary, on his first attempt, Pedro's mother answered the door. On the second attempt, one of his slaves answered but said he was indisposed. Undeterred, the notary watched the house over a period of weeks to see when Pedro's slaves left for the market to gauge the time when Pedro would be alone. The notary timed his service perfectly: Pedro opened the inner door to his house, at which point he was personally served.

56   Muñóz, *Práctica para procuradores*, 50–53.

57   Crown-appointed procurators received a modest salary of 100 pesos annually. It was impossible for them to exist on their appointed salary alone. As a point of comparison, procurators for Andeans (*procurador de naturales*) received an annual salary of 1,000 pesos, and the *abogado de indios* received 800 pesos annually. See Cobo, *Historia de la fundación de Lima*, 106–7.

58   Enslaved litigants' infrequent use of the free services provided by *procuradores de pobres* suggests that these officials were either ineffective or overworked – probably a combination of both.

59   The question of legal fees and churchmen had a lengthy history, particularly with regard to the crime of simony. Ecclesiastical personnel who were salaried could not charge for legal services. According to James Brundage, many decretalists condemned those advocates who received payment for their services from the poor but permitted payment by wealthier clients and patrons of the church (*Medieval Origins of the Legal Profession*, 190–201).

60   Alonso de Arcos, for example, appeared as procurator in the name of slave owners in religious establishments. Arcos also represented many enslaved litigants fighting those orders. Arcos may have built up a reputation as someone who knew the delaying strategies of the orders – the better to orchestrate or evade those delays.

61   With reference to medieval European courts, Brundage states that, "the maximum number of authorized proctors was seldom very large" (*Medieval Origins of the Legal Profession*, 357). According to Father Cobo's account, the *Real Audiencia* set a limit of four procurators ("El 5 de julio, se nombraron cuatro procuradores y en 9 estando en acuerdo, ordenó la Real Audiencia que los procuradores fuesen sin que pudiesen acrecentar más, y que hubiese procurador de pobres" [*Historia de la fundación de Lima*, 102]).

62   Johnson, "A Lack of Legitimate Obedience and Respect," 633.

63   In the study of protracted lawsuits in Buenos Aires, Lyman Johnson points out that legal fees could bankrupt an enslaved client – rendering the process negligible in terms of the freedom that was secured as a result of litigation ("A Lack of Legitimate Obedience and Respect," 648).

64 Pérez Perdomo, *Latin American Lawyers*, 9.
65 As Tamar Herzog notes with reference to *letrados* in Quito, "Most lawyers graduated in both laws (Roman and canon). Those who chose a single career usually chose to study canon law, which enabled them to occupy offices in the ecclesiastical hierarchy" (*Upholding Justice*, 22).
66 Legal studies in sixteenth-century Europe were hugely popular. The law faculties at two universities – Salamanca and Valladolid – attracted students from all over the peninsula and Europe. As Richard Kagan writes, "By the 1580s, law students at Salamanca numbered just over thirty-eight hundred, a figure that accounted for three-fourths of its total enrollment" (*Lawsuits and Litigants*, 142). Similar trends were reflected in thirteenth-century enrollments at the University of Bologna, the seat of the "Roman law revival" in southern Europe. See Brundage, *Medieval Origins of the Legal Profession*, 268–69. Two further considerations may explain the appeal of legal studies. In southern Europe, law was an open profession, which did not require proof of Old Christian blood to practice. The civilian legal traditions were also portable within Europe and throughout the Spanish Empire. As Brundage reminds us, canon law in particular had always functioned as the *ius commune* of Latin Christendom with jurisdiction that transcended political boundaries. Having both civil and canon law training along with a solid foundation in Roman law supplied a student with skills and trades that could be plied "in Riga, and Rouen, as at Rome" (*Medieval Origins of the Legal Profession*, 5).
67 Brundage, *Medieval Origins of the Legal Profession*, 219; Kagan, *Students and Society in Early Modern Spain*, ch. 5.
68 Martín, *Intellectual Conquest of Peru*, ch. 2. Unlike the judicial biographical traditions of prominent common law jurists, the judgments or instructions handed down by ecclesiastical or secular judges have never been viewed as a source of their scholarly corpus.
69 Notwithstanding the professoriate's unanimous support for Vega, the selection process for chaired professorships was fraught with heated rivalries between secular candidates and those who belonged to the religious orders. Religious orders formed an insuperable voting bloc, resolutely disqualifying secular candidates who were nominated by the viceroy and *Audiencia* to hold professorships in canon law, civil law, Quechua, and theology. The appointment process resulted in a checkmate between candidates supported by the religious orders and any secular candidate nominated by the viceroy to hold chairs in those disciplines. Other endowed positions in mathematics, art, and medicine were not contested by the orders. On the appointments process at San Marcos, see Glave, "Las redes de poder y la necesidad del saber."
70 After serving as provisor of Lima's Archbishopric court, Feliciano de Vega held two positions as bishop of Popayán and La Paz. He was named Archbishop of Mexico prior to his death in 1639. Vega has been prolifically studied by Lima's historians and biographers. Lincoln Draper portrays Vega as a quintessential bureaucrat: efficient, professional, aristocratic, and ambitious. This skillset served him well, as Vega ascended up the ecclesiastical ranks until he was appointed Archbishop of New Spain – a post recognizing his talents and intelligence. My examination of Vega's rulings as provisor reveals that it was physically impossible for him to be in Lima and in Popayán. I conclude that Vega never assumed his bishopric there although

he continued to use the title in his writings. For an interesting review of Vega's tenure as bishop of La Paz, see Draper, *Arzobispos, canónigos, y sacerdotes*, 27–54.

71 *Tinterillos* were common nineteenth-century legal intermediaries who served as legal practitioners to Andean plebeians. I have only seen the term "tinterillo" applied to one practitioner in the seventeenth-century records, and the use of the term was largely derogatory in connotation. On *tinterillos*, see Aguirre, "Tinterillos, Indians, and the State," 119–51. On notaries, see Burns, *Into the Archive*. On procurators, see Honores, "Legal Polyphony in the Colonial Andes." On scribes in criminal court, see Scardaville, "Justice by Paperwork."

72 See Burns, *Into the Archive*, 37, and Brundage, *Medieval Origins of the Legal Profession*. In a similar vein, Melissa Macauley characterizes the legal document as "that god-force of bureaucratic narrative reality that could harness distant state power to resolve plebeian disputes with elites and regional authorities" (*Social Power and Legal Culture*, 3). See also Dueñas, *Indians and Mestizos in the "Lettered City,"* and de la Puente Luna, "The Many Tongues of the King." As Dueñas points out, this epistolary activism built on the earlier sixteenth-century tradition of Andean chroniclers and activist priests who protested abuses and injustice by denunciation and appeals to the Catholic kings.

73 Scardaville, "Justice by Paperwork."

74 Burns, *Into the Archive*, 71. For Europe, see Brundage, *Medieval Origins of the Legal Profession*. The documents are stored in thick hidebound folios in (somewhat) chronological order and are housed in the Peruvian National Archive. It is often difficult to find the documents needed to complete the evidence in one lawsuit, since those documents could have been located in the *protocolos* or filed by a different notary than the one bringing the case forward. There is no index for the documentary subject matter bound in the folio. Archival investigation thus requires a painstaking page-by-page review of the entire set of documents produced during the notary's career.

75 Herzog, *Mediacíon, archivos y ejercicio*, 22–23. Herzog describes the peninsular development of public municipal archives that emerged at the beginning of the seventeenth century. In theory, this bureaucratic practice was adopted in the municipalities and cities of the Americas. Documents should have been collected according to the jurisdiction and locale, catalogued, and maintained by trained personnel (ibid., 19). However, as Herzog points out, the crown devoted no resources to maintaining archives in the Americas. Moreover, litigants and their advocates held onto notarial documents to ensure payment for legal services. Herzog traces the use of *censuras* in Quito as a way to obligate notaries and litigants to return documents, but the issuance of censuras depended on the bishop's goodwill. This could explain the popularity behind the practice of *censuras* in the Archbishopric of Lima – the dates coincide with the phenomena Herzog describes in Quito. *Mediación*, 26.

76 On notarial records as "fragments in the mosaic" of the lives of urban slaves and freed people, see Bowser, "The Free Person of Color in Mexico City," 331.

77 See Ribera and de Olmedilla, *Primera [segunda y tercera] parte de escrituras*, 105–11v. See also Moscoso y Peralta, *Aranzel de derechos eclesiásticos parroquiales, de hospitales, curia eclesiástica, y Secretaría de Cámara del Obispado del Cuzco*. Although writing in 1860, Manuel Atanasio Fuentes recorded virtually the same prices for notarial fees in Lima. See Porcari Coloma, *La ciudad de los reyes*, 70–72.

78 Currency conversion for *reales* into pesos were listed at 8 *reales* to 1 peso. See
    Cobo, *Historia de la fundación de Lima*, 108.
79 Like notaries, procurators were also embroiled in high-volume paperwork, and they
    also purchased their office. According to Father Cobo's calculations, the office of
    procurator was valued at 1,600 pesos. See *Historia de la fundación de Lima*, 124.
    We are not clear how much controversy the sale of procurator's offices engendered.
    Presumably, commodification of higher-level judicial offices was more controversial
    than the sale of what elites largely derided as paper pushers who merely operational-
    ized rather than embodied the king's justice. See Scardaville "Justice by Paperwork."
80 Brundage, *Medieval Origins of the Legal Profession*, 355.
81 AAL, Causas de negros, leg. 17, exp. 19, año 1673.
82 Lima's Archbishopric had six *racioneros*, all of whom enjoyed a stipend for their
    services. See Cobo, *Historia de la fundación de Lima*, 161.
83 "María de la Torre, parda esclava del Lic. Gaspar Román digo que como consta
    de la escritura que presento con la solemnidad necesaria, el dicho Lic. me compró
    del Josef de Alamo, religioso de la Compañía de Jesús con condición y cláusula
    que diese yo u otra persona por mí los cuatrocientos pesos de desembolso el
    dicho Lic. había de ser obligado a recibirlos y otorgarme carta de libertad, con-
    forme y porque al presente tengo los cuatrocientos pesos y quiero conseguir mi
    libertad. A Vmd. pido y suplico que se sirve de mandar que el dicho Lic. Gaspar
    Román reciba los dichos cuatrocientos pesos y en fuerza desta cláusula de la
    escritura me otorgue carta de libertad" (AAL, Causas de negros, leg. 17, exp. 19,
    año 1673).
84 AAL, Causas de negros, leg. 5, exp. 31, año 1628 ("Autos seguidos por Juan Pacheco,
    negro libre, contra Juan Hernández, clérigo presbítero sobre que declare sopena de
    excomunión el trato que hizo con Ana Jolofa, negra libre para dar libertad a la
    negrita Juana su hija, pagándole al dicho Hernández los 150 pesos pactados").
85 In other words, the court never deliberated or issued a finding that María or Juan
    failed to prove their cases. Neither case can be explained by administrative uni-
    formity – María's case was brought in front of Provisor Villagómez, and Juan's case
    went before Provisor Vega.
86 AGN, Protocolos, Antonio de Zuñiga, 1627. Carta de libertad included in the
    AAL case folio. Zuñiga's protocolos are no longer in existence, although his name
    appears in other lawsuits as a notary of the period.
87 For those who were already enslaved in arduous labor conditions, "hard labor"
    was considered a punishment when it was imposed in conjunction with banish-
    ment, effectively cutting enslaved people off from their community. As the records
    demonstrate, enslaved men and women often fought against exile by contracting
    marriage. See Chapter 2.
88 *Tercera Carta:*
    Y si pasados otros tres días después de haber sido así declarados por tales
    excomulgados, con ánimos endurecidos. . .os dejareis estar en la excomu-
    nión y censuras y porque creciente la culpa y contumacia, debe crecer la
    pena, mandamos a los curas y sus tenientes que en sus iglesias a las misas
    mayores, los domingos y fiestas de guardar teniendo una cruz cubierta con
    un velo negro y candelas encendidas os anatematicen y maldigan con las
    maldiciones siguientes:
    Malditos sean los dichos excomulgados de Dios y de su bendita madre.

> *Huérfanos se vean los hijos y sus mujeres viudas.*
> *El sol se les oscurezca de día y la luna de noche.*
> *Mendigando anden de puerta en puerta y no hallen quien bien les haga.*
> *Las plagas que envió Dios sobre el reino de Egipto vengan sobre ellos. La maldición de Sodoma, Gomorra, Datan y Aviron que por sus pecados los tragó vivos vengan sobre ellos. Amen.*

Aguirre and Montalban, *Procedimientos eclesiásticos*, 261.

89 If a petitioner wanted to reach someone within the cloisters, *censuras* were also read within the monasteries' chapels. *Censuras* were also read in other dioceses outside of Lima. The records show witness responses in Arica, Popayán, Panama City, and Tierra Firme. See Chapter 2.

90 Aguirre and Montalban, *Procedimientos eclesiásticos*, 263–65.

91 Herzog, *Upholding Justice*, 146–47; Muñoz, *Practica para procuradores*. Muñoz lists several categories of persons who were affected by *tachas*, including the excommunicated, hermaphrodites, rapists, abortionists, heretics, or other persons whom he deemed of dubious moral character (44–46). It is not clear why Margarita brought her case initially in the *Real Audiencia*, especially given the fact that Cristóbal Sánchez was a priest.

92 This suggests that the notary who took the original witness statements cooperated with Margarita in sending over the statements, since the witnesses should have come forth to give their own testimonies separately to the ecclesiastical court.

93 "Brígida de Córdoba por sí y en nombre de su hijo, Alejo de Córdoba, por su libertad, Censura, 7 noviembre 1669."

94 *Corregimientos* were administrative districts granted to peninsular nobles and criollo elites for a limited term and were highly prized positions for their rent-bearing potential. The larger and more populous the *corregimiento*, the greater its tributary payout. In 1666, according to an inspection ordered by Archbishop Villagómez, the *corregimiento* of Chachapoyas held 7,500 *naturales*. See Vargas Ugarte, *Historia de la iglesia en Perú*, 3:165.

95 "2 de marzo 1670, Ynez de Córdoba, morena libre, estando enferma en cama como a mas de diez oras de la noche, y dixo que a su noticia a llegado como de pedimento de Brígida de Córdoba parda se an leydo y publicado censuras sobre un trueque y cambio que hizo doña Francisca de Córdoba con doña Luisa de Córdoba su hermana, y lo que ella sabe es que la dicha doña Francisca queriendo irse a un corregimiento le dio a la dicha doña Luisa la dicha Brígida por trueque y tomándose por sí a la dicha Ynez, y no sabe si ubo escritura o no hasta ahora cuatro años oyó decir en diferentes ocasiones a la dicha doña Francisca que avía hecho trueque con la dicha doña Luisa de la dicha Brígida por esta declarante." Censura, Brigida de Cordova y su libertad.

96 Later *censuras* were brought by procurators "en nombre de" (on behalf of) their clients. However, the early wave of *censuras* issued in the boilerplate 1660s forms were self-petitioned.

97 In lawsuits brought by enslaved litigants or suits that relied on slave testimony, defendants often cast aspersions as to the *calidad* of the people testifying or pointed to relationships of dependence and servitude linking the witnesses with the petitioner that obligated them to lie.

98 Herzog, *Upholding Justice*, 147.

99 Burns, *Into the Archive*, 31.

100 Johnson, "A Lack of Legitimate Obedience," 638.

101 On Don Martín de Zavala, see Lohmann Villena, *Los regidores perpetuos*, 342. According to Lohmann's entry, Zavala also served as mayor (alcalde) of Lima in 1670.

102 Burns, *Into the Archive*, 77.

103 The orders of Santiago and Alcántara were militaristic religious orders that played a principal role in the holy wars against Muslims on the Iberian Peninsula. Their tribunal, the Santa Cruzada, was authorized by a series of papal bulls, and in 1615 the tribunal was transferred to the New World. On the history of the Santa Cruzada Tribunal in the Americas, see Benito, "Historia de la bula de la Cruzada en Indias." In the Americas, the Santa Cruzada was established as a subsidiary body of the Council of the Indies, the Holy Tribunal, and the Archbishoprics. Members of the orders were granted special dispensation to collect taxes and tribute from indigenous villages on the basis of their past history as soldiers of holy wars. This arrangement meant that their salaries were paid by *naturales*, from whom they collected tax and tribute, rather than the community of Catholics. Reminding us of Zavala's power as accountant (*contador*), Benito notes that "la pieza clave de todo el organigrama del Tribunal eran los contadores y tesoreros." Ibid., 73.

104 I explain the reasons behind the numbers of spousal unity suits in Chapter 2.

105 Neal Milner graphically likens popular approaches to litigation as "root canal work" writing that, "litigation, like root canal repair, is a painful process and most people are averse to it" ("The Intrigue of Rights, Resistance, and Accommodation," 320).

106 On complainants who "lump it" (as opposed to those who "like it"), see Galanter, "Why the Haves Come Out Ahead."

107 Lockhart, *Spanish Peru*, 61–62. Like many decrees, this was pointedly ignored. By the time the *Real Audiencia* was established in 1544, Lima, Cuzco, and Potosí housed a sizable legal community. See Honores, "Legal Polyphony."

108 Kagan, *Lawsuits and Litigants*, 18–19.

109 Ibid.

110 Ibid. According to Kagan, "Out of 6,000–7,000 cases each year, only 400 *ejecutorías* (judgments) were reached. Ninety percent of the lawsuits never obtained a final writ. Most were withdrawn or forgotten, because litigants ran out of money (frequently) or because an out of court settlement was reached" (93).

111 See Comaroff, "Colonialism, Culture and the Law," which sets out the foundations for nuanced inquiries of colonial law that avoid the bipolarities of law as domination versus law as salvation. For popular perceptions of due process and procedural fairness in Bourbon New Spain, see Scardaville, "Justice by Paperwork."

112 Bryant, "Enslaved Rebels, Fugitives, and Litigants"; Lane, "Captivity and Redemption."

113 On the baroque "theater-state," see Cañeque, *The King's Living Image*; Bennett, *Africans in Colonial Mexico*; and Osorio, "The King in Lima."

114 Bowser, *The African Slave in Colonial Peru*, 40–41; see also Bühnen, "Ethnic Origins of Peruvian Slaves," 64.

115 O'Toole, "As Historical Subjects."

116 O'Toole, *Bound Lives*, 47.

117 AGN, Cristóbal Aguilar Mendieta, Protocolo no. 54, años 1614–15, ff. 299–310v.

118 Ysabel assumed the surname of her owners, Joana de Aguilar and Joan Bautista de Guadalupe. The Hispanicized spelling of their names suggests they were Spaniards.

119 Such details of archival minutiae are important markers of social ascendancy and self-perception. In any official interaction, Anton was classified as a *ropero* (cloth seller), but when he presented himself to the court, he assumed the title of a royally licensed professional tailor (*oficial de sastre*).

120 AGN, Cristóbal Aguilar Mendieta, Protocolo no. 54, años 1614–15, ff. 299–301v. See also Bowser, *The African Slave in Colonial Peru*, 278. Bowser observes that Ysabel's price was inflated for the time. In his careful review of slave prices, he notes that other slaves paid 450–500 pesos for their freedom in 1615. Ibid., appendix B, 342. My review of slave prices also reveals that prices escalated after 1640, although rarely did they reach the 1,000 peso mark – even for females of reproductive age. See Chapter 6.

121 See Serra Silva, "María de Terranova," for the same observation about María de Terranova's liberty suit.

2

Conjugal Chains

> Quiero me casar, pero yo no sé con quién
> *Cásate con un botellero, si a ti se te cumbén*
> Pero ese botellero, a mí no me cumbén
> Botellero vende botella, puede venderme a mí también
> *Cásate con un carpintero, si a ti se te cumbén*
> Pero ese carpintero, a mí no me cumbén
> Carpintero corta madera, puede cortarme a mí también
> *Cásate con un panadero, si a ti se te cumbén*
> Pero ese panadero, a mí no me cumbén
> Panadero amasa harina, puede amasarme a mí también.
>
> Popular Afro-Peruvian song

On January 19, 1693, María Terranova protested the prolonged absence of her husband, Francisco, in Lima's ecclesiastical court.[1] Though Francisco's owner had received permission to take him outside of Lima, the court had issued only a nine-month travel permit. Eighteen months after Francisco's absence, María returned to the court, complaining that his owner had violated the couple's conjugal rights and the terms of the license.

On July 1, 1627, don Juan Gaspar del Aguilar sought permission from the ecclesiastical court to sell his slave Francisca Terranova outside of Lima.[2] According to don Juan, Francisca was an incorrigible drunk, a runaway, and a thief and was unfit for domestic service. In an effort to recoup his investment, don Juan decided to sell Francisca in the port city of Arica (Chile), where criminal or rebellious slaves were routinely resold to other buyers or consigned to hard labor for the crown. But Francisca was married and so could not be sold outside of the city and still fulfill her conjugal obligations.

Spousal unity complaints were among the class of cases most commonly brought by slaves in the sixteenth and seventeenth centuries (see Table 2.1). Given the church's exclusive jurisdiction over marriage, spousal

TABLE 2.1. *Spousal Unity Cases, 1593–1699*

Year	Spousal unity cases	Wife	Husband	Joint owner petitions	Total cases in folio (AAL, Causas de negros)
1593–1609	8	2 wives	4 husbands	2	33 exp.
1610–15	4	1 wife	3 husbands		32 exp.
1616–18	3		3 husbands		20 exp.
1619–22	6	3 wives	3 husbands		19 exp.
1623–29	21	5 wives	14 husbands	2	41 exp.
1630–35	16	5 wives	11 husbands		42 exp.
1635–39	22	5 wives	17 husbands		47 exp.
1640–42	14	3 wives	11 husbands		35 exp.
1643–46	17	4 wives	12 husbands	1	40 exp.
1647–52	17	5 wives	9 husbands	3	48 exp.
1653–54	14	6 wives	6 husbands	2	33 exp.
1655–57	9	4 wives	5 husbands		37 exp.
1658–63	12	3 wives	7 husbands	2	51 exp.
1664–67	1		1 husband		32 exp.
1668–69	1	1 wife			21 exp.
1670–72	4	0 wives	3 husbands	1	24 exp.
1673–74	4	2 wives	1 husband	1	29 exp.
1675–76	4	2 wives	1 husband	1	34 exp.
1677–79	3	1 wife	2 husbands		35 exp.
1680–83	6	2 wives	3 husbands	1	37 exp.
1684–86	7	3 wives	4 husbands		34 exp.
1687–90	24	8 wives	14 husbands	2	69 exp.
1691–93	15	6 wives	9 husbands		43 exp.
1694–99	39	22 wives	11 husbands	8	79 exp.
Total	270 Cases	93 Wives	153 Husbands	27 Owners	914 Exp.

unity proceedings took place in ecclesiastical courts. Enslaved couples were fully aware of their conjugal rights and acted swiftly to protect them. Lima's enslaved couples used the court to uphold their rights to conjugal visitation whenever the travel plans of their spouse's owner imperiled their ability to remain together. A comparatively small subset of couples sought to defend their rights to weekend and feast-day visitation if owners opposed the couple's union. Most complainants either sought injunctions to prevent their spouses from being shipped outside of Lima or claimed that their spouses' owners had violated the terms of their travel permits.

The sources for this chapter draw on 270 spousal unity petitions that were filed in Lima's ecclesiastical court between 1593 and 1699. I use the sources to examine the ways in which slaves appealed to their marital rights as an expedient mechanism with which to resist criminal sanctions and contest spousal separation. Note that Francisco's absence was supposed to be temporary, while "incorrigible" married slaves in resale proceedings faced permanent exile from the city. Though these were technically two different legal proceedings, both concerned the rights of enslaved married couples to remain within reasonable distances of each other to fulfill their conjugal obligations. Their owners had to comply with identical requirements for married slaves, even if one wanted to sell an enslaved spouse outside of Lima or send one spouse away from the city for a temporary (though extended) period of time.[3] Captains in the port of Callao could refuse to board a slave on their vessels without the license authorizing the enslaved spouse's departure. Francisco Terranova's owner had to ask the ecclesiastical provisor to issue a travel permit and pay a sizable bond before he could legally take Francisco outside of the city. Failure to secure such permission resulted in the threat of excommunion and ecclesiastical condemnation (*censuras*). These *censuras* would be read and prominently displayed in the parish church where the owner resided, and they would not be removed until the infraction was resolved to the court's satisfaction.

As I have noted repeatedly, slave owners did not take these *censuras* lightly. When Francisca Bran learned of her husband Pedro's unauthorized departure from the city, she denounced his owner, doña Isabel de Vilicia, to the court, and asked the court to issue *censuras* to compel doña Isabel to bring Pedro back to Lima.[4] These *censuras* excommunicated doña Isabel from the community of faith, preventing her from taking the sacrament or attending mass in the Cathedral or any place of worship until Pedro returned to the city. Doña Isabel importuned Provisor don Feliciano de Vega to remove the *censuras*, claiming that she had shipped Pedro out to Arica in the company of her brother-in-law because he had been in and out of jail numerous times. Given Pedro's "willfulness and incorrigibility" doña Isabel had no other option but to send him to Arica with a master who could control him. In her first response, doña Isabel conceded that she sent Pedro away without a license but pointed out that he would return to the city in eighteen months. Not surprisingly, Francisca protested, and doña Isabel appealed for a reasonable term (*plazo*), claiming that she was a fragile and confused widow bereft of male guidance and support to help her sort out the details of Pedro's return.

Seemingly unpersuaded, Provisor Vega gave doña Isabel two options: purchase Francisca and send her to Arica or return Pedro to the city. Doña Isabel subsequently agreed to embark Pedro on the next incoming ship so that he could fulfill his conjugal obligations to Francisca. Doña Isabel keenly felt the isolation and ostracism levied by the *censuras*, which motivated her to comply with the ecclesiastical orders and seek absolution. Other owners who departed from the city with slaves may not have been as affected by the *censuras* as doña Isabel.

Iberoamerican historians have commented favorably on the Catholic Church's protection of slave marriages.[5] The church proclaimed the right of Lima's slaves to marry in 1582, during the third Archbishopric synod (*tercer concilio limense*).[6] Of course, marriages between enslaved couples were recognized before 1582; however, the ecclesiastical proclamation was important. The revered Archbishop Toribio de Mogrovejo reminded owners that slaves were free to choose their spouses without impediment and that they could not be separated through resale or relocation for prolonged periods of time.[7] Marital protections constituted one of the few rights accorded to slaves under natural law.[8] The Archbishop's proclamation reinforced confidence among enslaved couples in the powers of the ecclesiastical court.

After 1582, slaves used the court's defense of their marital rights against their owners to argue with greater frequency for associated rights. Marital rights petitions were followed by demands for back wages, change of ownership, and contract enforcement; slaves articulated claims that were not necessarily based in any formal body of law granting slaves those rights. This accretion of custom followed a pattern of legal innovation and casuist reasoning in the absence of digests or glosses adapted to the conditions of slavery in the Indies.[9] Advocates frequently relied on the *Partidas* as the body of law that articulated the marital rights of enslaved couples, which textually was more favorable to enslaved couples than it was to the property rights of slave owners.

According to the *Partidas*, an owner who sought to separate spouses was legally obligated to seek a local buyer or offer the spouse's owner right of first refusal. The relevant title read:

Where two slaves who are married have two masters, one in one country and the other in another, and they are so far apart that where they serve their masters they cannot join one another and live together, the church can then compel one of the masters to buy the slave of the other. Where they are unwilling to do this, whichever one of them the church may select can be compelled to sell his slave to some man who is a resident of the town or community where the master of the other slave resides, and if no-one wishes to buy him, the church should do so, in order that the husband and wife may not be separated.[10]

If an owner made his travel plans known to the couple, the spouses filed a petition for legal transfer of ownership called *variación de dominio*.[11] Owners of slaves who protested the relocation of their slave's spouse sometimes joined the petition for *variación de dominio*. These petitions were either part of an initial plea for injunctive relief to prevent departure or part of a subsequent plea to return the spouse after an unlicensed or prolonged departure.

When one spouse acquired a new owner through inheritance or resale, the couple could file a preemptive claim to prevent their separation. Resale or inheritance often signaled a rupture in the equilibrium of the relationship that had been established between the enslaved and their prior owners, and it behooved the couples to put the new owners "on notice" that they knew their conjugal rights and were willing to go to court to enforce them.[12] In some cases, change of ownership prompted concubinary couples to formalize their union.

Owners invariably resisted this infringement on their property rights. Don Jerónimo Vosmediano protested the court's order that he was obliged to sell his slave Juliana to her husband's owner.[13] As Vosmediano pointed out, Juliana was not fungible: he needed her to nurse the grandchild with whom he had recently "been blessed." Vosmediano offered to post a sizable bond to ensure Juliana's return to the city after she nursed his grandchild.[14] However, Vosmediano's property claim was relegated below Juliana's rights to remain with her husband in the city. Her husband disputed the temporary nature of the relocation, arguing that a married couple's rights were not tantamount to goods that could be disposed of according to the owner's will. Juliana's husband also had irrefutable proof that Vosmediano had no intention to return to the city, as he apparently made plans consistent with permanent relocation to Arica. Consequently, the court ordered Vosmediano to sell Juliana to her husband's owner.

As favorable as the laws were to slave marriages, each case was assessed according to the merits and exigencies of the owner's relocation. As we dig deeper into the cases, we often find instrumental factors that accounted for an owner's willingness to find local buyers or offer a spouse's owner right of first refusal. Departing sellers with time-sensitive constraints could be persuaded to accept a lower payment for an enslaved spouse in lieu of incurring costly legal fees, securing bond payments, and facing the delays that injunctions entailed. In this regard, the owner of the spouse protesting the relocation would benefit from a lower purchase price. Many potential owners would also comment approvingly on the virtues of having the couple under one roof and dominion (*poder*) if another buyer competed for the purchase of only one of the spouses. Though this was not alluded to in the briefs, sole ownership of both husband and wife extended the possibility of acquiring children through the law of the slave womb.

As Alexander Wisnoski has shown in his review of marriage litigation in Lima, the courts balanced an owner's property rights with the couple's marital rights. According to Wisnoski, "Even as codified institutional norms permitted and encouraged slave autonomy and agency in regards to marriage, social forces constrained those avenues for justice and freedom."[15] If an owner offered a compelling reason for temporary relocation and paid a bond (*fianza*) to ensure the spouse's return, the provisor regularly granted the license. Bonds were assessed at 4 *pesos ensayados* for each day that the enslaved spouse was absent from the city and had to be paid before the license was granted. The initial grant of injunctive relief did, however, give the couple the chance to find a local buyer, protest the separation, and demand the payment of the bond.

Comparative scholars are often struck by slaves' use of legal avenues to fight against familial separation in Lima's courts vis-à-vis the virtual non-existence of legal remedies in North American courts. However, despite a long-standing debate regarding the civil law of slavery among historians, little attention has been devoted to the distinctive role of *marriage* within French, Spanish, and American slave regimes.[16] This is not to suggest that accounts of family and domestic relations are absent from the slavery literature.[17] Among ancient slavery scholars, for instance, the instrumentalist calculus of permitting slaves a family life is well studied.[18] Herbert Gutman's monumental work on the slave family is critical in establishing patterns of multigenerational family histories before and after Emancipation in the United States.[19] But marriage is surprisingly underexplored in comparison with the profuse scholarship on concubinage, illegitimacy, and other non-marital unions such as *barraganía, amancebamiento,* and *plaçage* in societies with slavery.[20]

The relative inattention to marriage could be explained by the prevailing idea that slaves married at low rates, as compared with Spaniards.[21] In addition, the prevalence of female-headed households among diasporic African communities has commanded considerable attention in the scholarly literature.[22] However, detailed empirical research of marriage records in Lima's largest parish – el Sagrario – reveals that slaves married at higher rates than Spaniards. As shown in Figure 2.1, 6,456 endogamous slave couples were inscribed in the Sagrario sacramental ledgers between 1565 and 1699. In addition, the Sagrario records indicate that 973 mixed-status couples (of whom at least one partner was enslaved) declared their intention to marry during that time period. A total of 5,571 marriage petitions for all Spanish parishioners were filed in Sagrario from 1565 to 1699. Data for four of Lima's five parishes (San Marcelo, San Sebastián, Santa Ana, and San Lázaro) are included in Table 2.2.

TABLE 2.2. *Slave Marriages, 1618–99, in Four of Lima's Parishes:* Libros de matrimonios de negros, mulatos e indios

Parish	San Marcelo 1632–93	San Sebastián 1618–99	San Lázaro 1632–99	Santa Ana 1632–99
1618–31		319		
1632–48	213	350	357	121
1649–59	249	23	175	52
1660–99	559	448	427	303
Total	1,021	1,140	959	508

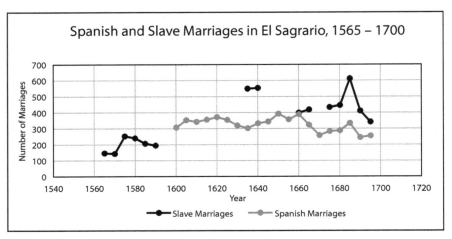

FIGURE 2.1. Spanish and Slave Marriages in El Sagrario, 1565–1700.

These marriage rates prompt historians to rethink the role of marriage in slaveholding societies. Here, I approach marriage and slavery as co-constitutive, and at times, competing institutions. The large numbers of endogamous slave marriages raise both ideological and material questions about the widespread popularity of Catholic marriages among African-born slaves and first-generation enslaved criollos vis-à-vis a preference for non-Catholic family formation patterns that also prevailed during this time. These marriage patterns suggest that slaves entered into marriage owing to assurances of the church's power to protect couples rather than to a fervent embrace of Catholicism. In contrast to North America, slave owners in Lima could not wield their power by threatening to separate slave spouses. The availability of legal protection for enslaved married couples constrained the power of their owners. The diminished threat of family disintegration was vital to the individual and collective well-being of enslaved couples. The church's defense of slave marriages profoundly shaped Lima's slave society, and it is perhaps this factor that distinguished urban Hispanic slavery most sharply from North American slavery.

Underlying the discussion about family life and slavery is the issue of slaveholder paternalism and benevolence, which can easily lead one down the slippery path into the benign Latin American slaveholding debate that raged between Gilberto Freyre and Marvin Harris.[23] I am not revisiting that debate here. Rather, my aim is to point out how amenable Hispanic American urban slavery was to marriage. I analyze the religious, legal, and economic context underpinning both the church and Limeño slaveholders' promotion of marriage in order to assess whether, in fact, marriage was the nefarious infringement on property rights so widely feared by many North American slaveholders.[24]

Reasonable objections could be raised against my proposition that Lima's slaveholders respected their slaves' marital rights. Doesn't Francisca's appeal and others like it demonstrate that owners simply applied for the license without intending to comply with the requirements? I think not. The number of injunctions or petitions filed by slave couples is surprisingly small compared to the total number of married slave couples. Others have objected to my argument – again not unreasonably – by pointing out that the numbers do not account for the underreporting of separation. However, given the low barriers to court entry and the support that couples' petitions for marital unity enjoyed, it seems more plausible that if a separated couple did not contest the separation, it was likely because the couple in fact wished to be separated. Clearly, family life created a degree of security in the life of enslaved peoples. The sizable numbers of married couples registered in el Sagrario's sacramental books suggest that the vast majority of owners respected their slaves' marital rights, did not interfere with their plans to marry, and did not seek to interrupt their conjugal unions. Why?

METHODOLOGY AND SOURCES

My survey of slave marriages is drawn from two archival sources: marriage petitions and the sacramental ledgers in five of Lima's six parishes between 1565 and 1699. All couples intending to enter into marriage were required by Tridentine law to file a marriage petition, called a *pliego matrimonial*. In the *pliego matrimonial*, couples presented their witnesses, testified to their eligibility to enter into the marriage without impediment of prior matrimonial promises or consanguinity, and gave their consent before a notary and priest. Parochial marriage ledgers recorded all marriages that were celebrated within the parish over a period of years.

Unfortunately, many marriage ledgers are either incomplete or lost. Therefore, I had to supplement marriage rate calculations with the *pliegos* where these were available. Santa Ana and Huérfanos, for example, did not begin keeping their own marriage books until the eighteenth century. I used marriage books from el Sagrario from 1565 to 1594 to estimate a comparable rate of marriage during the years in the seventeenth century for which there are neither petitions nor books. My survey also includes *pliegos* in which one of the intending spouses was enslaved.[25] I also counted marriages registered between freed blacks and marriages in which the black partner was free. Despite this thorough review, it is impossible to account for all marriages because of archival loss.

Marriage rate calculation also proved challenging because the census data did not align with the years for which there are marriage records. There are no records for slave marriages to measure against the 1613 census. We have census data and marriage records for the end of the century, although the 1700 census is problematic because its intended purpose was to assess the city's military preparedness. Women are suspiciously overrepresented, and blacks and *mulatos* are enumerated without regard to age or status.[26] However, I am not trying to undertake a definitive study in colonial demography. Rather I am attempting to use the extant marriage and population records to answer this chapter's overarching questions. What was the place of marriage in societies with slavery? Did marriage play a role in enslaved people's quest for liberty? What can marriage records between enslaved couples tell us about their diasporic and African-Atlantic identities?[27]

My interest is to discern the ways that enslaved couples' entry into marriage may have enhanced their manumission possibilities using pooled household income sources. This presumes that both owners and slaves accepted lifetime emancipation as prescriptively desirable and that self-purchase was financially attractive for both parties. As we have seen in the case of Anton and Ysabel Bran, marriage was critical to both the possibility of Ysabel's manumission and the couple's social mobility. But couples' marriage rights also enabled less economically prosperous enslaved men and women to resist exile or spousal separation, despite the outstanding orders for banishment or arrest. Given that marriage and family law profoundly shape the societies in which they function, it should come as no surprise that slaves' conjugal rights were the anvil that forged Lima as a society with slavery.

IMPERIAL LAW AND SLAVE MARRIAGE

Marriage performed normative and political work in societies with slavery. Throughout Latin Christendom, within imperial Rome, and in the Iberian colonies, slaves were encouraged to marry.[28] This is in marked contrast to antebellum North America, where slaves were deemed morally or legally ineligible to contract marriage.[29] The enduring preoccupation of imperial, antebellum, and republican regimes in promoting or prohibiting marriage among slaves raises a logical presumption that marriage performed critical regulatory functions in societies with slavery. Moreover, the *types* of marriages that were permitted both facilitated and perpetuated the establishment of racialized hierarchies.

Earlier generations of scholars studying the civil law's facilitation of slave marriage tended to approach marital eligibility as a moral and theological counterpart to slavery. The Iberoamerican impetus for slave marriages derived from the overwhelming preoccupation of viceregal and ecclesiastical authorities with channeling profligate sexual energies into "appropriate" marital unions. Catholic priests were anxious to promote slave marriages, but their prevailing concern was that slaves marry *other slaves*. In theory, endogamous marriage ensured a locally born slave workforce (in perpetuity), because of the law of the slave womb. Marriage reinforced patriarchal religious norms and reduced interethnic illegitimacy by preventing mixed status or exogamous relationships, widely thought by viceregal administrators and the clergy to produce delinquency and social unrest.[30]

This top-down imperative obscures the selective processes of spousal endogamy. In the *pliegos matrimoniales* filed by *bozal* couples in the parish of Santa Ana between 1650 and 1699, I recorded a 98 percent endogamous marriage rate between spouses with the same ethnonymic surname who indicated that they came from the same cultural and linguistic group (de la misma tierra y nación).[31] As Linda Newson and Susie Minchin's close study of Lima's slave importations demonstrates, those who remained in Lima were overwhelmingly from Upper Guinea, while hacienda slaves were from Angola.[32] Though these statistics are mired in unknowns about provenance, they still demonstrate that African-descent peoples chose to marry partners from their cultural area. Endogamy is an unfortunately flat term for the active attempts among displaced peoples to reproduce a semblance of their cultural and linguistic worlds.

An important associated rationale for slave marriage was rooted in market forces. Marriage was encouraged to stave off male rebelliousness: it performed a domesticating function among restive slaves. Again, these were externally driven incentives and policy considerations. In practice, as I argue here, slave couples also strategically entered into marriage, which – not insignificantly – undermined the overarching goal of maintaining a perpetually enslaved population. As Christopher Morris writes, "The aspects of slavery that could be most liberating and self-affirming for the slaves – family, economy, community – could become structures that made slavery profitable and enduring for the masters."[33] Given the fact that many Limeño slaves achieved their freedom through self-purchase, the expectation and legal opportunity for manumission created powerful incentives for slaves to marry.[34] It also strengthens the presumption that slavery and marriage were co-constitutive, because both institutions facilitated and rewarded compliance, virtue, and industry.

Regardless of enslaved or free status, marriage is an instance in which regulatory power is unleashed to create desirable social and legal categories of subjects – categories that are conditioned along racialized and gendered lines.[35] Thus, one task of many historians of domestic relations has been to weave together the rich feminist scholarship on the regulatory function of the marriage covenant (dictating who *should* marry and whom they could marry and who *could not* marry). Other scholars examine the role of marriage in ensuring the reproduction of patriarchal norms, particularly during periods of economic transformation, imperial expansion, and political upheaval.[36] My focus here departs from that of the canonical works of domestic relations, since slave marriages were not integral to the private accumulation of wealth, nor were they critical to the normative construction of patriarchal households.

SLAVERY, PROPERTY RIGHTS, AND MARRIAGE OBLIGATIONS

From a property owner's perspective, marriage presented a restriction on transfer or sale. It was a "missing" stick in the bundle of property rights that the
slave owner ceded to the church and the couple. A slave's marriage was listed
on the contract of sale, together with age, geographical origin, length of time
with the seller, previous owner, skills, known "defects" ("tachas"), and original
sale price. In the language of property law, marriage analogized the spouse to
a lienholder. But marriage could also be very attractive for slave owners: slaves
were less likely to run away from their owners and family members if they
were located within close range and were perhaps more compliant in their
duties. Married slaves were also more likely to purchase their freedom, making them an economically attractive – or at least a less risky investment – for
slaveholders of modest resources.[37]

Perhaps slaveholders would have been more resistant to marriage if the
restrictions on travel truly infringed on their property rights. But Hispanic
urban slavery was precisely that: urban. Moreover, slaveholding in Lima was
by no means an elite affair. Many modest households existed exclusively off
subcontracting their slaves or from the remittances of their slaves' day-wage
earnings (*jornales*).[38] Female slaves washed clothes, sold food and sweets,
labored in boardinghouses, bakeries, hospitals, convents and other religious
institutions, and the city's ubiquitous taverns. They were subcontracted as
wet nurses, seamstresses, and cooks. Ten percent of the city's population lived
within religious institutions, cloistered residents required significant amounts
of slave labor. Male slaves went back and forth from agricultural estates in the
outlying fertile valleys carrying water, firewood, and crops for consumption in
the city.[39] Other slaves paid their *jornales* by working in bakeries, hospitals,
artisanal workshops, and religious complexes. The port of Callao (the city's
locus of shipping, commerce, and maritime defense) was a site also heavily
provisioned by enslaved labor.

Colonial census and demographic reports reveal the existence of multiple
household industries and workshops within "residential" spaces.[40] One study
of the 1613 census notes the juxtaposition of shoemakers, tailors, seamstresses,
silk dealers, hosiers, button makers, milliners, trunk makers, confectioners,
lace makers, locksmiths, and silversmiths within one city block that measured
approximately 450 square feet. These small establishments were also dense
residential spaces for laborers and owners alike. Subleasing or proxy rentals
were common, with long-term leases averaging four years of tenancy. This suggests a degree of residential stability within the city for both the enslaved population and their owners.[41] These urban work-life residential patterns reflect
interethnic spaces that were dependent on the labor of enslaved and indigenous
apprentices and dependent wards adopted in a servile capacity within a household, known as "criadas," who were raised by a variety of elders who were not
their parents.[42] This does not imply that the composition of the household was

stable – its very nature was impermanent. However, the point is that people would have been rotating into the city and its hybrid residential-occupational spaces rather than migrating out of it.⁴³

As noted, the petty artisanal and commercial sector responded to local patterns of consumption. Elite Spanish families were loath to leave the city with its urbane comforts. However, landholding – particularly when it conferred indigenous labor and tribute – was also a source of prestige and wealth for Spaniards and aristocratic criollos. Appointments to administrative offices (*corregimientos*) and assigned tributary rights (encomiendas) were highly coveted by both groups.⁴⁴ As Eduardo Torres Arancivia and Guillermo Lohmann show respectively, 600 criollos applied for 85 *corregimientos* every year. These grants lasted between two and five years, depending on whether they were dispensed by the king or the viceroy.⁴⁵

In attempting to trace movements within the viceroyalty, I have tried to graft sale and transfer petitions of slave owners onto larger patterns of economic expansion and relocation. But it is difficult to trace the frequency with which slaves were resold in the event that their owners planned to relocate. Predictably, we see evidence of quick turnover in subcontracting agreements. Although Brigida de Córdova's *censura* did not specify the reason she was exchanged between two sisters, it is plausible that doña Francisca could not bring Brigida to the *corregimiento* because she was married.

The seventeenth century was a period of internal and regional commercial and agricultural expansion. Kenneth Andrien calculates that at least 245,000 Iberians migrated into the Peruvian viceroyalty by 1650.⁴⁶ Similarly, Jane Mangan traces the migration into Potosí of *peninsulares*, mestizos, and Limeños.⁴⁷ Mangan cites a 1611 census conducted in Potosí, which showed that the mining city had a population of 43,000 Spaniards and 35,000 creoles, in addition to 76,000 Andean *naturales*.⁴⁸ Contrary to the prevailing view of the seventeenth-century Spanish Empire as one of spiraling economic depression, Mangan and Andrien carefully document local elite and petty entrepreneurs' response to regional "booms" in expanding markets in the southern provinces, the northern estates of Trujillo, and the mining city of Potosí.⁴⁹ An in-depth review of economic cycles over the seventeenth century is beyond the scope of this chapter, but it is important to mention that economic historians have highlighted Peru's overall market diversity and internal buoyancy, even as they note that different regions experienced boom-bust cycles.⁵⁰

In light of demographic patterns in the seventeenth century, I speculate that transfers out of Lima would not have been infrequent.⁵¹ However, the only data we have to show slave transfers out of the city are those in the marital unification suits. We do have more solid historical sources concerning travel between Lima's haciendas and estates (*chacras*). The central valleys provided most of the wheat and other grains needed for consumption in the coastal cities. Though travel would have been prohibitive during the week, families could conceivably have maintained weekend relationships if men and boys worked on the *chacras* and *estancias* and women and girls remained in the city. Prior to their apprenticeships, children typically went back and forth between the valleys and the city as families diversified their holdings and income-bearing potential with their allotted agricultural plots.[52]

Grapes, olives, and peppers were grown in the southern coastal valleys to supply a robust domestic market.[53] Corn was an Andean staple that also furnished the ingredients for beer. Sugar and cotton were grown on northern haciendas, where sugarcane alcohol was also produced. Cattle ranching, along with the cultivation of corn, potatoes, and beans in the upper Andean regions, all supplied consumers in internal urban, coastal, and rural markets.

Slaves who worked on haciendas were purchased for that purpose.[54] Unmarried slaves were obliged to accompany their owners when they relocated to their new holdings. After the separation of the Portuguese and Spanish crowns in 1640, slave prices rose exponentially.[55] As Rachel O'Toole writes, "Coastal landowners lacked enslaved Africans when indigenous communities refused (or could not) supply their required labor quota. By the 1650s, coastal landholders were land rich but labor poor."[56] Given the labor shortage, we would expect to see a spike in spousal unity suits while the slave trade was suspended. Although the caseload was higher, it was not as heavy as the period toward the end of the century (see Table 2.1).

In sum, Spaniards immigrated to and relocated internally within upper Peru. Slaves married at high rates. If they accompanied their owners, they either did so without protest or they fought when the separation went beyond the stipulated period. Enslaved families would have been able to fight against their separation if they were part of well-placed households and were conversant with the legal lexicons I discuss later in the chapter. Conversely, rural-urban arrangements did not always preclude conjugal unions, especially with weekend visitations. A third possibility is that couples resisting separation became fugitives or fled their owners. Infuriated or frustrated owners like don Juan Gaspar del Aguilar frequently filed petitions requesting permission to sell a slave outside of the jurisdiction, alleging capture or fear of flight. With these possibilities in mind, we now turn to an in-depth study of legal conflicts within and over enslaved marriages.

MATRIMONIAL CONFLICTS

Contestations emerged over enslaved people's marital rights in relation to five issues: consent, mixed status, spousal relocation, children's manumission, and marital discord. Here, I address consent and marital discord cases before examining the relocation cases in greater depth. I analyze mixed-status marriages (marriages in which one partner was free and the other enslaved) in Chapter 3 and children's manumission in Chapter 4.

Legally, slaves did not need their owner's consent to enter into marriage, and they sued in court independently when that right was abrogated.[57] According to Partida Four, "Slaves can marry one another, and although their masters oppose it, the marriage will be valid, and should not be annulled for this reason if both give their consent."[58] Thus, Pedro Toledo was fully within his rights in indicting Catalina Congo's owner, who refused to grant the couple permission to marry.[59] According to Pedro, Francisco Osorio de Contreras physically assaulted him when he proposed to marry Catalina. Pedro's owner, Juan Pérez de Zumeta, brought suit on his behalf, reminding Osorio that he could not physically abuse Pedro nor prevent him from entering into marriage with Catalina. Pérez de Zumeta may have brought the suit on the grounds that his property would be damaged if Pedro was prevented from marrying Catalina, although from the extant proceedings, it seems more likely that Pedro appealed to Pérez de Zumeta because the latter had the social status to challenge Osorio's actions.[60]

Conjugal rights were also complicated by legal minority and mixed-status marriages. Pedro de Tapia tried to contract marriage with Luisa Augustina, a free *mulata*.[61] Pedro approached Luisa's guardian, Francisco de Ballesteros, to propose marriage. However, Ballesteros resisted, citing at first Pedro's enslaved status. But the condition of male enslavement was not fatal to contracting marriage with a free woman. It may have been socially indiscreet, but the children of the union would not have been affected by their father's status since enslavement was transmitted along matrilineal lines. Ballesteros continued to deny the couple permission to marry. In the face of Pedro's persistent appeals, Ballesteros claimed that Pedro had an ongoing sexual relationship ("trato carnal") with Leonor Augustina, Luisa's aunt, who remained behind in Panama City when the family moved to Lima. Many of Ballesteros's witnesses corroborated this story – all of whom were recent arrivals from Panama City. We have no ruling from Provisor Vega in this case, who apparently left the matter up to the parties to wait until Luisa came of age.

Historians of domestic relations have long studied the church's stance on consent in marriage. As James Brundage reminds us, "Consent [between the parties] was the sole essential requirement for Roman marriage."[62] Patricia Seed's well-cited study of consent and the public exchange of matrimonial promises in seventeenth-century New Spain also emphasizes the Catholic Church's support of consenting couples even when there was parental resistance.[63] Ecclesiastical magistrates were more likely to intervene in preventing unequal marriages among plebeian couples when the stakes of whiteness were higher.[64] Even the Royal Pragmatic issued in 1776, and extended to the Americas in 1778, exempted enslaved couples from requiring parental consent, together with "mulattoes, blacks, mestizos and members of other similar mixed races who are publicly known and reputed as such."[65]

Mixed-status couples could also appeal to the court to enforce their rights to spousal unity. Captain García de Sobarzo, who was moving to Arica, resisted the order to sell his slave María de la Concepción to a local Lima buyer.[66] María de la Concepción was married to a free *mulato*, who asked the court to issue *censuras* to prevent her removal from the city. Captain García claimed that since María's husband was free, he could follow María to Arica and still enjoy his conjugal rights. Technically, García was right. Conjugal unity laws protected only married couples who were both enslaved. In asking the court to absolve him of the *censuras*, García reasoned that he negotiated with María's husband to find a local buyer, but he was running out of time. Given his imminent departure, García offered to bring María's husband along to Arica, paying him a salary that essentially reduced him to servile status. Provisor Villagómez refused to issue García a travel license to leave with María de la Concepción. García had not made an offer commensurate with María's husband's wage-earning potential, and the couple did not want to relocate to Chile. Villagómez also alluded to gendered reasoning in his decision: it disturbed him that a husband would be forced to relinquish his livelihood to follow his wife. Throughout his lengthy career as provisor of the ecclesiastical court (1657–83), Pedro de Villagómez was a staunch defender of marriage. Villagómez's unwavering support of marriage worked in favor of enslaved couples seeking to enforce their matrimonial rights, but it was devastating to wives who wanted to dissolve an unhappy marriage.

The marital discord cases provide a window into the ways in which conventional gender roles of male headship and female subservience were negotiated between enslaved spouses. The conjugal contract was based on the husband's obligation to financially support and provide shelter for his wife, and the wife's obligation to remain faithful to her provident husband.[67] However, the financial insecurity of many enslaved husbands impinged on their ability to exercise their patriarchal roles. It was expected that women in slave families would be breadwinners, which in turn conditioned their experience of subordination. Throughout colonial societies, prescriptive patriarchy was very much a "work in progress" rather than a given reality with stable parameters, and appeals to multiple patriarchs could unsettle the pretensions of some to power as well as fortify the positions of others. Enslaved husbands' assertions of disciplinary power over their wives and children met with mixed results. In divorce cases, wives could appeal to their owners to shield them from violence by preventing their abusive spouses from entering the house. Outraged husbands could then complain to the ecclesiastical court, demanding that it enforce the conjugal rights that they claimed were violated by their wives' owners. In other instances, wives would remain in owners' households but appeal to the court to grant separation of matrimonial bed and board.[68]

Many of the cases brought by outraged husbands against owners or other superiors like parents or godparents contain disputed testimonies, and the wives are conspicuously absent from the record. As Magdalena Chocano and Alberto Flores Galindo show in their pioneering study of marital suits in the eighteenth century, husbands recruited the courts to reinstate their *potestad*, essentially compelling their wives to return to their power and control.[69] However, enslaved husbands could not compel their wives to return to the marital home. Neither could they allege abandonment of the matrimonial household ("abandóno del hogar"). Thus, they were limited to filing complaints for conjugal visitation and putative assaults on their masculine honor when their wives went out working as *jornaleras*.[70] Conversely, enslaved wives were able to bring claims of inadequate economic support, infidelity, and severe and extreme cruelty (*sevicia*). I describe these cases in greater detail in the next section of the chapter, but I briefly cite two cases here in order to highlight the dilemma of multiple patriarchs.

In 1632, Augustina de los Ríos called on her owner to prevent Juan de la Rua, her husband, from entering into the household for conjugal visitation.[71] Augustina presented six witnesses who corroborated her claim that Juan abused her. Augustina alleged that her husband abused her continually, but the incident that prompted this complaint was Juan publicly stating his intention to kill her.

One of Augustina's witnesses, Ysabel, testified that Juan was physically abusive toward Augustina in public. According to Ysabel, Juan appeared in the courtyard of the boardinghouse where both Ysabel and Augustina were washing their feet. He dragged Augustina out of the courtyard upstairs to their room by her hair, and a heated fight quickly ensued, with Juan drawing a knife and holding it against Augustina. Ysabel physically intervened between the couple, and within minutes, the other residents in the boardinghouse came to both women's rescue to save them from the wrathful Juan. Another witness, Juliana, decried Juan for abusing his wife without provocation. Juliana berated Juan for calling Augustina and her mother whores and for taking her hard-earned money on weekends during the year and a half that the couple had been married.

In reading through the witnesses' testimonies, we glean a tale of escalating domestic violence against a young woman who found protection in the solidarity of her coresidents from the abuse of her irascible husband. All of Augustina's witnesses grew up together and remained under the roof of her owner. In his response, Juan de la Rua claimed that he was forced to exercise discipline over Augustina, who repented her early marriage and refused to relinquish her youthful customs. Juan further asserted that Augustina's owner, mother, and friends "influenced her insolent and contrary behavior."

In 1642, María Terranova appealed to the court to prevent visitation after enduring twenty-six years of abuse from her husband, Francisco.[72] María Terranova's case gives us a snippet of her life with Francisco – which by all accounts was a relentless cycle of abuse, infidelity, and neglect. Although she had endured Francisco's beatings for decades, it was one incident in particular that precipitated María's complaint. Francisco – who had abandoned María for a new mistress – returned to the home and absconded with 150 pesos that María had hidden in a mattress.

By the time María sued for divorce, she was no longer enslaved. Her former owner, Juana Díaz, had freed María after ten years in her service. According to Juana's testimony, María earned enough *jornales* to free both herself and Francisco. Francisco's freedom had been paid for seventeen years previously, which suggests that the couple had made his freedom their priority. The couple had two children whom we presume were freed as well. María's witnesses included the *padrino* of the couple's nuptials and those to whom they served as godparents. Nine witnesses who testified in María's favor claimed that they knew María and Francisco because they hailed from the same ethnic and linguistic group (*por ser de la misma nación y tierra*).

Neither María nor Augustina pursued her case beyond the stage of witness presentation. As Nancy van Deusen points out, although the majority of litigants dropped their suits, "*95 percent* of these litigants were women, and their continued insistence is an indication that they considered [petitioning for divorce] to be an effective means to question the intolerable forms of oppression and violence they faced in their marriages."[73] Van Deusen's observations corroborate the patterns that we have seen in other areas of legal mobilization and reflect the value of the legal process for socially subordinate groups. Hapless wives, like enslaved peoples, approached the legal sphere with similar objectives: to seek reprieve from an intolerable, abusive owner/spouse by appealing to an intercessor who would remind the abuser of the limits of his power. Both petitions, filed in the wake of a catalytic event, put the abuser on notice that his actions had strayed beyond the limits of tolerable discipline.

According to Bernard Lavallé's study of Lima's marital discord petitions during the seventeenth century, the majority of petitioners appealed to the court during the first five years of their marriage.[74] Augustina de los Ríos conforms to that pattern, but María Terranova's case is unique because of the length of her marriage and long-term tolerance of her husband's abuse, infidelities, and financial profligacy. However, even María dropped her case after presenting witness testimony.

The presentation of witnesses seemed to suffice in these cases, as they did in the *censuras*. Witnesses expressed their disapproval of the men's behavior and character, openly denouncing these husbands in front of an ecclesiastical official. Clearly, neighbors and parishioners were aware of conjugal conflict, adultery, and abuse before a case was publicly aired. These testimonies demonstrate convincingly that neighbors monitored conflict between partners because it spilled over into the community. Outside the closed, corporate world of elite families, enslaved, plebeian, and *casta* couples lived closely together in a congested urban space, and brawls were virtually impossible to conceal. Indeed, in Augustina de los Ríos's case, the intervention of her coresidents saved her life. However, witness testimony in an official forum went one step further than community opprobrium or candid confrontation with an offender. It signaled to the offensive husband that his behavior was unacceptable and that people were willing to support his wife before the eyes of the law and God.

The legal determination of rights when the labor and offspring of the married couple belonged to others occupied much of the court's time. Although many Limeño slaves amassed enough capital to purchase their children's freedom over time, their children and grandchildren were regulated as part of the domestic arrangements of their owners until the children's freedom was paid in full. Children were simultaneously cheap and expensive.[75] Although their purchase prices were lower, children were expensive to clothe, feed, and educate. Cash-strapped owners happily deferred to fathers who wished to provide for their children after their third birthday, even when the children remained under the roof of the mother's owner.

It is with regard to children that the logic of property is shared throughout all slave laws. The children of enslaved spouses belonged legally to their mothers' owners. The common practice of renting out lactating enslaved mothers as wet nurses illustrates the split logic of property most sharply, since legally the mother's milk belonged to her owner and not to her child. It is important to note that parents could not assert their parental rights to resist relocation: an unmarried mother, for example, could not invoke her maternal rights to stay with her child.[76] True, the court might rule that if a child was young, the child needed to remain with his or her mother because of lactation. But this was not always the case, particularly for mothers without husbands. Juliana Bran's husband Gaspar Zape was able to assert his paternal *and* marital rights in court, but it was only when he offered incontrovertible evidence that Gerónimo Vosmediano lied about the temporary nature of his family's relocation that Gaspar prevailed in his paternal claim. If we remember, the case revolved around Vosmediano's property right to command Juliana to serve as a wet nurse for his grandchild, not for the couple's child, whom we presume would have accompanied Juliana to Chile.

Thus it is not surprising that many of the lawsuits I examine revolved around enforcing promises of liberty for children. Children like Margarita Florindes (whose *censura* proceeding I describe in Chapter 1) had no way of knowing the arrangements their mothers had made. Unscrupulous owners did not hesitate to keep freed children in their households and later sell them. More commonly (yet no less unscrupulously), owners simply availed themselves of the labor of freed children for decades. Similar observations hold true for the widespread practice of apprenticeships of children and young adults who were indentured for a period rather than permanently enslaved. As many historians of childhood have noted, slave families were dependent on the fates of at least two or three households: their own and their respective owners.[77] In short, they were partially dependent, semiautonomous familial units subject to competing claims to their fertility, labor, and capital.

MARRIED LIFE IN LIMA

How did slaves navigate their joint obligations to their families and their owners? What did it mean to sustain family life or a home while enslaved? We get fragmentary images of slave marriages through legal and parochial documents.

Although these sources are tremendously valuable, they do not give us the most accurate picture.[78] As John Noonan reminds us, legal historians, like pathologists, see the ravages of a diseased body rather than a healthy specimen when we study marriage through the lens of divorce.[79] Countless couples no doubt sustained robust, loving domestic relationships. These couples had no reason to come under the purview of the court, and so they elude our retrospective inquiries.

This is one of the conundrums of family history when reconstructed through court records: the law tells us very little about the lived realities of everyday domestic life. María and Francisco Terranova would have appeared very different in the archival record twenty-six years before when they filed their *pliego matrimonial*. Legal action gives us evidence of family life at the moment of rupture rather than intuitively guiding us through the joys and travails of the union itself. Divorce and annulment proceedings, for instance, give us images of the couple at the time of crisis and rupture. The *pliegos* are perhaps more dependable, since they reveal the constellation of the couple's close relations and friends who testified regarding their eligibility for marriage.[80] Wills provide posthumous evidence of affective relationships, although testaments self-consciously left the most favorable image of the testator in preparation for a good death. Testaments are notoriously unreliable for piecing together the rancorous and volatile nature of the testator's familial and interpersonal interactions that invariably emerged in probate.

With these caveats in mind, I now turn to the spousal unity cases. I then recount a number of cases in which owners sought to ship their "incorrigible" slaves outside of Lima for discipline and resale and describe how slaves stymied their owners' plans by contracting marriage. In the interstices of these cases, I tease out some of the details of how owners, enslaved couples, and children sustained both marriages and families within a society with slavery.

On April 14, 1625, Lucas Criollo sought to enforce his rights to conjugal visitation with his wife, María.[81] María's owner had in fact permitted the couple visitation on weekends and holy feast days, but Lucas argued that such limited visitation was appropriate only for enslaved couples living in rural haciendas who belonged to different owners. Urban enslaved couples, in Lucas's view, were entitled to cohabit in the house of the wife's owner throughout the week like other married couples.

Lucas solemnly declared that he had been married for ten years to María Caboverde according to the orders of the Holy Mother Church. Lucas's owner, don Juan de Salinas, was a *regidor* of Lima, a highly ranked viceregal official.[82] Don Juan de Salinas did not contest Lucas's nocturnal absences, presumably because he had other slaves to attend to his family's domestic needs or perhaps because he did not care to intervene in Lucas's marital arrangements. María's owner, however, protested Lucas's entry into his house on weeknights by punishing María with beatings and insults. In light of this harsh treatment, Lucas asked the court to notify María's owner of his entitlement to cohabitation during the weeknights.

María's owner, don Juan Bautistia Squiaca, was a procurator who was actively embroiled in litigation in the *Real Audiencia* and the Archbishopric court. Given both owners' official positions and their ongoing professional and social relationships, they could not disregard the court's initial summons in the way that so many other owners ignored the preliminary notifications that they were served. In his response, don Juan Squiaca denied preventing the couple's exercise of their conjugal visits but did concede he limited their visits to weekends and feast days as required by law. Squiaca protested Lucas's nocturnal cohabitation during the week, because he said it impeded his family's access to María's ministrations throughout the night. Squiaca accepted that María's primary duty would have been to attend to her husband's needs and not to his family's if the couple remained together during the week. Squiaca contended that if he allowed Lucas to spend the weeknights with María, then other slaves would think they were entitled to this same privilege, thereby depriving other owners of their domestic slaves' attentions. Underlying this argument was the perceived threat of opening one's house at night to male slaves, which would disrupt not only domestic peace but public order.

Lucas magnanimously responded to Squiaca's rebuttal by claiming that he was more than willing to help María attend to the Squiaca family during the night. He objected to the specter of public danger raised by Squiaca, who had invoked the threat of black male mobility after the nighttime curfew in his rebuttal. Lucas reminded the court that he was honorable and hardworking and finished with his duties at a respectable hour. As the proceedings wore on, both sides called witnesses to answer their interrogatories. All Lucas's witnesses were asked to attest to his upstanding character, and the case ended with a victory in Lucas's favor. As expected, Squiaca protested the ruling, and the case proceeded to the Andean city of Huamanga on appeal. Though the record is incomplete, the last order, dated eleven months later, affirmed the ruling in Lucas's favor.

Unquestionably, Lucas was not a typical litigant. He was enslaved in a high-ranking household, which explained his familiarity with the law and his confidence in its capacity to protect married couples. Lucas knew the law only entitled him to what Squiaca offered. However, he (rather cleverly) tried to distinguish himself from the agricultural laborers for whom he claimed the laws were drafted and then alluded to a customary practice of owners permitting urban slaves to cohabit during the week to strengthen his claim.[83] He also imputed a higher-class position to himself and María based on the social prominence of the households in which they served. Not to be outdone, Squiaca unwaveringly relied on the law in his own interrogatories. Despite Squiaca's reliance on legal formalism, however, the case seemed to end with a ruling in Lucas's favor.

Like many lawsuits, the record does not have a definitive sentence (*hallo* or *sentencia*). A generous (and perhaps optimistic) interpretation leaves it up to the parties to come to an agreement. However, the lack of a definitive outcome was not disastrous to Lucas's claim. To the contrary, we expect that Lucas made his point that other owners gave their married slaves license for weeknight cohabitation simply by going to court and asking Squiaca to prove otherwise. All of Squiaca's witnesses were from socially prominent positions, on par with or more highly ranked than Lucas's owner. Alternatively, Lucas may have been emboldened to protest Squiaca's harsh punishment of María by bringing this to the court's (and the public's) attention. Squiaca's recourse to the whip and harsh words would also be exposed by Lucas's complaint, perhaps to the detriment of his public reputation, since he was punishing a practice that his peers accepted and allowed. Enslaved litigants knew that their lawsuits were publicly discussed. As Lyman Johnson reminds us for the case of Buenos Aires, "Many [slaves] used their sworn testimonies to place an owner's most embarrassing and shameful actions before the public... The satisfaction that slaves could take from performing their anger and frustration to this broader public helps us better understand why slaves pursued these unequal legal contests."[84] Patriarchy and masculine honor depended on performance.

A second case of an owner's interference with a married couple's conjugal rights was intentionally punitive. The owner claimed that he had placed his slave Polonia in a bakery (*panadería*) to punish her, because she had convinced her daughter to hide her pregnancy and abscond with her child – his property. The ecclesiastical provisor was not sympathetic to the owner's claims and ordered Polonia released from the bakery so that she could resume married life with her husband. The provisor based his ruling in large part on the fact that the couple was older and had been married for a long time.[85]

The disciplinary resale case in which don Juan Gaspar del Aguilar, archdeacon of Arequipa, sought to sell his slave, Francisca Terranova, outside of Lima on the grounds that she was a drunk also involved slaves attached to high-ranked households. The owners' social positions account for similar patterns of compliance with the law regarding married couples.[86] Aguilar appeared to be at his wits end with Francisca.[87] Francisca's husband was an agricultural laborer in Lurigancho, and she constantly ran away to be with him.[88] For the ten months that she had been in Aguilar's service, Francisca had only spent eight days in his house. Don Juan incurred considerable expenses paying armed guards to recover her to no avail.[89] Francisca simply ran away again. The month prior to lodging his plea, Aguilar had Francisca imprisoned while he tried to find an alternate buyer. But everyone knew about her habitual runaway status and also feared her husband, who was an alleged troublemaker, "a negro with an evil nature" ("*un negro de mal natural*"). Consequently, Aguilar found no buyers for Francisca. Thus he asked the court to issue him a permit to send Francisca to Arica, where he would seek a buyer. In the alternative, don Juan proposed a disciplinary rationale for banishing Francisca, hoping that exile would give her pause to repent and amend her errant ways.

As I have mentioned, the ecclesiastical court always granted a reprieve to the spouse claiming the imminent departure of an owner, giving the parties time to state their claims and counterclaims. This reprieve functioned as a petition for injunctive relief, as it effectively enjoined owners from leaving the city with their slaves. Of course, some owners surreptitiously departed to avoid these regulations, however the logistics of departure or residential relocation were difficult to conceal. Some enslaved spouses got to the court too late, but they alluded to a vibrant informational network among slaves, *castas*, and plebeians that swiftly communicated an owner's plans to desert the city.

In 1679, for example, Juan de Mendoza complained to the court that his wife Susana's owner had removed her from Lima without his knowledge. Susana was reportedly seen in a roadside inn (*tambo*) heading south to Cuzco, chained in a carriage. Despite being in chains, Susana managed to tell many people at the inn about her situation, hoping word would get to Juan so he could report her master. Witnesses in the city indicated having seen Susana's owner making plans for an unauthorized departure when they testified at Juan de Mendoza's behest.[90] Other witnesses at the inn testified that they saw Susana in chains, which indicated her owner's illegal intent. More importantly, Susana's owner had not requested the court's permission to take her to Cuzco.

Seafaring captains in the port of Callao were not allowed to leave without the proper documentation for married slaves. Clearly, some captains turned a blind eye to the requirement, or slaves were smuggled out on false pretenses. Many cases recount how spouses desperately searched ships in Callao, armed with appropriate warrants to check for their husbands or wives who might be imprisoned within the ship's galleys.[91] Witnesses in Catalina Biafara's case confirmed that her husband, Gaspar, was on board an Arica-bound ship. Catalina went to the captain's house and the port authority with the court's injunction to prevent the ship from leaving Callao. The captaincy was prepared to comply with the court order, but Gaspar's ship had already set sail. We surmise from the case records that a financial penalty was assessed against the ship's captain who carried slaves without the proper authorization, although it is not clear how the penalty was assessed or levied.[92]

Slave-owning captains were not immune from spousal unity complaints. Captains could avoid the summons by taking leave, although (somewhat remarkably, given the coordination required) church courts did communicate with personnel in other dioceses to have the *censuras* read when the captains were docked in their jurisdiction.[93] This interdiocesan communication yielded occasional results – particularly between Lima and Arica. This makes sense given the frequent travel between the cities and the fact that Arica was the principal site for prisoners banished for hard labor to the crown.[94]

Other communication attempts were not so effective. Four cases recount enslaved spouses' arduous legal battles to return to their families in Mexico, Nicaragua, and Panama City. Alvaro de la Cruz, owned by a sea captain, litigated for ten years in an effort to return to his wife and children in Mexico

City. Alvaro presented numerous witnesses in Lima who knew him and his wife in Mexico City, and many of his witnesses were men who had spent considerable time in Mexico City. In ruling on one of his petitions, Provisor Feliciano de Vega ordered Alvaro's owner to sell him to an owner bound for New Spain. However, slaves with maritime experience were particularly favored, and Alvaro's owner showed no intention of selling him to anyone else.[95] Because Alvaro was at sea with his owner for such extended periods of time, his case remained unresolved. Alvaro may have given up out of sheer exhaustion, or he may have purchased his freedom in another jurisdiction.[96]

In another case, it was an intending bride who bargained with her groom's owner to find a suitable local buyer.[97] María de los Santos and Juan Josef de Moncado had declared their intent to marry by filing the requisite *pliego matrimonial*. The couple had secured the church's permission to marry when Juan Josef's owner announced that he would be leaving for Arica. They were unable to marry because Juan Josef's owner promptly imprisoned him in Callao. Because Juan Josef and María had not yet received the sacrament, the church could not afford them its protection. But the marriage petition that María presented was critical to the success of her complaint. And María was an enterprising and determined litigant. As she argued analogously, the court of the Holy Mother Church should defend couples faithfully *intending to enter into* marriage as vigorously as it defended lawfully married couples. She found a buyer for Juan Josef who paid the 525 pesos that his owner had paid earlier. María also convinced Juan's owner to move him from the prison in Callao into the city where other buyers could appraise him. María found a buyer within thirty-six hours, which was the *plazo* that the court granted her while they stayed issuing the permits to Juan's owner in order for her to look for an alternative buyer.

Although this was a singular case, it is significant that María was able expand on the customary right to look for a local buyer for a spouse whose owner was relocating and extend it to her betrothed.[98] The record reveals that María de los Santos belonged to don Miguel Nuñez de Sanabria, an *oidor* in the *Real Audiencia* and a viceregal adviser. Juan Josef's owner was an attorney with the same court.[99] Again, I maintain (as in the case of Lucas and María) that the working relationship between owners may have been critical in convincing Juan Josef's owner to negotiate with María. As I have already noted, in the majority of cases, if an owner offered a legitimate reason for the enslaved spouse's departure, then the church would issue the requisite license.[100] The owner would be required to pay a sizable bond to ensure the slave's return.[101] Both the bond and license created the expectation of return, six to nine months being the conventional length of time authorized by the travel permit.

DISCIPLINE, BANISHMENT, AND HOLY MATRIMONY

In disciplinary resale cases, owners also had to exhaust all local possibilities to find a buyer so that the couple could stay together. In the case of Francisca

Terranova, the ecclesiastical provisor in fact ordered don Juan Gaspar Aguilar to offer Francisca for sale to her husband's owner. Note that neither the *Partidas* nor the *Curia Philipica* dictated anything with regard to married slaves with criminal sentences of exile.[102] Nevertheless, the procedure of *variación de dominio* may have developed as customary practice in Iberia and the Americas analogously with the laws of conjugal unity for married slaves facing banishment. The seller had to demonstrate due diligence to find a local buyer before securing a permit from the church. The likelihood of finding a local buyer was slim, however, unless the seller was prepared to disclose the slave's alleged defects and take a much lower price.[103]

Lima's resale slave market operated on a trial basis; buyers could first "try out" a slave in their households and workshops to see if the slave was a worthwhile investment. As I discuss in Chapter 6, many redhibition cases mention this probationary period, so we presume that it became an accepted customary practice of the resale market. According to many contracts of sale, the prospective buyer paid the *jornales* to the owner during the trial period to compensate the seller for the temporary loss of income; this advance payment went toward the final purchase price.[104] Once the slave exhibited the allegedly defective behavior (running away, theft, drunkenness, illness), the new owner had a cause of action to bring a redhibition suit. Sellers unanimously claimed that the defect developed under the new owner's custody, pointing to the trial period when the defect should have been noted and the slave returned because of the buyer's dissatisfaction.

I discuss these redhibition suits in Chapter 6, but the suits only obliquely refer to marriage. When we view them together with the spousal unity suits, we get a clearer picture of the marriage regime and the church's power: a power that enslaved couples could harness to protect their marriages. Both categories of cases suggest that slaves destined for Arica or the southern provinces deliberately entered into marriage to prevent their departure or banishment. Owners took action to prevent their slaves from marrying because of its restrictive effects on their travel plans. As we saw in María and Juan Josef's case, the owner imprisoned Juan Josef as soon as the couple filed their marriage petition. Another outraged owner claimed, "These two slaves who I have in my service have gotten married on me, just to remain in the city."[105] In this case, the owner, Captain Don Juan Cavero, planned to relocate to his hacienda in Pisco because of the damage to his properties in Lima during the two severe earthquakes of 1687.[106] Cavero argued that Ana possessed no meaningful ties to Lima, as he had only recently brought her to the city from Panama. Cavero implied that Ana's marriage was of such short duration that it could not trump the affective ties she had formed within his household. Despite these arguments, the case ended with an order for Cavero to offer both Ana and María for sale to their husbands' owners.

In another case, Juan de Nolete alleged that his slave Pedro Bran had married without his consent to avoid being sent to Arica.[107] But the court reminded

Nolete that Pedro did not need his owner's consent to marry. Nolete urged the court to grant him a reprieve from the obligation to respect Pedro's marital rights, pointing out that Pedro was an accomplished baker whose skills were necessary as Nolete opened up a new cake-making business in Arica. Another owner asked permission to take his slave Juan de Mesa to Pisco, where he needed Juan's skills as a tailor as he attempted to deliver vestments to the church for an important ceremonial event.[108] The church had granted Juan de Mesa's owner a four-month permit, but he violated the terms of the permit by keeping Juan in Pisco for another four months. Juan's wife, Francisca Bran, complained repeatedly to the ecclesiastical provisor, who in turn persisted until the petitions and *censuras* elicited a response from Juan's owner.

These appeared to be legitimate marriages; they were long-term relationships that predated the spouse's departure. Similarly, María and Juan Josef's petition stated that the couple had been involved in an eleven-year concubinary relationship. Perhaps the imminent departure of Juan Josef's owner convinced the couple to marry. Again I suggest that the widespread practice of marriage is attributable to precautions taken by Limeño slaves to remain in the city close to children and loved ones. I doubt that the high marriage rate amongst slaves was exclusively due to the broad appeal of, or enthusiasm for, the marriage sacrament.

Ana Terranova's marriage may have been legitimate despite Cavero's claim about the short duration of the couple's courtship. Marriage rates spiked in the aftermath of the earthquakes in 1687 as priests exhorted all couples to solemnize their sinful unions. Conversely, Ana and María possibly took advantage of Cavero's property damage during the 1687 earthquakes to leave his service by marrying their husbands and thereby resist relocation to Pisco.

Other cases clearly indicate that the slave slated for departure entered into marriage solely to avoid banishment. In September 1676, Pascuala Criolla lodged a complaint against her owner for boarding her on an Arica-bound vessel in violation of her marital rights. Her owner, don Alonso Bolaños, responded that Pascuala merely chose to marry another slave while she was in prison in order to lodge her complaint.[109] Another couple contracted an "eleventh hour" marriage and found a priest willing to marry them within the jail's chapel.[110]

In an annulment proceeding, Juana Maldonado claimed that she was forced into marriage with Ignacio de la Cruz to prevent his banishment to Chile because his owner needed Ignacio's services in his *panadería* (bakery).[111] Ignacio had been exiled to Chile by the *Real Audiencia* for crimes against the public order, and his owner would have been deprived of Ignacio's earnings had it not been for the right of husbands to remain in the city close to their wives. Juana herself was imprisoned and working in the *panadería*. Faced with the prospect of threats and beatings from Ignacio's owner, Juana had no other choice but to comply with the marriage.

Although the couple fulfilled the Tridentine requirement of attesting to their consent and proffering witnesses, Juana confessed later in her annulment proceeding that these were false statements that she made under duress. In a rare move, Provisor Villagómez granted Juana's annulment petition. Nine years later, after repeated petitions and denials, Juana presented evidence from a young priest, who as a boy had spent time in the house of Ignacio's owner. The priest corroborated Juana's story that the marriage was never consummated and that Juana was forced into the marriage without her consent.

In a case similar to that of Pascuala Criolla, Juana Criolla's owner imprisoned her within the city jail for punishment and exile. However, Juana – in collusion with her lover – brought three *negros bozales* to the jail for her to choose a husband to marry.[112] Why Juana could not contract marriage with her lover is not explained in the record. Two of the three *bozales* refused to marry a criolla slave. It took Juana's lover repeated attempts to find a willing spouse. And the case contained surprising elements. The man Juana eventually married accused her owner, Josef de Mereguez of having a child with Juana. According to her husband, the reason Mereguez sought to ship Juana off was to get her away from her lover. Mereguez vigorously denied this accusation in his rebuttals, although Juana's witnesses also claimed that jealousy was the motivating factor in Mereguez's decision to send Juana away.

Finally, it bears mentioning that not all departing spouses left against their partner's will. Departure could be a solution to an unhappy and violent marriage. In three cases, owners sought permission to send their slaves to Chile because of marital strife. In 1694, Julian Angulo counterclaimed Francisco Congo's spousal unity suit.[113] Francisco had asserted his rights to conjugal visits with his wife María, who was Angulo's domestic slave. However, Angulo claimed that slaves' conjugal rights were contingent on the safety of the couple and their children and, by extension, the safety of the owner's household. This is one of three instances in the extant sources in which an owner sought to deny the conjugal rights of his slave and to secure permission to sell her outside of the city on the basis of marital discord. As Angulo claimed, he was more than willing to abide by the law but the situation between María and Francisco was growing so dangerous that he feared for his life and those of María and her children.[114] María did not testify about Francisco's abuse, and so we have to wonder about the veracity of Angulo's statements.

Two other owners alleged spousal disagreement as the reason for separating the couple. According to doña María Velazquez's plea, she sought permission to send her slave Antonio to Arica because of the discord between Antonio and his adulterous wife, Josefa.[115] Previously, Antonio had traveled to Panama – presumably without resistance from Josefa. During his absence, Josefa had a series of amorous affairs. Upon his return to Lima, Antonio tried to kill both his wife and her current lover and succeeded in maiming the lover. As a consequence, Antonio was sentenced to two years of hard labor in Chile. As with many cases, this one ended with a strange twist. Antonio returned to Lima after serving his two-year sentence and reunited with Josefa. We know this because of the repeated complaints Josefa brought to the court seeking Antonio's return.

CONCLUSION

The idea that marriage and slavery were compatible might seem odd given the weight of the Anglo-American experience in our scholarly conversations. But as I have argued, it is less remarkable in seventeenth-century Hispanic urban centers given the market dynamics of those particular societies and the unrivaled power of the baroque Catholic Church. The cases of Anton and Ysabel Bran, María Caboverde and Lucas Criollo, and Juan Josef de Moncada and María de los Santos remind us that the institution of marriage could be wielded by slaves themselves for their own intended purposes. Their cases provide us with further evidence of enslaved peoples' social navigation, community building, and participation in interethnic networks that undermined the divisive effort of viceregal administrators and slave owners and that shaped the experience of human bondage itself.

NOTES

1   AAL, Causas de negros, leg. 23, exp. 41, año 1693.
2   Ibid., leg. 5, exp. 22, año 1627.
3   See, for example, a notarized letter of consent from Juana Bautista de Salas to her husband's owner, granting him reprieve to travel to Mexico for two years. (AGN, Real Audiencia Protocolos, Gomez de Baeza, 1590.07.24).
4   Ibid., leg. 4, exp. 12, año 1621.
5   See, for example, Klein, "Anglicism, Catholicism and the Negro Slave."
6   The synodal councils were responsible for implementing Tridentine doctrines in Peru.
7   Vargas Ugarte, *Concilios limenses*, 3:77. Drawing almost verbatim on the *Partidas*, Lima's synod concluded that "ni los esclavos ya casados se envíen o lleven o venden en parte donde por fuerza han de estar ausentes de sus maridos o mujeres perpetualmente o muy largo tiempo, que no es justo que la ley del matrimonio que es natural se derogue por la ley de servidumbre que es humana."
8   In fact, we see many petitioners referring to their marital rights as their only right (su único derecho).
9   The earliest *Recopilación de leyes* for the Americas was not promulgated until 1680. See Altamira, *Técnica de Investigación en la historia del derecho indiano*, 22.
10 Burns, *Las Siete Partidas*, Partida 4, law 2, 902.
11 The right to look for a new owner was also known as *papel de venta* in Buenos Aires.
12 Ana de la Cruz put her husband's new owner on notice by registering their marriage. See AAL, Causas de negros, leg. 4, exp. 8, año 1620.
13 AAL, Causas de negros, leg. 5, exp. 37, año 1629. "Digo que sin embargo se ha de mandar guardar y cumplir el auto justificado a causa de que el susodicho pretende sacar a la dicha mi mujer de la ciudad, lo cual no puede ni debe hacer por ser a favor del matrimonio que los dueños de los esclavos no los saquen fuera del lugar donde viven los maridos o mujeres con quien están casados y en este caso que dispone la parte contraria que cada uno pueda cuidar de sus bienes como le pareciere no es de consideración decir que el susodicho se va por tiempo limitado porque lo hace con ánimo de no volver a esta ciudad."

14 According to Vosmediano, "Mi hija ya está en días de parir y la dicha negra tiene leche, y quiero que crie al nieto que Dios me diere" (ibid.).

15 Wisnoski, "It Is Unjust for the Law of Marriage to Be Broken by the Law of Slavery," 247.

16 For an extensive analysis of slave marriages in colonial Mexico, see Bennett, *Africans in Colonial Mexico*. For a study in Quito and Popayán, see Bryant, *Rivers of Gold, Lives of Bondage*.

17 The comparative lack of interest in marriage is due to the fact that it was buried within larger points of contention in the US slavery literature. Slaveholders' concern in promoting their slaves' family rights and domestic relations was seen as self-interested paternalism. Other scholars viewed the legal denial of the rights to family as the exemplar of a conflict-ridden violent slave system. For a classic rendition of the latter view, see Stampp, *The Peculiar Institution*. For paternalism, see Genovese, *Roll Jordan Roll*.

18 In his challenging review of "apologist" slavery scholarship in the ancient world, Keith Bradley turns to the Roman writer Columella, who recommended material and emotional allowances for slaves in terms of their rational return and incentives. Bradley writes, "Columella gives some indication of the means by which social contentment among slaves might be elicited: the [fostering] of family life among slaves, the prospect of emancipation from slavery" (*Slaves and Masters in the Roman Empire*, 25).

19 Gutman, *The Black Family in Slavery and Freedom*.

20 On concubinage in early colonial America, see Fischer, *Sex, Race, and Resistance in Colonial North America*, and Hodes, *Sex, Love, Race*. For Latin American concubinage, see Nazzari, "Jose Antonio da Silva"; Borchat de Moreno, "El control de la moral pública como elemento de las Reformas Borbónicas en Quito"; Martinez-Alier, "Elopement and Seduction in Nineteenth-Century Cuba"; and Rodríguez Jímenez, *Seduccíon, amancebamiento y abandono en la colonia*. For illegitimacy, see Twinam, *Public Lives, Private Secrets*; Dueñas Vargas, *Los hijos del pecado*; Mannarelli, *Pecados públicos*. For the intersections of sexuality and empire, see Stoler, *Carnal Knowledge and Imperial Power*, and Burton, *Gender, Sexuality, and Colonial Modernities*. For plaçage in Louisiana, see Martin, "Plaçage and the Louisiana *Gens de Coleur Libre*."

21 According to Burkholder and Johnson, "In Peru before 1650, less than 8 percent of slaves aged 20–25 and less than 15 percent of slaves aged 26–35 married; in both groups women married more frequently than men did. Among free blacks, marriage rates were similar to those of whites" (*Colonial Latin America*, 205).

22 This profuse body of scholarship analyzes the relationship between income-generation opportunities and female autonomy among urban enslaved women and free women of color. See, for example, Scully and Paton, *Gender and Slave Emancipation in the Atlantic World*. Other scholars emphasize the matrifocal nature of slave families in the British and French Caribbean and the northeastern provinces of Brazil. For Brazil, see especially Kuznesof, *Household Economy and Urban Development*, and Karasch, *Slave Life in Rio de Janeiro*; cf. Metcalf, "Searching for the Slave Family in Colonial Brazil"; Graham, *House and Street*; and Dore, *Gender Politics in Latin America*.

23 See Harris, *Patterns of Race in the Americas*, and Freyre, *Casa grande y senzala*.

24 Edwards, "The Marriage Covenant Is the Foundation of All Our Rights." Edwards compares the Reconstruction emphasis on urging slaves into formal marriage with its earlier proscription. As she writes, "Marriage was not only a civil right, but also the entering wedge into a broad range of social privileges. As such it carried the potential to destabilize slavery" (95). In a similar vein, Eugene Genovese comments on the failed attempt of proslavery leaders and jurists to recognize slave marriages. According to Genovese, one outspoken critic of the American law's lack of protection of slave marriages admitted that "marriage was not inconsistent with the institution of slavery as it exists amongst us, and the objection therefore lies rather to an incident than to the essence of the system" (*Roll Jordan Roll*, 52). Genovese explains that later attempts to "humanize the slave code with respect to marriage and literacy got nowhere. The slaveholders understood that such reforms threatened the economic viability of the capital and labor markets. No other issue so clearly exposed the hybrid nature of the regime, so clearly pitted economic interest against paternalism and defined the limits beyond which the one could not reinforce the other" (53).

25 The sacramental ledgers also record a number of couples as *esclavos indios*. I have not included those marriages here. Neither have I included endogamous indigenous marriages in this tabulation.

26 Pérez Cantó, *Lima en el siglo XVIII*.

27 See Bryant, *Rivers of Gold, Lives of Bondage*, who uses marriage petitions for similar ends in his study of Ecuador.

28 For imperial Rome, see Treggiari, *Roman Marriage*; Evans Grubbs, *Law and Family in Late Antiquity*; Corbett, *The Roman Law of Marriage*; and Falcão, *Las prohibiciones matrimoniales de carácter social en el imperio Romano*.

29 In New Jersey and New York, slaves were allowed to marry according to laws passed in 1809. (My thanks to Sarah Levine Gronningsater for bringing these laws to my attention.) The prohibition on slave marriages also did not apply to Louisiana, where slaves were allowed to marry with their owner's consent. Louisiana's married slaves, however, did not have the full contractual range of rights accorded to Lima's enslaved couples. For Louisiana, see Kelleher Shafer, *Slavery, the Civil Law, and the Supreme Court of Louisiana*. For Reconstruction efforts to marry emancipated slaves, see Edwards, "The Marriage Covenant," and Franke, "Becoming a Citizen."

30 See, for example, the sixteenth-century royal *cédula* issued for Peru: "Que los negros se casen con negras" (Konetzke, *Colección de documentos*, 1:210).

31 Nancy van Deusen records a similarly high percentage of endogamous marriages for San Marcelo. Her review of the *libros matrimoniales* for San Marcelo between 1640 and 1693 reveals a 93 percent rate of endogamous marriages among free and enslaved blacks ("The 'Alienated' Body," 6–8).

32 Newson and Minchin, *From Capture to Sale*, 68. Newson and Minchin base their findings on a close reading of Manuel Bautista's detailed records of slave trading into Lima between 1613 and 1635, when Inquisitors seized his assets.

33 On the "articulation" of family, economy, and community for slaves and owners, see Morris, "The Master-Slave Relationship Reconsidered," 987.

34 Note that there were no equivalent state-driven constraints on an owner's desire to manumit a slave as there were in the United States.

35 For the United States, see especially, Pascoe, *What Comes Naturally*, Cott, *Public Vows*, Hartog, *Man and Wife in America*, Grossberg, *Governing the Hearth*, and Yamin, *American Marriage*.

36 For representative works on Latin American family history, gender relations, and labor history relating to the impact of administrative policies on domestic relations, see, for example, Lavrin, *Sexuality and Marriage in Colonial Latin America*. For sixteenth-century Andean societies, see Vieira Powers, *Women in the Crucible of Conquest*. For late colonial Latin America, see Twinam, *Public Lives, Private Secrets*. For Brazil, see Caulfield, *In Defense of Honor*. For republican Peru, see Hünefeldt, *Liberalism in the Bedroom*. For colonial Mexico, see Boyer, *Lives of the Bigamists*.

37 See Hünefeldt, *Paying the Price of Freedom,* on economic strategies for familial manumission in the nineteenth century.

38 See Bowser, *The African Slave in Colonial Peru*, ch. 6.

39 *Chacras* in Lima's outlying areas complemented the production of larger haciendas that supplied important staple crops.

40 Panfichi, "Urbanización temprana de Lima" and Quiroz, *Artesanos y manufactureros en Lima colonial*. Quiroz writes, "La ciudad contó con curtiembres, ollerías, adoberías, ladrilleras, jabonerías, fundiciones y otros establecimientos con hornos ... De esta manera, la ciudad llegó a tener algunos talleres relativamente grandes ya desde el siglo XVII, pero numéricamente siguieron prevaleciendo las pequeñas y micro unidades de vivienda y producción. Esto permitió (o tal vez determinó) la difusión del trabajo domiciliario como una forma alternativa de organización industrial en Lima colonial" (39).

41 Duran Montero, "Lima en 1613, aspectos urbanos." Both the 1613 census and the 1700 *numeración* show sizable numbers of free *morenas* who rented rooms to other tenants. See Pérez Contó, *Lima en el siglo XVIII*.

42 Vergara, "Growing Up Indian." For a primary source from which to infer nonparental child-raising patterns of *criadas*, see *Numeración General*. For an interpretation of the census, see Cook's introduction to *Numeración General*. Studying these interethnic child-rearing and family formation patterns integrates historical narratives of black, Spanish, and indigenous social experiences – which still tend to be interrogated separately. These residential patterns also demonstrate that various practices that shaped past social and demographic orders resulted from the coordinated (and not oppositional) actions and efforts of members of mixed-status families and social units. For a nineteenth-century review of interracial conviviality, see Cosamalón Aguilar, *Indios detrás de la muralla*.

43 Historians have always been fascinated by Lima's chaotic and poorly regulated development (so evident in contemporary patterns). Throughout the centuries, Lima has been characterized by congested spaces of horizontal sociality, conviviality, and tension. See Panfichi, "Urbanización temprana de Lima," 24.

44 As Eduardo Torres Arancivia notes, the most sought-after administrative office was the *corregimiento*, because of the rent-bearing possibilities these held. "Sin lugar a dudas las mercedes más anheladas en aquella época fueron las rentas de encomiendas y los corregimientos. Los corregimientos de indios podían ser nombrados por el rey o por su virrey, aunque las diferencias entre uno y otro nombramiento eran la duración del cargo (por nombramiento mayestático un corregidor podía estar en el

cargo cinco años, mientras que por gracia virreinal solo uno o dos). El virrey tenía en su plantilla 52 corregimientos de las 85 plazas que existían, cifra que resultaba pequeña para los 600 candidatos que postulaban para ocupar una plaza" (*Corte de virreyes*, 111).

45 Lohmann Villena, *El corregidor de indios en el Perú bajo los Austrias*.
46 Ibid., 29.
47 Mangan, *Trading Roles*.
48 Ibid., 43.
49 Contrary to the widely held view that African-descent peoples did not migrate to the mining center of Potosí, Jane Mangan shows that there was a robust community of mestizos and *mulatos* (at least six thousand) as well as of slaves who came to the *sierra* via Brazil and Buenos Aires. African-descent peoples were thought to fare poorly in the frigid, high altitude, which explained the popular saying "El gallinazo no canta en puna" (see Bowser, *The African Slave in Colonial Peru*, 14). Viceregal policies also sought to segregate African-descent peoples from the *república de indios*. However, as Mangan notes, "Men and women of African descent adapted as well as Europeans to Potosí's altitude, and they engaged as vendors and consumers where they crossed paths with indigenous traders" (*Trading Roles*, 42). By far the largest migration patterns we see in the spousal unity petitions are on the coast, from Lima to Arica. Fewer petitions show movement to Potosí and Cuzco.
50 As Andrien writes with regard to the "boom" cycles of the seventeenth century, "Local economies were welded more tightly together, and were more diverse than in the past and there is no evidence of a sustained malaise" (*Crisis and Decline*, 40).
51 Ibid.
52 Married couples were granted agricultural plots on the haciendas for their domestic consumption and could use the plots for income generation. For urban-rural links between slave families, see Hünefeldt, *Lasmanuelos*. In Hünefeldt's fictional account of the Lasmanuelos, the family raises pigs on its allotted plot – generating enough revenue to purchase the freedom of one of their children – although not all. Pig rearing was key to familial enrichment – a pig in Lima sold for 40 *reales*. Another key investment for rural-urban families was a mule. In seventeenth-century Lima, a mule cost 125 *reales*. Owning mules facilitated familial mobility and male employment through muleteering and local transit. African-descent males who rode mules did not visually disturb the masculinist hierarchy that reserved horseback riding for Spaniards. We see evidence in the *cartas notariales* that families contracted mules on a rent-to-own basis until they could be purchased outright.
53 Rebecca Earle's excellent study of Iberian conceptions of food, *Body of the Conquistador*, puts Limeño patterns of consumption and tastes in perspective. The preference for bread and wine created strong internal markets in the urban areas.
54 Cushner, "Slave Mortality and Reproduction."
55 See Vila Vilar, "Los asientos Portugueses y el contrabando de negros."
56 O'Toole, *Bound Lives*, 9.
57 In fact, Limeño owners regularly appeared as witnesses testifying to their slave's eligibility to marry. Notarial records also reveal owners' involvement in their slaves' nuptials in the form of providing financial assistance or freeing the intending spouse. In 1607, Ana Carvajal decided to free her nineteen-year-old slave Juan Jiménez pending his entry into marriage: "Se va a casar con mujer honrada doncella

onesta y recogida y en renumeración y gratificación del buen serviçio que... me an hecho él y su madre" (AGN, Pedro Gonzalez Contreras, Protocolo no. 789, año 1607, ff. 1334-36v). An owner's resistance to a pending or contracted marriage also appears in some cases, but that did not invalidate the marriage. And enslaved women seeking to dissolve their marriages did cite their lack of consent when their owners forced them to marry undesired spouses. See AAL, Causas de negros, leg. 22, exp. 47, año 1690 (Pascuala Buitron v. Domingo Terranova). See also AAL, Causas de nulidades, leg. 35, año 1680 (Dominga Juana v. Domingo Folupo), and ibid., año 1660 (Juana Maldonado v. Ignacio de la Cruz), discussed in this chapter.

58 Burns, *Las Siete Partidas, Partida 4*, title 5, law 1, 901.

59 AAL, Causas de negros, leg. 1, exp. 31, año 1609.

60 Pedro de Zumeta was an official of the Holy Tribunal of the Inquisition.

61 AAL, Causas de negros, leg. 1, exp. 9a, año 1603.

62 Brundage, *Law, Sex, and Christian Society*, 34–37.

63 Seed, *To Love, Honor and Obey in Colonial Mexico*.

64 McKinley, "Illicit Intimacies."

65 The Royal Pragmatic issued in 1776 prevented unequal marriages between persons of different racial status and required parental consent for marriages of legal minors (under twenty-five years of age). See Socolow, "Acceptable Partners," 210. By 1803, "blacks and other mixed-bloods were included in the [new] *Pragmatica*" (212).

66 AAL, Causas de negros, leg. 20, exp 27, año 1682.

67 van Deusen, "Determining the Boundaries of Virtue," 375.

68 We see similar appeals to multiple patriarchs when the couple lived in the wife's familial household.

69 Flores Galindo and Chocano, "Las cargas del sacramento." The eighteenth-century divorce complaints that Flores Galindo and Chocano describe in their study share many of the characteristics of the complaints examined here. However, the husbands in the complaints they examine were not enslaved. As they observe, the husbands articulated their marital rights and control over their wives as though they had acquired a perpetual servant: "Los hombres parecen entender que con el matrimonio han adquirido un bien de uso, especie de sirviente a perpetuidad que, además de encargarse de las tareas domésticas y los hijos, debe ayudar al marido en la labor de mantener a la familia: lo que alguno denominaría eufemísticamente, 'las cargas del sacramento'" (411).

70 See Boyer, "Honor among Plebeians," 161–64, for a discussion of honor among slaves.

71 AAL, Causas criminales de matrimonio, leg. 2, exp. 8, año 1632.

72 AAL, Causas criminales de matrimonio, leg. 8, exp. 28, año 1642.

73 van Deusen, "Determining the Boundaries of Virtue," 375, my emphasis.

74 Lavallé, *Amor y opresión en los Andes coloniales*, 26. Van Deusen shows that "divorce petitions tripled and annulment requests doubled between 1651–1700" ("Determining the Boundaries of Virtue," 375).

75 I am eternally grateful to Karen Graubart for this observation.

76 I thank Cristian Villonga for urging me to clarify the difference between marital and parental rights.

77 Kuznesof, "The House, the Street, Global Society"; Premo, *Children of the Father King*.

78 Not surprisingly, Christine Hünefeldt's depiction of the Lasmanuelos family was constructed from legal and secondary sources.

79 Noonan, *Power to Dissolve*.

80 Bennett, *Africans in Colonial Mexico*.

81 AAL, Causas de negros, leg. 5, exp. 3, año 1625.

82 Don Juan de Salinas was appointed to the *cabildo* of Lima in 1623, where he served as *regidor* until 1640. See Lohmann Villena, *Los regidores perpetuos del Cabildo*, 2:280–81.

83 In his interrogatory Lucas asked his witnesses to verify the following: "Si tiene conocimiento que en esta ciudad los negros casados a quienes sus amos dan licencia van a dormir con sus mujeres todas las noches que tienen lugar sin que los amos de las esclavas se lo estorben ni impidan de manera contraria, y que se guarda de dejar salir los amos a sus negros esclavos solo los sábados y domingos a dormir con sus mujeres es con los negros chacareros por la ausencia que han de hacer venir de su chacra a esta ciudad pero no los que viven en ella por ser justo." AAL, Causas de negros, leg. 5, exp. 3, año 1625 (Interrogatory).

84 Johnson, "A Lack of Legitimate Obedience and Respect," 635.

85 AAL, Causas de negros, leg. 21, exp. 15-A, año 1686.

86 Arequipa is an important Andean city south of Lima.

87 Francisca was left to Aguilar by inheritance. Possibly Francisca's previous owner was more lenient with her conjugal visits.

88 Lurigancho was an agricultural area outside of Lima.

89 *Cuadrilleros* charged 4 pesos for every slave recovered. This amount is consistent with owners' claims for recovering runaway slaves. See Chapter 6.

90 AAL Causas de negros, leg. 19, exp. 29, año 1679.

91 AAL Causas de negros, leg. 5, exp. 28, año 1627.

92 Bowser suggests that captains were assessed freight charges as penalties if they were caught without the proper documentation for slaves on their ships, although his reference is to the fines for contraband slave trading.

93 For Realejo (Nicaragua), see AAL, Causas de negros, leg. 2, exp. 15, año 1611. For Mexico City, see ibid., leg. 1, exp. 1, año 1600, and leg. 4, exp. 37, años 1621–31. For Panama, see ibid., leg. 5, exp. 3, año 1612. It would be interesting to know whether the spouses also filed petitions with the ecclesiastical courts in their jurisdictions.

94 A communiqué from officials in Chile pleaded with Lima's alcaldes to not send any more *presidiarios* to Valdivia because of numerous breaches to the city's peace and social order ("Para evitar los perjuicios que el presidente de Chile a representado pueden servirse de suspender el envío de presidiarios a la Plata de Valdivia").

95 On enslaved ship pilots, see Dawson, "The Cultural Geography of Enslaved Ship Pilots."

96 Alexander Wisnoski examines the case of Juan de Villegas, also an enslaved husband seeking unification with his spouse in Mexico City. Villegas's case was resolved more favorably than the case of Alvaro de la Cruz. See "'It Is Unjust for the Law of Marriage to Be Broken by the Law of Slavery.'"

97 AAL, Causas de negros, leg. 24, exp. 65, año 1699.

98 See de la Fuente, "Slaves and the Creation of Legal Rights in Cuba," on the interplay of law and customary rights.

99 The prosopography on don Miguel Núñez de Sanabria is considerable. Don Miguel was a long-serving *oidor* to the *Real Audiencia* (1686–94), whose purchase of his office "inaugurated the systematic sale of *Audiencia* positions." See Burkholder and Chandler, *Biographical Dictionary of Audiencia Ministers in the Americas*, 235. Don Miguel purchased his office in 1687 for an exorbitant price of 17,000 pesos and paid an additional fee for being a native son (*dispensa de natural*). Juan Josef's owner, don Antonio Domínguez, was listed in the folio as an *abogado* of the *Real Audiencia*.

100 See Wisnoski, "'It Is Unjust for the Law of Marriage to Be Broken by the Law of Slavery.'"

101 Bonds (*fianzas*) ranged between 200 and 800 pesos.

102 The *Curia Philipica* was a widely used treatise on criminal and civil procedure in the seventeenth century. It was published in Lima in 1615.

103 In the buyers' complaints, they routinely claimed that the slave would be worth no more than 200 pesos – generally one half to a third of what they paid: "Siendo como en su poder era y fue cimarrona y ladrona y acostumbrada a irse con los hombres ... Que padeciendo los dichos defectos cualquiera de no ser provechoso por estos en su justo valor ni a común estimación no valía ni 200 pesos" (AAL, Causas de negros, leg. 12, exp. 21, año 1656).

104 A female slave's *jornales* were approximately 3 or 4 *reales* per day (8 *reales*=1 peso).

105 "Se me han casado las negras que tengo en mi servicio, María y Ana Terranova, solo a fin de quedarse a su voluntad en esta ciudad" (AAL, Causas de negros, leg. 22, exp. 3, año 1687).

106 Pisco is a city located south of Lima on the coast of Peru.

107 AAL, Causas de negros, leg. 10, exp. 17, año 1648.

108 AAL, Causas de negros, leg. 10, exp. 24, año 1649.

109 AAL, Causas de negros, leg. 18, exp. 26, año 1676. Witnesses in jail also corroborated the owner's story.

110 AAL, Causas de negros, leg. 21, exp. 9, año 1685.

111 AAL, Cauas de nulidades, leg. 21, año 1660 (Juana Maldonado v. Ignacio de la Cruz).

112 AAL, Causas de negros, leg. 24, exp. 34, año 1695.

113 AAL, Causas de negros, leg. 15, exp. 17, año 1694.

114 According to Angulo, "Desde que compré la dicha negra han sido tantas las pesadumbres y disgustos que el dicho negro me ha dado ... no abiendo ocasión para ello porque siempre he procurado la paz y permitiéndole que cohabite con su mujer los días que están dispuestos para ellos con que esta, A Vuestra merced, pido y suplico que en atención de las causas referidas se sirva de concederme licencia para poder permitir a la dicha negra fuera de esta ciudad así para asegurar la quietud de mi casa por los peligros que resulta la cohabitación de los cónyuges esclavos."

115 AAL, Causas de negros, leg. 24, exp. 69, año 1699.

3

Dangerous Dependencies

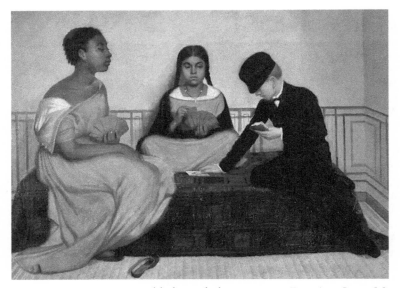

FIGURE 3.1. Las tres razas o igualdad ante la ley, ca. 1859, Francisco Laso, Museo de Arte de Lima.

Men sometimes decide upon marriage, thinking that they are marrying free women and marry slaves. Where a freeman marries a female slave not knowing that she is such, and her master brings a suit against her for her services, after her husband learns that she is of such a condition, he should not have carnal intercourse with her, even though she requests it. For if he should lie with her, even though she should be returned to slavery, he cannot separate from her.

"Concerning Men Who Marry Female Slaves Thinking
That They Are Free," Las Siete Partidas

On August 9, 1659, Juan González de Miranda sought to annul his marriage to Juana de Torres on the basis of mistaken identity. According to Juan, he married Juana de Torres thinking that she was the daughter of a noble, wealthy family from Panama City.[1] In fact, Juana de Torres was a domestic slave who had been brought to Lima from Panama City with a Spanish family possessing dubious pretensions to nobility.

Juan was not the only litigant that year seeking an annulment on the basis of mistaken identity. Out of twelve annulment suits brought to the ecclesiastical court of Lima in 1659, four litigants similarly claimed to have married enslaved women "in error." One litigant, Pascual de Dueñas, contracted marriage with María de los Angeles believing that she was a free mestiza of Andean and Spanish parentage. When Pascual tried to assert his conjugal rights, he encountered staunch opposition from María's owner.[2] Although Pascual secured ecclesiastical support favoring his conjugal rights, the property rights of María's owner encumbered his petition. Granted only the right of weekend cohabitation as opposed to the unlimited access to María that he desired, Pascual requested an annulment, resting his claim on "notorious" inequality (la notoria desigualdad) and mistaken identity (*error de persona*). Pascual, a free *mestizo*, was located higher on the socioracial scale than María, an enslaved *cuarterona de mulata*.

As discussed in the previous chapter, owners could not impede the marriages of their slaves. Drawing on Roman law precedent, mixed-status marriages among enslaved women and free men were subject to regulation – and a great deal of social disapprobation – because of the transmission of enslavement to the offspring and limits on inheritance. Yet the archival record demonstrates a high incidence of mixed-status marriages (see Table 3.1). And the *error de persona* cases show that it was possible to conceal one's enslaved status. How did Juana and María disguise their enslavement from the men they married? "Race," phenotype, clothing, physical labor, and work activities common to domestic servitude should have immediately marked them as enslaved. Moreover, these are claims arising in a marital context: we presume that free men had other means of accessing sexual favors of enslaved women that did not involve marriage.[3] How were the visible markers of enslavement manipulated or subverted to entrap naïve suitors "blinded" by love? Were these accusations of mistaken identity a convenient excuse for astute husbands who sought to annul their marriages: a difficult undertaking in an ecclesiastical court?

This chapter examines one annulment suit in detail, using it to illustrate a common set of arguments deployed by litigants in *error de persona* cases. My primary sources include the complete court record: the complaint, the rebuttal, the witness statements, the cross-complaints and the final judgment.

The *error de persona* cases that I have reviewed emerged exclusively in the context of domestic slavery.[4] I use the cases as a guide to explore the gendered paths to liberty and the dangerous calculus of dependency. Should an enslaved woman choose to stay with her owner, gambling on the chance of testamentary

TABLE 3.1. *Petitions for Marriage*, Libro de Expedientes Matrimoniales, *Arzobispado de Lima, 1650–1700*

| | | | Women | | | | | |
| | | | Enslaved | | | | | |
			Mulata	Negra-Criolla	Cuarterona	Quinterona	Zamba	Other
Men	Enslaved	Mulato	3	9	1		3	
		Negro-Criollo	1	18			5	1
		Cuarterón Quinterón	2	2				
		Zambo	1	4			1	
		Other		1				
	Free	Mulato	6	5			7	
		Negro-Criollo		10			1	
		Cuarterón Quinterón	8	14	2		2	
		Zambo	2	3			3	
		Indio	6	8			4	
		Mestizo	6	3			2	
		español	8	5	3		3	
		European		1	1			
		Other						
Total			43	83	7		31	1

manumission, or conceal her status and forge ahead with a spouse?[5] These cases do not suggest an easy or automatic quid pro quo association of affection with freedom. Rather, they point to the complex and emotionally fraught relationships people found themselves in as they negotiated status, labor, indebtedness, filial piety, surrogacy, ownership, gendered roles, and emancipation over a lifetime.

The *cartas de libertad* (letters of freedom or freedom papers) demonstrate repeatedly that prospects for testamentary manumission were inextricably bound up with household relationships established over generations between owners and their slaves. One woman protesting her wrongful enslavement in a *censura* case used evocative maternal idioms – "She raised me at her breast" ("Por haberme criado en sus pechos") – to substantiate her claim that her mother's owner had freed her at the baptismal font. The *cartas* between female owners and their domestic slaves use the language of maternal affection, not sexual intimacy. Thus, in many instances, enslaved women had to choose between marriage and an owner's maternal goodwill. These *error de persona* cases help us to understand how domestic slaves negotiated transactions in what I am calling the "economy of emotion."

As a general rule, historians of slavery do not like emotion.[6] Emotions are too similar to archival fictions and perilously close to paternalism. The equanimity of the historian's craft is inevitably ruffled when we analyze an owner's will that bequeathed an eiderdown and bedsheets to her slave. Is this bequest "evidence" of an emotional bond?[7] Historians of slavery are uneasy about sentiments like affection or intimacy, even as we problematize them or refuse to deploy them categorically. But in the following three chapters that chronicle cases of baptism, marriage, and death, I am willing to take emotion seriously, as a window to view how the gendered and racialized experience of inequality and enslavement affected men and women's intimate relationships.[8]

Unlike the marriage litigation cases I discuss in Chapter 2, *error de persona* cases must be evaluated in light of early modern Iberoamerican racial grammars. *Error de persona* was typically alleged in two situations. In the first scenario, the free partner in a mixed-status couple claimed to have erroneously married an enslaved person. In effect, the free partner accused his spouse of concealing her enslaved status prior to marriage. In the second scenario, the free spouse claimed that the other spouse's ambiguous phenotype duped him into marriage with a racially "inferior" partner. In a slaveholding society where racial stratification coexisted with a high degree of miscegenation, many *error de persona* cases alleged both racial fraud and status concealment. These cases enable us to explore the complex relationship between whiteness and freedom in a society with both significant numbers of freed people of color and those coded as *español* (given their indeterminate phenotype and uncertain parentage) but who remained enslaved.

Error de persona cases sought dissolution of sacred marital ties that could not be granted liberally if the institution of marriage were to retain its important regulatory function. The church was acutely concerned with the parity of the married couple.[9] But the church preferred to avert these "mistakes" by channeling procreative sexual relations into endogamous marriages. Even the most cursory review of parochial records (and a prolific historiography) reveals the failure of these best-laid plans.

Our inquiry into these cases of marital fraud could be informed by at least two different considerations. The first would be to query whether those seeking annulment based on marital fraud really endorsed the racial hierarchies that they subsequently proclaimed in court. But it is a daunting (if not impossible) task to deduce motivation from text, given what we know about notarial ventriloquism, "hidden transcripts," and public scripts. The cases require us to discern the sentiments of the petitioners themselves – sentiments as powerful as desire, hatred, ambition, envy, and perhaps love. Another alternative is to question whether these violations of the racial order imperiled the viability of the order itself. The interpellation of law and race is particularly salient in the ecclesiastical courts because it was the church that assumed the enumerative function of both assigning "race" at birth and adjudicating racial fraud claims in its courts.

Though partial and imperfect, the *error de persona* cases yield invaluable insights about interethnic intimacies. Together with baptismal, marriage, and divorce records, these cases show us how slaves, freed blacks, Iberians, criollos, mestizos, and *castas* fought, loved, and procreated up, down, and across the racial scale. The annulment cases provide a rich archival source for understanding the diversity within urban slave communities and highlight the tensions over race, honor, and status among plebeians. Unlike the accounts we have of the North American experience, this is not a story about the invocation of state force to police interracial relationships. This is about self-regulation of racial borders: about how individuals threatened by the effacement of those borders called on the law to reinstate racial hierarchies.

ANNULMENT AND DIVORCE IN ECCLESIASTICAL COURTS

Couples seeking to dissolve their marriages in an ecclesiastical court generally requested an annulment as the preferred option. To circumvent the likely denial of the annulment petition, the petitioner alternatively requested an ecclesiastical divorce in the initial pleading. Ecclesiastical divorce – *quoad thorum et mensam* – could be granted on the grounds of heresy, mutual decision to enter religious orders, adultery, and *sevicia* – cruel and inhuman punishment.[10] Ecclesiastical divorce simply meant that the court authorized a permanent separation of matrimonial bed and board; neither spouse was free to remarry. Conversely, annulment severed all bonds between the couple, restoring each party to the original prenuptial state. Annulment was a more difficult legal pursuit in ecclesiastical courts.

Given the Iberian ideal of marital parity, inequality between married couples was a permissible ground for annulment even before the 1776 Royal Pragmatic. Prior to this Pragmatic, racial impurity of *conversos* (or New Christians), illegitimacy, and economic disparity in family status could be proffered as evidence of marital inequality. In the case of complex marriage negotiations between socially unequal families, resistant elders could allege *error de persona* to annul a prenuptial contract or a clandestine marriage.[11]

Tomás Sánchez, an eminent seventeenth-century canonist, divided the law of error into categories of *personae* (error of person, "when one person is taken for another"), *conditionis* (error of servile condition, "when a free man marries someone he supposes is free and she really is a servant"), *fortunae* (error of fortune, "when he thinks she is rich and she is really a pauper. This can be called [error] of quality, since he was mistaken only about the quality of her wealth"), and *qualitatis* (error of quality, "when he believes he is marrying a beautiful noble virgin and she is actually misshapen, common, and corrupt").[12] Parents or guardians of the higher-status family typically raised these objections at the betrothal or prenuptial stage. But in the annulment petitions examined here, the higher-status partner raised the objections *after* the marriage had occurred. Indeed, our first petitioner, Juan Gonzáles de Miranda, sought an annulment six years after his marriage to Juana de Torres, having already fathered two children with her. The credibility of Juan's claim is not of interest here – it was unlikely that he would have been ignorant of his wife's status, especially given that, according to Juana in her rebuttal, Juan had lived at her owner's house continuously throughout their marriage.[13] What is interesting is that he and many other petitioners brought *error de persona* claims after celebrating marriages of considerable duration.[14]

IBERIAN RACIAL FORMATIONS IN THE AMERICAS

> Dios hizo el café e hizo la leche,
> pero no hizo el café con leche.
>
> Quien no tiene de Inga, tiene de Mandinga.
>
> Peruvian folk songs.

It is difficult to understand the legal rationale for *error de persona* cases without a clear idea of notions of race, blood, and *calidad* that developed in tandem with the consolidation of Iberian slavery in the Americas. Legal categories that developed in societies wherein enslavement was increasingly justified by appealing to racial attributes shaped the way that people thought about racial stratification. Ideas about race were inextricable from those that legitimated the enslavement of Africans and Moors and exempted indigenous peoples from servitude. But enslavement was not neatly coterminous with race, lineage, status, or birth condition. As Joanne Rappaport points out in her study of the *mulato* category in early modern Nueva Granada, people simultaneously connected physiognomy with genealogy, engaging in what she perceptively describes as the "performance of ethnoracial taxonomy."[15]

Confusion invariably arose with commingled populations of free, freed, runaway, *yanaconas,* indentured, *naturales*, apprenticed, servile, poor, enslaved, and noble.[16] Impoverished Spaniards (or those with negligible *hidalgo* status) married and consorted with free and enslaved black women and with indigenous noblewomen and girls.[17] Runaway slaves sought refuge in indigenous communities, founding families therein. Unsurprisingly, their offspring created more anomalies for apportioning rights, privileges, and duties on the basis of blood quantum.[18]

Many colonial scholars have focused on the eighteenth-century blood quantum charts that were developed and promulgated largely in New Spain to study the evolution of racial thinking in the Americas.[19] (See Figure 3.2). However, the *sistema de casta* charts were drawn up at least a century later than the *error de persona* cases I describe. And as Rappaport points out, the charts and paintings are essentially ones that grew out of the experience of race in New Spain. The Mexicanist lens has overdetermined how we view the *casta* charts.[20] The charts

FIGURE 3.2. Series No.18. Español. Quarterón de Chino. Unknown. Museo Nacional de Antropología, Madrid.

themselves represent only one aspect of the way early modern Iberoamericans thought about and experienced racial difference.

Presuming that there was ever a stable racial order (a questionable proposition), the solidity of the racial trinity (Andean, Spaniard, and *negro*) had already dissolved into capacious categories of mestizo and *mulato* in the previous century. By the mid-seventeenth century, these categories had fragmented into infinite equations based on quotients of hybridized blood.[21] María de los Angeles, for instance, was identified as a *cuarterona de mulata* in 1659.

None of these enumerations were "value free, objective descriptions of phenotype" or complexion.[22] (One might ask when enumerations were ever neutral, despite the claim that census data merely document and do not create race.) Clerics – charged by Tridentine decree to receive and register all Catholic souls – struggled to freeze identity at the moment of birth, devising such ambiguous categories as "suspended in the air" ("ténte al aire") or "I don't understand you" ("no te entiendo") – an obvious phenotypical anomaly. This was an attempt to forge "caste" out of phenotype, maternal identity, and whatever evidence about possible paternity was proffered by the newborn's mother and witnesses. When paternal identity was known or publicly acknowledged, clerics were able to determine the caste of an infant depending on the degree of blood admixture of both parents.

Exogamous sexual unions generally occurred outside of marriage. *Casta* was thus a racialized designation vested with the opprobrium of illegitimacy and lower social status. Granted, this reflects an elite perspective, but it undoubtedly influenced the way *castas* viewed themselves. Caste emerged as a way of thinking about "blood mixing" (vis-à-vis an ideal of blood purity) that articulated ideas of inequality and impurity commonly shared by priests, treatise writers, magistrates, prosecutors, colonial elites, and Iberian plebeians. *Casta* was not merely a designation of blood lineage – it was indicative of and encompassed one's status, descent, occupation, condition at birth, and networks of patronage. Caste categories were negotiable both in terms of the law and the broader community, but they were closely monitored and upheld by the parties themselves.

Despairing of the limited utility of the term "race" as a way of understanding the complex colonial categories of identity and frustrated by the erstwhile pigmentocratic approaches to caste, some scholars rely more heavily on the term "calidad" to "capture the multiple factors beyond phenotype (for example occupation, reputation, language abilities, dress) that qualified a straightforward racial classification."[23] I likewise use the word "calidad" as a barometer to measure social location that was not exclusively conditioned by elite notions of identity. *Calidad* referred to a person's general worth: his or her prestige, family connections, reputation, blood lineage, and honor. Caste was a factor of one's *calidad*, but *calidad* in turn was contingent on the concatenation of upbringing, appearance, virtue, modest seclusion, and religious devotion. *Calidad* was highly susceptible to social perception and could change over time as people amassed greater prestige and improved their economic position or as they fell on hard times.

Reputation, status, and honor were of course important among plebeians.[24] Plebeians, enslaved, and *casta* men and women also used *calidad* to dissolve their marital bonds.[25] In 1670, Inés de Escobar, a *mulata* slave, sought an annulment of her marriage on the grounds of "notorious inequality." Inés alleged in her pleadings that "I understood that my husband Antonio was *mulato*, but it turns out he is *morisco* of Berber parents, and a slave, and for this reason, he is so depraved and of poor habits and condition." Inés, a *mulata* slave, differentiated herself from her "depraved" Moorish husband by claiming a preferential place on the racialized religious scale differentiating Catholics and infidels.

Pascual de Dueñas invoked similar racialized hierarchies to establish inequality between him and his wife, María de los Angeles.[26] According to the endogamous scheme that Pascual outlined in his statement, he should have married a mestiza. He believed that María de los Angeles was a mestiza and filed for an annulment upon finding that she was an enslaved *cuarterona*. The court immediately dismissed Pascual's claim. No matter how indeterminate her appearance, María's surname identified her as someone of African-criollo heritage.[27] Pascual's identity as a mestizo was too capacious to claim racial hierarchy, as the mestizo of the mid-seventeenth century was born of parents of uncertain heritage. As David Cahill points out, the mestizo category in administrative use could have included *quinterones, tercerones* or even urbanized Andeans. However, as evidenced by these proceedings, "notorious inequality" became inflected with different socioracial meanings when plebeian couples sought court intervention to dissolve their marriages.

The crown explicitly prohibited marriages between certain groups, particularly between African-descent peoples and Andeans. Colonial authorities were deeply concerned about relations between African slaves and indigenous populations (perhaps even more so than they were about relationships between Africans and Spaniards), and they took pains to prohibit sexual relationships between enslaved men and indigenous women.[28] Indeed, the crown condemned mixed-status unions as "unsightly" and doubted whether they could be endowed with the legal status of holy matrimony.[29] But extensive miscegenation (largely through concubinary unions) urged the incorporation of hybrid mestizo categories into taxonomies of caste that retained core features of Iberian blood purity while accommodating mixed offspring. Without belaboring the point, miscegenation contravened the Iberian system of blood purity by which status and privilege were apportioned on the peninsula.[30] Legislators responded to this breach by relegating "mixed-race" offspring to the lower castes.[31] Consequently, viceregal and ecclesiastical authorities admitted the existence of mixed-race offspring but circumscribed their opportunities for upward mobility.

Mixed-status and interracial unions unfolded in an urban multiethnic milieu where whitening (*blanqueamiento*) had become increasingly critical to social ascendancy and where ethnic categories were in constant flux. As Karen Graubart points out, many people whose identities traversed the ethnoracial scale spent their lives in the "interstices of ethnicity provided by colonial hybridity."[32] However maligned interethnic unions were by lawmakers and the clergy, blood purity was an impractical means of allocating privilege in the Americas. Those who were nearly white – and thus closest to white privilege – were precisely those who were the most compromised in terms of blood purity.[33] There is no neat correlation between peninsular concepts of racial purity and colonial realities of social ascendancy through whitening. Nevertheless, we see numerous decrees inveighing against interethnic unions juxtaposed with the administrative recognition of increasingly complex fractions of caste.

It was precisely the marriages of those women and men who were nearly white in terms of phenotype and associated behavioral codes of *calidad* that were most heavily surveiled. These women were frequently identified as *quinterona de mestiza* or *cuarterona de mulata*, but this bureaucratic designation was at odds with their unstable public perception. Marriage to an *español* was the penultimate barrier to completing their whiteness and to securing their *calidad* and that of their children. That crossing virtually guaranteed their access to the most privileged social status in Iberoamerica, one that was vigilantly guarded by criollos of modest means, who understood and maybe even shared the pathological fear of contaminated blood with elite *peninsulares*. Emergent criollo elites and arriviste Iberians were often threatened by these marriages because they exposed the creaky edifice of their own claims to white privilege. Ecclesiastical law dealt harshly with those who tried to destabilize the boundaries that demarcated status and privilege, even if it meant contravening a deeply held principle regarding the sanctity of marriage. This severity conveniently suited the party seeking to escape his or her marital obligations.

Until the promulgation of the *Real Pragmática* in 1776–78, mixed-status marriage in the Americas was never illegal, though it was socially disreputable and imprudent for the upwardly mobile or ascendant classes.[34] But surprisingly (given our received wisdom on the subject of free men marrying enslaved women), the marriage records analyzed herein reveal a high percentage of mixed-status marriages between enslaved women and free men. Marriage records for Lima's el Sagrario parish during the period examined here (1650–1700) show 68 percent of enslaved women married free men, whereas only 32 percent of free women married enslaved men. In the seventeenth-century marriage petitions (*pliegos matrimoniales*), I identified 144 unions in which one partner was enslaved out of a total of 604 interethnic unions. (See table 3.1) Although the *error de persona* cases highlight the dangers of relying on this kind of data (and I reiterate that we should regard any enumerative statistic with great caution), these statistics suggest that 23 percent of interethnic marriages were mixed-status marriages.[35] The apparent lack of significance attributed to women's enslaved status by their free husbands prompts us to consider the possibility that marriage was a gendered path to freedom, along with concubinage.[36]

Legally, marriage to an enslaved woman bore consequences for the offspring of the couple. As the *error de persona* cases make clear, full disclosure of one's enslaved status was required or the marriage could be annulled under ecclesiastical law. In addition, the male suitor was required to exercise due diligence in ascertaining the condition of his bride. As the canonists held,

> Error about the condition, the family, or the fortune of the individual, though produced by disingenuous representations, does not at all affect the validity of marriage. A man, who means to act upon such representations, should verify them by his own inquiries. The law presumes that he uses due caution in a matter in which the happiness of life is so materially involved; and it makes no provision for blind credulity, however it may have been produced.[37]

Peninsular legal rules were drafted with an administrative goal of endogamous reproduction and hermetic coexistence in separate republics, but these rules were applied within divergent social realities and cultural milieus.[38] The *Partidas* provided an exit strategy for those who claimed to have married a slave *in error* but not in blind credulity.[39] Indeed, a spouse's claim that he or she was ignorant of his or her partner's enslavement was subject to strenuous proof. Arguably, within the social circuits of the Limeño aristocracy, marriage to a slave in error was infrequent. However, in the protean social strata where enslaved, freed, and free lived and worked together and where extensive intermixing yielded phenotypically ambiguous offspring, such "mistakes" were more common. Let us now turn to a detailed examination of these mistakes in the annulment petition of Pedro Ramírez and María Josefa Martínez.

THE ANNULMENT PETITION OF PEDRO RAMÍREZ AND MARÍA JOSEFA MARTÍNEZ

Oh what a tangled web we weave
When first we practice to deceive!

On May 12, 1682, Pedro Ramírez asked Provisor don Pedro de Villagómez to annul his marriage to María Josefa Martínez de Soto.[40] Pedro discovered María Josefa's true identity as a slave when he attempted to establish an independent household seven months after the couple married. Throughout the preceding seven months, the couple had lived with doña Beatriz de Tovar, María Josefa's owner. Doña Beatriz resolutely opposed Pedro's domestic plans and refused to let María Josefa go. As doña Beatriz maintained, she was not legally required to grant Pedro and María anything beyond weekend conjugal visits. After a brief exchange of petitions demanding and rebutting the legal basis for María Josefa's release, Pedro abruptly dropped his claim. One month later, Pedro sought an annulment of the marriage altogether. According to Pedro, it was inconceivable that a Spaniard of "good" parentage would willingly enter into marriage with a slave and contaminate his lineage.[41]

The legal determination of Pedro's case revolved around the credibility of Pedro's claim to marital fraud and *error de persona*. The curious point in this case was that everyone knew of María Josefa's enslavement except her suitor.[42] The courtship and marriage took place in the multiethnic parish of Santa Ana. We presume that criollos themselves (anxious about the slipperiness of their own claims to respectability) carefully erected barriers to prevent these kinds of "racial mistakes." During their courtship and marriage, it seems reasonable to assume that Pedro would have guessed or would have been told that María Josefa was in domestic servitude with doña Beatriz – particularly since everyone else in their very closely knit neighborhood knew that she was doña Beatriz's slave.

The subterfuge that Pedro decried indicates the porosity of racial boundaries and the residents' broader ambivalence about the boundaries themselves. Their silence may also suggest that the residents were more invested in their relationship with María Josefa than with Pedro at the outset of the marriage. In other words, the residents may have been prepared to accept the relationship and María Josefa's crossover into whiteness if Pedro or doña Beatriz had accepted it. But given the foundational assumptions of the racial order, it seems reasonable to presume that the residents would have alerted Pedro to the stain (*mancha*) in María Josefa's blood or her enslaved status before he entered into the marriage.[43]

In her rebuttal, María Josefa asked the court to find her marriage to Pedro true and valid and to deny the annulment petition. María Josefa (somewhat) coyly got around the fact that she never verbally disclosed her enslaved status by saying that Pedro simply never asked. María Josefa further contended that it was Pedro's responsibility to inquire into the status of the person with whom he sought to contract marriage, particularly at the time of petitioning the marriage license. Moreover, she maintained that Pedro could not have failed to notice that she was encumbered to doña Beatriz, given that the couple lived in the house of her owner. María finally argued that the condition of slavery was not itself an obstacle to marriage.

After María Josefa's tour de force, Pedro asked the provisor to summon María Josefa's friends and relatives to testify about their efforts to ensure that he remained ignorant of María Josefa's status. Pedro's legal strategy was twofold: to prove a deliberate cover-up by María Josefa's family to trick him into marriage and to establish the impossibility of discovering María Josefa's enslaved status given her Spanish phenotype and her virtuous and noble comportment. His first witness was Juana de Tovar, María Josefa's mother. Juana de Tovar's statement was not entirely persuasive to Provisor Villagómez. First, Juana clearly acted in her capacity as María Josefa's mother in the marriage negotiations with Pedro. Juana was identified consistently throughout the proceedings as either *mulata libre* or *parda libre*. It was thus impossible that Pedro could claim that his sole intention was to marry a woman whose parents were Spaniards, although his interrogatories asked witnesses to corroborate that point.[44]

Knowing that María Josefa was still enslaved, Juana tried to convince Pedro to marry one of her younger daughters, Ynéz. Ynéz was born after Juana had been manumitted by doña Beatriz's family and was therefore free. Pedro refused her offer of Ynéz, insisting that he wanted to marry only María Josefa. Juana admitted that on seeing Pedro's determination to marry María Josefa – presumably based on affection or infatuation – she deliberately withheld information about her daughter's enslaved status. Under oath, she confessed that even if Pedro had asked, she would have denied that María Josefa was a slave, fearing that this would have discouraged Pedro and ruined her daughter's chance of freedom: "hubiese perdido su remedio." Instead of telling Pedro the truth, she gambled on doña Beatriz's willingness to liberate María Josefa. In Juana's mind, if María Josefa were manumitted before the wedding, that would be tantamount to giving Pedro a free bride. Legally, if María Josefa were freed before the marriage occurred, her children would not be compromised by her former enslaved status.

Juana went straight away to doña Beatriz, putting Pedro's marriage proposal before her. The fact that a Spaniard of a "good family" wanted to marry María

Josefa could not have been lost on doña Beatriz. But doña Beatriz refused to grant María Josefa her *carta de libertad*. Juana begged doña Beatriz as a god-fearing and benevolent Catholic to liberate María Josefa, but doña Beatriz told her that it was not yet time. Given doña Beatriz's refusal, Juana seemingly had two alternatives: tell Pedro the truth or hope that doña Beatriz would release María Josefa from servitude when presented with the marriage as a fait accompli. Pedro's advocate crafted the interrogatories to elicit yes or no answers, which left Juana no room to rationalize her decision. Juana's sworn testimony that she willfully failed to disclose María Josefa's status because she privileged her daughter's freedom thus corroborated Pedro's insistence that he had been deceived into marriage by a conniving, ambitious mother.

Pedro's procurator drafted five questions that were posed to the witnesses in an interrogatory. Although the interrogatories are loaded with information intended to elicit the answers most favorable to the party posing them, they are often more interesting for what they assert than the answers themselves. For example, Pedro's second question asked the witness to confirm whether it was true that since birth, both Juana de Tovar and doña Beatriz had contrived to cover up María Josefa's enslaved status by dressing her like a *doncella* (chaste maiden of virtuous upbringing) and whether it was true that since María Josefa was so fair skinned that it was impossible for anyone to discern her true *calidad*.

Witnesses could embellish their statements in greater detail, but they tended to provide these more fulsome statements at the beginning when they were asked to state their general knowledge of the complaint. Procurators were entitled to draft their interrogatories. Witnesses would respond to these interrogatories by recording their testimonies with the notary handling the case. Both parties could publicly summon their own witnesses, but in this case, María Josefa did not produce any questions. Neither did she engage a procurator; all proceedings were recorded by the ecclesiastical notary. María Josefa merely responded to Pedro's legal actions – often in a dilatory fashion. Thus, we have a very limited rendition of María Josefa's side of the story, which is somewhat atypical in these records that have lengthy rebuttals and counterclaims.

Notwithstanding Juana's testimony, the provisor found merit in María Josefa's claim that it was Pedro's responsibility to determine the character and lineage (*calidad*) of the woman he sought to marry. One week after reading María Josefa's testimony, Provisor Villagómez recommended that the court deny Pedro's petition. Provisor Villagómez's response granted María Josefa the full benefit of the law, in his formidable defense of the holy institution of marriage:[45]

As María Josefa contends in her written brief, the said Pedro Ramírez solicited her hand in marriage, and according to reason and the law of the marriage contract, the contracting party bears the responsibility of examining and investigating the quality, lineage, and character of the woman he wishes to marry. We presume he followed the law, and knew the nature of the person he married, as is brought to our attention by the defendant. For these reasons, and in the defense of the matrimonial cause, we ask your Grace to deny the annulment petition and compel the said Pedro Ramírez to resume married life with María Josefa under pain of excommunion.[46]

Villagómez based his decision primarily on the law of marital contracts but also on the strength of María Josefa's plea, which urged the court to find the marriage valid. The fact that two months earlier Pedro had asked the court to issue an injunction ordering doña Beatriz to respect his conjugal rights undoubtedly colored Villagómez's view of the merits of Pedro's claim. Not coincidentally – given his role as Provisor of the Archbishopric court – Villagómez was the official who signed the order to doña Beatriz.[47] Thus, Villagómez made short shrift of Pedro's claim weeks later, concluding with a stern reprimand for Pedro to resume married life with María Josefa.

Seemingly undaunted by this development, Pedro appealed Provisor Villagómez's ruling. Pedro's response focused principally on Villagómez's point that it had been incumbent on him to investigate María Josefa's background and status. He offered extensive evidence of María Josefa's dress, circumspect behavior, mien, and public image – all of which befitted an elite *doncella* of seventeenth-century Limeño society. Ten witnesses confirmed his impressions of María Josefa's exquisite physical appearance and virtuous public persona and testified to her virtue and modest seclusion (*virtud y recogimiento*). By all accounts, doña Beatriz treated María Josefa as her own daughter: she outfitted María Josefa with the accoutrements, jewelry, and gold-embroidered shawls and veils worn exclusively by elite women. According to neighbors, María Josefa accompanied doña Beatriz to mass and all public events in her carriage and was always impeccably dressed.[48] As Pedro reasoned, he did investigate María Josefa's *calidad* with all the tools he had at his disposal. What he saw, heard, and inferred established her identity in his mind as a Spaniard and her eligibility for marriage.

Indeed, it bears noting that both Beatriz and María Josefa violated the sumptuary laws of the period that were promulgated precisely to avoid racial indeterminacy and to clearly demarcate social status. For example, a royal decree issued in 1612 proclaimed thus: "No *mulata* nor black woman, whether free or enslaved, can be bedecked or adorned in jewels, or gold or silver, nor can she wear pearls or silk dresses from Castile, nor silk gloves, nor can she be seen in accessories with gold or silver laced edges, under threat of one hundred lashes and confiscation of the prohibited items of clothing."[49] These laws attempted to limit the dress and jewelry choices of *casta* women, especially when they were attending mass.[50]

In his much cited *Diario de Lima*, Juan Antonio Suardo notes that the viceroy Conde de Chinchón was particularly disturbed by the ostentatious dress of elite Limeñas and *mulatas*. Very soon after the viceroy's arrival in Lima in 1629, he singled out two *mulata* women for public reprimand. The women were apprehended after they were encountered dressed in blue silk shawls and gold-tipped gloves. The viceroy had their clothing confiscated and imprisoned them while fining them 50 pesos each.[51]

Not everyone was as disapproving of the city's sartorial opulence.[52] As Father Bernabé Cobo writes with his characteristic enthusiasm for all things Limeño, "The elegance of the residents of this city in their dress and accessories is such that in general, one cannot distinguish between nobles and those who are not of that class, because they all dress with such luxuriance, since the pragmatics issued in Spain regulating dress codes are not proclaimed in Lima."[53] Cobo's observations lead us to conclude that the sumptuary laws, like so many other legislative acts, were neither proclaimed nor enforced in Peru.

Pedro echoes Father Cobo's observation in his rendition of María Josefa's appearance. According to Pedro:

I never knew that she was a slave, because her clothes, her accoutrements, her bearing, and the entire manner in which the said doña Beatriz treated the said María Josefa was that of a Spaniard, and I could never have been expected to understand that she was a slave, especially as she was held up in public for all to see as a Spaniard. Everyone saw her as I did, with the ornate shawls and fine accessories of a *doncella* when she attended mass or public festivities in the company of doña Beatriz. She appeared to be a Spaniard of noble *calidad*.[54]

Pedro also summoned María Josefa's younger half sisters, Ynéz and Augustina, who both corroborated Pedro's account of racial fraud and subterfuge. As they said, María Josefa's whiteness (*blancura*, sometimes referred to as "lúcidez"), her smooth straight hair, and her elaborate clothing enabled her to dissimulate *doncella* status.[55] From her appearance, those who did not know her could never guess her true status and *calidad*. In addition, María Josefa's racial performance was enhanced by doña Beatriz – whose status was not in doubt. Presumably, although the sisters looked very similar in terms of phenotype, María Josefa's whiteness was complemented by Beatriz's pedigree and her preferential treatment of María Josefa. Pedro disputed Villagómez's claim that he should have been able to discover the master-slave relationship that bound the two women. According to Pedro, doña Beatriz never indicated any opposition to their courtship, and María Josefa was free to come and go as she pleased. It was only when Pedro tried to whisk María Josefa away from doña Beatriz that he encountered resistance.[56] In light of this evidence, Pedro asked, how could he be faulted for failing to discern María Josefa's true status as a slave? Drawing on a gendered and racialized script of female sin and connivance (that had unequivocal purchase in an ecclesiastical court), Pedro portrayed himself as a powerless victim of marital fraud.

Pedro amassed a large number of witnesses to corroborate his version of the courtship: four *doncellas*, an Iberian petty merchant (*tratante de mercaderes*), two *cuarteronas de parda*, and one *cuarterona de mestiza*. The two remaining witnesses were Juana de Tovar and the indomitable doña Beatriz herself.

All ten witnesses lived in the Santa Ana parish in close proximity to doña Beatriz's house. Six of the nine female witnesses were part of María Josefa's age cohort or younger, ranging from fourteen to twenty years of age. All of the witnesses made reference to the *carta de libertad* that granted Juana de Tovar her freedom. We presume that with their assistance or collusion, Pedro was able to procure the *carta de libertad*. On June 15, Pedro introduced the *carta de libertad* manumitting Juana de Tovar as evidence of María Josefa's enslaved status. Juana had been manumitted twenty years previously, and María Josefa was born four years prior to Juana's freedom. By law, she retained the status of her mother at birth.

The credibility of Pedro's *error de persona* claim ultimately rested on María Josefa's convincing performance as a free *doncella*. Common to these *error de persona* cases, magistrates evaluated how the women were perceived in the community by eliciting numerous witness testimonies, given their ambiguous appearance and parentage.[57]

It is interesting to note that despite Pedro's capacity to summon witnesses, he did not call on anyone who knew *him* personally prior to the marriage. From the record, Pedro strikes the reader as virtually anonymous. In other words, Pedro was never asked to corroborate or verify his own honor or *calidad*. He claimed legitimate birth, Spanish parentage, and residency in the Santa Ana parish, but those claims were never supported by the testimony of his parents, family members, priests, or business associates. We never learn what he did for a living, if anything. He willingly entered into marriage negotiations with a *mulata* mother with no promise of a dowry (*dote*). He did not have sufficient financial resources to establish an independent household upon marriage and had to rely on María Josefa's owner for a place to live, even though he was in a city wherein he claimed status as a *vecino*.[58] Given that all his witnesses were people who knew María Josefa, his claim that he was a resident of the Santa Ana parish was apocryphal to say the least. Nonetheless, his dubious residency status did not imperil or even compromise his honor or *calidad*. From the way his interrogatories were worded, everyone concurred that Pedro, as a member of a "good family" ("un hombre de bien"), would not have compromised his lineage through marriage to a slave.

Once again, the neighbors' silence is telling, given their volubility after Pedro summoned them to testify. Their responses suggest that they endorsed the racial hierarchy on which Pedro rested his claim. But if they were that invested in the racial hierarchy they subsequently espoused, an interethnic marriage of a Spaniard "de bien" with a slave would precariously tip the racial scale so that nonelite Spaniards would seek to recalibrate it by exposing María Josefa's status. It bears repeating that the successful outcome of Pedro's claim rested on his ability to prove conspiracy among all involved to cover up María Josefa's status.

As Pedro built his case with increasingly strong evidence, Provisor Villagómez also proceeded with his investigation and reviewed the earlier conjugal rights

proceeding filed in April 1682. Apparently Provisor Villagómez was not convinced that Pedro could have been deceived for so long and agreed with María
Josefa that Pedro should have suspected that she belonged to doña Beatriz
prior to contracting the marriage or soon thereafter. Villagómez suspended
proceedings at the end of August, ordering doña Beatriz to testify whether she
had consented to the marriage between Pedro and María Josefa. Doña Beatriz
had never been asked directly whether she consented to the marriage before
it was contracted, which was precisely what Villagómez needed to know to
rule on the validity of Pedro's fraud claim. Doña Beatriz's refusal to liberate
María Josefa was, as we have seen, cryptically recorded in Juana's testimony.
But doña Beatriz's responses in the interrogatories were equivocal on the issue
of her consent.

In her statement, doña Beatriz claimed that upon learning of the impending
marriage plans she consulted her confessor to see whether she could impede
the marriage by placing María Josefa in a convent. Her confessor said no,
pointing out that entry into a religious order itself demanded a divine oath.
The same rules of marital consent applied to religious service: guardians,
parents, or owners could not morally or legally avoid an undesired marriage
by forcibly placing their charges in holy confinement. Furthermore, her confessor noted, religious confinement would effectively remove María Josefa
from her household. Doña Beatriz thus had no option but to accommodate
Pedro in her home if she wanted to keep María Josefa by her side and in her
service. As a devout Catholic, doña Beatriz decided that the lesser of both
evils would be to provide the couple with a place to live to eliminate any
threat of immoral cohabitation. From reviewing doña Beatriz's statement,
Villagómez could have reasonably inferred that she accepted the marriage
by allowing the couple into her home. Further, in his view, Pedro could not
credibly maintain his claim of *error de persona* given that he lived in a home
where his wife was in domestic servitude.

Doña Beatriz presumably had no great love for Villagómez, who had issued
a declaratory judgment favoring Pedro's conjugal rights petition back in April.
But until her summons, doña Beatriz had been surprisingly quiet. She testified
once on July 3, responding to Pedro's summons. But in that statement, doña
Beatriz merely recounted her conversation with Juana de Tovar during which
she discouraged Juana from pursuing marriage negotiations with Pedro.

Juana de Tovar and doña Beatriz clearly had a long-standing relationship.
They were both forty years old and had grown up together in the same household. From the terms of the *carta de libertad,* it appears that Juana had been
doña Beatriz's childhood companion as well as her personal slave. Juana was
very young when she gave birth to María Josefa – at most thirteen or fourteen
years old.[59] María Josefa did list a father who bore her last name in her marriage petition, but for all we know, he could have been a male within the Tovar
household where Juana served. By all accounts, doña Beatriz loved María
Josefa and treated her like her own child. At times, Beatriz referred to herself

as María Josefa's spiritual parent. A childless and unmarried *doncella*, Beatriz raised María Josefa in a manner befitting genteel Limeños, educating her and giving her accoutrements that Juana could not have given her. Although Juana was free, two of her daughters remained in Beatriz's service, limiting Juana's maternal role and influence. If they were both thinking as conscientious mothers, a "good marriage" should have been as pleasing to doña Beatriz as it was to Juana. So, why then would she refuse to let María Josefa go?

Doña Beatriz vigorously maintained that she opposed the marriage, both before it took place and after, but the situation did not escalate into a full-blown lawsuit until Pedro tried to remove María Josefa from her home and service in April. Doña Beatriz affirmed that she raised María Josefa from birth to serve her as a dutiful daughter.[60] Even in this statement alternating between authorial and reported speech, the notary recorded the blurry distinction between filial piety and diligent servitude.[61] And María Josefa had been an exemplary charge until she married Pedro. Rebutting the presumption that beatific owners ought to manumit their slaves, Beatriz averred that manumission was possible only for wealthy, powerful women with many slaves at their disposal. In short, Beatriz was at pains to prove both her Christian piety (which should have swayed her to manumit María Josefa) and to refute any hint of egoism or selfishness in claiming her property rights in María Josefa. Hence, she referred to herself as a *pobre doncella* who could not afford the luxury of parting with her slave who she had brought up like a daughter to take care of her in her old age.

As soon as Villagómez suspended the proceedings, Pedro urged the court to rule in his favor by claiming it was immaterial whether doña Beatriz had in fact consented to the marriage. As it turns out, the marriage was a clandestine one, presented to doña Beatriz as a fait accompli. But the problem for Pedro was that since he was party to the deception, it was becoming increasingly hard for him to claim that he had been ignorant of María Josefa's status. According to doña Beatriz, both Juana and María Josefa requested permission for María Josefa to go to the Cathedral for confession. In truth, María Josefa was going to give her statement of consent, accompanied by her mother. That María Josefa claimed to be going to the Cathedral to confess, rather than to the church in Santa Ana, may have raised Beatriz's suspicions, as it seems that was the time she sought the advice of her own confessor. That week, Pedro and María Josefa married in secret in Santa Ana. The priest and ecclesiastical notary who issued the license clearly violated the Tridentine rules requiring the posting of banns. Villagómez suspected that something had gone amiss for such a violation to have occurred. To complicate matters further, it was Villagómez's uncle (the Archbishop of Lima) who signed the *Auto* authorizing the couple to marry upon confirmation from the ecclesiastical notary.

On October 12, Villagómez asked for the *pliego matrimonial* to be introduced into the proceedings. All couples had to establish the exchange of consent and their ability to contract their intended marriage free from the impediments of preexisting matrimonial promises, surviving spouses, devotional oaths, and consanguinity. After the exchange of consent, banns had to be posted in each parish where the petitioners had resided for at least six months for three consecutive Sundays. Among elite families, betrothals (*esponsales*) involved complex negotiations, but for couples where there was no dowry, they were more straightforward affairs. In the *pliego matrimonial*, dated September 27 1681, Pedro solemnly attested to his intention to marry María Josefa in compliance with the will of God and the holy church:

Pedro Ramírez, resident of this city and legitimate son of Pedro Ramírez and doña Paula de Ocampo, declare that in order to serve the Lord, our heavenly Father, I intend to enter into marriage according to the law of our holy Church with María Josefa Martínez de Soto, *cuarterona*, resident of this city, and illegitimate daughter of Cristóbal Martínez de Soto and Juana de Tovar. Before Your Grace, I ask that you send for the said María Josefa to receive her consent and that you gather information from us both, confirming that we are both single and without impediment to marriage in order to issue the marriage license. I ask that you exempt us from the three banns required by the Holy Council of Trent so that any of the priests of our holy parish Santa Ana can perform our marriage.[62]

Pedro's statement was typical of the declarations of intent to marry of the time, but two points stand out immediately. First, he informed the notary of María Josefa's status as a *cuarterona* and also as the illegitimate daughter of Juana de Tovar and Cristóbal Martínez de Soto. Second, Pedro requested an exemption from the Tridentine rules so that the priests of Santa Ana could perform the marriage without posting banns. The notary, who also verified María Josefa's consent and eligibility to contract marriage, duly recorded Pedro's marriage petition. That same day, the notary recorded three witness statements testifying to the couple's eligibility to marry and alleging their illicit cohabitation.[63] The couple's prenuptial proceedings went smoothly, and one day later, Archbishop Villagómez declared them free to marry. Moreover, the Archbishop granted Pedro the exemption, authorizing them to marry without requiring that the couple post their banns in the parish on three consecutive Sundays. The couple's marriage was recorded in Santa Ana on September 30, 1681.[64]

Though it is unstated in the *pliego matrimonial*, we reasonably assume that the Archbishopric's notary expedited the marriage to ameliorate the harm of the couple's alleged carnal sins. The priority of the church was for the fornicating couple to legalize and sanctify their union.[65] Archbishop Villagómez tended to authorize a marriage petition if his notaries were persuaded that there was no striking disparity in social status and if other conditions of consent and consanguinity were fulfilled. Court personnel were encouraged during this period to exercise particular caution in approving marriage petitions, precisely because the population was so mobile.[66] But the Archbishopric's notaries expedited the proceedings if there was the allusion of illicit cohabitation or in dire circumstances like the impending death or relocation of one of the parties. Moreover, it was only within the Archbishopric's offices (located in the Cathedral) that such an exemption was granted.[67]

It is important to note Pedro's legal savvy. He knew the potential benefits of disclosing immoral cohabitation, and he went directly to the Archbishopric's office in the Cathedral to request the exemption. Certainly, banns should have been posted in Santa Ana, where of course doña Beatriz would have seen them. Couples who did not want the banns posted proffered evidence of their cohabitation to get around the rules.[68] In fact, many plebeian couples merged confession with their statements of consent, attesting to their sinful cohabitation as the reason they sought to enter into holy matrimony.

Villagómez summoned Pedro de Carvajal, a notary of the Archbishopric, who had been in charge of the couple's *pliego matrimonial*. Carvajal testified that he had indeed recommended the license and approved the dispensation because of the "mal estado" of the petitioners. Carvajal also confirmed that he received María Josefa's statement of consent in the Patio de los Naranjos – the part of the Cathedral abutting the Archbishopric's administrative offices – on that day.

As far as Carvajal was concerned, there was no problem with the proceedings at the time. Pedro declared his intent, and María Josefa gave her consent in the presence of her mother. Three witnesses swore to the couple's eligibility to contract the marriage. Moreover, there was verbal testimony regarding illicit cohabitation. But for the subsequent annulment petition, no one in the Archbishopric would have given second thoughts to the couple's prenuptial proceedings. The vast disparity in status that Pedro subsequently alleged was not apparent to Carvajal at the prenuptial proceedings. Thus, we can only surmise that when it was brought to the court's attention, neither Villagómez nor his staff believed Pedro's allegation of prenuptial fraud. Although the church was willing to mitigate the sin of illicit cohabitation, its court was predisposed to deny any petition that dismantled the sacred conjugal union. Thus, Villagómez presciently called for the marriage petition to build his case against Pedro's claim to annulment.

Upon review of the petition, he emphasized the witnesses' unanimous statements about the illicit cohabitation between Pedro and María, marking "Look!" ("OJO!") in the margins of the three statements that Carvajal had recorded. Two days later, on October 14, Villagómez urged the Archbishop to deny Pedro's annulment claim. He wrote:

There can be no basis for the said annulment given the information received upon issuing the marriage petition. We find that the couple indulged in illicit cohabitation, according to three witnesses. It is not possible that in this state, the said petitioner Pedro Ramírez could ignore the *calidad* and condition of the said María Josefa, with whom he intended to contract marriage. Neither can it be presumed that when both parties attempted to contract marriage in secret, coming to the Patio de los Naranjos so as not to attract the attention of doña Beatriz, that both parties were not acting in concert. By these terms and having expressed the presumption in favor of marriage, we ask your Grace to deny this petition for annulment of the holy matrimonial state.[69]

Pedro's reaction to Villagómez was swift and indignant. Throughout the preceding five months, Pedro had steadily built up his case of fraud. He had overcome the hurdles raised by María Josefa, but unfortunately, Pedro fell into a trap of his own making.

At this point, the problem became one of complicity in prenuptial fornication with three divergent views on the matter. Villagómez was clearly convinced that prenuptial fornication had preceded the marriage and thus justified the union. Somewhat predictably, Pedro denied the prenuptial fornication and claimed he had no knowledge that the witnesses had made allegations of that nature in their statements. This denial is implausible, since the three witnesses testified on the same day that Pedro declared his intention to marry María Josefa. But in denying the fornication he was then guilty of a premeditated attempt to conceal the marriage from doña Beatriz. Presumably, he would not have gone to such lengths to conceal the marriage or deliberately lie about his carnal sins if he were in fact unaware of María Josefa's relationship to doña Beatriz. Neither would he have requested the exemption from posting banns if he did not want to conceal the marriage from doña Beatriz or from someone else. Besides, Pedro's racial fraud claim was clearly deficient – Pedro listed María Josefa as a *cuarterona de parda* on the petition. In his response, Pedro conceded that he knew María Josefa was a *cuarterona*, but insisted that while he was willing to descend a notch down the racial scale, he would never have contracted marriage with a slave.

Once apprised of Villagómez's judgment, Beatriz was outraged at the effrontery of those who suggested that carnal sin had occurred under her roof. She was equally disturbed by those who besmirched María Josefa's virtuous reputation, given that it reflected poorly on the rectitude of her own tutelage. Doña Beatriz's bristling indignation resonated throughout her statement:

I must formally assure the court that in the custody and care in which I have raised my said slave she has been a chaste and modest virgin of honorable upbringing. Moreover, she has always been extremely virtuous, such that after I die, she will continue to uphold the customs and behavior in which she has been raised. Moreover, in my household, and in my care, nothing so remotely sinful would have been permitted, let alone imagined.[70]

Doña Beatriz was so incensed that the marriage would have been expedited because of the suggestion of licentious behavior that she, like Villagómez, demanded to see the marriage petition. She immediately disputed its legal validity. Apparently, two of the three witnesses (identified as *españoles*) who attested to the couple's state of carnal sin (*mal amistados*) were María Josefa's brothers. The third witness, also an *español,* was María Josefa's close cousin. Despite having been asked in the *generales* if they had any relation to the parties, the three men deliberately concealed their fraternal relationship to María Josefa. As a consequence, their perjury invalidated their subsequent statement of the couple's marital eligibility and illicit concubinage. The fact that her brothers and cousin urged the court to legalize their sister's profligacy is not surprising – indeed, as guardians of her honor, they could not be expected to do otherwise. The problem was that they concealed their relationship to María Josefa, which then compromised the veracity of their testimony.

Pedro was jubilant upon hearing Beatriz's revelation. Again, Pedro claimed ignorance that the three witnesses were close family members. In his rejoinder to Provisor Villagómez, he pointed out sanctimoniously (and somewhat redundantly) that the solemnity of the marital contract demanded the utmost respect and honesty on the part of all involved. He then reiterated his earlier denial regarding the illicit fornication, now fortified by doña Beatriz's assertions of the moral rectitude of her charge. Indeed, he claimed that he could not even speak with María Josefa alone, given Beatriz's vigilant watch.

Pedro's earlier statements in which he attempted to justify his failure to notice that María Josefa was in Beatriz's thrall did not suggest that there were such restrictions when they were courting. As he claimed then, María Josefa was able to come and go as she wished during their courtship with absolutely no objection from Beatriz.[71] Notwithstanding these disclosures, Pedro remained silent about why he why he requested the exemption to expedite the marriage and why he named these three men as witnesses in the first place. In general, only close friends who could attest to the eligibility of the couple to contract marriage were called on to testify – it was an honor and a demonstration of friendship to serve as one's witness.[72] We can only conclude that Pedro had no reputable witnesses or long-standing friends of his own to testify on his behalf.

And what of María Josefa's role in the subterfuge? Clearly, she was not ignorant of her brothers' perjury and may have played an active role along with her mother in crafting their testimony. María Josefa's motivations are probably the hardest to decipher in this murky case of marital fraud.[73] Very early on in the proceedings, although she insisted on the validity of their marriage, she expressed regret over the ruptured relationship with doña Beatriz. In the April proceedings wherein Pedro sought to assert his conjugal rights, María Josefa alluded to her fine clothing as items that doña Beatriz withheld and chided Pedro for his complaint. She noted that she probably would have gained her freedom from doña Beatriz but for her marriage to Pedro.[74] Here, it seems that doña Beatriz withheld the elaborate clothing that she had formerly bestowed on María Josefa in addition to prohibiting María Josefa from leaving her service to set up a household with Pedro. More importantly, doña Beatriz refused to manumit her.

For nine months, María Josefa was in the unenviable position of serving two masters: her owner and her husband. Later, she faced the prospect of being chastised by her owner for foisting Pedro on them and being trapped in a marriage in which she was repudiated by her husband.

Villagómez finally called on María Josefa in January 1683 (the following year) to testify. The proceedings had been considerably delayed because Pedro was unable to answer Villagómez's interrogatories. At the end of November, Pedro sent word that he was gravely ill, asking his three doctors to testify regarding his serious medical condition. When pressed by Villagómez, María Josefa confessed that no prenuptial fornication had occurred and that her brothers had lied in their witness statements. María Josefa echoed the rendition of her circumspect life under Beatriz's tutelage, saying that her brothers lied about the prenuptial fornication because of their ardent desire to see her free.[75]

One month later in February, Villagómez annulled the marriage between Pedro and María, finding that Pedro had proven his case of marital fraud. The litigation was not cheap: Pedro was assigned court costs of 2,074 *reales*.[76] The hefty legal fees raise the presumption in Pedro's favor, as he would not have expended that much money if he were not convinced of his right to prevail in this case. But Pedro did not live to relish his legal victory. Pedro never recovered from his illness and died before hearing the final judgment. And thus, the archived record ends with a petition from María Josefa four years later on November 28, 1687. In that petition, María Josefa requested the original *carta de libertad* that belonged to her mother, Juana, which had been submitted by the late Pedro Ramírez in their annulment proceeding.

ON WIVES, TERMITES, AND WIDGETS

It is at once challenging and frustrating to subject lawsuits to retrospective analysis, and particularly so in the case of fraud. Perhaps in recognition of our human frailties, the law establishes some guidelines for transacting parties with regard to disclosure, misrepresentation, and due diligence. Classic treatises and formalist approaches hold that failure to disclose information that is calculated to deceive the other party will invalidate a contract on equitable grounds.[77] But even under the strict individualist logic of caveat emptor (a potentially harsh doctrine for the gullible, lazy, or unsophisticated), the contracting party must also exercise a diligent effort to discover any flaws or imperfections in order to mitigate his risks.[78] In a transaction as binding as marriage, the contracting party should assume the responsibility of ascertaining the virtue, reputation, or status of the woman whom he intends to marry if this is indeed important to him, as a precaution against conniving and unscrupulous brides.

One could reasonably argue here that the doctrine of caveat emptor is an inappropriate one to apply to Pedro's legal claim – after all, wives are neither the proverbial termites nor widgets. I am nonetheless persuaded to apply the doctrine to this case because Pedro alleged that María Josefa willfully misrepresented a material fact for her personal gain. (Whether she gained anything from the marriage remains a mystery. There is no record of doña Beatriz's last will and testament, and no *carta de libertad* exists for María Josefa in the notarial documents. I speculate – with a heavy dose of solidarity with María Josefa – that maybe in the fateful earthquakes of 1687 that wracked the city of Lima, she went looking for Juana's *carta de libertad* to solicit her own freedom. But the records are silent and her freedom remains unknown.)

Interpreting willful misrepresentation is a perilous task in the case of status concealment or racial fraud, because so much depended precisely on what Pedro should have known or tried to discover according to the racial logics of the time. Short of protections for the "feeble-minded," courts do not look kindly on those who are deliberately foolish or reckless and then seek legal redress for their "blind credulity." In this regard, we presume that if Pedro were as concerned as he subsequently claimed to be about the purity of his lineage, he would have been more careful to investigate María Josefa's background, particularly in marriage negotiations with a *mulata* mother. In Provisor Villagómez's mind, what Pedro should have known was a straightforward, commonsensical matter – not unlike a prudent homebuyer inspecting for termites. In Pedro's mind, common sense failed because María Josefa defied the racial logics of the period. In terms of dress, appearance, and adornment, María Josefa visually communicated an identity that was calculated to deceive onlookers – although those who were close to her knew she was enslaved.

Even in the most generous reading of Pedro's efforts or intelligence, it is unlikely that he was as clueless as he insisted about María Josefa's identity. María Josefa never changed her story. Pedro simply never asked. If Pedro had exercised due diligence *and asked*, someone would have apprised him of the situation – either out of envy, malice, or genuine concern for the disparity of the union.

In the close-knit neighborhood where Pedro would have been trying to establish connections, there would have been no shortage of gossiping tongues. María Josefa was not the newcomer in the parish – she could not assume a new racial identity or reinvent her status like Juana de Torres, a recent arrival from Panama. The neighbors certainly stated their disapproval of what they agreed was racial subterfuge in their statements to the court. Granted, when pressed by administrative authorities, people tend to give responses that echo or conform to official mandates about socially respectable behavior, and so some skepticism is warranted in reading through these interrogatories. Nonetheless, the witnesses made remarks about Beatriz's favorable treatment of María Josefa that revealed envy, disapproval and animosity and granted Pedro a great deal of latitude in bringing the lawsuit.

The neighbors might not have had much invested in Pedro, but, as noted, they ultimately expressed an investment in the racial hierarchy of a society with slavery and sought to recalibrate the hierarchy that the relationship between doña Beatriz and María Josefa disrupted.

If anyone violated the racial order, it was doña Beatriz in her treatment of María Josefa. I do not pretend that the relationship between Beatriz and María Josefa was completely harmonious and altruistic or that power was equally distributed between both women. Such claims would be untenable and totally unsupported by the record. Beatriz countered Pedro's domestic plans by asserting her property rights in María Josefa. The distances between them were clearly marked: Beatriz was a propertied *doncella* and fully endowed with the "honor" bestowed by Iberoamerican society. María Josefa was enslaved, illegitimate, and without honor. Beatriz allowed Pedro and María Josefa to live with her, but it was clearly under her terms. But her insistence that she needed María Josefa to serve her rings somewhat hollow, given that Beatriz had at least two other domestic slaves in her household (one was another of Juana's daughters who was not as favored as María Josefa). It is true that slaves were status symbols for the Limeño elite, but Beatriz's rectitude is incongruent with the ostentatious displays of a vain, frivolous Limeña aristocrat.[79]

The relationship was more complex than the conventional dichotomies of the master and slave. Can we explain Beatriz's actions without accounting for emotions like maternal love, or even jealousy? Or in a society in which, ultimately, people were held as property, would Beatriz have been prepared to act as a calculating owner – willing to resell or rent out María Josefa if her financial exigencies so required?

Further questions arise when we expand our focus to include Juana. Did Juana intend to undermine Beatriz's maternal role by negotiating a marriage with Pedro that would remove María Josefa from Beatriz's control? Was Beatriz competing with Juana – María Josefa's biological mother and Beatriz's former slave – for María Josefa's filial loyalties? Recall Beatriz's fulminating statement: "*I have raised my said slave... Moreover, she has always been extremely virtuous, such that after I die, she will continue to uphold the customs and behavior in which she has been raised.*" This is a particularly maternal relationship that Beatriz portrays. She intends María Josefa to play the role of the dutiful daughter, even after she dies. Juana has no place in this script, she is effectively written out of it.

I reiterate that it is risky for us to delve too deeply into motivation because the record does not support much beyond speculation. The annulment suits brought by Juan González de Miranda and Pascual de Dueñas were easily disposed of, even though all these plaintiffs alleged marital fraud and were indeed married to enslaved women. Pedro endured three denials before prevailing in his case. Villagómez was only willing to extinguish the marital bond when María Josefa confessed that she lied about the prenuptial fornication that had convinced the Archbishopric to expedite the couple's marriage petition.

Ecclesiastical courts, like any administrative agency, ought to adhere strictly to procedure. The Archbishopric's court was particularly important to the administrative objectives of the viceroyalty: court personnel were expected to be judicious *letrados* and men of the cloth. Villagómez's family credentials were impeccable; he had connections to the highest ranks of viceregal and ecclesiastical administration. Villagómez himself was an unwavering, high-profile, passionate proponent of the moral authority of the Archbishopric. When plaintiffs prove a procedural defect or prove that that their opponents are "working the system" to circumvent procedures that should be strictly upheld, the plaintiffs generally prevail in their cases. Here, the laxity of the Archbishopric's officers in following Tridentine procedure was the decisive factor in the outcome.

This does not mean that the court did not endorse the ideas of racial hierarchy that Pedro proclaimed in the proceedings. Clearly, status, class, and gendered hierarchies shaped the topography of colonial Lima, and enslaved women were not immune from these considerations when they came before the court. But the court was not in the business of policing racial fraud – that was left to the community. The Archbishopric court was a high-volume court in which hundreds of litigants sought intervention in their marital affairs. Villagómez was concerned with upholding the overall mission of the court, which was to preserve the sanctity of marriage.

In sum, there is more to these cases than the recondite record will ever reveal. The interesting aspect of these *error de persona* cases is their very possibility – they depict the mobility of the racial landscape in which owners, slaves, freedmen, Andeans, and Spaniards lived. María Josefa was literally an embodied contradiction: she was living proof of the unsustainable nature of racial boundaries. We will never know what Pedro really knew about María Josefa. All we know is that multiple outcomes were possible from this tangled web of deceit and contested intimacies as women like María Josefa navigated between marriage and slavery in their pursuit of freedom.

NOTES

1 AAL, Causas de nulidad, 9 de agosto, 1659, exp. 37. Note that cases of annulment (causas de nulidad) and divorce (divorcios) are archived according to the year in which they were brought. There are no separate files (legajos) for these proceedings.
2 AAL, Causas de Nulidad, 9 de septiembre, 1659.
3 Colonial historians have generally agreed with Verena Martínez-Alier's thesis that enslaved women were less desirable marriage partners. According to this thesis, black and *casta* women acquiesced to the concubinary arrangement with Spaniards because it guaranteed a degree of status for their children (who would be born whiter, leading to progressive whitening over generations). Being attached to a higher status male also demonstrated their social ascendancy. See Martínez-Alier, *Marriage, Class and Colour in Nineteenth-Century Cuba*, ch. 4. The degree of choice and agency that enslaved women had in negotiating freedom through the exchange of sexual favors is, of course, debatable.
4 McKinley, "The Unbearable Lightness of Being (Black)." See also Lavallé, *Amor y opresión en los Andes coloniales*.
5 In reviewing wills in New Spain, Frank Proctor showed that testamentary manumission was likely when a slave and her children had been in domestic service for an extended period of time. See his "Gender and the Manumission of Slaves in New Spain."
6 This is not to detract from the productive historical scholarship about emotions, merely to bracket the paternalist objections in slavery studies. For a thoughtful review on the field of emotions and history, see Barbara Rosenwein's "Worrying about Emotions in History."
7 AAL, Monasterio de la Santísima Trinidad, leg. 4, exp. 7, año 1646.

8   van Deusen, "The Intimacies of Bondage."

9   The formal position of the church on parity between marital partners was not universally shared or uniformly enforced. Indeed, in the period before the Royal Pragmatic was issued, many priests upheld matrimonial promises between couples of unequal status over the objection of parents and elders. See Socolow, "Acceptable Partners," Saguier, "Church and State in Buenos Aires in the Seventeenth Century," and Seed, *To Love, Honor, and Obey in Colonial Mexico*.

10 X [= Liber Extra = Decretales Gregorii IX] 4.19.5 Ex litteris tuis, Clement III (1188–91); JL 16645 and X 4.19.7 Quanto te, Innocent III, May 1, 1199; Potthast, *Regesta pontificum romanorum*, 684, for papal edicts pertaining to divorce.

11 See Twinam, *Public Lives, Private Secrets*, and Nazzarri, "Sex/Gender Arrangements and the Reproduction of Class in the Latin American Past."

12 "Quadruplicem esse errorem. Primum personae, cum una persona pro alia supponitur. II conditionis servilis, cum contrahens liber existimat contrahere cum libera et est ancilla. III Qualitatis, cum credit se contrahere cum pulchra, nobili virgine et est deformis, plebeia, corrupta. Ultimum fortunae, cum putatur dives et est pauper. Qui error potest dici qualitatis. Cum tunc in qualitate divitiarum sola errettur" (Sánchez, *Sancto matrimonii sacramento disputationum*, 2:69). See also de Penyafort, *Summa on Marriage*, 30–31, for a widely cited canonical legal source on error.

13 AAL, Causas de nulidad, año 1659 ("Juana de Torres responde al escrito y demanda de nulidad de matrimonio puesta por Juan Gónzalez de Miranda"). After the provisor confronted Juan with his wife's testimony, Juan admitted that someone had advised him that if he wanted to get out of his marriage, he should go to court and allege *error de persona*. Clearly, it was becoming well known among unhappy spouses in mixed-status and interracial unions that *error de persona* was a legal basis for annulment.

14 Strictly speaking, the litigants should have alleged *error de condición*, although they uniformly refer to *error de persona*. When inequality of condition was the basis of annulment, litigants sometimes referred to their spouse's "defective" condition of slavery ("en su defecto de ser esclavo").

15 Rappaport, "Asi lo paresçe por su aspeto," 605–6.

16 *Yanaconas* were mobile Andean laborers without claims to land who bore no tributary obligations.

17 On the sexual unions between conquistadors and Inca noblewomen, see Vieira Powers, *Women in the Crucible of Conquest,* and van Deusen, "The Intimacies of Bondage."

18 It bears repeating that "race" signified differences as they were defined in religious and cultural terms. During the sixteenth century, the legitimacy of slavery was grounded in the curse of Ham – the biblical rationale for enslavement as the original sin of Africans fused with Aristotelian ideas about natural slavery and the possession and presence of Mediterranean slaves that were a constant feature of Iberian life. These were largely justifications that reflected the overall imperative of economic growth through the importation of a large nonnative workforce, but I am particularly interested in the social mutation of the previous category of "slave" as a captive of holy war to an object of commerce that emerged as ideas of race and blood mixing were negotiated in the Americas.

19 As shown in the eighteenth-century *sistema de castas* chart, children of mixed
European, indigenous, and African ancestry were classified in (at least) sixteen categories. The charts were accompanied by a series of stylized oil paintings depicting a
racially mixed couple in European clothing with their offspring. Only one Peruvian
series of paintings was produced (compared to the hundreds that circulated in New
Spain), commissioned by the Viceroy Manuel Amat y Junyent in 1770. (See Figure 3.2).
Romero de Tejada, *Los cuadros de mestizaje del Virrey Amat*, 27. Another set of illus-
trations together with the chart reprinted here was produced between 1767 and 1780.

Troncos   Español
             Negro
             Indio
I)   De Español y Negra redunda Mulato
     De Mulato y Española Testeron o Terceron
     De Terceron y Española Quarteron
     De Quarteron y Española Quinteron
     De Quinteron y Española, blanco o Español común.

II) De Negro y Mulata Sambo
     De Sambo y Mulata Sambohijo
     De Sambohijo y Mulata Tente en el Ayre
     De tente en el Ayre y Mulata, Salta atrás

III) De Español e India, Mestizo Real
     De mestizo e India Cholo
     De Cholo e India tente en el Ayre
     De tente en el Ayre e India, Salta atrás

IV) De Indio y Negra, Chino
     De Chino y Negra, Rechino o Criollo
     De Criollo y Negra, Torna atrás

                              Gregorio de Cangas
                         Tablas de mestizaje, ca. 1767

20 Rappaport, "Asi lo paresçe por su aspeto," 605.
21 Graubart, "Hybrid Thinking."
22 Ibid., 329.
23 See Fisher and O'Hara, *Imperial Subjects*, 11. For an early pigmentocratic
    approach, see Mörner, *Race Mixture in the History of Latin America*.
24 See, for example, *The Limits of Racial Domination*, and Johnson and Lipsett-
    Rivera, *The Faces of Honor*.
25 AAL, Divorcios, año 1670.
26 Cahill, "Colour by Numbers," 341. On the ambiguities of the mestizo category in
    the 1613 census, see Graubart, "Hybrid Thinking," 225–27.
27 On the ethnic designation of surnames for Mexico, see Cope, *The Limits of Racial
    Domination*, 67. For a discussion of Afro-criollo and diasporic names, see O'Toole,
    "To Be Free and Lucumí."

28   See Bowser, *The African Slave in Colonial Peru*, 153. According to Bowser's analysis of early colonial sanctions, the punishment for sexual relations between African men and indigenous women was castration (ordinance of 1551). In the case of sexual relations between African women and indigenous men, the punishment was a hundred lashes for the first conviction. If there was a second conviction, African women's ears were to be cut off. Free persons of color of both sexes faced the lash on the first offense and exile on the second.

29   The *Recopilación* contained numerous laws for slaves and free blacks but only modified the extant laws on manumission in one significant instance. The *Siete Partidas* conferred freedom on a slave who married a free woman with the consent of the owner, provided that his slave status was disclosed to his wife (Burns, *Las Siete Partidas*, 4, title 5, laws 1, 3, 4, 901–902). As Alan Watson notes, in 1515, the crown extended freedom to slaves who married indigenous women in the Indies, but in 1538, it retracted the conferral of freedom through marriage (*Slave Law in the Americas*, 48). Underscoring the contrary nature of viceregal lawmaking concerning slave marriage, Watson mentions that another law passed by the *Real Audiencia* in Hispaniola in 1526 reiterated the provision in the *Siete Partidas* conferring freedom on the marriage of a slave man and free woman (49). The 1526 *cédula* was passed in conjunction with the importation of 200 slaves – 100 men and 100 women – into the island, and the *Audiencia* specifically documented its intention to limit freedom to those who married endogamous partners. The legislation was ambiguous – indeed silent – on how those female slaves would be free so as to confer freedom on their husband in conformity with the *Siete Partidas*.

30   Martínez, *Genealogical Fictions*.

31   Entry into religious orders, university, or upper-level military administrative posts was prohibited for those of illegitimate parentage, *castas*, and Andeans. When economic pressures created needs for additional sources of revenue, wealthy *castas* could appeal to the crown for a royal dispensation of honorary whiteness. See Twinam, "Purchasing Whiteness," for a detailed study on *gracias al sacar* petitions. Silvia Espelt-Bonbín's recent "Notaries of Color in Colonial Panama" shows how *pardos* and *mulatos* circumvented the royal decrees against their entry into the notarial profession. Like Twinam, Esbelt-Bonbín discusses the situated nature of "pardo-ness" by challenging the prevailing idea that the dispensations were granted as a response to the crown's economic necessity. She also questions the view that economically prosperous professional people of color like notaries, militiamen, or surgeons sought the dispensation of their African origins in order to practice their craft (39–41).

32   Graubart, "Hybrid Thinking," 232.

33   Estenssoro Fuchs, "Los colores de la plebe."

34   The *Real Pragmática* of 1778 was part of the Bourbon reforms both on the peninsula and in the colonies; they were intended to modernize the colonial economy and strengthen royal metropolitan power in the face of criollo demands. The *Pragmática* significantly encroached on the church's autonomy by consolidating the power of secular courts over the temporal aspects of marriage. The crown adroitly maintained its strategic alliance with the church by leaving the sacred aspects of marriage in the hands of the ecclesiastical courts. Both church and crown

were exceedingly concerned with asserting "moral control" over the colonial population, and legislation was passed to penalize "crimes against public morality." See Borchat de Moreno, "El control de la moral pública."

35 On endogamy and intermarriage among mestizos and *mulatos*, see Seed and Rust, "Estate and Class in Colonial Oaxaca Revisited."

36 The chart's surprisingly high percentage of mixed-status marriages reaffirms that plebeians have always displayed more disregard for racial barriers. Sociologist Edward Telles has written that patterns of marriage and residence among the poor and working class – what he calls "the horizontal dimension of sociability" – are much more integrated and egalitarian, even in societies like Brazil with a great deal of disparity and economic/class stratification (*Race in Another America*, 173–214).

37 Ayliffe, *Paregon juris canonici anglicani*, 362–64.

38 Martínez, *Genealogical Fictions*, ch. 4.

39 "Where an accusation is made for any of the reasons aforesaid, it is not ... an accusation ... but rather a mistake, where the party thought he was marrying a person who was free, and married a slave" (Burns, *Las Siete Partidas*, Partida 4, title 5, law 3, 902).

40 AAL, Causas de nulidades, leg. 37, año 1683 (Ramírez c. Martínez, 12 de mayo, 1682).

41 "No es creíble que siendo español de calidad había de manchar mi sangre con una esclava de mala nota" (ibid.).

42 Founded in 1568 as the urban population outgrew the Cathedral, the parish of Santa Ana was located to the east of the Plaza Mayor. For a detailed review of the founding of the parish and its constituency, see Bernabé Cobo's study *Historia de la fundación de Lima*, 126, 199. Since status, race, and ethnicity were spatially reproduced in colonial Lima, the aristocracy lived in *solares* (city plots) located in close proximity to the Plaza Mayor. Although imprecise, it was possible to calculate the level of elite status and prestige Spaniards enjoyed by their residential proximity to the Plaza Mayor. According to Cobo's description, the Plaza Santa Ana was dominated by those *españoles* in the meat trade (53). Santa Ana encompassed the Cercado as a subparish. Formally, the Cercado and Santa Ana comprised one parish, but the Cercado was set aside for *naturales* and continued to attract Andean migrants to the city throughout the colonial and republican period. Santa Ana's hospital was established to care for the Andean population. Santa Ana also had a large black population. In Bowser's review of late sixteenth-century parish records, Santa Ana had the second largest population of blacks and *mulatos* in Lima (*The African Slave in Colonial Peru*, 339). These demographic facts taken together give us insights into the multiethnic composition of and the concomitant multiethnic relationships within this parish.

43 On gossip between horizontal and vertical communities, see Ramos, "Gossip, Scandal and Popular Culture in Golden Age Brazil."

44 "Si saben que el dicho Pedro Ramírez es hijo de padres españoles tales que si hubiera tenido conocimiento del error de la persona no hubiese venido en el contrato y celebración del casamiento porque su yntención es y ha sido casarse con mujer española." On the gender-specific nature of the "Spanish" designation, see Kuznesof, "Ethnic and Gender Influences on 'Spanish' Creole Society."

45 Doctor don Pedro de Villagómez was well versed in all aspects of ecclesiastical law and governance. Villagómez was a *peninsular* and the nephew of the
Archbishop of Lima, also named Pedro de Villagómez. In Lincoln Draper's profile
of the personality traits of the high clergy, Villagómez strikes one as an evangelizer who believed passionately in the proselytizing mission of the Archbishopric.
In contrast, Draper classified Feliciano de Vega (our other long-serving provisor)
as a distinguished bureaucrat rather than an evangelizer. Like Vega, Villagómez
served as rector of the University of San Marcos (1655), and was then appointed
as provisor of the ecclesiastical court in 1657 (see Mendiburu, *Diccionario
histórico biográfico del Perú*, 8:328). Villagómez served in that capacity until
1683. In 1680, he was appointed as the governor of the Archbishopric court by
Archbishop Melchor de Liñan y Cisneros. Villagómez was also appointed bishop
of La Paz in 1657. In 1683, he was named priest of Our Lady of Santa Ana parish
in Lima and served as a *visitador* in an idolatry investigation in 1650 during the
extirpation campaigns launched by his uncle. See Mills, *Idolatry and Its Enemies*.

46 "Porque como dice la dicha María Josefa en su escrito en que contesta la demanda
el dicho Pedro Ramírez solicitó el casamiento y como quiera que según la razón
del contrato a él le toca el examinar la calidad y prendad de la mujer con quien
había de contraer el matrimonio, se presume muy conforme a derecho que despúes
se celebró fue con el conocimiento de quien era y no parece que fue de entender
lo contrario de las instancias y diligencias que se insinuaron en el escrito de con-
testación presentado por la mujer. Por todo lo cual y lo mas que hace queda a favor
de la causa matrimonial: A Vmd. pido y suplico declare no haber lugar la dicha
nulidad y mande con el apremio de las censuras que el dicho Pedro Ramírez haga
vida maridable con la dicha María Josefa Martínez por ser justicia que pido y por
la defensa desta causa matrimonial."

47 On the responsibilities of the ecclesiastical court with regard to marriage, annulment, and divorce, see Vargas Ugarte, *Concilios limenses*.

48 AAL, Probanza de doña Ana de Barrios Urrea, española doncella, 4 de julio, 1682.

49 "Que ninguna negra ni mulata, libre ni cautiva, pueda traer ninguna joya de oro
ni plata, ni perlas ni vestidos de seda de Castilla, ni mantos de seda, ni pasamanos
de oro ni de plata, so pena de cien azotes y de perdimiento de tales vestidos, joyas,
perlas y lo demás" (Konetzke, *Colección de documentos*, 2: 182). On the inattention to sumptuary laws in Lima, see Walker, "'He Outfitted His Family in Notable
Decency.'"

50 See Bowser, *The African Slave in Colonial Peru*, 153, and Cantuarias Acosta, "Las
modas limeñas."

51 "Que se haga exemplar castigo deste excesso y desverguenza" (Suardo, *Diario de
Lima*, 1:17).

52 Walker, "'He Outfitted His Family in Notable Decency.'"

53 "El trajino y lustre de los ciudadanos en el tratamiento y aderezo de sus personas es
tan grande y general que no se puede en un día de fiesta concocer por el pelo quien
es cada uno; porque todos, nobles y los que no lo son, visten corta y ricamente...
porque no llegan acá las pragmáticas que se publican en España sobre los trajes"
(Cobo, *Historia de la fundación de Lima*, 72).

54 "Nunca llegué a conocer que era esclava porque los tratos, los vestuarios y lo
general con que la dicha doña Beatriz trataba a la dicha María Josefa era de española, y nunca se pudo entender fuese esclava respecto a lo dicho y así teniéndola

al pueblo y viéndola con los ornatos de española como era llevarla con manto a la iglesia y festividades públicas constantes que la habían de tener por española y de buena calidad."

55 The Spanish word "disimular" could be clumsily translated as "passing." According to Covarrubias's *Tesoro de la lengua española,* "disimulo" means "encubrir con malicia." "Passing" functions as one of several terms to designate the visual instability of race and gendered identity. In terms of clothing – important in the determination of María Josefa's identity as free and *española* – individuals don clothing that is gendered, raced, and classed to successfully convince the public of their identity. In the colonial context, "whitening" (i.e., racial drift), not passing, is the objective.

56 "Se puso dificultad a la salida respecto de querer apartar la casa para buscar la vida."

57 In this sense, the proceedings closely mirrored the racial determination trials conducted in the United States described by Ariela Gross, in which local juries deliberated over cases of racial identity on the basis of performance, "common sense," and blood quantum. As Gross reminds us, "Racial knowledge resided not in documents but in communities, and it required reputation evidence to determine" (*What Blood Won't Tell,* 24).

58 Residency status was important for males. *Vecinos* were granted voting rights and could serve in official administrative capacities. *Naturales* or *residentes* were tied by birth to a certain place, but they were not necessarily vested with the full rights of citizenship. *Moradores* could be born elsewhere but enjoyed residency rights within a community. See Herzog, *Defining Nations.*

59 María Josefa appears in the record to be anywhere from eighteen to twenty-seven years old. When María Josefa gave her notarized consent to the marriage, she claimed that she was only eighteen years old, thereby dating her birth after Juana's manumission. However, all the witnesses – Juana included – confirmed that María Josefa was between twenty-four and twenty-six years old.

60 "Desde que la nació, la ha tenido con sujeta de hija para el efecto de que me sirviese y asistiese como lo ha estado haciendo desde que tiene uso de razón."

61 On the notion of intertextuality in notarial statements, see Jouve Martin, *Esclavos de la ciudad letrada.*

62 "Pedro Ramírez, natural desta ciudad, hixo legítimo de Pedro Ramírez y de doña Paula de Ocampo, digo para mas servir a Dios nuestro Señor, tengo tratado de contraer matrimonio según horden de nuestra santa madre yglesia con María Josefa Martínez de Soto, quarterona, natural desta ciudad, hija natural de Cristóbal de Martínez de Soto y Juana de Tovar. Y así ante Vmd. pido y suplico mande que a la contenida se reciba consentimiento y a ambos información de como somos solteros y se nos despache licencia para que qualquier de los curas de mi señoría Santa Ana nos pueda casar dispensando en las tres amonestaciones que dispone el Santo Concilio de Trento" (AAL, Expedientes matrimoniales, año 1681).

63 AAL, Pliegos matrimoniales, consentimiento y probanza de testigos, año 1681.

64 AAL, Libro de matrimonios de españoles, Santa Ana, año 1681.

65 Sánchez, *Amancebados, hechiceros y rebeldes,* xxv.

66 Vargas Ugarte, *Concilios limenses tercer concilio, Cap. 34 Del contraer matrimonio,* p. 337. When reviewing the *pliegos,* it seems that particular care was taken in the case of widows to verify the death of the former spouse. Widows whose spouses

died outside of Lima, whether in Spain or in other colonial sites, tended to present numerous witnesses testifying to their eligibility to contract a new marriage.

67   Rípodas, *El matrimonio en Indias*, 79–81; Vargas Ugarte, *Concilios limenses,* Sexto Concilio Limense, Caps. 9 & 10.

68   For similar machinations after the *Pragmática* was enacted, see Rípodas, *El matrimonio en Indias*, 65. For seventeenth-century petitions, see McKinley, "Illicit Intimacies." Pilar Latasa notes that the clergy was on notice that enslaved couples pretended they were parishioners of a church in which they did not worship in order to evade their owners' opposition to their marriages. "Se advierte de la facilidad con que los esclavos trataba de encubrir sus casamientos para no fueran conocidos por sus amos. Con ese fin, suelen irse a casar a parroquias ajenas y diciendo que son feligreses dellas" (Latasa "La celebración del matrimonio en el virreinato peruano. Latasa cites Lima's synod convened in 1613, *De sponsalibus et matrimonis*, cap. 4: "Del recato que ha de haber en los casamientos de negros por los engaños que usan. Y que ninguno a sabiendas se atreva a casar en feligrés ajeno" (245–46).

69   "Digo que se ha de declarar no haber lugar la dicha nulidad por la información que se hizo para dar la licencia para que los dichos se casasen. Se hallará que para haber de dispensar en las amonestaciones dicen los testigos que estaban dichos contrayentes en amistad ilícita= y no es verosímil que estando en ella ygnorase el dicho Pedro Ramírez la calidad y condición de persona de la dicha María Josefa con quien trató de contraer matrimonio=ni es de entender que la diligencia de venirse a que en el Patio de los Naranjos se le recibiese el conocimiento para efectuar dicho matrimonio no fue cautelosa de ambas partes procurando que Doña Beatriz de Tovar, ama de la dicha María Josefa no procurase impedirlo= en cuyos términos y abiendo por expresado lo que puede favorecer la causa matrimonial a Vmd. pido y suplico no aber lugar la dicha nulidad de matrimonio."

70   "Así formalmente puedo y devo asegurar que en la custodia que he tenido y criado de la dicha mi esclava ha sido no solo de doncella sino es de virtud exemplar con ánimo de disponer de ella después de mis días en la forma que pudiese conserbarla en el buen ejemplo en que se ha criado.... Además de que en mi recogimiento, casa y obligación, nunca pudiese caber semejante pecado, y no solo permitirlo mas ni pensarlo."

71   "Totalmente con las acciones de libre salía todas las veces que se ofrecía sinque la dicha doña Beatriz diese una palabra sola en contrario."

72   See Bennett, *Africans in Colonial Mexico*, ch. 4, and Cosamalón Aguilar, *Indios detrás de la muralla.*

73   Many of these cases emerged at the moment of separation, when the husband attempted to establish an independent household with his wife. The husbands' demands for independence and separation expose the codependency of the master-slave relationship. Marital alliances – particularly newly formed ones – disturbed the household rhythms established over decades between slaves and owners. In their responses, wives either resisted the move or were inscrutably silent about it. Their silence is in marked distinction with those cases in which wives actively sought injunctions against their owners for denying their conjugal rights discussed in Chapter 2. In these annulment cases, the wives expressed no interest in moving, no doubt because they wished to avoid alienating or infuriating their owners or perhaps because they astutely realized that the contested

marriage was not their conduit to freedom. Owners and husbands recruited the courts (albeit for different purposes) as a neutral third party with the power to impose the sought-after domestic arrangement. On the imbrication of domesticity, gender, and social hierarchy, see Milanich, "Whither Family History?"

74 "Con la dicha doña Beatriz no solo hubiera conseguido yo mi libertad sino es que no hubiera perdido por su causa muchas utilidades y conveniencias granjeadas desde mi niñez... Porque aunque es cierto que la dicha mi ama no tuvo noticia del dicho casamiento y cuando se le dio fue después de lo celebrado, esto no puede ser de fundamento porque ordinariamente sucede casarse de la misma calidad muchas españoles y estándolo cumplen con las obligaciones del matrimonio" (Responde María Josefa, f. 36).

75 "Con el deseo ardiente de ver remediada dicha hermana suya lo hicieron."

76 Over half of these costs were *arançeles* (notarial fees). The court also fined María Josefa's brothers for perjury (f. 63, 9 de enero 1683, al margen).

77 See, for example, *Laidlaw v. Organ* 15 U.S. 178 (1817).

78 The contemporary law of contract and tort is less tolerant of the harsh individualism of caveat emptor. See Kennedy, "Distributive and Paternalist Moves in Contract and Tort Law with Special Reference to Compulsory Terms and Unequal Bargaining Power."

79 Beatriz was not an aristocrat, although she hailed from a wealthy clerical family with enough financial assets to own a coach.

4

Freedom at the Font

> Let it be known by whoever sees this letter that I, doña María de la Asunción, widow of Fernando López de Miranda, resident of this City of Kings, swear that I have a slave named Francisco, who is only eighteen hours old. The little boy Francisco is my godson. I blessed him with holy water after he was born. His mother, Catalina Miranda, morena criolla, is my slave. I love the said Catalina Miranda because of everything she has done for me, and because she has served me with such loyalty and goodness, I want to grant this child his freedom. He was born in my house and received at birth by my hands. Let it be known that henceforth, this letter proves that he is free from the captivity into which he was born, from now and forevermore. I hereby grant Francisco his freedom, and swear that I do so of my own free will.

On August 21, 1706, Juan Antonio de Arriola filed suit in Lima's royal court to clarify his wife María Albina's legal status.[1] According to Juan Antonio, María Albina's godfather had freed her at the baptismal font with her owner's knowledge and consent. Her godfather, don Antonio Caro, paid María's owner 100 pesos for her purchase price, insisting that he would not serve as her godfather if she went to the baptismal font as a slave. María's owner, don Diego Camaño, accepted don Antonio's terms and María was inscribed in the baptismal books of Piura as free.

María's baptismal manumission occurred when she was a young child – she was not more than three years old. But when María was five years old, she became reenslaved. In 1665, don Diego "gifted" her family to his goddaughter doña María de Lara y Figueroa, who was entering the Monasterio de la Santísima Trinidad in Lima. María, along with her parents Catalina and Antonio Criollo, were to minister to doña María's needs in the convent.

Although María was legally free, she was also dependent on her parents because of her young age. There is some confusion in the record as to whether her parents protested her reenslavement while they were still in Piura or whether instead they understood the full implications of the donation. Indeed, the *carta de donación* was clear that the family was a "loan" to doña María. Upon her death, or if she left the convent, the family would revert to don Diego's ownership and custody.[2] Don Diego provided 2,000 pesos for doña María's dowry (*dote*), and the gifted slaves became part of the convent's labor pool. Catalina and Antonio became day-wage laborers (*jornaleros*), while María served doña María as a religious servant (*donada*), remaining in the convent for over eighteen years.[3]

Catalina and Antonio did not want to leave María behind in Piura. The distance between both cities spanned more than 500 miles – a lifetime apart in terms of seventeenth-century travel. (see map 4.1) The parents had to bring their child in order for the family to stay together. According to one witness, Catalina later lamented that her daughter had been part of don Diego's beneficent gift but consoled herself with the knowledge that María had received a religious and virtuous upbringing in the cloistered environment. Many witnesses concurred that Catalina said that securing such an upbringing was her purpose in bringing her daughter along.[4] Catalina also believed doña María de Lara was a virtuous Catholic and so was confident she would respect her daughter's baptismal freedom.[5]

In 1683, Juan Antonio de Arriola and María Albina married. Juan Antonio was a free, prosperous *pardo*, who purportedly had earned a great deal of money (*pesos de buen caudal*) as an assistant sea captain.[6] Prior to their marriage, Juan Antonio diligently tried to ascertain María Albina's status, consulting with don Diego. By 1683, Catalina and Antonio were dead, and María Albina reverted to serving in don Diego's household. Consequently, marriage negotiations took place with don Diego, who acted as surrogate parent. Juan Antonio offered to pay María's purchase price, but don Diego reassured him that he had already freed María Albina and that the *carta de libertad* was on file with the notary who drew up the document. Juan Antonio went in search of the document, but he discovered the notary who recorded the *carta* had fallen into dementia and so was unable to help him. Juan Antonio pressed don Diego for a copy, but the only document don Diego could produce was the original *carta de donación* of the gift of the family.

Upon reading the *carta de donación*, Juan Antonio realized that María Albina had been freed twice: once at the baptismal font and another time through manumission by grace. In 1683, Juan Antonio brought his first suit on behalf of his wife for personal services rendered to doña María de Lara while doña María was interned in the Monasterio de la Santísima Trinidad.[7] Given the lack of documentation attesting to María's free status, it was incumbent on Juan Antonio to make the best case possible by claiming payment for personal services. Had María been enslaved, she would not have been entitled to payment for the years she served in the convent.

Over the course of twenty-three years (1683–1706), Juan Antonio filed a number of lawsuits to clarify María Albina's status. The lawsuits took different

MAP 4.1 Map of Peru.
Map by: David Cox.

paths and ultimately converged when Juan Antonio used the personal services complaint filed in 1683 as proof and justification for the 1706 status determination proceeding.[8] By 1706, the couple had six children and two grandchildren. Their ages ranged from twenty-two years to eight months. The freedom of the couple's children and grandchildren was compromised by María's uncertain legal status. At stake in Juan Antonio's 1706 lawsuit, therefore, was the freedom of his entire family. It was vital that María be declared free before the time of her marriage so that enslavement was not transmitted to the couple's offspring.

When they discovered that the documents they needed were not available, Juan Antonio and María summoned an impressive number of witnesses to testify that María had been freed as a child and that the couple had relied on that grant of freedom to conduct their lives as freed people. This was prudent legal strategy, since Juan Antonio rested his claim on a reliance argument.[9] According to the *Siete Partidas*, "Where the slave of any person goes about unmolested for the space of ten years, in good faith and thinking that he is free, in the country where the master resides ... he becomes free for this reason."[10] Despite the absence of any documents explicitly guaranteeing María's freed status, everyone in the couple's social network regarded her as free. Indeed, the record indicates that María lived her life unencumbered by the confusion as to whether she was free or enslaved.

As we go through the record with Juan Antonio, we become acutely aware of the slippery and ambiguous terrain of quasi emancipation traversed by so many slaves, a terrain that was particularly treacherous for those who were freed as children and then reenslaved. Quasi emancipation here does not refer to a legal status but rather to tensile bonds of dependency tethering putatively "freed" people to their former owners. We are reminded of Rachel O'Toole's point that "the achievement of legal manumission did not mean liberty for enslaved women... The struggle to obtain autonomy illustrates a segmented freedom as women moved in and out of supplying intimate labor to heirs, patrons, and former owners."[11] Baptismal manumission was embedded in other multigenerational relations of dependency that were common features of the conditional nature of colonial manumission practices. Therefore, studying baptismal manumission helps us to understand the relationships between and among parties who conferred freedom on a child while retaining the services of one or both of the parents.

Slavery scholars are focusing renewed attention on *cartas de libertad* granting deferred manumission, notarial self-purchase contracts, and wills and testaments to examine the multifaceted dynamics of lifetime emancipation.[12] Whereas studies of childhood manumission traditionally associated the conferral of freedom with paternity and sexual relationships between enslaved women and free men, a more nuanced view of age, gender, and household relationships emerges when the *cartas* are examined in tandem with baptismal records and *censuras*.[13] This chapter explores the dynamics of mixed-status parent-child relationships, infused as they were by slavery, dependency, and freedom. In particular, the chapter is concerned with the impact of baptismal manumission on legal claims to freedom that were brought later in life. In what follows, I suggest that a higher probability of reenslavement ensued from baptismal manumission if the child remained in a familial unit that was enslaved or tied to the same household. In other words, baptismal manumission was akin to constructive reenslavement.

Most societies deemed children as dependent and in need of control and tutelage by social superiors – this was acutely the case for children of slaves in colonial Latin America.

For many children born to enslaved parents, freedom at the font was one step in a trajectory toward liberty. Using María Albina's case as background, this chapter examines 148 cases in which children born to enslaved mothers were inscribed as free in Lima's baptismal books for slaves, *mulatos*, Indians, and españoles in El Sagrario between 1640 and 1699. The chapter also incorporates twenty-two *censuras* alleging childhood emancipation and baptismal manumission. Where possible, I used *cartas de libertad*, wills and testaments, *censuras*, subsequent legal proceedings and administrative petitions involving the parties to track the status of manumitted children and to evaluate the relationships that bound the parents, owners, and freed children together. Although each case is *sui generis*, the cases and *censuras* demonstrate extended relationships involving enslaved mothers and grandmothers, owners and godparents, and freed children.

SEARCHING FOR SLAVERY'S MIDDLE GROUND: FREED CHILDREN OF ENSLAVED MOTHERS

Much of the scholarly literature within Atlantic legal history on reenslavement is concerned with the fate of enslaved peoples after public emancipation.[14] Another stream of literature focuses on jurisdictional tensions between free soil regimes and slave states and the consequences of freed people's travel into slave territory.[15] With particular regard to slave children, historians of slavery in the United States have examined the rise of coercive apprenticeship and indenture arrangements to illustrate the precarious nature of emancipation in the aftermath of the Civil War.[16] Others have looked at reenslavement in jurisdictions favoring gradual emancipation.[17] Reenslavement scholars use these divergent case studies to comprehend the "vexed and permeable boundary between slavery and freedom."[18] By focusing on the fate of children within enslaved families, we can trace the interconnected worlds of freed people and slaves on what Barbara Fields evocatively called the "middle ground."[19] Perhaps nowhere is this middle ground as pronounced as in the mixed-status family.

Technically, "mixed status" simply meant the coexistence of free and enslaved people within one family unit. Prior to the "boom" in childhood studies, enslaved children were analyzed as part of the laboring unit of their family. Departing from this trend, Gilberto Freyre treats enslaved children separately in his epic study of the extended plantation family in northeastern Brazil.[20] While Freyre's views on the benign nature of sexual paternalism and racial democracy have been excoriated over the years, his work has been (justifiably) recognized for its focus on the slave-owning household as a sociopolitical site of cultural production and power. More importantly, Freyre draws attention to children as agents of intercultural and racial exchange.[21]

The combination of paternalism, tutelage, unpaid labor, childhood companionship, kinship and gender relations, and indeed, the infantilizing of enslaved peoples renders childhood's lens a particularly apposite one through which to examine slavery. Cases involving children shed light on relationships between freed children and enslaved mothers (María Albina and Catalina, María Albina and her own children) and on the impact of mixed status on social mobility (Juan Antonio and his family). Like the *error de persona cases* examined in Chapter 3, all baptismal emancipation cases emerged in the context of domestic servitude. Legal proceedings based on grants of childhood emancipation highlight the ways in which household labor relations were couched in the discourse of protection, dependency, kinship, reciprocity, and discipline.

María Albina's case combined different aspects of the three strategies customarily used by formerly enslaved peoples to support their claims to freedom: providing documentary proof, demonstrating the financial means to purchase their freedom, and calling on witnesses who could vouch for their freed status.[22] As we have seen repeatedly, when one of these three components was weak or missing, claimants had to fortify the others to prevail in their cases.

Juan and María Albina marshaled thirty witnesses who unanimously attested to an event during which she was freed and who testified that there were subsequent occasions when don Diego made clear his intent to free her. Like the witnesses summoned by Pedro to support his claim of *error de persona* against María Josefa, the witnesses in this case emphasized the performance of freedom on the part of Juan and María Albina. The claimants' witnesses used habitus, religious piety, and virtue to construe freedom in the absence of documentation. All the witnesses insisted that Juan Antonio and María Albina acted like free people, that they never paid a daily wage (*jornal*) to anyone, that they were masters of their own time. María's *calidad* was of a kind that her friends, confessors, and neighbors attributed to a free woman of color.

Relevant to the determination of María Albina's case was Juan Antonio's initial offer and financial ability to purchase her freedom. Equally important, María Albina's case was litigated in a legal context favoring the presumption of liberty when questions of status arose. Such a presumption indicates a markedly different jurisprudential stance than that of North American common law or even the 1685 *Code Noir*. In the judges' determination of her case, the number of people whose liberty depended on María Albina's status was paramount in the *Audiencia's* decision to find in her favor.

Despite these factors that persuaded the court to find María Albina a free woman, we are mindful nonetheless of the circumstances that gave rise to her case in the first place. María Albina was freed, reenslaved, freed again on some indeterminate date, and then legally declared free. These de trop manumissions remind us that children's fates were decided on different terms than those of adults. Liberty was not a primary factor in the calculus for the welfare of plebeian children whose life trajectories depended on the fortunes of the adults in their midst. In the retrospective calculations of María Albina's peers and associates, the fact that she was a child going into religious service was important. They perceived the benefit of such service as being greater than her freedom. No one else besides Juan Antonio seemed perturbed that María Albina worked for nearly twenty years without wages. In people's minds, María Albina accrued the benefit of virtue and *recogimiento,* even though she was inside la Santísima Trinidad working as an enslaved *donada.*

I argue that we do not fully appreciate the logic behind María Albina's reenslavement if we overlook the powerful practices associated with religious enclosure for colonial dependents, elite women, and their families. Indeed, a gendered study of urban Iberoamerican slavery would be incomplete if it failed to consider the experience of religious enclosure and servitude. Let us now turn to the cloistered world of Lima's religious institutions where thousands of enslaved children and legal dependents made their homes in the seventeenth century.

HOLY LABORING WOMEN: ENSLAVED *DONADAS* IN LIMA'S CONVENTS

When María Albina arrived as a child in Lima, she must have been awestruck by the grandiosity of the city and baroque splendor of the Monasterio de la Santísima Trinidad. As Nancy van Deusen writes, "The number of monasteries and convents, the architectural grandeur, the fascination with symmetry and order, and the ritual and public fanfare were all valid expression of Lima's religiosity and of the city's persona."[23] According to Juan Bromley's historic survey of the baroque city, there were 43 churches and convents and 200 chapels, including private sanctuaries.[24] These religious complexes corresponded to the organization of the city into six parishes. Limeños defined where they lived by locating their home's proximity to one or more religious establishments.[25] The only other geographical reference that competed with religious landmarks was a large or imposing home owned by a prominent citizen of the city.[26]

One out of ten Limeños lived within religious enclosure.[27] These vast religious complexes relied heavily on enslaved labor in the kitchens, laundries, refectories, and private *celdas.* (see Figure 4.2). Although the word "celda" is correctly translated as "cell," *celdas* were in fact private dwellings within the convents. *Celdas* varied in size and grandeur according to the wealth and status

FIGURE 4.1. Convento de Santa Catalina. Author's photograph.

of the novitiate's patron. In Lima's largest convent, La Encarnación, *celdas* ranged from one room with a kitchen and patio to two-storied dwellings with rooftop patios, balconies, private gardens, and prayer rooms. Wealthy residents also had their own orchards and raised their own poultry.[28]

Lima's convents and monasteries also subsidized their earnings by allowing secular women like doña María de Lara to reside in their own private *celdas* within the cloisters. Indeed, although religious institutions generated considerable revenue through extended credit (*censos*), dowries, donations, and religious endowments (*capellanías*), secular residents also provided substantial revenue for the convents' operational expenses.[29] Thousands of foundling children, slaves, indigenous neophytes and dependent women all contributed their labor in what Kathryn Burns has aptly called the "spiritual economy." According to van Deusen's careful study of Lima's religious institutions, la Santísima Trinidad had a high occupancy rate of slaves, *donadas*, and servants, at times even surpassing the labor force of the larger convents. In 1690, la Santísima Trinidad had over 250 servants for a population of 120 nuns and novitiates.[30]

Even though they comprised the labor force for the arduous domestic work demanded by nuns of higher status, the historical record reflects a degree of respectability that inhered to *casta* and enslaved women through their association with religious institutions. For many women of color, entry into the cloisters ensured a modicum of upward mobility.[31] All the witnesses in María Albina's case attributed her rectitude and virtue to her moral upbringing and

FIGURE 4.2. Interior of a nun's celda, Convent of Santa Catalina.
Image credit: Kelly Donahue-Wallace.

Christian education in the Santísima Trinidad.[32] María Albina's social mobility
was linked to her *recogimiento* rather than her marriage to a free prosperous
pardo. That the witnesses privileged her religious education over her marriage
is surprising, given the gendered grammar of the time.[33]

Female religious institutions were vital to Spanish hegemony and also to
slavery.[34] Monasteries were key sites of regulation, religious inculcation, and
tutelage, places that harnessed the church's powerful imaginary in order to
normalize racial inequality and gendered subordination. The racial hierarchies and inequities of the secular world were thus mirrored in the cloistered
environment. "Rebellious" and "wayward" women and girls were routinely
placed in the monasteries to be punished and reformed.[35] In 1606, the Mother
Abbess of La Encarnación asked the city council (*cabildo*) not to send her any
more *negras* or *mulatas*, because of all the trouble and expense entailed in their
supervision and discipline.[36] Not infrequently, enslaved women and girls in the
cloisters protested their confinement by claiming lack of consent and duress,
language that resonated with legal norms of limited autonomy regarding religious internment.

Given this hybrid public interiority, monasteries and convents were spaces
where legal dependents were insulated from external pressures.[37] Several

lawsuits brought by enslaved spouses and parents demonstrate that attempts to extricate family members interned in the convents tended to be unsuccessful.[38] Owners were also thwarted in their efforts to remove slaves once they were inside the cloisters.[39] Indeed, religious orders presented formidable legal opponents, and only the most persistent enslaved litigants could prevail in their proceedings.

In general, complaints brought by enslaved litigants against religious orders revolved around unenforced promises of freedom, disputed testamentary bequests of slaves to the orders, and nonconsensual confinement. A patron had to solicit the abbess's permission to emancipate a slave or her child, since they were regarded as community property. Religious orders were able to stymie efforts to release enslaved women (and children in particular) not only because of the power they exerted in colonial society but also because of the regulatory role that the orders exercised over all manner of colonial dependents. This power was derived from the widely held view that religious internment was beneficial to legal dependents bereft of powerful or significant patrons. We see this in María Albina's case, but also in others. Numerous bequests of servant-wards (*criadas*) were couched in terms of beneficence, even though the bequests were made with the family's honor, reputation, and celestial ascendancy in mind. The wording used in these petitions was carefully framed to appeal to the cloister's maternalist mission, even though the patron reserved the services of the *criada* for his daughter or protégée.

Kathryn Burns insightfully describes the reframing of religious maternity by looking at the practice of child-rearing within the convents: "For [nuns], mothering did not require conjugal sex or secular marriage, and family did not require a patriarchal head of household. Their experience of motherhood … and their recasting of family relations placed them at the head of their own households."[40] The nuns' male religious superiors repeatedly called these unconventional maternalist practices into question. In 1695, nuns in Las Descalzas were admonished for permitting enslaved mothers to raise their children inside the *celdas* of their owners.[41] The Archbishop and ecclesiastical procurator launched an official investigation into the matter. We see no evidence, however, of the nuns' yielding to these inquisitions. Indeed, the cloisters' institutional power was a double-edged sword: erecting an imposing shield to protect enslaved women and children who were inside while keeping other claimants to these families outside their impenetrable walls.

The confluence of maternalism, slavery, servitude, and Catholic hegemony is evident in the practice of donating slave children to convents so they could be raised inside. Our baptismal sample includes children freed by nineteen professed nuns, who remained laboring alongside their mothers within the cloisters until they were released by the nuns. Though these bequests did not signify a qualitatively different fate from the perspective of the enslaved women and children (they were no different from routine bequests that transmitted property to heirs) the fact that cloistered slaves were community property made it much more difficult for an enslaved *donada* or *criada* to purchase her freedom from the orders.

Inside the slaveholding *celda*, the liberty, autonomy, and upward mobility of enslaved *criadas* and *donadas* were closely related to the weight of the bonds that linked the mother and child to their professed or lay owners. From an impressionistic reading of these baptismal records and the *cartas de libertad* that supported the grant of freedom at the font, the most favorable outcome for the manumitted child was contingent on the strength of the owner's position within the cloisters and the length of service that the child's mother had with the family.[42] In addition to the ubiquitous phrasing "for the love I have for her" ("por el amor que le tengo"), we see evidence of strong emotional ties expressed repeatedly in manumitting documents alluding to generational household formation: "born in my home" ("nacida en mi casa") or "received by my hands" ("recibida en mis manos").[43] Sebastiana Tellez Avila, a claimant in a 1656 *censura* case, used the phrase "raised at her breast" ("criádola a sus pechos") to substantiate her claim that she had been freed at the font.

Another lawsuit brought by Juana Godinez claimed that her owner, the abbess of La Encarnación, granted her freedom on the condition that she remain within the convent. If Juana chose to leave, she would have to pay 400 pesos to the convent for her freedom. In her lawsuit, Juana insisted that it was her desire to remain within the cloister, but as a freedwoman, which was her owner's wish.[44]

Juana's case was atypical of many of the baptismal grants of freedom to children born in the convents. Her successful outcome (though hard won) was undoubtedly related to the powerful position of her deceased patron. Many owners imposed restrictions and conditions on a child that bound her to servitude until the end of her owner's life. Failure to provide companionship and service resulted in the revocation of liberty. As one owner declared: "Let it be known that while I am alive, Graciela must remain by my side and in my company. She cannot ever run away or leave the convent, even when she comes of age, because if she does so, this letter of freedom will become null and void."[45] This case was all the more poignant because Graciela's liberty was granted by two sisters, both of whom insisted on tying her to their sides until their respective deaths. For childless women, this insistence on care work and companionship was a common feature of baptismal manumission agreements, even taking precedence over service to the orders.

BAPTISMAL MANUMISSION AND *CARTAS DE LIBERTAD*

A deeper analysis of childhood manumission patterns demands a multilayered accounting. In my analysis I draw on a patchwork of *cartas de libertad*, *censuras*, wills and testaments, and third-party purchase transactions. Of the 148

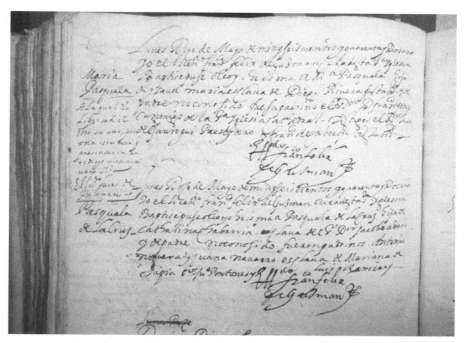

FIGURE 4.3. Partida entry, Libro de bautismos, María Pascuala, 1642. The priest's comment in the left margin shows that María Pascuala's owner had granted her a notarized carta de libertad, and mentions the name of the notary.

baptismal entries that I examined, 58 entries had associated *cartas de libertad* in the notarial records (*protocolos*). In addition, twelve of the baptismal entries were sufficiently detailed about the circumstances accompanying the child's manumission to qualify as a *carta de libertad*. (see Figure 4.4). Other entries included annotations and references to *cartas de libertad* in the margins of the registries, indicating an intention to free a child during the course of the owner's life or perhaps alerting the priest that a full inventory of documents conferring freedom either existed elsewhere in a notary's records. (see Figure 4.3).

The simultaneous existence of multiple manumission records in Lima seems distinct from patterns described by slavery scholars in Brazil, where, as Douglas Libby and Alecanstro Graça Filho note, "a child *alforriada na pia* almost never bothered to obtain notarized manumission papers later in life for the simple reason that, according to the long-standing tradition, his or her baptismal register was virtually equivalent to a *carta de alforria*. As one cleric put it, 'this same register will serve as a *carta de liberdade*.' "[46] In two *censuras* from 1686, Bernandina Chaparro and Juana de Sacramento alleged their baptismal registers as proof of their manumission, but it was not the exclusive basis for the appeals.

TABLE 4.1. *Baptismal Books for* Negros, Mulatos, *and* Indios, *El Sagrario,* *1640–99*

Status at baptismal font	
Slave children of known parents	3,196
Free children of free/d parents	114
Slave children of mixed-status parents	110
Slave children with unknown fathers	5,058
Adult slaves	3,582
Children freed at font	36
Abandoned children of unknown parents (*niños expósitos*)	496
Total baptisms	12,592

TABLE 4.2. Libros de españoles, *1640–99*

Slave children freed at font	112
Cartas de libertad	58

TABLE 4.3. *Children Freed at the Font: Baptismal Registers and* Cartas de libertad, *1640–99*

Terms of manumission	Male owner	Female owner
Gratis	16	19
"Love of a child"	9	22
Money received from relative/godparent	3	18
Freed after owner's death	5	5
Child freed, mother remained enslaved	13	19
Child freed and donated for religious service	2	0

In his extensive study of slave manumissions in colonial Bahia, Stuart Schwartz examines 1,160 *cartas de alforria* issued between 1684 and 1745.[47] While not focused exclusively on slave children, Schwartz analyzes the patterns of age, gender, and ethnicity emerging from the records. Over half of the *cartas de alforria* were issued for children under thirteen years of age (54 percent). Schwartz concludes that paternity was not the underlying motivation for the children's emancipation, despite language within the *cartas* that invoked affect or sentiment. He factors in the low purchase price for children – an effect of their high mortality rates – as a reason behind their frequent manumission. Schwartz writes, "This economic consideration, when added to feelings of affection towards children, probably motivated slave owners to manumit slaves at an early age."[48]

We draw similar inferences from Lima's baptismal records. The *cartas* allege affective feelings for either the child or mother, but at the same time the owner received money from a relative for the child's freedom. Thirty-five owners freed the children of their slaves without monetary benefit. However, all but one of these owners retained the services of the mothers.[49] On the basis of the 148 baptismal registers alone, 101 children were freed by female owners. Male owners freed the remaining forty-seven children. Male owners who freed children included prominent members of Lima's aristocracy: Viceroy Conde de Lemos, canonist Sebastián de Loyola, *oidor* don Juan de Padilla, and cantor Joan de Sivico.[50]

Enslaved mothers mobilized preexisting relationships to encourage their owners to grant baptismal manumission through purchase with monies provided by the child's relative or godparent who was in a financial position to pay for the child's freedom. The widow doña Maríana de la Serna freed her slave's son in exchange for monies paid by his godparents.[51] Another owner, doña Ana de Rivera, returned to the parish to inscribe the child in the baptismal registers of free births, although the day before the child had been christened as a slave. Doña Ana insisted that the priest correct the inscription, as it was her will and

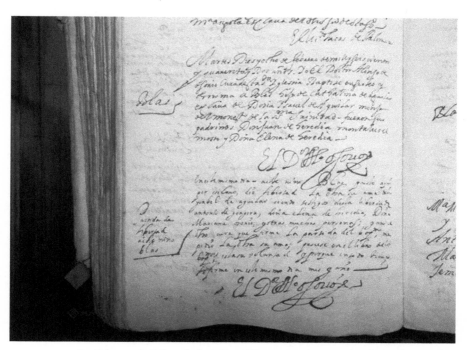

FIGURE 4.4. Partida entry, *Libro de bautizos, Negros, mulatos and indios*, El niño Blas, February 18, 1642.

intention to free the child of her slave.[52] Two female owners freed children of their slaves on consecutive occasions, although they explicitly stated their intention to retain the services of the mothers. Gracia Gamarra (alternately described as *negra libre* and *morena libre*) freed two of her slave's children in 1660 and 1663.[53] Another owner, the professed nun doña Isabel del Aguilar, followed suit in 1640 and 1648 – freeing children borne by two different slave mothers in her possession.[54]

Six owners (male and female) used the baptismal occasion to announce delayed manumission. In an entry suggesting similar circumstances to María Albina's, don Blas de Aguilar gifted a child whom he freed at the font to his novitiate ward ("la donó a su entenada").[55] More strikingly, three baptismal manumissions were corroborated by notarial documents decades after the date of baptism.[56] These corrections in status were made in the margins of the baptismal books in the year that freedom was finally granted. These manumissions no doubt coincided with an owner's demise or with the fulfillment of a contingency that had to be fulfilled in order for full emancipation to be granted.

These cases strengthen the presumption that reasons besides paternal sentiment accounted for baptismal manumission. What resonates throughout these records is more appropriately characterized as "maternalism," expressed through a broad range of colonial child-rearing patterns.[57] In addition to child donation for religious service, these practices included surrogacy, apprenticeship, exchange (*trueque*), and child circulation, practices premised on patronage and the culturally appropriate devolution of child-rearing responsibilities to social superiors. Undoubtedly, these cases are numerically insignificant when compared with the baptisms of slave children of unknown fathers. I suggest however, that the performance of baptism as a public ritual and its weight and solemnity in baroque Catholicism, together with the collective knowledge of a child's parentage, created broad (and at times extensive) social networks for children in mixed-status families. Those networks and their collective knowledge could be mobilized later to substantiate a claim to freedom (as in María Albina's case) or to attest to an owner's privately held convictions and intentions to free a child.

PROVING CHILDHOOD EMANCIPATION AND BAPTISMAL MANUMISSION THROUGH *CENSURAS*

In 1672, Catalina Conde, a *mulata* slave, asked the ecclesiastical court to issue *censuras*, summoning any witnesses who possessed knowledge of or evidence relating to her paternity.[58] Fourteen witnesses, many of whom lived outside of Lima, heard the *censuras* read at mass and responded to her request for evidence. At issue was whether Catalina could prove that she was the illegitimate daughter of the deceased don Alonso Conde de Salazar and whether don Alonso's publicly acknowledged wish to free her carried enough evidentiary weight to secure her liberty. Catalina petitioned the court to issue *censuras* attesting to her paternity to strengthen her case against don Alonso's widow, who refused to honor his promise of testamentary manumission.

Catalina was the product of an illicit relationship between the deceased Alonso and his slave, María Bran. As the story unfolded, each witness was able to fill in parts of the relationship that took place prior to Alonso's marriage to his legitimate wife, largely in the Chancay Valley outside of Lima. All the witnesses – not all of whom seemed to know each other – independently corroborated Alonso's lifelong desire to emancipate *la mulatilla* Catalina. Catalina was able to provide evidence regarding her father's reiterated desire to free her despite the absence of a *carta de libertad*.

In his last will and testament, dated 1662, don Alonso stated explicitly that he freed Catalina (who was at that point fourteen years old) along with her suckling child ("su crío de pecho"). Don Alonso later stipulated in a codicil to the will that Catalina was to serve his widow doña Violeta and their children for eight years after his death, after which time she would be free. Ten years after don Alonso's death, doña Violeta refused to free Catalina. Witnesses attested to strong words and insults between the two women and a lifelong hatred that doña Violeta harbored toward Catalina. Don Alonso's sister chided his bereaved widow for failing to honor her brother's wishes. Yet the pressure was not enough to sway Alonso's widow to grant Catalina her freedom. The knowledge of Catalina's paternity had to be made public by multiple people who knew about the affair in Alonso's feckless youth when he was much less prosperous and faraway from Lima's prying eyes.

One of the male witnesses was Alonso Conde's son, who identified himself as a forty-year old Spaniard and resident of Chancay. This son was also illegitimate, although neither his paternity nor inheritance was at stake. According to the son, Alonso confessed to his relationship with María and his desire to free María and their children to a visiting priest. Apparently, Alonso had fallen gravely ill as a young man during his time in Chancay and thinking he might die and desiring to depart this world with a clear conscience, he confessed his sin. Other witnesses remembered that during an ecclesiastical inspection of the parish of Chancay in 1646, Alonso was indicted by the *visitador* Pedro de Villagómez for his concubinary relationship with María.[59]

Many of the cases that depend on childhood grants of freedom or paternal recognition revolved around people's memory of events and required the petitioner to "sculpt[] the raw material of memory into a convincing case."[60] Although we have spent considerable time discussing *censuras* as a means of summoning witnesses, we need to look more closely at what witnesses said when they came to relieve their consciences.

It is useful at this point to draw together some common themes and observations about the circulation and crafting of testimonies in the life of a lawsuit. Three general themes converge in the sociolegal and historical scholarship about witnessing: the way knowledge is publicly circulated, the gendered nature of talk, and the importance of the character (*fama*) of those who bore witness.[61]

As historians we rely heavily on witness testimony to reconstruct social worlds, reaffirm shared memories of events, and to chart the multiple and criss-crossing paths to the events that precede a lawsuit. What we rely on is gossip. Yet as Chris Wickham reminds us, "Gossip has a bad press. There is a strong tendency to say that people should not gossip, and that the act of gossiping is idle and trivial."[62] Gossip is denigrated as women's talk – the work of idle wagging tongues, and a sin against God.

According to the laws of evidence, people who had direct knowledge of an act such as notaries or those called to witness a document had unassailable proof.[63] Direct or full proof was preferred in court, but public and notorious knowledge was nearly as acceptable.[64] Notaries and priests were eyewitnesses to private acts and were often called to testify, but most witnesses trafficked in community knowledge. Knowledge that was public and notorious had to be distinguished from gossip: what someone heard or what people whispered about. Donald Ramos usefully describes the role of gossip (*murmuracão*) in the evidence-gathering process as one that traversed horizontal and vertical communities. Gossip moved knowledge that was known by a few people linked by horizontal social bonds into the public zone of admissible evidence. As Ramos writes, "It was sufficient for witnesses to report community knowledge through expressions such as "I know because it is widely known" or "I heard it said that it happened." These witnesses were perfectly acceptable since they reflected the community's awareness of the transgression."[65]

We have thus two approaches to witness testimony. On the first, witnesses were called on to corroborate the version of the story that the petitioner told. On the second, witnesses confirmed that the alleged acts occurred because they were public knowledge or that the acts could be construed as meaning something about which there was public agreement. Our cases are rife with both versions.

On one hand, witnesses – whether summoned through *censuras* or responding to the petitioner's request – corroborated the version of the story that the petitioner told. Nowhere in the hundreds of cases I researched for this book did a witness make a "surprise revelation." Remarkably, no witness statements in civil cases proved inconsistent – in contrast to the testimonies extorted under torture (*tormento*) in criminal trials during which suspects and witnesses changed their stories multiple times. This does not necessarily mean witnesses were schooled or told what to say. As I explain in Chapter 1, anyone called to witness for a lawsuit was expected to support the person on whose behalf they gave testimony. On the other hand, when people came to give their testimony, they reiterated and reinforced popularly held knowledge or supplied an interpretation of actions that corroborated the petitioner's story. Echoing Ramos's points in the case of Brazil, witnesses often confirmed that what they knew was "commonly held knowledge" ("público y notorio").

Don Alonso's relationship with Catalina's mother, María Bran, certainly occupied the sibilant zone of *murmuracão* and *susuros*. The immoral nature of Catalina's paternity had to be balanced with people's acceptance of it. The witnesses (both male and female) claimed that don Alonso's sister told his wife on many occasions that he meant to free her. Alonso's son testified that he had always treated Catalina "as his sister" ("como hermana suya"), because everyone told him that Catalina was don Alonso's child. This evidence, coupled with the terms of the testament, would be sufficient for the court to compel doña Violeta to grant Catalina and her son their liberty.

Whispered rumors or *susuros* were contrasted with what witnesses called *voz pública*. María Albina's case fell squarely in the zone of public knowledge, with no hint of scandal or *susuros*. People knew that María Albina was freed at the font, even though they never witnessed this act. They knew she came to Lima in the service of doña María de Lara and in the company of her parents because this was knowledge gleaned from those who knew her mother and her patron. Others in her neighborhood knew or inferred that María Albina was free because she lived her life according to the rhythms and practices of a free woman of color; she acted in ways that they equated with an emancipated person. None of these people were actual eyewitnesses to the baptism. Nor did anyone have visual proof that a *carta de libertad* existed. In order to be believed, the people who testified had to be credible and honorable themselves.[66] It was important to flood the case file with credible and honorable witnesses in order to prevail in one's case.

Many cases lacked both eyewitnesses and knowledge that was public and notorious. The only factor that moved Catalina's case into realm of publicly held knowledge with moral (if not legal) consequences was the spiteful disregard of a dead man's testamentary mandate to free his child. Other *censuras* publicized knowledge that never left the private realm of conscience. The lawsuits or *censuras* prompted a public recognition of private compacts – especially those that resulted from intimate negotiations of liberty.

Was there "women's" talk or, to put this question another way, did men and women talk about events differently? In certain contexts of course they did. Particularly in commercial disputes, inquisitorial proceedings, and concubinage accusations, men and women demonstrated different kinds of knowledge. Many men denied any knowledge of acts such as lovers' trysts or sexual couplings that they deemed beneath their dignity or interest. However, the cases that I describe in this book are at their core intimate.[67] It is difficult to pinpoint differences in what men knew and testified about as opposed to their female counterparts because the subject matter of these cases belonged to private or interior compacts. Even in domestic abuse cases described in Chapter 2, men bore witness to husbands who mistreated their wives.

Perhaps it is more useful to think about the ways that men and women expressed emotion. In the baptismal context, men and women expressed their sentiments toward the children being freed in very different ways. In three separate documents bestowing manumission by grace to children of his slaves, don Sancho de Castro declared the following:

> Let it be known by whoever sees this letter that I, General don Sancho de Castro, resident of this City of Kings, state that I have a *mulata* slave named Josepha de Castro, who has given birth to a daughter named Baltazara de los Reyes. In light of the faithful service of her mother and her many other efforts worthy of remuneration, and because I hold nothing but goodwill toward her, I have asked doctor Don Martín de los Reyes, attorney of the Real Audiencia to serve as her godfather. Let it be known that henceforth, it is of my own free will that I grant this letter of freedom to Baltazara, in recognition of her mother's services to my family, on this fourth day of her life. From this day forth, she is free from the subjection and captivity into which she was born.[68]

Although formulaic, the wording of these *cartas* carefully portrayed the owner's position and munificence. And of course, this public persona or masculine sense of honor could be exposed in court when the donor or the "Great Man" failed to live up to his word. Not surprisingly, we have a *censura* brought by Sebastiána Tellez against don Sancho de Castro's family, remonstrating the heirs for their failure to honor their patriarch's wishes to free her granddaughter.[69]

As we have seen repeatedly in the cases and *censuras* brought by adults who were freed as children, baptismal manumission was not coterminous with autonomy or emancipation. Legal action forced people to reconcile their private acts with the honor and beneficence attendant to their office and their public persona and the memory of their lineage. As in the case of Margarita Florindes against a powerful opponent like don Martín de Zavala, moving these private compacts, unscrupulous dealings, and changes of heart into the public sphere exposed an owner's undesirable traits: his callousness and caprice and, by extension, his untrustworthiness and diminished honor.

AMBIGUOUS PATRONS: "UNKNOWN" FATHERS AND BAPTISMAL MANUMISSION

Given our interest in mixed-status families, it behooves us to look more closely at those who were registered as freed children of enslaved parents in the baptismal books. In the marital context, the designation of mixed status meant a free person whose spouse was enslaved at the time of the nuptials.[70] In the baptismal record, the designation also encompassed the familial unit of children like María Albina who were freed at the font but born to enslaved parents. Mixed status generally signified exogamous couplings that produced illegitimate children born to slave mothers. However, it bears mentioning that not all mixed-status families followed the same pattern: María Albina's parents were both married and enslaved. A year's records for el Sagrario (1663) shows more clearly the variations in status and condition from the data consolidated in Table 4.1.

TABLE 4.4. Negros, Mulatos, *and* Indios, *El Sagrario Baptismal Register, 1663*

Slave children of enslaved parents	43
Enslaved children of unknown fathers	74
Adult slaves	74
Free children of free/d parents	1
Parents' condition unknown (*expósitos*)	1
Indian slave mother and unknown father	4
Mulata slave mother and unknown father	8
Quarterona slave mother and unknown father	2
Free black mother and unknown father	1
Slave father and free *zamba* mother	1
Free *parda* mother and unknown father	2
Free children of slave mothers	2
Total entries	213

According to Table 4.4, twenty entries could potentially qualify as unions producing mixed-status children. This raises a couple of questions. Did high rates of illegitimacy indicate paternal exogamy? Were unknown fathers free or freedmen? Extramarital unions between enslaved and free individuals may have been socially indiscreet, but they were neither fatal nor calamitous for purposes of filiation, especially among plebeians. Out-of-wedlock paternity did not diminish the reputational honor of plebeian men. Moral condemnation of extramarital unions was not strong enough to diminish high rates of illegitimate births.[71] Yet condemnation seemed to silence paternal expressions of affect or sentiment, whereas it did not among women.

Women's sentiments were no doubt amplified by their conformity with gendered maternalist norms. Indeed, the parameters of legal language loom large in the ecclesiastical context, validating certain affective expressions and effectively silencing others. As Barbara Rosenwein observes, "People lived in 'emotional communities,' they made evaluations about other's emotions, the nature of the affective bonds between people that they recognize, and the modes of emotional expression that they expect, encourage, tolerate and deplore."[72] Moreover, these emotional communities shaped expressions within the same society. Eating together at the same table, paying for a mattress and providing a suit of new clothes every year, or arranging for a sought-after apprenticeship with a master artisan could all be acts construed as tacit paternal recognition of an illegitimate child that later would carry evidentiary weight in court.

Rarely do we see a *carta de libertad* or a baptismal entry bestowing freedom from a male patron with the expression ""because of my love for her" ("por el amor que le tengo"), likely because these words were seen as unbefitting of masculinist sentiment. Two couples who freed children of their slaves at the font reiterated their love for the mothers and also alluded to payments received for the children from unnamed patrons who bore the children goodwill ("hacerle bien y buena obra").[73] The anonymous nature of these patrons raises the distinct possibility that they were sons or male family members of the manumitting couple whose identity remained unrecorded in the ledgers and notarial documents.

The statistically high percentage of unknown fathers presents unique difficulties when one seeks to assess paternity solely on the basis of baptismal records.[74] Since we can only reasonably surmise the reasons behind the records' ambiguity, let us confine our discussion to cases where the law demanded silence: that of priests who fathered children with their domestic slaves.[75]

Given the iniquitous nature of these relationships, we infer paternity through baptismal manumission or through subsequent bequests during a child's life. In some instances, ecclesiastical lawsuits provide felicitous sources of biographical information. Ecclesiastical courts exercised personal jurisdiction over priests, and their domestic slaves did not hesitate to publicize the peccadilloes of their masters in lawsuits forcing the issue of their children's emancipation. Three of the twelve masters in our baptismal sample were priests freeing the children borne by their enslaved mistresses. As discussed at the beginning of this book,

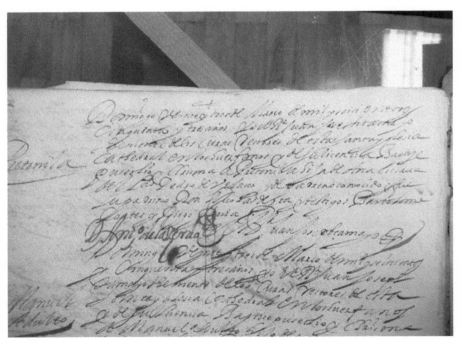

FIGURE 4.5. Partida entry, Petronila de Velasco, *Libro de Bautizos, Negros, mulatos e indios*, Huerfanos, March 23, 1653.

Pedro de Velasco freed both his children, Petronila and Juan Asunción, in 1653 and 1656, respectively. Were it not for Ana de Velasco's subsequent lawsuit in 1659 accusing her owner of defloration and inhumane treatment, we would have no evidence of her children's paternity.[76]

Other records are similarly circumspect. In 1672, the priest Nicolas Rodriguez freed the son of his slave, "saying it was his will that the child be free after his death" ("dijo que era su voluntad fuese libre ese niño después de sus días"). Attuned to these nuances (or euphemisms), we suspect that the third priest in the sample, Julian de Heredia, was similarly motivated by paternity. Julian simply stated that he freed the child María "because she was the daughter of his slave Felipa" ("por ser hija de una esclava suya llamada Felipa").

One baptismal grant of manumission had its provenance in a relationship that spanned three decades. On June 6, 1632, Provisor Feliciano de Vega indicted Sebastián de Loyola for public and notorious concubinage with a *mulata* slave. At that time, Loyola was a priest who had been denounced by witnesses in the parish for arranging nocturnal trysts with an enslaved woman who remained nameless because she was married.[77] One night, a church sheriff (*alguacil ecclesiástico*) followed Loyola to his mistress's house and waited for him until he left at dawn. The *alguacil* confirmed that he caught Loyola in flagrante delicto with "the married woman." Confronted with this evidence, Provisor Vega censured Loyola and fined him 20 pesos. Vega warned Loyola to keep away from his mistress and threatened Loyola with two years of exile if he did not follow orders. However, that was not the full extent of Loyola's crime. He was also censured for orchestrating the disappearance of the witness proofs and papers in his case. Though he paid the modest pecuniary fine, Loyola refuted the charges of concubinage and denied any involvement with the mysterious disappearance of the written evidence.

Loyola clearly did not break off his relationship. In our sample of sacramental ledgers in 1656, we see that don Sebastián de Loyola freed a child born to Joana de Loyola, his slave, at the baptismal font.[78] By 1656, Loyola had been promoted to prebendary (*canónigo*) of the Archbishopric, which was one of the endowed positions within the Archbishopric.[79] That Loyola was able to pass the interviews regarding his moral fitness given the salacious accusation against him (and the "disappeared" proceedings) two decades earlier strains credulity.

In 1659, three years after freeing Joana's child, Loyola died.[80] While Loyola's assets were being crated for shipment to Spain, many valuable items were reported stolen by the trustees of his estate. The trustees asked for *censuras* to be read to aid in the recovery of Loyola's property. Among the first witnesses to be interviewed was Joana de Loyola, the housekeeper (*ama de llaves*) of the late Sebastián. Joana was never accused of theft – rather it was Loyola's *sacristan* who was ultimately indicted for stealing the missing items. However, the investigator interviewed two men in their mid-twenties who Loyola freed upon his death: Luis and Pascual. The investigator also interviewed Guillermina de

Loyola, a chatty young witness who identified both men as her brothers and the sons of Joana de Loyola, all of whom were freed by the late Sebastián de Loyola.

BAPTISM AND SOCIAL NETWORKS OF ENSLAVED FAMILIES

Sábado, primero de enero del año mil seis cientos, yo el Bachiller Juan de la Roca, cura desta santa iglesia catedral en ella puse olio y crisma a Jacinta hija legitima de Leonardo Mandinga y de María Mandinga, esclavos de Esteban Pérez a la cual bautizó luego que nació la comadre Ana de Santiago por estar en gran peligro. Fueron sus padrinos Antón Biafara, esclavo de Rodrigo de Castresana, y Juana Biafara, esclava de Álvaro de Álvarez.[81]

On Saturday January first, 1600, I, Juan de la Roca, priest of this holy Cathedral anointed Jacinta with oil and chrism. Jacinta is the legitimate daughter of Leonardo Mandinga and Maria Mandinga, both slaves of Esteban Perez. Because of the precarious state of her life and health, Ana de Santiago, Jacinta's godmother baptized her at birth. Her godparents are Anton Biafara, slave of Rodrigo Castresana and Juana Biafara, slave of Alvaro de Alvarez.

Baptismal records have long served as fruitful historical sources for reconstructing family relationships and social networks among enslaved subjects. Slave baptismal registers recorded the age of the child (or adult), parentage that was publicly acknowledged, ethnic and racial designations of the child and her parent/s, previous or in extremis baptism, names of the godparents, their consent and eligibility to serve as spiritual parents, and the presence of witnesses. Baptism created ties of spiritual kinship between families and godparents (*compadragzco* or *compadrío*) that carried defined legal consequences and material obligations.[82]

The wealth of biographical and demographic data offered by baptismal records have made them invaluable to colonial historians of gender, diaspora, illegitimacy, and kinship.[83] In the case of illegitimate slave births, clerics recorded what they were told about the child's parentage, leaving the condition of the father unknown so as not to foreclose subsequent legitimation.[84] (see Figure 4.5). If a child was freed prior to arriving at the font, that decision was noted in the registers – even though the child's baptism was entered into the books for slaves, *mulatos,* and Indian births.[85] Baptisms for adult slaves were comparatively short entries, indicating truncated social networks given the brevity of the slave's presence in Lima.[86] An adult slave's baptismal register often served as evidence of the first catechism.[87]

In our baptismal sample, many entries allegedly granted gratis manumission, as if the sanctity of the baptismal occasion would have been besmirched by the exchange of money. However, these were not gratis manumissions. We see evidence of payment and conditions attached to a child's baptismal manumission when we match the *cartas de libertad* to the baptismal registers. Payment ranged from 50 pesos to 150 pesos, although there were two cases that report relatives paying 200 pesos.[88] Eight entries memorialized an agreement on a purchase price with eventual freedom. Others simply stated that the mother remained in the owner's service although the child was freed.

As frequently noted, slave owners' language in all the written instruments overwhelmingly reflected a sense of benevolence, goodwill, and Catholic piety, even when they received payment in full for their slaves' purchase. Manumission instruments characteristically included phrases such as "because of the love and goodwill I have for him" ("*por el amor y voluntad que le tengo*") and most commonly "to serve our Lord" ("*por servicio de Dios nuestro Señor*"). The *cartas* depict a relationship in which the path from purchase and acquisition at birth to liberty was intricately bound up with an owner's patronage and largesse. Rather than a quid pro quo for payment and services rendered, manumission was legally couched in terms of the reward for faithful service and compliance with the laws of God and nature. Even the laws of slavery demanded obligation and reverence in return for emancipation. According to the *Siete Partidas*, "because liberty is one of the most honorable and precious things of this world, those who receive it are obliged to love, obey and honor their masters who emancipate them."[89] As Robin Blackburn observes, "Like other gifts, it left the recipient of freedom deeply beholden. The servile relationship was transmuted into that of patron to client. The exercise of the power of manumission could confirm the legitimacy and benevolence of master and sovereign power."[90]

The high percentage of gratis baptismal manumission may coincide with the child's lower purchase price, as Schwartz speculated in the Bahian case. Baptismal records, as I have noted, indicate manumission bestowed by grace more frequently than the testamentary records. The lack of contingencies in the baptismal context plausibly supports the thesis that baptismal manumission was easier to revoke than manumission by testament or that freedom at the font was regarded as a "deposit" on eventual freedom in the arc of an enslaved person's life. Baptismal manumission seems to be qualitatively different than testamentary manumission because of the stage of life in which these emancipatory acts took place.

Arguably, the comparison of baptismal and testamentary manumission is inapposite given the structural conditions of dependence (age, condition, status) accompanying childhood. A child had to remain within close range of the parish in which she or he was manumitted to rely on the baptismal grant of emancipation. Birth and baptism were not simultaneous: in extremis baptism often predated the formal ceremony and entry into the baptismal books by months if not years.[91] Parents, godparents, patrons, and owners had to record the child's manumission by grace or by purchase. Drafting and formalizing the *carta de libertad* implied advance planning and coordination before the baptism. These were circumstances out of a child's control. Without a formal document, baptismal emancipation by virtue of the owner's wishes had to be very public for parol evidence to count.[92] In María Albina's case, the witnesses stated that everyone knew María had been freed at the baptismal font because it was her godfather's explicit desire and a condition of his accepting the responsibility of godparenthood. But the witnesses refrained from complaining about the donation, citing it as a benefit for María. Freedom granted at a young age was something relatively easy to lose – contingent on an owner's beneficence or an emancipator's presence.

Papers were also easy to lose. In María Albina's case, the family had not been careful with the records as it moved from Piura to Lima. Indeed, the absence of documentation in this case is surprising, especially given the significance of notarial records in the lives of enslaved people in the lettered city. Even though geographical relocation ostensibly explained the absence of baptismal records, both María Albina and don Diego should have been more diligent about securing a copy of the subsequent manumission instrument – if indeed one existed. Don Diego's repetitive – or perhaps cumulative – indications of intent to free María Albina suggest that childhood liberty and deathbed emancipation were steps in an arc toward freedom for children born to enslaved parents. It was uncertain whether María Albina knew that she was free while inside the Santísima Trinidad. Notwithstanding her legal status, María Albina was unequivocally bound to don Diego. As we recall, don Diego conducted the marriage negotiations with Juan Antonio, acting in loco parentis while she was under his tutelage.

Similar bonds of patronage between former owners and slaves appear in other cases within our sample. One of the owners from our sample who manumitted her son's slave in 1649, Angela de los Ríos, also appeared as a protector of that child's aunt Augustina in the divorce proceeding I discuss in Chapter 2. Dependency and inequality framed – if not permeated – the social interactions between former owners and freed persons. Drawing on natural law's premise of obligation and "reverence," owners demonstrated a continued sense of entitlement to their slave's services and loyalties even when payment of the slave's purchase price formally terminated their relationship. In a stratified society, it behooved former slaves to count on the protection and patronage of social superiors in case they were needed in times of inevitable financial, physical, or conjugal stress. And owners derived the lifelong benefit – indeed, the entitlement – of access to the intimate labor of their former slaves under the powerful premise that enduring ties of loyalty and affection enveloped all members into one family.

CONCLUSION

I have used the extant sources here to understand how children experienced slavery and liberty in baroque Lima. These cases highlight the ways in which the dynamics of domestic servitude simultaneously encompassed obedience, violence, and protection.[93] María Albina's case allows us to focus on the status of quasi emancipation for one category of legal dependents in urban slaveholding societies. As many scholars of female religious communities have shown, convents were also collective domestic spaces. In this vein, I have characterized the *celda* as a type of slave-owning household: a space comprised of dense social networks that reflected the city's secular hierarchies of age, status, generation, caste, and *calidad*.

However, the question inevitably remains whether María Albina's case is generalizable or just rich. How can we use rich cases and extrapolate from those to draw larger conclusions?[94] I have suggested that María Albina's case demonstrates the weak staying power of baptismal manumission vis-à-vis self-purchase and have also posited that it was less robust than testamentary manumission. Despite the different life stages at which the grants of liberty occurred, it is clear that affective, lengthy household relationships were key components of the manumission process. While historians are productively engaged in debates surrounding the gendered and generational forms of domestic and intimate work qua labor, cases like María Albina's illuminate the conundrum of legal freedom and continued bondage within the interior of the slave-owning household.[95] Baptismal manumission simultaneously invoked an owner's paternalist sentiment and his or her material interests in retaining the labor of both mother and child that was germane to domestic slavery.

Only one owner – in all the cases described here – simultaneously freed a mother and child at the font. Fractional freedoms loom large in this domestic tableau and in the context of religious enclosure more broadly. As the baptismal records indicate, manumitting children while keeping their mothers enslaved in domestic servitude rendered mothers more dependent and tethered to their owners by powerful bonds of loyalty and compliance.[96] These were uniquely gendered arrangements, accessible to men, women, and children in different ways. Fathers no doubt paid for their children's freedom when they could, and slave-owning fathers freed their children through proxies and without legal fanfare. However, from the extant records, the primary role on the baptismal stage belongs to women as principal and supporting actors.[97]

Proponents of both life-course analysis and cultural history have influenced my reading of childhood manumission cases. By definition, manumission is a unilateral legal process: agency is only expected of the one doing the manumitting. Great Men like don General Sancho de Castro would declare with pomp and formality to their notary that "it is of my own free will that I grant this letter of freedom," but this was the public face of manumission. It tells us nothing about the relationships that preceded the act or the hard-earned payments that went toward a child's freedom. In a society in which liberty was highly prized and in a legal framework in which the condition of enslavement was regarded as against nature and against God, manumission was a heavily charged process. We see litigants summoning up every shred of evidence of affect that they could muster to prevail in their claims.

Manumission is larger than slavery – I do not accept Orlando Patterson's contention that manumission does slavery's ideological dirty work.[98] Patterson suggests that the dialectic between manumission and slavery rendered manumission "central to the invention and social construction of the most important secular value in Western civilization, namely, freedom."⁹⁹ Yet on closer look here, and in the following chapter, I conclude that manumission had its own dynamics and transactional realities that all accepted – whether owner or owned – and to which they conformed their lives. The laws of manumission both accommodated and maintained multiple degrees of slavery and freedom. Manumission was not a frozen institution: its dynamics and transactional realities created ripples of activity, of movement, even of opportunity. Ultimately, manumission incorporated degrees of freedom and bondage that allowed María Albina a life – on the margins of bondage – but outside them.

NOTES

1   AGN, *Real Audiencia*, Causas civiles, exp. judiciales, leg. 32, cuad. 692, año 1683.
2   This caveat may have been originally inserted to get around the rules that prohibited novitiates from owning property given their vows of poverty. See Burns, *Colonial Habits,* ch. 2. The rules for propertied laywomen (*seglares*) entering into convents were less clear – doña María remained a *seglar* in la Santísima Trinidad until her death.
3   On the hierarchy of servants within the cloisters, see Nancy van Deusen, "The Lord Walks among the Pots and Pans."
4   "Que se criase con temor, recogimiento y buena enseñanza."
5   "Testigo, Hermana Isabel de Acosta, beata: D. Diego Camano a esta ciudad trajo en su servicio a la dicha Catalina, madre de la dicha María Albina, y le oyó decir la dicha Catalina muchas veces por la comunicación que esta testigo tenía con ella respecto de haber sido antes esclava en la casa donde esta testigo se crió, lamentándose de que el dicho su amo hubiese hecho donación de la dicha su hija a doña María Lara siendo libre desde la pila, pero se consolaba con decir que allí se criaba en recogimiento y en virtud y en compañía de la dicha doña María de Lara que era una señora virtuosa, la cual por último la declararía libre."
6   See Dawson, "The Cultural Geography of Enslaved Ship Pilots," for a ship pilot's earning potential.
7   Juan Antonio brought another suit in 1686 against the *albaçea* of don Diego Camano's estate for personal services in which he added on the years that María Albina served don Diego after she returned to his household. Don Diego passed away in 1684.
8   In one of the proceedings, doña María de Lara Figueroa protested Juan Antonio's "giving María Albina ideas about her freedom and seeking to despoil her of her property." See AGN, *Real Audiencia*, Causas civiles, exp. judiciales, leg. 243 cuad. 912, año 1683 ("Autos seguidos por doña María de Lara y Figueroa contra doña Juana de Luza, viuda del capitán don Antonio Caro de Rodríguez sobre la posesión de una esclava"). In that proceeding, doña María attributed María Albina's legal challenges to the pernicious influence of don Antonio Caro's aunt, doña Juana de Luza, who tried to assert ownership over María on the basis of don Antonio's earlier payment for María as a child. But as we know, this was don Antonio's payment to *free* María, not to purchase her. Indeed, the record includes a complaint

lodged by don Antonio's aunt against doña María de Lara as the *albaçea* of Caro's estate. Given these multiple claims to María that ensued early in the couple's marriage, Juan Antonio's 1683 lawsuit could have been a preemptive one to stay future claims to the children he might have with María Albina.

9 A reliance argument is a legal ground in tort or contract law to enforce a promise if the plaintiff relied on the defendant's promise to his or her detriment. See *Black's Law Dictionary*, 671.

10 Burns, *Las Siete Partidas*, 4, title 12, law 7, 983. As with much of the *Partidas*, this title combines arguments that take both equity and law into account. Alfonso clearly contemplates the reasonable time that a property claim may be brought, and balances this with the inequity of permitting that claim to be enforced.

11 O'Toole, "Manumitted but Not Free."

12 For Mexico City, see, Proctor "Gender and the Manumission of Slaves in New Spain." For Lima, see Jouve Martín, "Death, Gender, and Writing." For an early study on Bahia, see Schwartz, "The Manumission of Slaves in Colonial Brazil."

13 For a thorough examination of the relationships between enslaved women and free masters in Minas Gerais, see Higgins, *"Licentious Liberty" in a Brazilian Gold-Mining Region*. See also Schwartz, "The Manumission of Slaves in Colonial Brazil," Nishida, "Manumission and Ethnicity in Urban Slavery," and Scully and Paton, *Gender and Emancipation in the Atlantic World*.

14 The most studied cases are those reenslavement suits emerging in the aftermath of the Haitian Revolution. See Scott, "Paper Thin," Jones, "Time, Space, and Jurisdiction in Atlantic World Slavery," and Nessler, "They Always Knew Her to Be Free.'"

15 Conversely, travel onto free soil could lead to liberty. See *Somerset v. Stewart*, Kings Bench, June 22, 1772, for the iconic case conferring freedom by embracing the free soil principle. See also Peabody and Grinberg, "Free Soil," Peabody, *There Are No Slaves in France*, and Wong, *Neither Fugitive Nor Free*.

16 Mitchell, *Raising Freedom's Child*; Jones, "Ties That Bind, Bonds That Break"; Fields, *Slavery and Freedom on the Middle Ground"*; and Brewer, *By Birth or Consent*.

17 Gradual emancipation was a popular political choice in the aftermath of Latin American republican wars, representing a return to conservative practices after reneging on the promise of freedom that led blacks and *pardos* to reject regalist forces in the revolutionary wars. See Blanchard, *Under the Flags of Freedom*. Another gradualist emancipation policy was the free womb law enacted in the new republics throughout the nineteenth century. See Abreu, "Slave Mothers and Freed Children," and Cowling, *Conceiving Freedom*. Although arguably many of the individual arrangements between slaves and owners that pivoted around delayed manumission were informed by the spirit of gradual emancipation, it was not a stated policy within the baroque colonies.

18 Johnson, "Resetting the Legal History of Slavery."

19 Fields, *Slavery and Freedom on the Middle Ground*, 35.

20 On Freyre's influence in the field of family history, see Milanich, "Whither Family History?"

21 Today, children are legitimate subjects of historical inquiry in the Americas. See Gonzalez and Premo, *Raising an Empire*, and Hecht, *Minor Omissions*. Though

not with specific regard to slave children, Nara Milanich depicts the embedded labor relationships of child-rearing and servitude through what she calls "tutelary servitude" in nineteenth-century Chile. See, Milanich, "Degrees of Bondage."

22 See Nessler, "They Always Knew Her to Be Free,'" 91.

23 van Deusen, *Between the Sacred and the Worldly*, 155.

24 Bromley and Barbagelata, *Evolución urbana de Lima*, 10–43.

25 Witnesses identified their place of residence not by an address, but by asserting their home's proximity to religious landmarks: "Que dijo vivir por las espaldas del Convento de Santa Clara or junto a las Recolectas de Santo Domingo."

26 As Cristina Ratto observes, "sobresale la extensa superficie que ocuparon los conventos de clausura … *Llegaron a invadir alrededor de un quinto de la superficie de Lima*" ("La ciudad dentro de la gran ciudad," 76, my emphasis).

27 Escobar Gamboa, *Padrón de los Indios de Lima en 1613*. Although colonial enumeration was misleading in certain respects, retrospective studies conclude that the census data reliably document Lima's religious population. See Pérez Cantó, *Lima en el siglo XVIII*, ch. 3.

28 See Ratto, "La ciudad dentro la gran ciudad," 83–88.

29 In chapter 2 of *Colonial Habits*, Kathryn Burns extensively studies this pattern of secular subsidies in Cuzco's monasteries to establish what she terms the "spiritual economy."

30 van Deusen, *Between the Sacred and the Worldly*, 174.

31 The records for Las Descalzas, a medium-sized monastery, document the self-petitions (*autos de ingreso*) of ten freedwomen of color to become *donadas* from 1600 to 1699. Although the records do not stipulate the petitioner's path in each case, we presume that the women began as *criadas* and then climbed the cloister's hierarchy. For example, in 1684, the free *parda* Nicolasa María de la Cruz self-petitioned to be accepted as a *donada*, "porque se crió en el Monasterio" (AAL, Monasterio de las Descalzas, leg. 6, exp. 32, año 1684).

32 As van Deusen explains, "Well aware of their place in the social hierarchy, … those women and children raised in convents and destined to serve others defined themselves or were described by their owners as *recogida* and honorable" (*Between the Sacred and the Worldly*, 136). Divorce records also show that lower-status women took refuge in monasteries, especially those institutions that provided protection for widows and divorcees.

33 María Albina's trajectory is more consistent with the status of a *criada*, although all witnesses referred to her as a *donada* in remarking on her rectitude and Christian habits in their testimonies – a distinction of which people of the time would have been very much aware. But it is clear that Maria Albina was a donated servant, not one who was in religious service.

34 We should remember that religious orders were among the largest slave owners in Peru, relying in part on the imperative to indoctrinate newly arrived African slaves (*bozales*). See Macera, *Instrucciones para el manejo de las haciendas Jesuitas del Perú*.

35 See van Deusen, *Between the Sacred and the Worldly*, 71–78.

36 "La Abadesa de la Encarnación pidió al Cabildo que no diesen licencia para que entrasen en el convento más negras o mulatas. Decía en su memorial que ya había 66 de las primeras y 48 de las segundas, de las que solamente son del convento 7

negras, las dos horras y cinco esclavas. Agregaba que son muchos los inconven-
ientes que se seguían de esto y muchos los gastos que le ocasionaban al convento"
(Córdoba y Salinas, *Teatro de la Santa Iglesia Metropolitana*, 155).

37 Nowhere was the church's protective force field more pronounced than in the context of ecclesiastical immunity, which granted sanctuary to those fugitives fleeing
criminal prosecution once they arrived on hallowed ground. For slaves seeking
sanctuary in colonial Lima, see McKinley, "Standing on Shaky Ground."

38 See, for example, AAL, Causas de negros, leg. 5, exp. 4, año 1624 ("Autos que sigue
Pedro de Ávila, de casta mina, que se notifique a doña Ana Rivadaneyra, religiosa
de velo negro del Monasterio de la Santísima Trinidad, para que venda a su esclava
María o la saque del Monasterio para que pueda hacer vida maridable con él, su
marido").

39 See, for example, AAL, Causas de negros, leg. 6, exp. 2, año 1630 ("Autos que sigue
doña Bernarda de Valenzuela contra su hermana Juana de Valenzuela, monja secular del Monasterio de la Encarnación sobre que le restituya la mulatilla llamada
Jerónima que se la sustrajo y la tiene dentro de la cláusula").

40 Burns, *Colonial Habits*, 14.

41 "Autos que sigue el promotor fiscal celador de los monasterios sobre que las religi-
osas no tengan en sus celdas negras criando sus hijos ni ningún niño sea esclava o
libre de cualquier raza o casta" (AAL, Monasterio de las Descalzas, leg.8, exp. 13,
año 1695).

42 Van Deusen also links the fate of the *donada* to the power of her patroness within
the cloisters ("The Lord Walks among the Pots and Pans," 152).

43 For a representative *carta de libertad* demonstrating multigenerational relationships, see the declaration made by doña Antonia de la Asunción in 1690: "Sepan
cuanto esta carta vieren, yo doña Antonia de la Asunción, monja del Monasterio
de las Descalzas ... tengo por mi esclavo a un cuarteroncito nombrado Joseph
Pascual que es de edad de quince días, *nieto de una mulatilla mi esclava* nombrada
Damiana, y por el buen servicio que me han hecho las dichas Damiana *y la dicha
su hija* Gregoria *madre del dicho cuarteroncito* y por el mucho amor y voluntad
que le tengo al susodicho y hacerle bien y buena obra ... por el tenor de la presente
otorgo, ahorro y liberto de la esclavitud y cautiverio... para que desde hoy en
adelante sea libre y horro" (AGN, Joseph de Figueroa Dávila, Protocolo no. 574,
año 1690, ff. 133-133v, my emphasis).

44 AAL, Monasterio de la Encarnación, leg. 16, exp. 16, año 1697 ("Alonso de Arcos
en nombre de Juana Godínez en la mejor forma que proceda del derecho, parezco
ante Vmd y digo que como consta del instrumento que presento, la doña Beatriz
Godínez de Luna, siendo abadesa del monasterio de la Encarnación desta ciudad
y a mi parte le dio libertad para después de los días de su vida con cargo y calidad
de que no salga de la dicha clausura porque en ella quiso se portarse como libre y
si quisiere salir de la dicha clausura se a dado cuatrocientos pesos de a ocho reales
sin que pueda ser vendida en mas cantidad según lo referido").

45 "Carta de libertad, doña Ana Delgado, religiosa profesa de velo negro en el convento de la Purísima Concepción y doña Mariana de Arcarrus, seglar en él, a
Gregoria Delgado. *Que mientras viviese yo la dicha otorgante haya de estar en
mi compañía y no haya de poder huir a otra parte ni salir de la clausura del dicho
monasterio teniendo edad para ello porque haciendo lo contrario se a de entender*

por ningún valor ni efecto esta carta de libertad" (AGN, Joseph de Figueroa Dávila, Protocolo no. 570, año 1687, ff. 362-64v).

46 Libby and de Alecanstro Graça Filho, "Notarized and Baptismal Manumissions." See also Libby and Andrade Paiva, "Manumission Practices in a Late Eighteenth-Century Brazilian Slave Parish." Libby and Paiva note in their review of the São José records that 90 percent of manumissions were for Africans over forty years of age.

47 Schwartz, "The Manumission of Slaves in Colonial Brazil," 615.

48 Ibid., 616.

49 Don Juan Gabriel de Irazábal y Flores freed his slave's son in 1688 and accepted 600 pesos for her freedom later that year. Both the son and mother's freedom were paid by the child's godfather. See AGN, Mateo España, Protocolo no. 431, año 1688, ff. 90–90v and ff. 869v–70v.

50 For children freed by Viceroy Conde de Lemos, see AAL, Libros de bautizos de esclavos, años 1663–65, 3/4/1672; for Cantor Juan de Sivico see ibid., años 1658–65, 15/2/1662; for Canónigo Sebastián de Loyola, see ibid., años 1650–58, 2/11/1656; for *oidor* don Juan de Padilla, see AAL, Libros de bautizos de españoles, 6/04/1670 and 8/07/1674.

51 AAL, Libros de bautizos de esclavos, años 1665–73, 25/9/1668. In addition, doña Ana mentioned her children's consent to the boy's manumission.

52 Ibid., años 1689–98, 23/2/1689.

53 Ibid., años 1658–65, 22/8/1660 and 21/11/1663.

54 Ibid., años 1637–43, 18/2/1642; ibid., años 1641–49, 1/3/1648.

55 Ibid., años 1689–98, 15/8/1693.

56 Doña Ana María Salazar freed the daughter of one of her slaves in 1678; that daughter was subsequently manumitted in 1692. The recorder amended the baptismal entry, noting that on July 9, 1692, doña Ana María decided that Ursula la Rosa should be free (ibid., años 1672–83, 12/11/1678).

57 I draw on Susan Pedersen's useful description of maternalism as "a framework in which educated and usually well-to-do women, drawing equally on their faith in women's superior moral and motherly capacities and on a long experience of single-sex philanthropic work, sought to protect those women and children who were presumed to be less fortunate or more vulnerable" ("The Maternalist Moment in British Colonial Policy," 180). For a useful discussion of maternalism in slave ownership, see Foster, "Women Slave Owners Face Their Historians."

58 AAL, Causas de negros, leg. 16, exp. 21, año 1672.

59 AAL, Causas de amancebamiento, leg. 4, exp. 19, año 1646. Ecclesiastical inspections were carried out periodically by visiting magistrates to investigate claims of crimes against the faith, which included concubinage. In the 1646 proceeding, Alonso had been denounced by parishioners for "bringing a single black woman María Bran from Lima to Chancay and keeping company with her in his house in scandalous concubinage." According to the record, Villagómez was not in charge of the *visita*, although it should be expected that people's memories would be subject to error given the twenty-five-year lapse of time.

60 Smail, *The Consumption of Justice*, 227.

61 Medievalists have extensively studied the themes of *fama* and *infamia*. For an excellent collection, see Fenster and Smail, *Fama: The Politics of Talk and Reputation in Medieval Europe*.

62 Wickham, "Gossip and Resistance among the Medieval Peasantry," 9.

63 Hevia Bolaños, *Curia Philipica*, § Prueba, Juicio Civil, 79–85.

64 As Wickham notes, "It was what everybody knew so it was socially accepted as reliable" ("Gossip and Resistance among the Medieval Peasantry," 4).

65 Ramos, "Gossip, Scandal and Popular Culture in Golden Age Brazil," 892.

66 Witnesses could be disqualified because of their enslaved or dishonorable status that relegated them to a lower social group. See Chapter 5.

67 Don Alonso's sister attested to his glowing pride when he beheld his grandson for the first time, and remarked how much he resembled his grandfather: "Teniendo en brazos el dicho don Alonso un niño de tres meses poco mas o menos que es hijo de la dicha Catalina Conde le dijo el susodicha a esta declarante, ha visto usted cosa mas parecida a Alonso Conde que este niño?" (doña Francisca Rosales, *testimonio*, 11/7/1672).

68 AGN, Bartolomé Espina, Protocolo no. 440, años 1684–85, Carta de libertad graciosa.

69 *Censura*, Sebastiana Tellez Avila, Año 1656. Although this is the same family, in this case it was the matriarch, doña Ana Sancho de Avila, who manumitted Sebastiana's granddaughter. Sebastiana's *censura* was filed in 1656. Possibly, this action prompted the General's public manumission two decades later. General don Sancho freed three of his slaves' children in the 1680s.

70 The category is conceptually clearer in the marriage context, since the majority of slave records exhibit marital endogamy. Alida Metcalf's study of slave marriages in Santana de Parnaíba, São Paolo, documents an endogamous rate of 89 percent ("Searching for the Slave Family," 288). For Lima's records, see ch. 2.

71 See Mannarelli, *Pécados públicos*, and Twinam, *Public Lives, Private Secrets*.

72 Rosenwein, "Worrying about Emotions in History," 842.

73 AGN, Juan Beltrán, Protocolo no. 215, ff. 45–45v, año 1699: "Decimos que por quanto tenemos por nuestro esclavo a Eusebio Joseph cuarterón que será de edad de un mes nacido y criado en nuestra casa hijo de una mulata esclava nombrada Gertrudis y respecto de los buenos servicios que nos a hecho la dicha mulata de que le estamos sumamente agradecidos y también por haber nacido en nuestra casa el dicho Eusebio y tenerle amor y voluntad hemos determinado darle carta de libertad al susodicho así por las razones referidas como *porque una persona que le quiso hacer éste bien* nos a dado cien pesos de a ocho reales porque le otorguemos la dicha libertad" (my emphasis).

74 Colonial historians have pointed to the remarkable disparity in the rates of illegitimacy between Western Europe and Latin America, particularly (though not exclusively) among plebeians. Seventeenth-century illegitimacy rates in England ranged from 1 to 2 percent, as opposed to 30–60 percent of births in Latin America for the same time period. See Kuznesof, "The House, the Street, Global Society." Illegitimacy rates between northern Portugal and Brazil were, however, parallel. See Ramos, "From Minho to Minas." Ramos's study of parochial ledgers shows that the northern parishes of Portugal had higher rates of illegitimacy, partly reflecting patterns of male emigration to Brazil. According to Ramos's analysis of the parochial records, Guimaraes had an illegitimacy rate of 25 percent in the early nineteenth century, and a rate of 14 percent from 1680 to 1689 (645). See also Brettel, *Men Who Migrate, Women Who Wait*.

75 As Twinam notes, priests were among those men whose illegitimate children frequently appeared in legitimation petitions (*cédulas de gracias al sacar*) (*Public Lives, Private Secrets*, 115).

76 See Introduction for a discussion of Ana María de Velasco's lawsuit.

77 In these concubinage accusations, a married woman's name was never mentioned publicly, the intention being to protect her husband's honor. The evidence here suggests that it was Joana.

78 Libro de Bautismo, El Sagrario 1650–58, 2/11/1656.

79 According to Alexandre Coello, "Había diez canónigos, cuatro de los cual eran de oficio u oposición – magistral, encargado del púlpito: doctoral o asesor jurídico, lectoral, o teólogo del cabildo, y penitenciario, encargado de administrar el sacramento de la penitencia para algunos pecados, y seis de gracia o merced – que cobraban de salario tres mil pesos anuales de plata ensayada" ("El cabildo catedralicio," 332).

80 Bermúdez, *Anales de la catedral de Lima*, 112.

81 AAL, Libro de bautizos de esclavos, el Sagrario, años 1588–1600.

82 See Helmholz, "Baptism in the Medieval Canon Law."

83 Scholars have paid close attention to the baptismal category of *niños expósitos* as a means of tracing the interpellation of gender with social status, ethnicity, illegitimacy, and sexuality. See, for example, Twinam, "The Church, the State, and the Abandoned."

84 On the difference between *hijos naturales* and *hijos de padres no conocidos*, see Dueñas Vargas, *Los hijos del pecado*, Kuznesof, "Sexual Politics, Race and Bastard-Bearing in Nineteenth Century Brazil," and Twinam, *Public Lives, Private Secrets*. As these scholars note, administrative silence regarding filiation was not fatal to legitimation if a child's paternity was not prevented by consanguinity or marriage.

85 Mixed-status baptisms are not recorded in a way that conforms neatly to racial divides. Rather, they reflect the priest's scribal idiosyncrasies. There is no reason why the 112 children of slave mothers who were freed at the font would have been recorded in the sacramental registers for *españoles*. In her study of the *gracias al sacar* petitions brought in the eighteenth and nineteenth centuries by *pardos* and *mulatos* seeking royal dispensations of whiteness, Twinam suggests that lighter skinned babies or *expósitos* with consanguineal links to Spaniards were inscribed in Spanish baptismal books. Twinam also mentions the frustration expressed by Venezuelan elites about the genealogical imprecision of the Spanish books (*Purchasing Whiteness*, 138).

86 Given the imperative of baptism for all slaves arriving in the New World, either in Cartagena or in their African ports of origin, we presume the baptisms of adults were rebaptisms.

87 A typical adult's register read: "Yo Diego de Salazar, cura beneficiado desta santa iglesia de la ciudad de los reyes en ella habiendo primero catequizado a Antón negro de la tierra Angola de edad de 26 años, esclavo de Pascual Martín. Fueron sus padrinos Luis de Valladolid criollo esclavo de Juan de Valladolid y Isabel Criolla desta ciudad, esclava de Ana de Ribera, y dello doy fe y firmo" (AAL, Libros de bautizos de esclavos, años 1588–1600.

88 See AGN, Pedro Pérez Landero, Protocolo no. 510, año 1696, ff. 517–17v; AGN, Francisco Moscoso Lázaro, Protocolo no. 1162, año 1675, ff.164v–65.

89 Burns, *Las Siete Partidas*, 4, title 22, law 8. Interestingly, for those freed by testament, Alfonso distinguishes between the reverence due to the owner who directly frees her slave, and the freedman's lack of obligation to the "heirs and strangers" of the testator.

90 Some scholars have argued that manumission was a poisoned "gift." See Blackburn, introduction to *Paths to Freedom*, 9.

91 Richard Helmholz analyzes the confusion that accompanied those who moved from one parish to another without proof of baptism. Canon law was clear that a person could not be baptized twice, and neither could a person claim to be baptized without proof. To get around the problem of uncertainty, a person would be proclaimed as conditionally baptized and then formally baptized anew by a priest ("Baptism in the Medieval Canon Law," 125). We see numerous entries of conditional baptism in the parish records. Because these baptisms took place in a city with numerous priests, I interpret these "emergency" or conditional baptisms principally as evidence of the fragile health of the mother and the newborn. Other contingencies may be at work, however, particularly if mothers wanted to conceal parturition from owners.

92 "Parol evidence" refers to the verbal expressions of a contracting party extrinsic to a formal written instrument. See *Black's Law Dictionary*, 580.

93 See Lauderdale Graham, *House and Street*.

94 On the perils of microhistory's reliance on rich cases, see Lepore, "Historians Who Love Too Much," and Kuehn, "Reading Microhistory."

95 See, for example, the special issue in the *Hispanic American Historical Review*, "Labors of Love: Production and Reproduction in Latin American History."

96 Foster, "Women Slave Owners Face Their Historians," 307–8.

97 As explained earlier, this is not necessarily the case throughout Iberoamerica: the records from Bahia, New Spain, and La Plata show greater male rates of child manumission.

98 Orlando Patterson has repeatedly dismissed the question of whether manumission is a gift or contract as moot. For Patterson, the more significant question is whether the act of possession – the experience of power and domination inherent in the condition of enslavement – could be passed on from master to slave. Along with other "idealist-realist" slavery scholars, I construe the myriad forms of manumission attendant to slave systems as reflecting both a fundamental antagonism between liberty and bondage and the law's inability to control the slave's double character ("Three Notes of Freedom," 16–29).

99 Ibid.

5

Till Death Do Us Part

Testatio et mens are two Latin words which mean, in Castilian, evidence of a man's will. From these words the term testament is derived, for in it is contained and clearly set forth the will of the party who makes it, through his appointing by it his heir, and dividing his property in such a way that he deems proper that it should be distributed after his death.

Las Siete Partidas, Part. VI, Tit. I

On May 3, 1682, Micaela de Torres declared herself of sound mind and judgment but suffering from the ailment that God had seen fit to bestow on her and from which she would not recover.[1] On that day, Micaela considered a proposition offered to her by her lifelong slave, Margarita de Torres, to accept 300 pesos for the freedom of her sons Feliciano and Pedro. Margarita also asked Micaela for her *carta de libertad*, which Micaela granted, acknowledging, "the love and devotion with which Margarita had served her and nursed her during her illness." Micaela accepted Margarita's proposition of payment for the children's freedom, again "in recognition of the tenderness and affection with which she had raised the boys." Margarita made an initial payment of 150 pesos for her sons' freedom, and Micaela signed a notarized document declaring the family "forever free of servitude and captivity." That document became the subject of a nine-year lawsuit. Micaela declared:

The said Margarita has asked me to grant her a letter of freedom and has also offered to give me two hundred pesos for the price of Feliciano, and one hundred pesos for Pedro, which is their current value, and what they will be worth in the future. In order to do right by the boys, so that they can secure their freedom together with the said Margarita, their mother, who has been a good slave to me, and because of the love and goodwill that I have for her, I want to do this. To wit, in drawing up this present document, in the most proper legal manner, voluntarily and of my free will, good faith, and without duress from any person, I grant, and recognize that with this letter, I free

Margarita. Pray that it be known forthwith that the said Margarita is free from captivity, together with her two sons, the *mulatos* Feliciano and Pedro. And that they should be known to all as free persons, not subject to captivity, who can appear as legal persons, to contract freely, to make their own testaments and dispose of whatever goods that they may acquire according to their wishes.[2]

The document was duly notarized and signed, followed by Micaela's last will and testament dated on the same day.[3] Both the *carta de libertad* and the testament were drafted and witnessed by a notary on the day before she died. This was Micaela's only testament, although the detail with which she enumerated her assets suggests that she put a great deal of thought into the disposition of her property. Micaela made a number of pious bequests and paid for thirteen elaborate masses ("misas cantadas y veladas") for the repose of her soul. The masses were celebrated both in the rural parish of Huaura where she lived and in the church of San Lázaro in Lima where she was interred.

Micaela's letter is representative of many *cartas de libertad* issued from a deathbed that simultaneously expressed the owner's "love and appreciation" of the slave's devotion and lifelong service. It was somewhat atypical in that Micaela imposed no conditions on Margarita's freedom beyond accepting the 300 pesos in consideration for the boys. Many testamentary bequests included additional conditions of service to the household, especially in cases where there were surviving spouses.[4] This document simply freed Margarita and made no requirement of any additional years of service.

Testamentary devises of freedom generally established the owner's Catholic piety and benevolence and expressed a desire to ascend to heaven with a clear conscience. Many people dictated testaments from their deathbed as they died at home surrounded by their loved ones and confessors. Notaries were present to record and bear witness to the testator's will. More instrumentally, many owners used the promise of testamentary grants of manumission as an incentive to secure their slaves' loyal and continued service. In other words, the promise of a deferred grant of freedom meant that a slave would likely not opt for either self-purchase or flight and so ensured an owner a stable, lifetime income from day-wage payments. As Ruth Pike notes for sixteenth-century Sevillan owners, "Manumission by will had distinct advantages, for the master retained the services of the slaves as long as he needed them; the prospect of freedom encouraged good conduct on the part of the slave; and the slaveholder could depart this life with a freer conscience."[5]

Although self-purchase was the most common route to freedom in colonial Lima, testamentary manumission was granted with much greater frequency to female domestic slaves. José Jouve Martín notes that out of the 3,120 individuals who were enumerated as "freed blacks" in seventeenth-century Lima, 1,762 were women and 553 were men.[6] This stark gender imbalance in the rates of manumission undoubtedly had to do with family strategies privileging women's freedom and also with the affective relationships between enslaved women and their owners.

Many scholars interpret the sources as suggesting that enslaved women bartered sex for the delayed promise of freedom for both themselves and their children – or at a minimum – a lowered purchase price. I read the sources somewhat differently. They suggest to me that delayed manumission, *pursuant to legal action urging freedom*, was the "default" arrangement of less economically prosperous owners and their domestic slaves. In other words, enslaved women used the legal process to prompt their owners to honor or make publicly known the existence of a private promise of freedom. This is consonant with my broader hypothesis that recourse to the court was a particular kind of stimulus to bring about eventual freedom.

While we cannot speculate about the degree to which these were consensual or forced relationships, we surmise that higher rates of manumission for women in domestic servitude – whether testamentary or self-procured – resulted from affective ties. These clearly included negotiations for sexual services and delayed liberty in the context of long-standing relationships.[7]

This chapter explores both the legal and spiritual aspects of testamentary manumission of domestic slaves through the lens of Margarita de Torres's lawsuit. This case disturbs the unilateral narrative of testamentary manumission by calling attention to the legal struggles of enslaved peoples who sought to enforce testamentary bequests of freedom despite the heirs' resistance to honoring the decedent's wishes. Here, I scour the legal record to write in the efforts of the slaves themselves to assume control of their disposition rather than relegating them (doubly) to mere chattel or to objects of distribution in the intergenerational transmission of wealth.

This chapter and the one that follows moves the reader along a gradient from the slave's character as person to the slave's character as property. I use this case to explore a stark realist conundrum: Margarita's ability to be free rested on the legal certainty (if not celebration) *of Micaela's property rights in her* and Micaela's unencumbered freedom to dispose of her property as she saw fit. Within this disfigured landscape of property and probate, Margarita launched a battle and secured her liberty but not without a nine-year odyssey through the courts.

TESTAMENT, INHERITANCE, AND MANUMISSION

Where did testators derive a legal obligation to bestow and bequeath their property – including their slaves? Following this, was there a legal obligation in the civil law of slavery to manumit slaves via testament? Under Roman law, slaves could be freed by *vindicato, censu*, and *testamento*.[8] The Fourth *Partida* expanded the grounds for emancipation and *inter vivos* grants of manumission to include fealty to the crown, malfeasance of the master toward the slave, marriage to a free person, and a host of other contingencies.[9] Nevertheless, as Ruth Pike's comments indicate, by the sixteenth century, testamentary manumission remained a favored option on the peninsula.[10]

The civil law made ample provisions for testamentary manumission. The Sixth *Partida*, which deals with rules on succession, wills, and executors, makes numerous references to the contingencies of slaves and testators.[11] It incorporates much of Justinian's writings on succession, although methods of resolving the potential conflicts between heirs and slaves are not explored with the same rigor as they are in the *Digest*.[12] Nevertheless, both legal codes contemplate the questions raised by the confluence of testament, manumission, and inheritance. The musings of the lawgivers on this subject demonstrate the extreme importance placed on the testament in Roman law, on the sacramental requirements of testaments in ensuring a proper Catholic death, and on the provisions for manumission in the civil law of slavery.[13]

Scholars have long held that testamentary devises of freedom were more frequently upheld – though by no means uncontested – in civil jurisdictions. Closer research shows, however that differential legal stances on manumission are attributed to timing, rather than formalist reasons. Manumission was less frequent in common law jurisdictions during the eighteenth century, as lawmakers in the United States responded aggressively to local fears of growing freed populations by foreclosing testamentary avenues to manumission. After the 1660s, both common law and statutes in the United States shifted and congealed, in pace with the US colonies' gradual transformation from a society with a relatively small enslaved labor force to a "society with slavery."[14] As such, the point about timing largely explains the legal differences in probate law in common-law jurisdictions.

As Kathleen Brown notes, until the 1660s, slavery in Virginia remained legally ill defined. No systematic law or public policies existed to prohibit manumission in the early seventeenth-century US colonies. Telling the story of Mary Johnson, who earned her freedom under similar conditions found among urban slaves in Iberoamerica during the same time period, Brown notes that, "In 1622, no laws limited Mary's opportunities from procuring her own freedom."[15]

Both Mariana Dantas and Keila Grinberg critically revisit the difference between civil and common-law systems with regard to manumission using sources from eighteenth-century Baltimore and the Brazilian cities of Sabará and Rio de Janeiro. Grinberg notes the similarities in slaves' ability to achieve manumission through bringing freedom suits against their owners in urban areas in both the northern United States and Brazil.[16] These examples demonstrate that the similarity of the material conditions of urban slaves created frameworks in which legal discomforts about slaves as res or persons could be exploited in courts to win one's liberty regardless of whether a slave was in a civil or common law jurisdiction.[17]

With reference to testamentary manumission, common-law jurists regarded the testator's freedom as foundational to interpreting disputed wills and codicils. As early as 1715 in Baltimore, Dantas notes, the growth of the freed colored population caused lawmakers alarm, and they considered prohibiting manumission. However, others contended that it would be "hard to restrain any Owner to sett free any well deserving Negro or Molatto slave, … no Owner being at Liberty Otherwise to recompence the good Actions of a well deserving Slave."[18] The extant jurisprudence arose at a time when the British Atlantic was increasingly committed to continued and perpetual enslavement. It also did not have a well-developed legal tradition of manumission. Therefore, common-law jurists adhered to the canons of construction in property, contract, and probate to settle disputes over testamentary manumission.

The common-law stance on testamentary devises struck a balance between absolute fidelity to the testator's intent – a primary rule of construction in probate law – and the political and economic exigencies of slavery as an institution authorized by law. The axiomatic rule of construction in the common law of probate is that the intention of the testator should govern, providing this can be done without contravening public policy. As such, jurists strove to limit their deliberations strictly within the confines of the law – based largely on fidelity to the testator's wishes. Simultaneously, a growing number of statutes designed to limit the growth of the free black population gave rise to many judicial invalidations of testamentary manumission.[19] But it is important to note that these were not borne of common-law precedent. Rather, they were statutes that drew on a well-developed British tradition of vagrancy and poor laws to police resistant and restive populations.[20]

In sum, both civil and common-law systems recognized the magnitude of the testamentary conferral of freedom, given its implications for the heirs of the estate. In addition, both systems protected the absolute property rights of the owner. Judicial deliberations were based on the owner's discretion in disposing of his property, and little consideration was given to the enslaved person's role in bringing about that disposition beyond fraud or duress. Heirs and executors routinely objected to the manumission of slaves as a result of "fraud and deceit" ("fraude y dolo"), indicting slaves for their pernicious influence over the testator in the unfolding drama in probate or reducing them to mere property to satisfy outstanding debts.

However, testamentary dispensation of the decedent's property gave rise to a host of contested claims, most often vociferously voiced by slaves themselves. Although the fate of enslaved peoples depended on the testamentary provisions that their owners made when they were alive, many owners died intestate or with insufficient funds to cover their debts. Slaves, as assets, were seized and appraised to pay or reduce any outstanding debts against the estate. However, in the case where a slave had already amortized his or her purchase price and paid toward it with earnings, that slave was encumbered by the contract and could not be sold. This became a contentious point in probate, leading to scores of lawsuits and numerous *censuras*. These legal actions justifiably draw our attention to the robust efforts of slaves to enforce promises or deeds of manumission against greedy executors.

In a more ambiguous situation like the one faced by Margarita de Aguirre (discussed in chapter 1) in which there was no notarized, written document available, it behooved the litigant to show the wishes of the deceased to strengthen the litigant's claim to freedom against a recalcitrant executor by asking the court to issue *censuras*. Those who responded to the *censuras* revealed deathbed promises or penultimate efforts to emancipate slaves. Priests who administered last rites could be summoned into ecclesiastical court to strengthen a litigant's claim to freedom. Given the presumption favoring testamentary manumission, recalcitrant executors faced the prospect of being labeled impious Catholics, which carried extralegal but strong sanctions in a religious society.

One *censura* brought by Pascuala Arias is instructive on the latter point. Pascuala claimed that Archbishop Fernando Arias de Ugarte freed her and her mother by testament in 1637. Pascuala appealed for *censuras* to be read in 1674 – nearly forty years later – to substantiate the earlier testamentary grant of manumission. In his will that he drafted in 1637, the Archbishop did in fact free all his slaves.[21] He explicitly stated that his estate contained enough assets to cover his debts and care for his heirs. He implored his trustees to honor his testamentary bequest of liberty to his numerous slaves. Apparently, however, the Archbishop changed his mind one year later, and he executed a closed will. He did however leave a codicil in which he stated his intention to free two legitimate daughters of his faithful slave, Urban.[22]

I presume that Pascuala was one of Urban's daughters, although she also could have been one of the children of the slaves who relied on the testamentary promise in 1637. Pascuala was unable to legally open Archbishop Arias's will. However, in asking for the *censuras* to be read, Pascuala made public reference to this codicil that bound the Archbishop's trustees to free Urban's daughters. It also revealed the Archbishop's expressed intent in his earlier promise to free his slaves. Pascuala's case only contains the one-page handwritten *censura*, but the significance of an enslaved woman suing the heirs of an Archbishop – the highest ecclesiastical authority in Lima – to press for her liberty in court is tremendous.

BEING OF SOUND MIND, I DO SOLEMNLY DECLARE, THAT THIS IS MY LAST WILL AND TESTAMENT, MADE OF MY OWN FREE WILL

The singular legal focus on the testator's intent (and by extension the testator's freedom to dispose of his property as he saw fit) is derived from the view that a will is the ultimate contract between the living and the dead. Sir Henry Maine insisted on the idea of the immortalization of the testator through inheritance – a process through which the dead live on through their property.[23] Nonetheless, contested inheritance suits were very much affairs of the *living*, of those who were aggrieved by the dispensation and testamentary bequests of assets and chattel to which they felt entitled. Moreover, it was a legislative decision to intervene on behalf of the living, to remedy their dispossession and disinheritance. Dower and curtesy laws were enacted to prevent the deliberate impoverishment of surviving spouses, notwithstanding the testator's expressed intent.[24] Probate judges, though deferential to the testator's will, entertained claims about the testator's mental infirmity from aggrieved or disinherited heirs.[25]

The civil law of succession placed more restrictions on the testator's ability to disinherit his next of kin, children, and spouse, leaving him discretion over only one-fifth of the estate.[26] The volume of legislation designed to prevent disinheritance and the subsequent litigation around succession demonstrate that courts have perennially been involved in policing the boundaries between the living and the dead.

Of course, the Catholic Church has long exercised jurisdiction over the boundary between living and dead. Though a secular document, the Catholic testament begins with a solemn invocation of the Holy Trinity.[27] Indeed, it was a required element in preparing for death, fusing together the spiritual and emotional with the material.[28] Micaela's testament provides the reader a public image of her as pious and beneficent – an image not necessarily borne out in piecing together her life in the archival record.

Micaela left a considerable estate to her daughters: Ana, Ynez, Ysabel, and María. The four daughters and the executor (*albaçea*) of the estate brought a consolidated suit against Margarita, claiming that the *carta de libertad* was invalid, extracted under duress on Micaela's deathbed.[29] The executor further alleged that Micaela's confessors had advised her that she could not grant Margarita's freedom without consulting her heirs, who had to agree to the terms of the *carta de libertad*. Given the daughters' opposition to manumitting Margarita and her sons, the executor declared that the *carta* was of no consequence. The executor concluded with a demand to remedy the theft (*despojo*) from Micaela's estate by delivering Margarita and the boys to their rightful owners.

Alleging their mother's indecision was not strictly speaking an instance of sound legal reasoning. Nevertheless, the daughters sought to strengthen their case by claiming duress in conjunction with Micaela's demurral. The parties were entitled to argue on the basis of whatever legal claim they thought would be most effective for their case. Duress and mental incapacity may have invalidated the *carta de libertad* if the promise to free the boys was regarded as part of the deathbed bequest of freedom to the family. Despite the proximity of the conveyance to Micaela's death, the money received from Margarita for the boys' freedom was evidence of a contractual promise.[30]

According to the law of succession, the will and the *carta de libertad* were both valid.[31] There was no subsequent instrument or codicil to revoke the will, and Micaela clearly made her testament in full possession of her mental faculties. Perhaps the daughters' case against Margarita's manumission would have been stronger on equitable grounds had Micaela disinherited her children.

However, Micaela's will made provisions for her daughters, although most of her wealth had been transferred through their dowries (*dotes*) decades earlier.

Micaela's executor stayed the disposition of the estate, suspending the appraisal and liquidation of Micaela's assets. He asserted the sisters' possessory rights over the entire estate, including the right to claim *physical* possession over Margarita and the boys. Margarita astutely prevented the sisters from asserting such possession over her and her sons by filing her lawsuit. But this is getting ahead of our story. In the following section, I follow the motions and pleadings of this lengthy legal battle, using Margarita's motivation and objectives as a focal point.

SUING THEIR WAY TO FREEDOM? THE LEGAL BATTLE OVER MICAELA'S LAST WILL AND TESTAMENT

On May 5, 1682 (two days after Micaela's death), Margarita responded to the executor's complaint. Margarita's procurator, Diego Esteban Berrocal, filed an *amparo*: an expedited legal proceeding to counteract the swiftness with which the heirs sought to claim possession over the estate.[32] Berrocal asked the court to issue an injunction against the heirs, introducing the *carta de libertad* into evidence. Berrocal reasoned that the *carta de libertad* was obviously valid, since the testator was fully within her proprietary rights to dispose of her property in the way that she pleased. Berrocal also objected to the executor's merging the inheritance claim with the dispute over the validity and legality of the *carta de libertad*. He asked the court to bifurcate the proceedings: to decide on the instrument's legality first and then rule on the composition and dispensation of the estate. Later that day, the panel of judges in the *Real Audiencia* reviewed Berrocal's petition and agreed to bifurcated proceedings. The magistrates of the *Audiencia* also enjoined the sisters' attempt to curtail Margarita's freedom or interfere with her ability to pursue her legal claim. More importantly, the judges asserted jurisdiction over the proceedings, advising the sisters that any communication between the parties had to be mediated through the *Audiencia*.[33]

This dealt an important blow to the sisters' attempt to take possession over Margarita and her two sons. In essence, the court temporarily secured Margarita's liberty by refusing to turn her over to the sisters until they made a determination on the disposition of the estate. The *Audiencia* reserved judgment on the question of whether Micaela's estate was overly compromised by Margarita's freedom to cover her outstanding debts. The legal question then became whether Micaela was free to manumit Margarita with the discretionary part of her estate (called the *quinto*), after her debts were paid.

After this initial victory, Margarita's procurator filed a more detailed complaint in which he set out a series of counterclaims. First, Berrocal objected to the sisters' allegation that there were insufficient funds to satisfy the debts against Micaela's estate. He reminded the *Audiencia* that Micaela agreed to free the two boys for the sum of 300 pesos and that she received money from Margarita toward that purpose. The boys' manumission therefore was not an act of *libertad graciosa* as it was in Margarita's case – it was a contractual agreement.

Second, Berrocal alleged that the sisters had absconded with Micaela's most valuable goods immediately following her death so that the inventory did not accurately reflect the entirety of Micaela's estate. Berrocal argued that a calculation of the worth of the estate should be made that included the money paid in consideration for the boys' freedom, in addition to the absconded goods, before it was decided whether Micaela had exceeded the *quinto* in manumitting Margarita.

Finally, and most damningly, Berrocal disputed the sisters' eligibility to inherit the whole share of Micaela's estate. He claimed that the four sisters were all illegitimate: products of adulterous unions with men who were not Micaela's husband. If this statement could be proven, it would mean that the sisters were not entitled to any share, since illegitimate children (*adulterinos*) were not entitled to inherit at all because of their iniquitous origins.[34] Berrocal did not allege the existence of any legitimate children. Rather, he disputed the daughters' ability to inherit, given their illegitimate, adulterous status.

Clearly, by the moral standards of seventeenth-century Lima, allegations of illegitimacy (and by extension, Micaela's adultery) were grounds for libel and calumny. Berrocal himself would not have possessed this type of information to invalidate Micaela's will. Although the parties were free to allege claims they thought most favorable to their case, it would have been professionally irresponsible for Berrocal to make such a calumnious accusation without "hard" evidence.[35] (Recall the close-knit professional communities in which procurators like Berrocal circulated, and the fact that their livelihoods depended on a high volume of referrals. He could have ruined his reputation with such a calumnious claim.) Margarita presumably shared information that she knew regarding Micaela's intimate affairs and the paternity of her daughters. Berrocal contended that Micaela lied in her testament about the legitimacy of her daughters.[36] He claimed, "Given that the daughters are not legitimate, but fruits of an impaired and punishable union, they cannot inherit either by will or through the laws of intestacy."[37] The guardian ad litem appointed to Margarita's two sons also advanced the same claim with even more explicit and condemnatory language: "Although it would be extralegal to apply the death penalty to the crime of adultery, it is enough that public opinion supports the husband meting out this type of punishment. Moreover, this damaged and criminal union excludes the children from testamentary succession."[38]

The executor's suggestion of fraud and duress paled in comparison to the gravity of Berrocal's accusation of illegitimacy and Micaela's adultery.[39] Margarita could have made false accusations in a desperate attempt to prolong the case. Or she could have been telling the truth. Lifelong domestic slaves like

Margarita became integrated into an intimate set of relationships, and they witnessed the private lives of their owners on a daily basis, becoming privy to their habits, secrets, and conflicts. If Micaela regarded Margarita as her confidante, Margarita would have been known about her owner's adulterous affairs. Theirs was a customary intimacy that reflected aspects of the domestic relationship, especially because sex was not the bind between the two. But how would the revelations of a perfidious slave measure against the declarations of a pious, dead, slave-owning woman, who although she was not of elite status was certainly located well above Margarita in the hierarchy of colonial Lima? Would the *Audiencia* – elite judges allied with the slave-owning classes – respond with superior disdain in an effort to discredit Margarita's ability as a slave to make these claims? As it turned out, they did not. Upon reviewing these surprising revelations and developments, the *Real Audiencia* granted both parties forty-one days to summon witnesses and present evidence in their case.

Alonso de Arcos, the procurator representing the four sisters, responded (understandably) with tremendous indignation. The sisters did not regard the taint of dishonor lightly, and they requested extra time to gather the necessary evidence to disprove Margarita's allegation. Arcos needed to summon witnesses in the rural valleys of Huaura and Vilca, in the parishes where the sisters were baptized and where Micaela resided prior to her death. Another exchange of papers confirmed both parties' agreement to extend the jurisdiction to Huaura, and the sisters made good-faith efforts to present certificates of baptism (*partidas*). But it was not before the following year that baptism records were introduced as evidence. Three of the four sisters presented notarized documents stating that they were the legitimate daughters of Micaela de Torres and Juan de César. Ana's baptismal statement read: "On the 15th of August 1639, I baptized Ana, the legitimate daughter of Juan César and Micaela de Torres with oil and chrism. Present were Juan Gales, her godfather, Lic. Domingo Camacho, and the Councilman Juan García."[40] All three baptismal statements recorded the presence of witnesses and designated the girls as "legitimate daughters" of Micaela and Juan.

Neither Berrocal nor Ortíz (the boys' guardian ad litem) were swayed by the presentation of the baptismal certificates. As they pointed out, the fact that the children were recorded as legitimate does not mean that their father was present at their baptism. They maintained that Juan and Micaela had separated years before, whereupon Micaela had relocated to the valleys of Vilca and Huaura. According to their briefs, everyone in Vilca and Huaura knew the girls' real paternity. Berrocal raised the specter of a broader conspiracy in covering up the girls' illegitimate status and implicitly enveloped the priests in this shroud of deception.

Although this would probably have been a point of contention in an ecclesiastical court and investigated more thoroughly, the suggestion that priests covered up illegitimacy at the font was not the main focus of Berrocal's response.[41] He cast more aspersions on the parties listed as witnesses to the baptism. Thus, corroboration required summoning even more witnesses to attest to the moral rectitude of those named in the baptismal certificates. The process of summoning witnesses through *censuras* and public calls (*publicación de testigos*) unfolded throughout the year. *Censuras* were read in Huaura's main Cathedral on three consecutive Sundays in November 1683.[42]

DEAD WOMEN TELL NO TALES? PIECING TOGETHER
FRAGMENTS OF MICAELA'S LIFE

When Nicolasa de Torres attended mass at the Holy Church of San Francisco on November 7, 1683, she heard the priest exhort his parishioners to come forward with any information that they had in the case against Margarita. Later that week, Nicolasa went to relieve her conscience and testify before the notary in Huaura. Technically, the *censuras* were read at the four sisters' behest, although anyone who had information pertinent to the case could testify and alleviate his conscience.

Under oath, Nicolasa told the notary that she entrusted 50 pesos with Josef Riberos in order to free Pedro de Torres. Nicolasa said that Josef had given the money to Micaela, along with a message promising to pay the remaining monies for Pedro's purchase price. Six other witnesses responded to subsequent *censuras* read at Sunday mass. They unanimously confirmed that Micaela had received 150 pesos from various sources to pay for the boys' freedom. Barragán de Llosa, a priest, testified that he personally gave Micaela 150 pesos for the boys' freedom. Barragán also knew that Nicolasa had paid 50 pesos on the day that he baptized Pedro – bringing the amount Micaela received for the boys to approximately 200 pesos.

Presumably, Josef Riberos was Pedro's father, and Nicolasa was the boy's aunt. Many of the witnesses were related either to Margarita or to the boys' fathers. It is not surprising that families would pool together resources to purchase a child's or a loved one's freedom, seizing the opportunity presented by an owner's imminent demise.[43] And from the record, it is not clear whether Margarita intended to pay the remaining 100 pesos for the boys. She no doubt gambled on Micaela's death and offered a one-time payment that she procured from the boys' fathers and their paternal relatives.

This case depended on confirming the veracity of over forty witnesses who were summoned or appeared with testimonies about what they knew. In addition to soliciting testimonies via *censuras*, both parties drafted interrogatories for their witnesses. The sisters asked witnesses to confirm the fact that Micaela never received any money for the boys' freedom. They claimed that the money paid was actually repayment of loans that Micaela had extended earlier to the boys' fathers. In this register, they asked the witness to corroborate outstanding debts owed to Micaela by the boys' relatives.

In their third question, the sisters asked whether the witness knew that Micaela only claimed she accepted the money to give the *carta de libertad* more legal weight. They did not ask the witnesses in this round of interrogatories to testify about their paternity, leaving us with the impression that having presented their *partidas*, they did not intend to ask witnesses to verify their legitimacy.

Margarita's interrogatories posed questions to elicit the witnesses' knowledge of the payments to Micaela, and to corroborate her version of the theft of Micaela's more valuable assets. The questions asked the witnesses to verify Micaela's expressed wish to free Margarita as a reward for her lifelong service and filial devotion.[44]

Margarita's third question spoke directly and at length to the sisters' paternity. Did the witnesses know that Micaela and Juan César were married according to the laws of the Holy Church? Further, did they know that Micaela and Juan separated by mutual accord? Did they know that the said Micaela went to Vilca, where she lived for some time? And in that time, did they know that she initiated an illicit friendship with Juan Gales, with whom she had two daughters, Ana and María? Could they confirm that Juan Gales recognized Ana and María as his daughters, because it was public and notorious knowledge to all who lived in Vilca and Huaura? Margarita's next question in connection to the issue of paternity asked the witnesses to state whether they knew that after breaking off the illicit friendship with the said Juan Gales, Micaela then embarked on another immoral relationship with Juan Barreto in Huaura, and bore Ynez Barreto out of that union. And did the witness know if after leaving Juan Barreto, Micaela commenced a friendship with Francisco de Aguilar, with whom she bore Ysabel del Aguilar? And finally, could the witness verify that the said Ynez and Ysabel were raised publicly as daughters of the said men, and that Juan César lived in Lima throughout the entire time until his death as a "vagabond and wastrel" ("andando en la tropa de pobres")?[45]

Ten witnesses responded to Margarita's call. Some witnesses lived in Lima, others testified in notaries' offices in Vilca, where Micaela had lived prior to moving to Huaura, and others went directly to Berrocal's office in Lima. Some were identified as *españoles*, others as *pardos* or *mulatos*. All *casta* witnesses were free. The witnesses corroborated some parts of the affairs with various men, depending on when they knew Micaela or whether they knew the partner with whom she was putatively involved at the time. None of the ten witnesses could answer whether the sisters had absconded with Micaela's valuables, as they were not present at the events immediately following Micaela's death. All unanimously swore that Micaela never maintained a marital household with her legitimate husband Juan César. And there was consensus among all witnesses that Micaela wanted to free Margarita for her lifelong service and devotion.

If we believe these witness statements, Micaela lived a remarkably nonconformist life for a woman in colonial Peru. This is not to say that other women did not live nonconformist lives, but they were usually elite courtesans or *castas* without honor. By the end of her life, Micaela was a woman of considerable means, who proudly informed her friends that she could provide dowries for her daughters independently of their fathers. In Huaura's rural households, Micaela appeared to be well regarded, which leads us to presume that wealthy women could live lives that cut across the patriarchal grain with impunity.

What can we make of this version of events for feminist history? The incompleteness and instability of colonial patriarchy spring irrepressibly to mind. Unfortunately, those observations must wait. The sisters disputed this scandalous rendition of their mother's life by casting aspersions on the moral standing of Margarita's witnesses. Each of Margarita's Spanish witnesses was compromised by consanguineal relationships to her sons' fathers. Most of the *casta* witnesses were impeached as unreliable because of their poverty and their feckless Catholic faith. Another of the witnesses was discredited because he was publicly regarded as feeble minded (*sonso y distraído*). In sum, the sisters' more highly regarded witnesses disqualified each of Margarita's witnesses. Those who were social equals disclaimed the testimony of Feliciano and Pedro's relatives. All of the sisters' witnesses – *honorable* men and women of good habits, faith, truth, and solemnity – restored Micaela to her circumspect position as caring and solicitous wife, mother and slave owner – a maternal role that was acceptable for a woman of her status within colonial society.[46]

The panel of judges convened in June 1685 to rule on Margarita's case.[47] The *Audiencia* ruled in the sisters' favor. In a short, terse statement, the panel found that the *carta de libertad* granted to Margarita was null and void. Though it was unstated, we presume the court annulled the *carta* for excessive disposition of the discretionary share. In contrast, the *Audiencia* held that the *cartas* written for Pedro and Feliciano were valid. They concluded with an order to deliver Margarita to the heirs of Micaela's estate. Berrocal immediately appealed the judgment and asked the court to release Margarita on bail. Margarita's bond was posted, and she was able to continue her lawsuit with the surety (*fianza*) and the court's approval.

In another exchange of papers, the sisters demanded that Margarita deliver two young children whom she had borne after Micaela's death. Because Margarita technically reverted to the condition of enslavement, any children she bore in that interim would follow their mother's status. The sisters conceded Pedro and Feliciano's freedom – they did not appeal the *Audiencia's* ruling with regard to Margarita's older sons. However, the sisters tried to compel Margarita to deliver the children she subsequently bore into their custody, even though Margarita was "freed" on bail. Margarita did not respond to their summons, and we see no evidence in the proceedings of her capitulating to their demand with her children in tow.

In fact, Margarita disappeared from the record for another three years. Following the petition to release Margarita on bail filed in 1685, Berrocal appealed to the *Audiencia* for an appraisal of Micaela's estate. Berrocal refused to accept the *Audiencia's* ruling with regard to the discretionary fifth share before the sisters submitted an accurate inventory of the decedent's estate. He calculated that if Margarita were valued at 400 pesos, her value was equivalent to the amount of the *quinto*. Micaela would then have been able to manumit Margarita with the discretionary fifth share.

In a petition unrelated to Berrocal's appeal, one of the sisters revoked the power of attorney that she had granted to Alonso de Arcos. In 1686, Ynez Barreto asked the court to withdraw Alonso de Arcos, stating no other reason than her peace of mind (*quietud*). Four years after Micaela's death, Ynez presumably had grown tired of the extended litigation and of the expense involved in retaining Arcos.[48]

For most of 1686, the parties disputed the value of Micaela's estate with the characteristic dyspepsia that accompanied legal squabbles over succession and inheritance in probate.[49] However, this exchange of documents was not principally concerned with Margarita's possession. In other words, this protracted dispute in probate occurred while Margarita was technically "freed" on bail. It would have been considerably more arduous if Margarita had been languishing in jail while the parties harangued over her value.

Later that year, it seems that the sisters got word that Margarita was about to give birth to yet another child. Arcos filed a complaint, asking the court to arrest Margarita so that the sisters could assert possession over Margarita and the child about to be born. Citing humanitarian motives, Arcos justified the plea for Margarita's detention as a means of assuring her safe parturition.[50]

The court ignored Arcos's appeal, but the judges did respond favorably to Berrocal's call for an accurate inventory of Micaela's estate. On February 15, 1688, the *Audiencia* ordered the executor to liquidate Micaela's assets so that the magistrates could rule on the disposition of the *quinto*. They made no mention of Arcos's allegation that Margarita was about to give birth or that she had borne other children. But the order was important for both sides. It heralded an end to the litigation. For Berrocal to prevail in his argument about Micaela's right to dispose of the *quinto*, Margarita had to comply with the terms of her appraiser. This meant that Margarita had to be *physically* apprehended so that she could be appraised.

In theory, an appraisal was a neutral exercise. Two appraisers were appointed – one by the slave and the other by the owner – to present their valuations to the court. Neither party could therefore object to the value adjudged or indict the process for price-fixing. However, for those resisting reenslavement, the appraisal was not without risk. For the past six years, Margarita's "freedom" had been contingent on her avoiding the court as well as its authorities. Indeed, Arcos was jubilant on learning that the *Audiencia* called for Margarita's appraisal. He reminded the court that the sisters had issued repeated summons for Margarita's apprehension to no avail. She simply never appeared. According to Arcos's protests, Margarita falsely claimed that her children died out of a malicious intent to despoil the sisters of their rightful property. On at least two occasions, Arcos's request for Margarita's detention coincided with a rumor of her pregnancy. Margarita had compelling reasons to elude the court's authorities.

Arcos promptly named an appraiser, who coincidentally had testified on the sisters' behalf years earlier. Josef de Cubillas submitted an appraisal for Margarita and her two sons in an inflated amount of 900 pesos. This did not appear to be based on a *physical* appraisal.[51] After this appraisal, Micaela's assets proceeded to auction in the city's *Almoneda* the following year (1687). The durable goods fetched a poor price at auction, and Berrocal justifiably complained that the inventory did not reflect the inevitable deterioration of Micaela's assets.[52]

There followed successive rounds of counterclaims disputing the value of the estate; in the end the estate was valued, although not without contestation, at 10,543 pesos. After deductions for pious bequests, legacies, debts, and funeral expenses, approximately 1,400 pesos remained. The *quinto* was thus calculated at approximately 288 pesos – an amount that was far exceeded by Cubillas's appraisal of Margarita and her sons. Berrocal appealed the valuation of the estate and proffered a more reasonable figure of 500 pesos for Margarita and the boys. He then tried to negotiate a payment schedule whereby Margarita would make prorated payments in exchange for her freedom. These negotiations occurred in a seeming flurry of activity in August 1687. Yet again Berrocal and Arcos quibbled over the computation of the discretionary share and disputed the discounts made in the auction.

Margarita successfully avoided apprehension until the battle over the estate was settled. No doubt at Berrocal's urging, she finally appeared before a notary in the town of Ate on June 14, 1688. There, she was interrogated about the whereabouts of her children. She submitted to an appraiser (*tasador*) who was appointed by Berrocal.[53] She was reprimanded for obstruction of justice in light of her dilatory response to Arcos's summons ("acusa de rebeldia").

It is at this point that we get a clear picture of Margarita. We learn from the document that Margarita was thirty-six years old. She could not sign her statement, because she was illiterate. She had given birth to three sons since she initiated the lawsuit. One son, named Josef, died when he was three weeks old. She was unable to give him a proper Catholic burial, because she was confined to bed (*en su reposo*) after the birth. She informed the priest of his death in order for his name to be recorded on the *tablilla* (entryway tablet) of the Church of San Lázaro in Lima. Her other child, also named Josef, died when he was one and a half years old. Margarita remembered with exactitude when this child died, because his death coincided with the great earthquake that ravaged the city on October 20, 1687.[54] The second Josef was not interred either, but a mass was celebrated for his soul's repose in the convent of the Monasterio de la Concepción – presumably as part of the services and pious acts for the earthquake victims. The third child, named Cayetano, was living in Huaura and was six years old. If Margarita's calculations were accurate, Cayetano presumably was born the year that Micaela died and so Margarita would have been pregnant with Cayetano around the time of Micaela's death. Given the law of the slave womb, Cayetano would have assumed his mother's status as Micaela's property. If indeed Margarita was aware of her pregnancy, we intuit that she had a legitimate motive to conceal her condition from Micaela.

After this statement, the parties resumed the process of computing Micaela's estate with renewed vigor. In what strikes the reader as a callous move, Arcos argued that the estate should reflect the value of Cayetano and the children who died. Arcos reminded the court that if Margarita had responded to his calls, she would have given birth in safe, attended conditions and the estate would have been enriched in value. There was no reason that his clients should be unjustly disadvantaged because of Margarita's negligence. Berrocal objected to this inclusion, reasoning that Margarita had not disappeared out of spite to endanger her children. In a telling phrase, Berrocal argued that Margarita also had a vested interest in their survival.

But the court did not agree. On June 20, 1690, the *Audiencia* reviewed all the figures, including Berrocal's counteroffer, and fixed the family's value at 470 pesos. By this point, Margarita had borne yet another child, as the court assessed her with the child that she was nursing (*la cria de pecho*). The newborn was valued at 80 pesos, despite his precarious mortality.[55] Berrocal accepted the court's assessment, although he pointed out that Margarita could not afford to pay the sum of 470 pesos. He tried to negotiate prorated payments, and arranged for Margarita to be released on bail (*fianza*). Arcos understandably resisted these negotiations, particularly since Margarita had been so adept at eluding his orders throughout the preceding eight years. Instead, Arcos called for Margarita, Cayetano, and the newborn to be delivered to his clients immediately.

The record ends with an ironic twist. In 1691, we see the last will and testament of Ynez Barreto, who passed away in 1689. In her testament, Ynez declared:

As one of the four daughters of Micaela de Torres, I am entitled to the one-fourth of the five hundred pesos assigned to the value of the *mulata*, Margarita de Torres, legitimate wife of Juan Sánchez Vanegas. And because of the great love and goodwill that I have always had and have toward the said Margarita, and because I have raised her since she was born in the house of my said mother, and where she served with such refinement and loyalty that would have been worthy of great remuneration, and in recognition and compensation of that service, of my free will and gratitude, I am certain that with the fourth part of five hundred pesos, Margarita de Torres will be freed.[56]

ON AGENCY, ADMINISTRATIVE BACKLOG, AND RESISTANCE (NOT NECESSARILY IN THAT ORDER)

The cases of Margarita de Torres, Catalina Conde, and María Josefa Martínez provide glimpses of the daily lives and unseemly secrets, powerful sentiments, beliefs and *mentalités* of the litigants who battled in court. Between the lines of stentorian proclamations from the *Real Audiencia* and bitter recriminations from the procurators, we see tempestuous love affairs, dashed hopes and fears, petty jealousies, and unimaginable anguish. In the span of six years, Margarita lost two children, survived two earthquakes, and earned enough *jornales* (although how she did is not known) to pay for Berrocal's legal services. If I have been successful in telling the tale of Margarita's legal odyssey, it should be clear just how insecure the liminal state of quasi emancipation could be for enslaved people. The case itself encompassed more than 500 written pages (*fojas*) of notarial script, making it something of a paleographic nightmare.

The slow wheels of justice were patently clear in this case, but I confess that the protracted nature of Margarita's lawsuit struck me as simultaneously frustrating and unsettling. Although I have asserted that the slow pace of justice was at times beneficial to enslaved litigants, Margarita's case demonstrates just how tied she was to Micaela's family, which continued to bicker over her purchase price, deny her liberty, and lay claim to her children. We presume Margarita returned to Ynez Barreto's household at some point in 1686 when Ynez recused herself from the lawsuit. Although both Micaela and Ynez claimed that they regarded Margarita with affection because she had been raised in their household, it is not clear that the other sisters shared that sentiment. Ysabel, for example, left her sister Ana Gales as her *albaçea* upon her death in 1691. Ana was the sister who insisted on Margarita's continued enslavement and who was most zealously represented by Alonso de Arcos. Was Ynez's beneficence meant to sway the other surviving sisters to grant Margarita her freedom or to cede their interest in her? Perhaps the case was not about Margarita at all but about the sisters' relationships and interpersonal rivalries, especially if the allegations about their illegitimacy were true.

The documentary record is incredibly rich in some details and unforgivably vague in others. For instance, it is difficult to assess Berrocal's legal prowess. After expending an inordinate amount of time gathering witnesses who could testify to the four sisters' illegitimacy, Berrocal abruptly abandoned this line of inquiry. The record yields no insight as to why he changed his strategy to focus on Micaela's disposition of the discretionary share of her estate. Was the accusation of illegitimacy and adultery a tactic designed to prolong the case? The rhythm of Margarita's litigation was marked by chronic delays punctuated by spurts of activity. Administrative backlog is a dear friend – indeed the salvation – of any overworked legal advocate. The more protracted the process, shrouded in bureaucratic red tape, the more likely one's client will be able to avoid detention or other grim punishment invariably issued by the magistrate. And yet the accusation was so preposterous, given the gendered grammar of the time, it just might have been true.

As we noted before, social historians appreciate cases with abundant witness testimony – even when they are frustratingly inconclusive, blatantly untrue, or contradictory – because they reveal the constellation of relationships around which the litigants' social world revolved. But in this case, the reader is cursed with too much information – the profusion of witness statements obfuscated rather than clarified the *mentalités* of the litigants or their social worlds. To be clear: Micaela may have genuinely felt the sentiments she expressed toward Margarita and her children in the *carta de libertad* that she penned. Throughout the various testimonies collected during the nine-year legal battle, it was clear to all the witnesses that the women had a close relationship.[57] But Micaela was a shrewd businesswoman who accepted a price for the boys that was higher than market value at a time when the expenses for their upkeep were high and their survival chances were low. She capitalized on the price that Margarita was willing to pay because the boys' freedom was worth more to their family than to anyone else.

The record is more generous – though inconclusive – with Micaela. She prided herself on her ability to raise and provide for four daughters independently, exuding an entrepreneurial spirit that was decidedly at odds with the indecisive, demure testator portrayed by her children. Many of the witnesses presented by both the sisters and Margarita were people indebted to Micaela, leaving us with the impression of a prosperous *rentier*-landholder-moneylender. Extrapolating from the size of her estate, we deduce that Micaela was active in the regional economy and that she profited handsomely from her agrarian holdings in wheat and livestock.[58]

The reader is most frustrated when trying to assemble a composite sketch of Margarita, who was after all the focal point of this litigation. We have only fleeting images of her rather than an in-depth portrait. She appears obliquely as an object of litigation, spoken for and about by others. All the documents filed on her behalf resolutely (and tautologically) asserted that she was free: "In the name of Margarita de Torres, free mulata, I bring this action for her liberty."[59] We infer her resistance and agency through her very absence in the record. The details of Margarita's reproductive life are apparent, but we know nothing of the affective relationships that gave rise to those pregnancies.[60] The only evidence of her emotional life is expressed through those who owned her and sought to reenslave her.

What emerges from the record in crystalline detail are the profound urban-rural links between Lima's court system and the rural valleys of Huaura, contradicting the widely held notion that rural slaves did not have access to the urban resources that might help them attain their freedom.[61] Christine Hünefeldt has painstakingly shown the efforts exerted by slave families to maintain links between city and hacienda in the nineteenth century. Granted, the character of the relationship between owners and slaves and the conditions on the hacienda facilitated those links, but the networks of kin, labor, and parish attenuated the distance that Margarita had to traverse in her legal battle.[62]

One final observation has been hinted at throughout this chapter: the vital importance of the *amparo* in the lives of enslaved subjects. For nine years, Margarita's fate hinged on the ruling of the *Real Audiencia*, a body made up of men who were literally delegated to represent the body of the sovereign and

dispense his mercy. The *Real Audiencia* was concerned with affairs of governance, peninsular-criollo intrigue, economic crises, the growth of Dutch capital
and the threat of English privateering in the race for the Atlantic, and so in
all likelihood, they expressed little more than a desultory interest in the plight
of their *amparo* petitioners during their sessions. But they were keenly aware
of, and deeply invested in, their mandate to administer the "justice" of the
Catholic kings to their subjects.

Generations of historians challenged this Golden Age narrative of justice,
indicting the judicial machinery of the monarchist state (courts, magistrates,
and inquisitors) for its exercise of arbitrary and despotic power. In response,
much has been written to reorient the notion of colonial and republican legal
systems as bastions of corruption, inefficiency, and tyranny.[63] Yet viewed even
in its most favorable light, enlightened despotism, coupled with benign inefficiency, cannot provide fertile ground for sowing the seeds of legal mobilization, judicial activism, let alone faith in the "rule of law." But the machinery of
viceregal protection was not out of Margarita's reach. Litigants like Margarita
initiated legal action by appealing to the *Real Audiencia* with the expectation
that the *amparo* would protect her against her owners. Legal action catalyzed
other lower-threshold processes that enabled Margarita to operate on the outer
edges of bondage.

No romanticized or triumphalist view of agency or legal mobilization follows from the fact that Margarita was able to press her claim. I am not making
grand claims about symbolic legitimation and capricious state power. Once
Margarita took the initiative, notaries and procurators – responsible for the
daily work generated by the majestic trappings and mystical regalia of the
Audiencia – acted on her behalf. They provided her with relatively easy access
to courts, judicial expertise, and the rule of law.

NOTES

1 AGN, *Real Audiencia*, Causas civiles, leg. 239, cuad. 899, año 1682.
2 "La dicha Margarita me ha pedido que le otorgue carta de libertad y por ello ha
   ofrecido darme por el precio del Feliciano dos cientos pesos y Pedro por el precio
   de cien pesos, que es el valor que tienen y puedan valer adelantado, y por hacer-
   les bien y que consigan libertad juntamente con la dicha Margarita su madre, y
   haberme sido buena esclava la susodicha y por el amor y voluntad que he tenido
   en ella, lo quiero hacer. Por tanto por el tenor de lo presente en aquella forma que
   mejor haya en derecho, de mi agrado, buena fe, libertad sin fuerza ni apremio de
   ninguna persona, otorgo y conozco por esta presente carta, que la horro. Se ruega
   siempre jamás liberto de cautiverio a la dicha Margarita y a los dichos Feliciano y
   Pedro, mulatos, sus hijos, para que como personas libres y sin sujetos al cautiverio
   puedan parecer y parecen en juicio, a tratar, contratar, y hacer sus testamentos y
   disponer de los bienes que tuvieran libremente."
3 According to the seventeenth-century *Concilios Limenses*, when death was imminent, a priest was to be called in to administer last rites. A notary was also to be

summoned to record the decedent's will, to prevent intestacy, and to prepare for a Catholic burial. See Ramos, *Muerte y conversión en los Andes.*

4 As in the baptismal context, many testamentary bequests were not outright grants of freedom (*libertad graciosa*). One testator placed the condition of service on her surviving spouse in addition to receiving 300 pesos from her slave for her freedom. See AGN, *Real Audiencia*, Causas civiles, leg. 261, cuad. 980, año 1689: "A la vista del pleito del testamento y codicilo de doña María Sánchez, consta que no se dejó más bienes que la dicha negra nombrada Felipa, con cargo de que hubiera de servir a Pedro de Ochoa, su marido, todos los días de su vida, y que después de ellos, dándole trescientos pesos sea libre en calidad y circunstancia."

5 Pike, *Aristocrats and Traders*, 182.

6 See Jouve Martín, "Death, Gender, and Writing," 106.

7 In the Brazilian context, not all domestic relationships resulted in freedom for women. Scholars have revisited the data that dispute easy associations of sex with freedom. For instance, Kathleen Higgins notes that testaments from eighteenth-century Minas Gerais reveal that in many alliances between enslaved women and Portuguese colonists, fathers bequeathed their property to their illegitimate children, often without freeing the mother through testamentary manumission. See Higgins, *Licentious Liberty*, and Nishida, *Slavery and Identity*. The Portuguese laws of inheritance allowed fathers to transmit property to illegitimate children with few entails on their estate. This ensured that property could be transmitted without the messiness of marriage or even testamentary bequests to the mother and her family. Because of womb enslavement, illegitimate children inherited property in a condition of mixed status – technically enslaved but propertied.

8 *Vindicta* and *censu* were state-sponsored interventions in that they involved the proclamation of the praetor or the censor to accept and record the declaration of freed status. In contrast, testament was a private act of emancipation. See Watson, *Slave Law in the Americas*, 28, and Buckland, *The Roman Law of Slavery*, ch. 21. Constantine added a fourth method: *manumissio-in-ecclesio*, which was an owner's declaration in front of the congregation or the bishop to free his slave. See Oppenheim, "The Law of Slaves," 393.

9 See Burns, *Las Siete Partidas*, 4, titles 1–9. See also Phillips, *Slavery in Medieval and Early Modern Iberia*, ch. 6.

10 Recent historical work on Mediterranean slavery repudiates Pike's inference about the frequency with which testamentary manumission was granted. Debra Blumenthal shows that for fifteenth-century Valencia, out of 417 contracts of sale for slaves, only 57 were recorded as freed through manumission ("The Promise of Freedom in Late Medieval Valencia," 52). Blumenthal's evidence suggests that self-purchase was the route to freedom.

11 See van Kleffens, *Hispanic Law until the End of the Middle Ages*, 201.

12 See, for example, Justinian's response to the question whether testamentary manumission affected the amount of the forced share of inheritors: "The quarter will of course be calculated after debts and funeral expenses are deducted, whether testamentary manumissions count so as to reduce it further still, is a point to consider. Then, how does the matter stand? The *Lex Falcidia* does not interfere with testamentary manumission; it may reasonably be assumed that the quarter in our case is to be taken after deducting the amount lost by manumissions" (*Digest*, 1.6.329).

13   According to medieval historian Thomas Kuehn, "the revival of Roman law in the Middle Ages created a … renewed loathing of intestacy. To the Roman desire not to die intestate was seemingly added a powerful impetus from the Church to use the testament to settle one's moral and charitable accounts, [and to] see to burial and memorial masses" (Kuehn, *Heirs, Kin, and Creditors in Renaissance Florence*, 13).

14   To compensate for the lack of a genealogical tradition of slavery and manumission, British colonists turned to the law of nations and combined this with the common law's deep wellspring of vagrancy legislation. See Tomlins, "Transplants and Timing."

15   See Brown, *Good Wives, Nasty Wenches, Anxious Patriarchs*, 108.

16   As Grinberg writes, "Between the early 1790s and the early 1820s, many slaves from cities such as Baltimore and Rio de Janeiro acquired their freedom or initiated lawsuits against their masters … [d]espite differences between the Anglo-Saxon and the Roman legal systems" ("Freedom Suits and Civil Law in Brazil and the United States", 66–67).

17   My intervention here trains a comparative lens on the topic of testamentary manumission by focusing on the civil law system. Although the time periods studied by Dantas and Grinberg are later than the period under review here, they take important steps in the direction of hemispheric or comparative work on the law of slavery and the legal treatment of emancipated peoples. For a more recent exploration of the comparative law of slavery, see de la Fuente and Gross, "Comparative Studies of Law, Slavery, and Race in the Americas."

18   See Dantas, *Black Townsmen*, 97.

19   New Jersey's lawmakers were more circumspect about the testator's rights and passed legislation to ensure that the freed population would not pose a financial burden to the state's coffers. A March 14, 1798, New Jersey statute declared: "*And be it enacted,* that if any person, by his or her last will and testament, shall give his or her slave freedom, such slave, being at the time of the death of the testator or testatrix, sound in mind, and not under any bodily incapacity of obtaining a support, and also not under the age of twenty-one years, nor above the age of forty years, to be certified in manner aforesaid, then such freedom shall be good and effectual in law" ("An Act Respecting Slaves," in *Laws of the State of New-Jersey*, 374). By the 1850s, many states in the Union had passed statutes restricting manumission by testament or deed, reflecting a commitment to hereditary slavery and permanent bondage. Acts prohibiting manumission were passed to prevent a new class of public charges, following the logic that owners were obliged to provide their slaves with food, clothing, and shelter. These acts were also related to the fear and distrust of "idle and slothful freed blacks." See Parker, "Making Blacks Foreigners." Some states invalidated deathbed grants of manumission. Arkansas and Louisiana absolutely prohibited the manumission of slaves by 1860. Many states enacted stringent vagrancy laws, and freed blacks risked reenslavement if found "wandering and strolling about, or leading an idle, immoral or profligate course of life." Other acts required that the testator also have enough assets to satisfy his debts. In the case of inter vivos manumission, statutes obligated owners to transport their newly freed slaves out of the state or post bond to guarantee their "orderly behavior." (Act of May 1782, Commonwealth of Virginia, ch. 21). Thus, in deciding on future or conditional grants of manumission, US probate judges strained to interpret the owner's intent from both the "plain meaning" of the will and from the statutory

regulations of the period that sought to limit the presence or growth of a freed black population.

20 Tomlins, "Transplants and Timing," 409.

21 AGN, Francisco de Cepeda, Protocolos, año 1637 (testamento cerrado). Since the will was a closed one, there was no point looking there. However, I figured that there must be other records left by such a prominent figure as Archbishop Arias, especially for Pascuala to ask for the *censuras*. I found the codicil pertaining to Pascuala's father, Urban, in the *Protocolos* of notary Diego Jaramillo, año 1638, another notary who worked with elite members of the Archbishopric.

22 "Por quanto Urban mulato nos a servido de tres años a esta parte con mucha fidelidad y cuidado queremos que nuestros albaceas y herederos le procuren rescatar dos hijas legitimas que tiene en una esclava su muger en que les encargamos pongan toda diligencia de suerte que esto tenga efecto."

23 Maine, *Ancient Law*, ch. 6.

24 Dower and curtesy laws grant surviving spouses a life estate in the deceased spouse's assets to cover their needs, even if that spouse died intestate. See *Black's Law Dictionary*, 258 and 201.

25 The classic textbook example of the common law right to disinherit one's surviving heirs arises when the eccentric wealthy decedent leaves her fortune to a pet charity or to the beloved pet itself. See, for example, the legal controversy engendered by Leona Helmsley's decision to disinherit her numerous grandchildren and leave her fortune of US$12 million for the upkeep and care of her pet lapdog Trouble. For a historical treatment of eccentric testators, see Susana Blumenthal's study of "deviant wills" in nineteenth-century probate, "The Deviance of the Will."

26 The distinction between the restraints on testamentary freedom in the civil law vis-à-vis the common law is well documented. For a comprehensive review on forced heirship in the civil law, see Pelletier and Sonnenreich, "A Comparative Analysis of Civil Law Succession." See also Hayton, *European Succession Laws*, for a contemporary review. The percentage left to a testator's discretion varies in the civil law, depending on the code, country, and historical time period. In seventeenth-century Lima, the discretionary portion was called the *quinto*, corresponding to one-fifth of the estate. This seemed to prevail in the Spanish colonies, derived from the *Partidas*. See Dainow, "The Early Sources of Forced Heirship," and McKnight, "Spanish *Legitim* in the United States."

27 See, for example, Kellogg and Restall, *Dead Giveaways*. The formulaic nature of the testament was part of the church's insistence on uniformity and standardization after the Council of Trent. Both confessional manuals and model testaments were disseminated widely in the Americas to facilitate the conversion efforts of the clergy. Sarah Cline's study of Fray Alonso de Molina's 1569 model testament ("Fray Alonso de Molina's Model Testament and Antecedents to Indigenous Wills in Spanish America") that was circulated in New Spain demonstrates the key role of will making in evangelization and its integration into more pluralistic forms of belief surrounding indigenous mortuary rites and processes.

28 Ramos, *Muerte y conversión*.

29 "Digo que justicia mediante y hablando como debe ser mandado que se entreguen dichos esclavos a mis partes y se debe hacer así porque todo ha sido una deposición y fraude que se ha fabricado en perjuicio de mis partes" (transcript, f. 8).

30 Legal scholars have disagreed as to whether manumission is a gift or a contractual promise to convey freedom. Many courts chose to regard testamentary manumission as a bequest to the slave. In the self-purchase context, however, where money was paid toward one's freedom, disputes were clearly governed by contract law.

31 Burns, *Las Siete Partidas*, 6, titles 1–25.

32 Through Berrocal, Margarita filed a writ of *amparo*, what in contemporary legal parlance would be akin to a protective order. The word "amparo" is derived from "amparar," which literally translates to "support" or "protect." In the seventeenth century, these proceedings sought the protection of the court against inflictions of physical harm, particularly from superiors, or intervention on behalf of weaker parties. Jurisdiction was delegated to the *Real Audiencia* and ecclesiastical courts so that they could act swiftly on behalf of the aggrieved. See Lira González, *El amparo colonial y el juicio de amparo mexicano.* Many comparative legal scholars have likened the writ of *amparo* to the common law writ of *habeas corpus,* and *amparo* is extensively studied as a critical element of Latin American human rights jurisprudence. In postrevolutionary Mexico, the writ devolved jurisdiction over constitutional rights and protections to federal courts, primarily as a means of diffusing insurrectionary grievances. See Rosenn, "Judicial Review in Latin America," and Fix Zamudio, "The Writ of *Amparo* in Latin America." On the *amparo* in indigenous lawsuits in seventeenth-century Mexico, see Owensby, *Empire of Law and Indian Justice in Colonial Mexico.*

33 "Vista por el señor presidente desta real audiencia, reconoce el amparo y no mezcla el juicio con la de posesión de bienes con la libertad, que las herederas de la dicha Micaela de Torres no les inquieten, ni perturben, y que si tuviesen algo que pedir, lo hicieran en esta Real Audiencia en la forma contenida en dichos autos" (transcript, f. 37).

34 Burns, *Las Siete Partidas*, 4, title 9. As Ann Twinam points out, elite parents who had children out of wedlock worried constantly about legitimating their offspring for inheritance purposes. If it were possible by administrative fiat, deception, or clerical collusion, adulterous parents sought to categorize their children as natural children (*hijos naturales*), a category that although socially disreputable did not complicate their inheritance. Others registered their children as *expósitos* (orphans) or of unknown paternity (*hijos de padres no conocidos*), which left the birth condition deliberately vague and did not foreclose inheritance or even subsequent legitimation. See Twinam, *Public Lives, Private Secrets*, and Mannarelli, *Pecados públicos.*

35 I have only seen Berrocal represent three other enslaved litigants in cases recorded at the AGN. Alonso de Arcos – the sisters' procurator – was much more active in both the *Audiencia* and the ecclesiastical forum. But although many testamentary disputes followed squabbles over the *quinto*, I have not seen any accusations of adultery as the basis for disinheritance. It does raise a presumption in Margarita's favor that Berrocal did not typically assert adultery as a reason for his client to prevail in other cases.

36 Micaela in fact declared in her testament that "Yten: fui casada y velada según orden de la santa madre Iglesia con Juan César de la Cruz, natural de Burgos, y durante dicho matrimonio, tuvimos por nuestras hijas legitimas a María Gales, Ysabel del Aguilar, Ana Gales e Ynez Barreto, declaro las por mis hijas legítimas y dicho mi marido declaro todo" (transcript f. 19).

37 "Pues no lo son sino adulterinas, siendo hijas de dañado y puñible ayuntamiento, no pueden heredar por testamento ni ab intestato conforme a derecho" (transcript f. 53). Here, the designation of the daughters as *adulterinas* relates to the accusation that Micaela, as a married woman, bore her children out of adulterous unions. Children of adulterous unions could not be legitimated by their parents' subsequent marriage, and their inheritance prospects were compromised. See Twinam, *Public Lives, Private Secrets*, 128–36. Some historians argue that under Portuguese law, parents of *adulterinos* could leave specific testamentary bequests that were not classified as "inheritance"or that they could make payments toward the maintenance of a child. For Brazil, see Lewin, *Surprise Heirs*.

38 "Aunque no sea tan cierta y asentada en derecho la pena de muerte, basta que se la pueda poner el marido pues conforme a la opinion común esta posibilidad, que el ayuntamiento sea dañado y punible para que los hijos quedan excluidos de la sucesión testamentaria" (transcript, f. 53).

39 Women in adulterous concubinary relationships prompted moral outrage and suffered severe legal consequences that far outweighed those directed at men. See Wertheimer, "Gloria's Story." This does not imply that adulterous men were exempt from social opprobrium, but feminist colonial historians and social scientists of the contemporary period note the gendered double standard for extramarital relationships that prevailed in the past and persists in the present. In the colonial context, adulterous concubinage was complicated by issues of race and gender. For historical reviews of concubinage and illegitimacy, see Kuznesof, "Sexual Politics, Race and Bastard-Bearing in Nineteenth-Century Brazil," Dueñas Vargas, *Los hijos del pecado*, and Mannarelli, *Pecados públicos*.

40 "El 15 de agosto de mil seiscientos treinta y nueve, bauticé, puse olio y crisma a Ana, hija legítima del Juan César y Micaela de Torres, fue su padrino Juan Gales, testigos al Licenciado Domingo Camacho y el Alférez, Juan García." According to the sacramental ledger, Juan Gales was present as a *padrino* (godfather), who paid the baptismal fee (*limosna*), although according to Margarita and subsequent witnesses, this was Ana's real father. As discussed in Chapter 4, the baptismal certificate was a formulaic document, duly noting that the priest had anointed the child's head with oil and holy water and stating who was present at the baptismal font. *Recording* the baptismal certificate in the parish register involved more detailed classification regarding parentage/paternity, "race," and status.

41 By Tridentine decree, priests were directly responsible for registering all Catholic souls within their flock, rendering the church responsible for enumeration and census taking in the Americas, especially in rural pueblos. The crown repeatedly exhorted colonial officials to maintain parochial records. See *La Recopilación de las leyes de los reinos de Indias de* 1680, lib. 2, title 1, law 31. Priests were encouraged to baptize all newborns before they were one week old. The priests' alleged collusion in covering up the sisters' illegitimate status was not the principal issue here. Such collusion does, however, conform to the larger pattern that so angered the colonial administration and that encouraged them to find ways to rein in and discipline rural, nonconformist priests. See Villegas, *Aplicación del concilio de Trento en Hispanoamérica*, Rípodas, *El matrimonio en Indias*, and Vargas Ugarte, *Concilios limenses*.

42 Margarita filed a subsequent petition in the ecclesiastical court in order to have *censuras* read at mass. In 1683, we see a petition from Margarita de Torres in

which she mentions her pending case in the *Real Audiencia* but asks the court to grant her the reading of *censuras* in her case (AAL, Causas de negros, leg. 20 exp. 33, año 1683).

43 Hünefeldt, *Paying the Price of Freedom.*

44 "Por lo bien que ésta le sirvió, curándola en sus enfermedades y asistiéndola como si fuera su hija."

45 "Y si saben que la dicha Micaela de Torres fue casada según orden de la Santa Madre Iglesia con Juan César de la Cruz y durante dicho matrimonio se separaron voluntariamente sin cohabitar y la dicha Micaela de Torres se fue a vivir en la villa de Huaura, donde residió continuamente hasta que murió, y en este tiempo tuvo amistad ilícita con Juan Gales de quien tuvo por hijas a las dichas Ana, María y las reconoció por tales y fue público y notorio en dicha villa que fueran sus hijas. Digan si o no. Y si saben que habiendo acabado la amistad con el dicho Juan Gales se mal amistó la dicha Micaela de Torres con Juan Barreto y después con Francisco de Aguilar, de quien tuvo por hija a la dicha Ysabel del Aguilar e Ynez Barreto, y se criaron públicamente como hijas de los susodichos y en todo el tiempo referido estuvo en esta ciudad el dicho Juan César de la Cruz sin hacer vida maridable con la dicha Micaela de Torres y andaba en la tropa de pobres, así que murió, digan que si o no."

46 Here, I use honor to signify the public, reputational status with which members of the elite or Hispanicized colonial society regarded each other. This was not behavioral honor or "virtue" that could apply to plebeians. For the intersection of plebeian and elite honor codes, see Johnson and Lipsett-Rivera, *The Faces of Honor.*

47 The panel comprised four prominent members of the *Real Audiencia*: don Juan Ximénez de Lobatón, don Juan de Peñalosa, don Mateo de Cuenca Mata Ponce de Leon, and don Pedro Fraso.

48 On August 30, 1689, we see a notarized statement from Ana Gales, testifying that her sister Ysabel had died and named her as the *albaçea* of her estate (transcript, f. 312).

49 Micaela's assets were not sold at public auction until 1687, and the formal liquidation was dated June 18, 1689 (transcript, f. 309).

50 "Alonso de Arcos, en nombre de las hermanas Ana y María Gales, Ysabel del Aguilar, e Ynez Barreto, se sirva de declarar por esclava de dichas mis partes juntamente con el ultimo hijo que tuvo, respecto de que la susodicha esta para parir, y se temen mis partes de que ha de ocultar el parto o que ha de suponer haberse muerto en gran perjuicio de las partes que defiendo como lo hizo con otro hijo que tuvo se ha de servir Vmd mandar o que se ponga en la cárcel para dar la providencia que mas conviene la seguridad del parto" (transcript f. 219).

51 Nine hundred pesos was an inflated appraisal for Margarita and her children. Prices for slaves increased exponentially in the seventeenth century after the dynastic shifts in the Portuguese monarchy in 1640 and the brief cessation of the slave trade between 1615 and 1640. See Vila Vilar, *Hispanoamérica y el comercio de esclavos.* Rachel O'Toole's thorough review of slave sales in Trujillo, for instance, demonstrates that Peruvian planters paid on average 650 pesos for an able-bodied male slave between 1640 and 1730. See *Bound Lives*, 10. Slave scarcity led to contraband slaving, primarily supplied by the Dutch, who capitalized on the political unrest between Spain and Portugal to gain a greater share of *asientos* (royal licenses issued for the importation of slaves). The Dutch

opened up new markets in Luanda and Benin and used their strategic location on the island of Curaçao as a base for contraband slaving after 1634. Local economic booms within upper Peru – precisely in the agrarian valleys where Micaela's lands were located – depended on unpaid, tributary, or low-wage labor. Despite the pressing labor needs of the region, purchase records for slaves have not shown such a high premium paid for a female slave who was presumably unskilled. For Lima's slave prices, see Chapter 6.

52 Micaela left three other slaves who were old and sickly in her estate and who were sold for 100 pesos each. But there appeared to be no real exchange of money, since the bill of sale was registered as a transfer of property to Micaela's executor and daughters. Berrocal justifiably objected to the executor's "flexible" accounting technique.

53 Berrocal assigned Diego de Mendieta as *tasador*. Mendieta was also the person who posted Margarita's bond (*fiador*) in 1682.

54 There were two severe earthquakes in Lima in 1687, and one did in fact occur on October 20, as Margarita testified.

55 On December 14, 1688, the court issued the following order: "Auto:- Dixeron que hazen la tasación de los dos esclavitos en la manera siguiente=el esclavo Josef, zambo, que murió de edad de dos años en ciento y cincuenta pesos=el esclavo recién nacido de pecho que según dice tiene tres meses lo tasaron en ochenta pesos, cuales es la verdad= y lo afirman" (transcript, f. 306).

56 "Sepan cuantos esta carta vieren como yo Inés Barreto, mujer legitima de Andrés del Peso, vecino desta villa de Carrión de Velasco, en presencia del dicho mi marido, y con licencia que le pido y demando para otorgar todo lo que irá declarando en esta escritura= y el dicho Andrés del Peso doy y concedo a la dicha Inés de Barreto mi mujer legitima la licencia según y para el efecto que me la pida. Como una de las cuatro hijas de la dicha mi madre, me pertenece y me toca la cuarta parte de herencia de los 500 pesos y 8 reales en la que se tasó Margarita de Torres, mulata, mujer legitima de Juan Sánchez Banegas, por su libertad en conformidad de la sentencia de vista y de revista, dada por los señores oidores de la Real Audiencia. Y por el mucho amor y voluntad que he tenido y tengo a la susodicha por haberla criado desde que nació en la casa de la dicha mi madre, y que ha asistido y servido con finesa y lealtad que son dignos de muy grande remuneración y en recompensa de ella de mi agrado y buena voluntad y como cierta y sabidora que soy, con la cuarta parte de 500 pesos, estará libre Margarita de Torres" (transcript f. 342).

57 One of the witnesses, Maria Francisca, *negra libre*, described herself as a close friend and confidante of Micaela and said that in repeated conversations Micaela had told her that Margarita should serve no one after she died.

58 Huaura's fertile valleys attracted Spanish settlers and investors eager to profit from a booming internal market. As Kenneth Andrien reminds us, "the growing demand for foodstuffs, the widespread network of markets established by the Europeans in the highlands and along the coast, the availability of good land, and the eagerness of Spaniards to gain the wealth and prestige that landholding promised, all led to the growth of the rural economy. These profitable agricultural and pastoral enterprises made a vital contribution to the prosperity and self-sufficiency of the vice-regal economy" (Andrien, *Crisis and Decline*, 19).

59 "En nombre de Margarita de Torres, mulata libre, en los autos que sigue sobre su libertad y lo demas deducido."

60 The high mortality rate of her offspring is confirmed by other grim statistics show-ing abysmally low survival rates for newborn babies. Records of birth rates on Jesuit haciendas, where slaves' health conditions were thought to be relatively favorable, were also low. See Macera, *Instrucciones para el manejo de las haci-endas jesuitas del Perú*. Nicholas Cushner also discusses the low fertility rates on the Jesuit haciendas, though his research is in conversation with a previous line of scholarship within historical demography comparing the natural increase of the slave population in North America with Latin America. See his "Slave Mortality and Reproduction on Jesuit Haciendas in Colonial Peru."

61 On legal activism of enslaved litigants in Popayán, see Bryant, *Rivers of Gold, Lives of Bondage*.

62 Hünefeldt, *Paying the Price of Freedom*, 38.

63 See, for example, Owens, *By My Absolute Royal Authority*, Scardaville, "Justice by Paperwork," and Owensby, *Empire of Law and Indian Justice in Colonial Mexico*. With particular regard to slaves' protections and absolutist justice, see Bennett, *Africans in Colonial Mexico*.

6

Buyer Beware

I, Felipa Clavijo, *parda libre*, bring this redhibitory action against doña María Pardo, who gave me her word that Juana Criolla was neither a runaway nor a thief. Two days after I brought Juana to my house, she ran away and was absent for twenty days until the authorities brought her back to me. I have not been able to tame her nor bend her to my will. She has run away twice and at present is still missing. I demand that the seller return my 700 pesos.

They deliberately hid from me that Juliana was a habitual runaway and had always suffered from this vice under her previous owner. Juliana came into my hands over a month ago, but she immediately ran away. She was gone for thirty-seven days until the officers brought her back to me, and I was obliged to pay them 12 pesos for her recovery. And although I did not whip her or given her any reason to run away (indeed, I have tried to break her in with love and kind words), she ran away again soon thereafter. She has not returned since, and I find myself without Juliana or my money, and I conclude that I have been greatly swindled.

This chapter examines redhibition cases brought against cloistered and religious sellers of "defective" domestic slaves in the ecclesiastical court.[1] Redhibition cases were causes of action between buyers and sellers over defective merchandise.[2] Under Roman law, the *actio redhibitoria* was a special edict that regulated the sale of slaves. According to an early study, "The vendor was under a duty to declare any physical, mental, and moral defects with which a slave might be afflicted, and had to stipulate that no latent defects existed except those that were declared." Redhibition cases show a striking similarity across centuries, societies, and lawmakers. In effect, redhibition as a cause of action based on implied warranties was worked out almost exclusively around slave purchases and rescission – similarly to the way that rules of possession were developed around foxes and whales.[3]

Given these protections for aggrieved or remorseful buyers, redhibition cases were among the most popular classes of litigation involving slaves that were brought to courts.[4] Buyers alleged two categories of defects to cancel the purchase: undisclosed illness that predated the sale, and undesirable qualities manifested by the slave that rendered her unfit for domestic service. Sellers counteracted the charges of nondisclosure by claiming that the defect emerged during the new owners' tenure. In most rebuttals, sellers claimed that the buyers were notoriously cruel or malicious, causing the slave to flee. By casting aspersions about the harshness and brutality of the new owners, sellers implied that with proper care and supervision, slaves would be obedient and productive. In contesting responsibility for manifestations of illness, sellers alleged that insalubrious conditions in the new household had led to the slave's debilitation or illness.

Disgruntled buyers seldom alleged the existence of a singular defect – rather they bundled together illness with other undesirable traits like theft, drunkenness, and insubordination to strengthen their complaints. Aggrieved buyers complained about undisclosed health defects, but these defects were principally raised in conjunction with a slave's flight (see Table 6.1). The sparse number of judgments raises the presumption that it was difficult for either party to prevail in these suits on the basis of flight alone. Only twenty-five redhibitory actions have final judgments, and two parties publicly agreed to settle their lawsuit.[5]

We proceed along the gradient from person to property, not in an ineluctable arc toward property as slavery's terminus but to use the redhibition context to explore the simultaneity of the slave as property and person. As Ariela Gross notes, it is at the moment of sale or hire when slaves were most "property-like" to their owners.[6] Given its stark legal rationale in property law, many scholars have used redhibition in tandem with the slave auction block to highlight the conundrum of the slave as property, mobile capital, and person. But here, I pick up the loose skeins of redhibition and reweave them into the tapestry of domestic slavery. In particular, I look at powerful yet understudied players in the internal resale market: laywomen, monasteries, and religious personnel. How were domestic slaves traded or resold when they were deemed defective in some regard? Within the context of religious slaveholding, what can these transactions tell us about relationships between buyers and sellers, or about the ability of enslaved peoples to exert some control over the conditions of their work and family life within the boundaries of bondage?

The protagonists whom we have studied thus far have all engaged with the legal system as a means of navigating their relationships with adversaries and social superiors. However, in redhibition suits, the enslaved person was the object rather than the instigator of the lawsuit.[7] And yet, despite the appearance of these suits as property disputes between owners, slaves themselves prompted many of these claims. The defective merchandise had a human face, with individual personalities, illnesses, moods, "vices," and habits. As such, redhibition cases provide an opportunity to explore facets of protagonism that we have not yet considered.

Lima's domestic resale market operated on a trial period basis for one to two weeks. During that time, the potential buyer would "try out" a slave to see if she was a good fit for his household needs. Many sellers indignantly refuted the accusations of latent defect by pointing out (somewhat reasonably) that the buyers expressed satisfaction with the slave's services during the trial period. Were slaves and new owners on their best behavior for the trial period? Did new owners flex their disciplinary muscles immediately to assert dominance or conversely feign kindness to woo the slave into a false sense of security?[8] Emotions emerged during the difficult adjustment period that was intended to "ease" the slave into her new situation. As Juliana Conga's owner declared, "I have tried to break her in with love and kind words without whipping her to break her spirit." But Juliana simply ran away again.[9] Don Bartolomé (Juliana's owner) could have exaggerated his leniency, or perhaps Juliana was simply unwilling to remain enslaved in his household. Although the cases are replete with witness testimonies, very rarely did the slave herself testify.

Slaves in redhibition suits rejected the paths to liberty outlined in previous chapters. They refused to ingratiate themselves with their new owners. They did not negotiate more favorable terms based on affect, let alone filial piety. A slave's "rebellious" behavior and comportment precluded the possibility of her working toward self-purchase. Under more grim circumstances, slaves were deemed defective because they had an illness that made them physically unfit for hard labor. Eleven cases sought restitution for the death of a slave, including one suicide.[10] Hence, we delve into these cases looking for paths to liberty that were forged primarily by running away or by displaying objectionable characteristics like excessive drunkenness, stealing, and laziness – the quintessential weapons of the weak.

The most useful way to introduce the arguments raised in these suits is to immerse ourselves in a few typical redhibition cases. To this end, I first summarize two representative cases in the next section. Then I analyze Lima's resale market for domestic slaves, slaves who were sold by clerics, laywomen (*seglares*), and mother abbesses from the cloisters. I go on to examine the disciplinary environments of Lima's nefarious bakeries (*panaderías*) wherein runaway, rebellious, and incorrigible domestic slaves were imprisoned awaiting resale. The mother abbesses placed the most noncompliant women and girls in the bakeries as a punitive or precautionary measure, enabling us to trace the disciplinary spaces navigated by enslaved women. I then review slave prices as reflected in redhibition suits and apply a gendered lens to examine the flight patterns of runaway slaves. Because many of the buyers alleged illness as a basis for cancellation of the sale, I also explore the conditions the slaves were described as having using the framework of humoral pathology that served as the dominant medical paradigm during the early modern period. The chapter concludes with a reflection on the challenges of writing about protagonism – or, the weightier term for this, "slave agency" – in the context of these sales.

My rendition of these cases is guided by two overarching questions. What would liberty look like to Juliana? Who was Juliana? We have no record of her in baptismal or marriage books or any other accounts of her interactions with ecclesiastical or secular authorities. She is referred to in the redhibition suit simply as Juliana "of Congo, roughly twenty-two years of age" ("de tierra conga veintidos años poco mas o menos"). According to the official record, two ships left Central Africa in 1607, both of which were destined for the Spanish Americas.[11] Don Bartolomé bought her for 420 pesos, which he agreed to pay in two installments: one in November and the other by Christmas of 1607. We know nothing of her previous owners or when she arrived in the Americas, since she was quickly sold without any guarantee of defects (*tachas*). None of the three men involved in her transaction was prestigious enough to leave behind a discernible paper trail in the prosopographical tradition that would allow us to construct her life history through their legacies.

At twenty-two years of age, we presume Juliana was no stranger to the ardors and drudgery of domestic work. Why would she not opt for a pragmatic negotiation with don Bartolomé in light of her other alternatives? If we believe don Bartolomé (albeit a big "if"), he was inclined to treat her fairly – even kindly. I want to leave aside the obvious possibility that don Bartolomé's "love and kind words" euphemistically masked sexual violence. If don Bartolomé were a predatory rapist, the rationale for Juliana's flight is clear. Whatever the results of the lawsuit, Juliana would be have been immediately branded as a defective slave and imprisoned in a *panadería*. The seller would have returned don Bartolomé's first installment, and Christmas celebrations would have unfolded in the City of Kings without much disruption.

I presume that Juliana desired her liberty just as much as María Josefa Martínez, even though each woman adopted a different strategy with her respective owner. Juliana's calculus as a domestic slave was specific to her options and possibilities, but her flight was fueled by a desire for liberty. Perhaps Juliana found protection in the communities of runaways (*cimarrones*), or she may have had a male protector within one of the criminal gangs of *bandoleros* that preyed on Lima's residents. Juliana's seller may have prevailed in the case because the transaction was explicitly based on caveat emptor principles.[12] Running away and surviving as a *cimarrona* was only feasible when fugitive slaves had a community to which they fled.

Armed with decades of historiography about slave resistance and revolt, we have a greater appreciation for the protean forms of subversion.[13] To broaden our scope beyond strategic surrender and calculated compliance, let us now turn our attention to Ursula's case and consider other paths to liberty.

DRUNK AND DISORDERLY

In 1618, don Joseph de Castilla Altamirano purchased Ursula Criolla and her two-month-old son from the cleric Diego de Morales for the sum of 600 pesos.[14] According to don Joseph's complaint to the court, Ursula was an inveterate drunkard, "who drank herself senseless" ("se priva del sentido natural cuando se emborracha"). Moreover, don Joseph maintained that Ursula's drunken vice was a preexisting condition developed under Morales's ownership. Don Joseph brought his suit within a timely period, and after three accusations of *rebeldía* for his dilatory response, Morales responded to the summons.

In his defense, Morales claimed that he had purchased Ursula for 500 pesos when she was pregnant and that she never displayed any such drunk and disorderly conduct. Morales countered that don Joseph had ample time to evaluate Ursula's behavior, since she served in his house for the customary two-week trial period. After satisfactorily serving her trial period, don Joseph finalized Ursula's purchase. Finally Morales argued that he had many offers for Ursula, and he sold her to don Joseph at a fair price. As he declared, Ursula was worth much more than the 600 pesos he received because "she was sold with a young child and had breast milk" ("la vendí con cria y leche").

In the typical back and forth that characterized these cases, a few details became crystal clear. Ursula was in Morales's possession for a relatively short period after she arrived in Lima from Panama City. Four or five months later, Morales put her up for sale, although he swore that during the short tenure in his household, Ursula was "honest, clean, and compliant" ("fiel, limpia y segura"). According to Morales, Ursula was happy in his house. If she developed any of the alleged defects during don Joseph's employ, the onus was on him because it was widely known that don Joseph worked his slaves very hard.

CHOOSING AMONG OWNERS

In 1642, doña Francisca del Pulgar sued the Monasterio de la Santísima Trinidad for selling her Magdalena Conga, a slave she alleged had runaway vices and proclivities, as well as a defective arm.[15] This case was less straightforward than Ursula's, not least because the seller was interned in the Santísima Trinidad, and the order represented her interests in court. Nevertheless, the case illustrates many issues faced by female slaves who demonstrated *tachas* and so it is worth spending some time on the details of Magdalena's experience.

Doña Francisca purchased Magdalena Conga for 500 pesos almost a year prior to bringing her suit. Doña Francisca paid 300 pesos at the time of sale and agreed to pay an additional 200 pesos in two subsequent installments. It is not clear why Magdalena's owner was obliged to sell her – the record is silent in this regard. Though she belonged to the Santísima Trinidad, Magdalena had always worked as a *jornalera* outside of the cloister.[16] Doña Francisca complained that Magdalena fled within eight days of being in her power.

The principal witness in the case was doña Catalina Manrique, a nun who subcontracted Magdalena at her behest and unbeknownst to Magdalena's owner. Doña Catalina swore that Magdalena returned to the Santísima Trinidad weeping and showed her scars where doña Francisca had paid a lasher (*verdugo*) to whip her.[17] Magdalena begged doña Catalina to purchase her to work in her rural plot of land (*chacra*). Doña Catalina consented to Magdalena's entreaties either out of self-interest or genuine sympathy – and most likely a combination of both. In a long convoluted statement, doña Catalina claimed that she tried to purchase Magdalena from doña Francisca, but she proffered numerous excuses as to why Francisca did not receive her offer.[18] As a result of this breakdown in communication, doña Francisca had no knowledge of nor had consented to Magdalena's laboring on doña Catalina's lands. Magdalena was soon captured as a fugitive and imprisoned in a *panadería*.

However, the wages paid by the *panaderos* were lower than what doña Catalina had offered. Presumably, doña Catalina and doña Francisca eventually communicated about doña Catalina's offer. Doña Francisca subsequently responded affirmatively to Catalina, and *both* Magdalena and Catalina negotiated a lowered purchase price, in addition to drafting a permit for Magdalena to remain in the countryside gathering firewood without threat of apprehension.[19] The negotiation unfolded in 1642, when slave prices were steadily increasing – Magdalena would have fetched almost double the price that she would have in 1640 (see Table 6.5). Hence it is important to note Magdalena's instrumental role in lowering her price to an amount she was capable of paying for her liberty.

During the first month, Magdalena remitted 50 pesos in day wages (*jornales*) and alternated between gathering wood and husking corn to supplement her wages. Unfortunately, Magdalena was captured again a few months later without her permit (*conque*). Magdalena was so outraged at her arrest that the *alguacil* imprisoned her for insolence and insubordination (*soberbia*). Magdalena was forcibly returned to the city with the *alguaciles*, who held her in a *panadería* for three months.

The case ends without a judgment. But we can make some educated guesses about the lawsuit from doña Catalina's lengthy (albeit confused) testimony. Magdalena was unhappy with doña Francisca after her whipping and returned to the Santísima Trinidad, where she sought to change owners and perhaps even her entire line of work. Having lived in the cloisters for most of her life, Magdalena would not have been bereft of allies and potential patrons among the Trinitarias.

If we believe doña Catalina, Magdalena was exceptionally well suited for work traditionally associated with male slaves: gathering firewood and cornhusking. No mention was ever made of her defective arm, which was probably pretextual "bundling" given her subsequent dexterity in the fields. She earned wages that must have been supplemented by children or a male partner. At that rate (50 pesos a month) she would have earned her freedom in less than one year. It raises suspicion that Magdalena would have gone voluntarily to doña Catalina's lands. Most slaves refused to leave the city where they had built up networks of labor and kin over a lifetime for the countryside.

I suspect that Magdalena had support networks where doña Catalina's lands were located, and this prompted her proposition to doña Catalina to trade owners. Unfortunately, doña Catalina's testimony about the exchange was too convoluted to make much sense, but these kinds of trades (*trueques*) and subcontracts were not uncommon. In the redhibition context, *trueques* often led to allegations of fraud or uneven exchange. Doña Francisca willingly agreed to trade Magdalena after she was imprisoned in the *panadería*. Magdalena would have become known as publicly "defective" as a runaway given her repeated imprisonment. As such, it would have been difficult for doña Francisca to secure another buyer without disclosing her *tachas*.

FROM THE CLOISTERS TO THE SECULAR WORLD: SALES OF *CRIADAS* IN LIMA'S MARKET FOR DOMESTIC SLAVES

Sellers of domestic slaves who were sued in the ecclesiastical court were overwhelmingly monasteries, laywomen (*seglares*), and religious personnel. This was not merely a function of ecclesiastical jurisdiction. Monasteries were frequent sellers of domestic slaves. Consonant with the child circulation patterns discussed in Chapter 4, buyers preferred to purchase domestic slaves (*criadas*) who were raised in monasteries. Buyers regarded the mother abbesses as honest in their dealings and as purveyors of well-trained domestic slaves. At times, buyers who purchased *bozales* and young female slaves placed them within the cloisters for a training period so that they could learn domestic skills that would later be employed in their households.[20]

The nuns raised children of less fortunate circumstances and put the girls on the market once they acquired domestic skills or reached an age where they could earn a *jornal*. Criollas raised in convents were sought after and fetched a premium price.[21] Slaves who were community property could be put on the market after the demise of their owner or patron if they did not wish to profess as *donadas* and remain in the convent.

It appears that female slaves who subsequently contracted marriage were not allowed conjugal visits within the cloisters, as a slave's marriage was often cited as a reason for the sale.[22] While women's reproductive capacity was viewed favorably – and rewarded financially – some of the nuns seemed less enthusiastic about accommodating the sexual relationships that gave rise to the pregnancies.

Seglares who lived within the cloisters also sold their slaves when financial circumstances necessitated a sale. Laywomen had the pronounced advantage in redhibition suits, as they were able to rely on legal representation provided by the orders. Clerics, departing functionaries of the ecclesiastical administration and the Holy Tribunal, and prebendaries also appeared as sellers, although in fewer numbers. In sum, enslaved women and children were not only a source of labor within the cloisters; they represented financial assets for the orders as well.

When young female slaves rejected life in the cloisters, they were sold under caveat emptor principles. In 1669, María Victoria was sold for 800 pesos with her child because she refused to live in the convent.[23] Another cloistered owner, doña María Ignacia, was so angered by her slave's recalcitrance that she put her up for sale with full disclosure about her bad habits.[24] She sold Polonia, together with her six-year old daughter, for 550 pesos because Polonia was allegedly behind on all her day-wage payments. This was an extremely low price for an enslaved woman and child in 1692, revealing the owner's last-ditch attempts to extract whatever residual value she could out of an absentee and noncompliant slave. Even with the disclosure and the deflated price for the mother and child, the buyer sought to return Polonia and reclaim his money. At the time of the suit, the buyer complained that Polonia disappeared almost immediately from his employ and had been absent for three years in the countryside.

As members of the religious community, clerics and abbesses were careful not to be seen as motivated by crass profit when transacting slave sales.[25] Selling "defective" slaves stretched the boundaries of the discourse of religious tutelage that legitimated access to dependent and enslaved labor. Religious actors sought to distinguish or distance themselves from speculators and traders who were especially reviled. Until 1640, traders who held the royal license for slave trading (asientos) were of Portuguese origins and were often viewed with suspicion and disdain as New Christians. The presumed distinctions that ostensibly separated owners and traders lead us to believe that Limeños tried to distance themselves for fear of guilt by association.[26]

Religious and lay sellers often claimed that they were reluctant to sell the slave in question – who was invariably referred to as a skilled domestic – but that the other party insisted on the sale.[27] Sometimes sellers received the "defective" slave as part of an inheritance and sold her at public auction to exonerate themselves of the blame in failing to disclose tachas.

Sellers' dissemblance of their financial exigencies belied the circumstances that precipitated the sale in the first place. Of course, not all sellers refused to acknowledge financial gain. The transaction records listed the conditions that authorized the seller to put the slave on the market – sellers provided proof that attested to the absence of liens and mortgages and full ownership. The transaction also contained records of the original purchase price, and so it was easy to see when sellers made a profit or sold at a loss.

Even when financial gain was evident, it was couched in language calculated to make the seller seem indifferent about the pecuniary profit. We might expect this posturing among elite buyers and sellers. However, the pretense was upheld between parties of unequal status as well. Anton Jolofo, a free *bozal*, purchased a slave (also called Anton Jolofo) from the cleric Pedro de Guzmán.[28] Soon thereafter, Anton brought a redhibitory action against Guzmán, accusing Guzmán of selling him a defective slave who was too weak to withstand the arduous physical labor required for his job. Guzmán contended that Anton approached him with an entreaty "to purchase a slave from his same land" ("por ruegos que le tuvo el dicho negro su pariente de la misma tierra y nación"), and that the slave went willingly with Anton for the same reason. In this rendition of events, the seller was doing a magnanimous deed by reuniting two kinsmen rather than profiting from the transaction.

Since redhibition cases came about as a result of one party's putative dishonesty, the only way to defend one's honor was to discredit the other party through accusations of cruelty, ignominy, and negligence. Because the sellers in these proceedings were either members of the clergy or religious institutions, many parties had ongoing social and professional relationships. Thus, the aspersions cast by each side were calibrated according to the investments the parties had in their relationships with each other and in such a way that enabled them to maintain their honor and prestige. In his review of the records, Frederick Bowser surmises that the parties settled amicably, although the rancor that often suffused the accusations of fraud and deceit belied any sense of friendliness.[29] However, parties involved in long-term professional or kinship relationships preferred to settle in order to preserve those relationships.

Some aggrieved parties clearly had "buyers' remorse," and those claims were easily dismissed. Doña María de Morales bought María Carabalí and her two children for 700 pesos.[30] She paid 350 pesos as a down payment, and arranged to pay the rest in two installments. However, she tried to back out of the contract by alleging the defect of bedwetting in one of the young children and by referencing her fear of María's wrathful husband. Neither condition was enough to compel a rescission, since neither was an actual "defect." Plausibly, Maria's daughter was distressed by the marital strife between her parents or feared her father's anger, which caused her bedwetting. In this vein, the conjugal stress could have been unpleasant for the Morales household, but we discussed other cases in Chapter two where beleaguered wives used their owners to restrain a husband's wrath.

It is interesting nonetheless to consider what owners "should" have disclosed and to explore how parties who knew each other previously negotiated the limits of caveat emptor. Doña María purchased María Carabalí from a cleric who had inherited María Carabalí and her children from his aunt. María Carabalí was also pregnant at the time of her sale. Doña María clearly regretted purchasing the entire family and assuming their travails and vicissitudes. No doubt, she initially thought it was a great deal to get a lactating mother with young children so cheaply. But they had not been long enough in her employ to incite her to protect María from her husband, as in the cases considered in Chapter 2, and doña María sought to rid herself of the family before her remaining payments came due.

In cases like this, sellers proffered evidence – either through rumors or through the testimonies of lenders – that the buyers were overleveraged and could not afford to keep the slaves whom they purchased on credit. Since redhibition often resulted in a default judgment of a lowered price, an indebted buyer may have been motivated to bring a claim of latent defect in order to cancel the remaining payments.

Other cases that were overturned included buyers who waited too long to make the claim against the seller. Witnesses were brought in to strengthen the claims of both parties and (as expected) corroborated the version that they were summoned to verify. In the redhibition context, many witnesses were enslaved. This raised the practical problem of *tachas* – hence judges had to rely on witnesses who were bound to lie on behalf of their owners. Both sides then trafficked in notions of plebeian virtue in presenting their enslaved witnesses: slaves were either persons of "good customs and morals" or vile, sharp-tongued, and bad Christians.[31]

Except for a few cases of alleged unequal or fraudulent exchange (*trueques*), redhibition cases did not involve skilled slaves. "Good help" remained within the household in a quasi-family-retainer status or else purchased their liberty through thrift and considerable sacrifice.[32] None of the "defective slaves" in these redhibitory actions had started down the path of self-purchase. They were unskilled *jornaleros* – many of whom were new to Lima – who had not yet accumulated the social or monetary capital for their self-purchase.

DOMESTIC DISCIPLINE

> Give us this day our daily bread, and forgive us our debts.

Domestic servitude did not solely consist of a slave remaining within a stable household performing the arduous labors of care work. Just as I stretched the contours of the household to include cloistered *celdas* in Chapter 4, I now extend the boundaries of domestic servitude to include the city's *panaderías*, where rebellious women were routinely committed to perform hard labor.

In many sectors of the colonial economy, notably in New Spain, Quito, and Puebla, slaves, *mulatos*, mestizos, and indigenous people were consigned to textile mills (*obrajes*), which essentially functioned as penal workhouses.[33] Lima had few *obrajes*, but the city was filled with *panaderías*, which also were the equivalent of penal workhouses. Every neighborhood square had a place where its residents bought their daily bread. Bread was essential to the reconstitution of Iberian life in the Americas and doubly so in an important viceregal city like Lima.[34] To satisfy this insatiable need, the city turned to prison labor. As they intoned the familiar lines of the Lord's Prayer, Limeños knew that the dough of their daily bread was kneaded, rolled, and baked by imprisoned slaves under harsh and inhumane conditions.[35] The public specter of the *panaderías* and their ubiquity no doubt extracted compliance on the part of many women, but it motivated others like Juliana to fight and flee.[36]

Limeños did not clearly delineate spaces of carceral punishment from ordinary or everyday spaces.[37] Indeed, the city had only three prisons – that of the *Real Audiencia*, the subterranean cells of the Inquisition, and the Archbishopric – all of which were located in the main city center. In contrast, *panaderías* permeated Lima's physical space. The *panaderías* were replete with chains, coffles, and leg restraints for captured slaves.[38] Runaway slaves who spent extensive time in the restraints of a *panadería* developed ulcerated sores and edema in their legs. In some cases, sellers would release runaways from the restraints when the wounds were partially healed and put the slaves on the market. One runaway, Paula Criolla, was returned because she had developed "elefancia" in her legs. Paula's condition was out of the ordinary for such a young woman (she was twenty-two years old), but the edema could have developed as a result of excessive restraint. The mother abbess admitted that Paula had run away on two previous occasions from Santa Clara.[39] Paula had been restrained in a *panadería* awaiting resale.

Scholars of defective slave sales have referred to the process of reselling rebellious or infirm slaves as "reading the slave body."[40] Sellers refuted claims of runaway history by showing the absence of scars from chains and coffles (*grillos*) used by the *cuadrilleros* to capture runaway or rebellious slaves. Conversely, buyers pointed to the scars from whips and restraints in the *panaderías* as proof of the fact that the seller had failed to disclose the slave's insubordination and fugitive status.

Rebellious women were very rarely incarcerated. These cases unfolded centuries before the implementation of reformist projects inspired by penal correctional thought of the nineteenth century.[41] In the early modern city, incarceration was unprofitable for any slave owner.[42] Owners were responsible for feeding their slaves while imprisoned, and they also were expected to post the bond of 1 peso a day for a slave who was apprehended to cover her expenses.[43] More importantly from the owner's perspective, an imprisoned slave could not earn a *jornal*. As soon as a slave proved troublesome or "incorrigible," she was placed in a *panadería*. The owner was assured a daily (albeit lowered) wage, and the *panadero* assumed the responsibility and expenses associated with her confinement.[44] The owners of the *panaderías* paid the lowered daily wage of 1 peso – which was half of what *jornaleros* earned in Lima's "open" market. This arrangement ensured that *panaderos* and owners continued to extract both labor and capital from an imprisoned slave.

Domestic theft was one of the most commonly committed petty crimes by women and girls. However, domestic theft was rarely a matter for judicial resolution, let alone incarceration. Rather, punishment was privately arranged in the spaces of interior, everyday life.[45] Because domestic theft represented a breach of trust, it was left to the *patrón*, mother abbess, or guardian to impose

TABLE 6.1. *Slave Prices and Alleged Defects, 1600–99 (n = 110)*

	Male	Female	With child	10–18 years	19–40 years
Bozal	22	29	7	5	51
Criollo/a	18	22	4	14	40
Runaway/vices	21	25	4	9	42
200–500 pesos	22	15	2	8	1
525–780 pesos	16	25	5	5	21
800–1000 pesos	22	211	54	6	7
Illness	26	30	7	13	43
Death	10	1	0	0	11

discipline. But breach of trust went in both directions: an owner had to provide for his dependents' physical and material needs to claim that his slaves
violated their compact. Slaves could defend themselves against charges of theft
by claiming that they only took what they needed for sustenance from their
owners.[46]

Susana Criolla's buyers complained to the court that she was a thief and a
runaway who stole bread, eggs, cloth, and meat from their household and fled
over the walls at night. Susana also purportedly stole from other *criadas* in the
buyer's household, causing an uproar that prompted her flight.[47] However, no
charges were brought against her, since her theft was limited to food from her
owner's household. The buyers found it difficult to uphold a charge of latent
defect, although they complained bitterly that the mother abbess who sold
Susana deliberately withheld information about her thieving nature.[48]

Buyers in the redhibition suits alleged defects for fifty-one women and forty
men, split almost evenly between criollos and *bozales*. Forty women, four of
whom were mothers with children, were denounced as runaways. Since most
aggrieved buyers alleged both illness and vice in their complaints, it is nearly
impossible to draw any conclusions about subaltern subversive strategies like
running away, stealing, or "faking lunacy."[49] Nevertheless, the evidence suggests that most buyers brought claims to settle accounts when a slave fled the
new household.

In working through the redhibitory claims brought on the basis of flight,
I found it useful to divide enslaved runaways into three categories. Women
in the first group like Magdalena had a stable community to which they fled.
These women did not intend to become permanent fugitives. Runaway slaves
in the second group were primarily newcomers to Lima like Juliana, who were
not yet ensconced within the multigenerational networks that would have provided stability and access to better-paying *jornales*. The third group was comprised of repeat or habitual runaways who fled to the maroon communities
(*palenques*) or to haciendas outside of Lima. Polonia fits most comfortably
into this category.

Although this division is helpful for heuristic purposes, female and younger runaways moved fluidly in and out of spaces of domesticity, discipline, and imprisonment. Male runaways fled to the city's taverns (*chinganas*) and neighborhoods where they could hide and to *chacras* in the valleys of Lima. Regardless of age or gender, all captured escapees were imprisoned in the city's *panaderías* until their owners paid the cost of their recovery.

Enslaved women in the first group either returned to the house of their previous owners seeking a revocation of the sale or sought the protection of another ally. Women like Magdalena were denounced as "runaways," but we know she returned to the Santísima Trinidad to recruit a new patron. In 1640, Clara Folupa scaled the walls of her new owner's house, swinging from a rope that someone had placed over the walls for her. Unfortunately, she broke her leg during her getaway.[50] Clara declared her intent to return to her former owner and was obviously desperate to leave the household into which she had been sold.

A runaway's reversion to her former owner raised a legal dilemma. When a slave ran away, it was incumbent on the buyer to establish that she had a publicly known runaway or fugitive history. One act of escape was insufficient to force a rescission.[51] Judges were aware that new sales presented a flight risk. However, the law demanded that buyers present their case early enough to refute charges of dormancy. Once a case was formally admitted for review, the judges gave the parties time to locate and recover the runaway, work out an interim solution, and return the money to the seller minus the time spent and expenses incurred in the slave's recovery.

Since magistrates were reluctant to revoke the sale, the likely result of a redhibition suit was that the price of the defective slave would be reduced or the slave would be resold under caveat emptor principles. Every slave – no matter how defective – had residual value. Interim solutions for less desirable slaves devolved to the vagaries of the resale market in the city's *panaderías* and public works while buyers and sellers haggled in court. When sellers exhausted these options, restive and defective slaves were shipped off to Chile's presidios, rural haciendas, or exiled from Lima altogether.[52] As Chapter 2 shows, many slaves tried to prevent this fate by contracting a marriage that would allow them to remain in the city.

Sellers sometimes alleged that women with children were guaranteed not to run away. The putative stability of the mother-child unit enhanced their desirability from the buyer's point of view. Indeed, buyers like doña María de Morales and don Joseph de Castilla purchased enslaved women with their children as part of a "package deal." In addition to the children whom the buyer acquired at a low cost, a woman's reproductive future and her lactation could bring a higher purchase price. A woman could both be rented out as a wet nurse and feed the family's infant together with her own.[53]

In one case brought in 1668, the buyer claimed that he purchased a twenty-two-year-old slave whom he thought was pregnant so that she could nurse his own child.[54] He eagerly bought Feliciana for 800 pesos upon learning that she had borne four children in six years and was pregnant with a fifth. However, Feliciana miscarried during her fifth pregnancy, and the buyer subsequently discovered that two of Feliciana's children had died. He brought his redhibitory action after Feliciana's miscarriage, when she had no milk left to nurse his child. Despite the fact that he waited over a year to bring his claim, surprisingly, the buyer prevailed. In one of the rare occasions where the slave herself testified, Feliciana corroborated the buyer's claim that she had not been able to nurse his child as a result of her ill-fated pregnancy.

Younger slaves, whom I have categorized as falling between ten and eighteen years of age, were sold for higher than expected prices, especially in the latter decades of the century.[55] In 1658, fifteen-year-old Tomasa was sold for 800 pesos – an extremely high price for a young unskilled slave. Tomasa, who had come from Panama one year earlier, was apparently an artful dodger. Almost immediately, she slipped out of the Monasterio de Santa Clara and refused to return.[56] The buyer accused the mother abbess of only disclosing Tomasa's unwillingness to remain in the cloisters, not her fugitive history.

Repeat runaways had two choices: they could flee to the *chacras* or they could remain in the city hiding in plain sight. Because the city's outskirts were patrolled by slave-hunting *cuadrilleros*, runaways tried to make their way further north or south to the coastal haciendas and join makeshift *palenques*.[57] Bounty-hunting *cuadrilleros* relentlessly combed the city and highways looking for runaways, and their teams often included former runaways themselves who were intimately familiar with the routes and networks of *cimarrones*.[58] Those who remained in the city could more easily evade capture by *cuadrilleros*. Given the city's dense residential patterns, runaway slaves could avoid detection in predominantly black neighborhoods like Malambo and San Lázaro. But remaining in these communities as a fugitive was contingent on survival networks that could help the fugitive find ways to earn his or her keep.

Fugitives who fled the city had more extensive geographical networks, but they also had to live within reasonable distances of haciendas, roads, water, and rural communities. Throughout the Americas, the survival of *palenques* depended on geographic invisibility and dense vegetation for camouflage, as well as symbiotic relationships with surrounding communities for periodic raids and provisions.[59] However, these conditions did not widely obtain in southern Peru. Outside of Lima's fertile valleys where the *chacras* were located, the topography of the southern Andes was bleak and arid – an inhospitable environment for self-sufficient agriculture and camouflage.[60] *Palenques* surrounding Lima were thus few and far between, and enslaved runaways tended to live either on the margins of or within the haciendas – which always needed labor – where they could then partake of the same sources of food, water, crops, and transportation routes that supplied the haciendas.

Moreover, once outside of Lima, it was difficult for persons of African descent to maintain invisibility because of the policies of the two republics that prohibited blacks from living among *naturales* in Andean pueblos.[61] Free-roaming African-descent peoples were suspected as being out of place and could be reenslaved and imprisoned for failure to carry a permit (*conque*). If we remember, Magdalena was imprisoned for three months for failing to carry her *conque*. Rural African-descent peoples belonged to haciendas where they remained nominally under the control of Spaniards. *Zambos* (Afro-Andeans) were more easily camouflaged, and indeed, the record shows that *zambos* were among the groups most likely to "palanquearse." *Zambos* had media-tors among their mothers' communities, despite the constant remonstrations against allowing African-descent peoples and Andeans to commingle. Andeans who were alienated from their communities (*yanaconas*) also formed tempo-rary alliances with runaway slaves.[62] The administrative record is replete with fears regarding the assembly and union of these two groups as founts of indis-cipline and rebellion, and their movements were constantly surveiled.

SLAVE PRICES IN LIMA, 1600–1699

Redhibitory actions provide us with a fortuitous source to review slave trading within Lima throughout the seventeenth century: a period that is compara-tively understudied in light of fragmentary and incomplete sources. We have reliable notarial records of sales and transactions in Lima while the Portuguese *asentistas* controlled the trade.[63] However, records are much less reliable after the dissolution of the Spanish and Portuguese crown in 1640.

These tables show prices for slaves during the period before and after the dissolution of the Portuguese and Spanish crowns. The redhibition records reflect that slave prices double after 1640. In addition, the most valuable slaves were females of reproductive age, particularly in the latter half of the cen-tury. Limeño buyers paid even higher prices for female slaves than they did for skilled male slaves, highlighting the premium paid for women's reproductive potential. Even "incorrigible" slaves like Polonia and her child could still fetch 550 pesos toward the end of the century. See table 6.5.

Throughout the century, slaves had multisited points of entry to the Americas that reflected the informal trade routes and networks of interimpe-rial trade and contraband.[64] By its nature, contraband is notoriously difficult to quantify, and the extant historical sources are coy about provenance. As a result, we know far less about the provenance of slaves after 1640 in the Spanish colonies. Nonetheless, the scholarly consensus is that slaves destined for Lima disembarked in Portobelo, Tierra Firme (modern-day Venezuela), Jamaica (which was a Spanish colony until 1655), and Curaçao before they got to Cartagena.[65] Recall the mobility of the parties in Ursula Criolla's case.[66] Both don Joseph and Ursula had recently relocated to Lima. Ursula came from Panama City in the service of a cleric who moved to Lima to take up a post within the Archbishopric. Don Joseph had to find witnesses who knew Ursula when she was with her previous owner in Panama to corroborate her "public

TABLE 6.2. *Slave Prices in Redhibition Suits, 1600–40, 10–18 Years Old (n = 10)*

	Buyer beware	Male	Female	With child	Total
Bozal		2	1		3
Criollo		6	1		7
200–520 pesos		7	1		8
525–700 pesos		1	1		2
Total	0	8	2	0	10

TABLE 6.3. *Slave Prices in Redhibition Suits, 1600–40, 19–40+ Years Old (n = 37)*

	Buyer beware	Male	Female	With child	Total
Bozal	3	15	14	3	29
Criollo	0	4	4	1	8
200–520 pesos	3	19	11	1	30
525–700 pesos	1	0	7	3	7
Total	3	19	18	4	37

TABLE 6.4. *Slave Prices in Redhibition Suits, Prices 1640–99, 10–18 Years Old (n = 9)*

	Buyer beware	Male	Female	With child	Total
Bozal		2	0		2
Criollo	1	2	5		7
200–520 pesos	1	1	0		
525–1,000 pesos		3	5	1	
Total	1	4	5	1	9

TABLE 6.5. *Slave Prices in Redhibition Suits, Prices 1640–99, 19–40+ Years (n = 56)*

	Buyer beware	Male	Female	With child	Total
Bozal		8	17	4	25
Criollo	2	12	19	3	31
200–520 pesos	4	6	5	0	11
525–1,000 pesos		14	31	7	45
Total	6	20	36	7	56

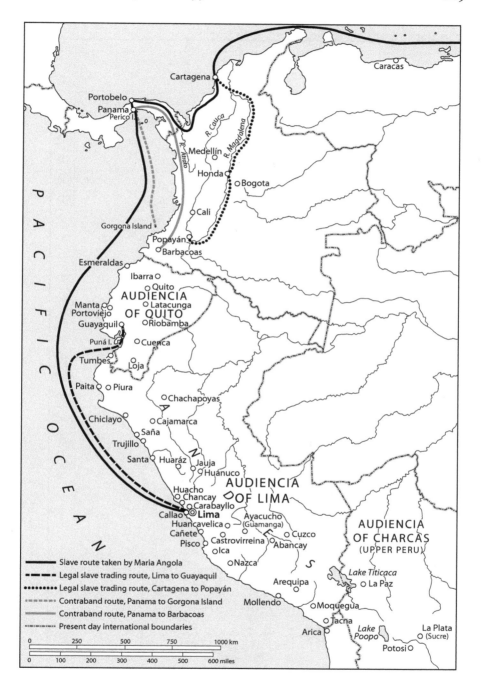

Caracas

Cartagena

Portobelo
Panama
Perico I.

R. Cauca

R. Atrato

R. Magdalena

Medellín

Honda

Bogota

Cali

Gorgona Island

Popayán

Barbacoas

Esmeraldas

Ibarra

Quito

AUDIENCIA
OF QUITO

Latacunga

Manta

Portoviejo

Riobamba

Guayaquil

Puná I.

Cuenca

Tumbes

Loja

Paita

Piura

Chachapoyas

Chiclayo

Cajamarca

Saña

Trujillo

Santa

Huaráz

Jauja

Huánuco

Huacho

AUDIENCIA
OF LIMA

Chancay

Carabayllo

Callao

Lima

Ayacucho
(Guamanga)

Cuzco

AUDIENCIA
OF CHARCAS
(UPPER PERU)

Huancavelica

Cañete

Castrovirreina

Abancay

Pisco

Ica

Nazca

Lake Titicaca

La Paz

Arequipa

Mollendo

Moquegua

Tacna

*Lake
Poopo*

La Plata
(Sucre)

Arica

Potosi

P A C I F I C   O C E A N

A N D E S

——— Slave route taken by Maria Angola

– – – Legal slave trading route, Lima to Guayaquil

•••••• Legal slave trading route, Cartagena to Popayán

·········· Contraband route, Panama to Gorgona Island

——— Contraband route, Panama to Barbacoas

·–·–·– Present day international boundaries

0   250   500   750   1000 km

0   100   200   300   400   500   600 miles

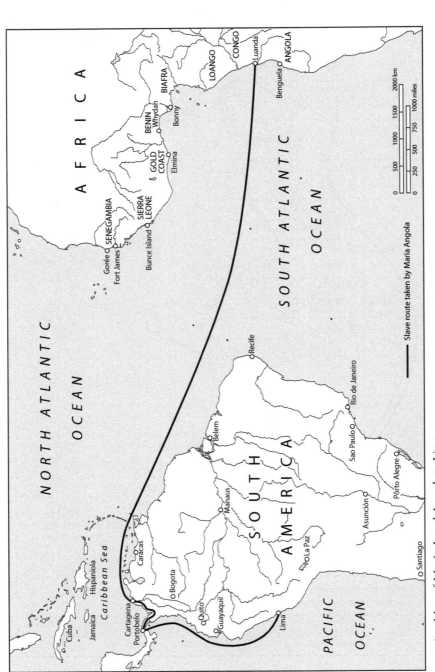

MAP 6.1 Map of María Angola's path to Lima.

Map by: David Cox, Smuggling and Slave trading routes from Central Africa to Lima.

and notorious" drunkenness there. Don Joseph was himself a recent transplant from New Spain. None of the parties – with the exception of Morales – had lengthy ties to Lima.[67]

In redhibition suits, Lima's owners were seemingly confined to the internal resale market, but the boundaries of that market extended to Buenos Aires, Cartagena, Tierra Firme, Portobelo, Panama City, and other Atlantic sites into which slaves were imported. (see map 6.1). One seller in a 1652 redhibitory action refuted the accusation that she sold her slave María Angola with an incurable illness. As the seller claimed, Maria Angola walked from Portobelo (Panama) to Cartagena together with "a group of slaves" ("un armazón de negros") before arriving in Lima. The seller, doña Isabel de Medina, bought María Angola for her personal service in the Monasterio de la Concepción, where she remained interned for a few months. María Angola married quickly after her arrival in Lima. Doña Isabel claimed that she would not have sold María Angola but for the inconvenience occasioned by her marriage.

According to doña Isabel's rendition, a hale and hearty María virtually bounded out the slave ship that transported her from Central Africa and then sprinted across the Americas rather than being shackled and marching hundreds of miles in a convoy overland from Portobelo to Cartagena and then shipped to Lima.[68] We are reminded of Jennifer Morgan's point that Europeans imbued African women's bodies with superhuman strength and powers that naturalized their capacities for hard manual labor and multiparity.[69]

ACCOUNTING FOR ILLNESS AND DEATH

Buyers alleged preexisting health conditions in fifty-six cases as grounds for revoking the sale. See table 6.1. What appear to our modern medical sensibilities as palsy, edema, deafness, strokes, or epilepsy were conditions portrayed as physical and undisclosed defects. As mentioned previously, buyers routinely bundled together flight and illness to prevail in their suits. In my reading of the records, however, only thirty-nine of the fifty-six cases were genuinely based on illness. Eleven cases were brought as a result of the slave's death, and the remaining six were cases in which illness was bundled with flight. At other times, dissatisfied buyers protested the sale claiming that slaves were "broken" or had faulty limbs, alleging this as an undisclosed infirmity. Unless buyers purchased slaves sight unseen, it was hard to maintain that they had no knowledge of a physical defect like a limp, a blind eye (*tuerta*), deafness, or a broken hand or foot.

Buyers who tried to rescind a sale on the basis of illness had to proffer the expert opinion of a doctor (*protomédico*) that the slave was in fact incurable and that medical treatment had been applied to no avail.[70] The

FIGURE 6.1. Frontispiece, *Tratado de las siete enfermedades*, Alexo de Abreu. [1623].

alleged health conditions merit a sustained study, and regrettably I do not
have the space here to do them justice. Nonetheless, they provide unique
insight into the corporeal and lived experiences of enslaved peoples, as well
as the cultural and spiritual resources that comprised early modern medical
practices.

Buyers complained that enslaved men and women had undisclosed defects
in their "secret parts" or "shameful parts" ("partes secretas" or "partes vergon-
zosas"), defects that manifested themselves in pustules and bubonic symptoms
(*mal de bubas*) and tumors in the groin, underarms, and neck. Syphilis and
yaws could also be known as *mal de bubas*.[71] A few male *bozales* were afflicted
with Guinea worm, a disease with African roots that was most likely contracted on the slave ships.[72] Others – men and women, old and young – were

diagnosed with swelling or edema in the lower extremities (dropsy), scabies, seizures leading to heart failure, and upper respiratory disorders.[73]

According to early modern medical humoralism, human health was contingent on the balance of four humors that circulated within the body.[74] Human bodies were comprised of blood, phlegm, black bile, and yellow bile. Health was defined as the equilibrium of the humors and their interaction with the earthly elements (fire, air, earth, and water). When someone fell ill, it was related to humoral imbalance combined with disequilibrium with one of the earthly elements.

There is no evidence from the records that Spanish medical practitioners who testified to the courts believed that the African or Andean body differed from the Iberian in its propensity for affliction.[75] Treatment for slaves, such as bloodletting and purgatives to restore the equilibrium, was identical to that prescribed for Spaniards. Diet and air played a large part in curative and restorative healing practices. Heterodox medical practices and beliefs also encompassed spiritual or miraculous healing, which provoked anxieties among the clergy about the blurry lines between acceptable faith and idolatrous practice.[76]

Iberian humoralism and popular Catholicism were compatible with appeals to intercessors such as ancestors, deities, and spirits, though beliefs in the powers of such entities were potentially idolatrous. Clerics sought to redirect Andean and African beliefs that supernatural powers bore responsibility for illness and misfortune by promoting the veneration of local saints who would intercede to cure physical ailments.[77] The miraculous thaumaturgical and intercessory powers of local saints of African-descent like Fray Martín de Porras, Ursula de Jesús, and Estephanía de San Joseph gave rise to cultlike followings.[78] Less well-known healers – Andean, creole, Iberian, and African – built up reputations associated with divination, incantation of prayers, astrology, peninsular "witchcraft" practices, and amatory magic.[79] Midwives, who treated a wide array of obstetric and reproductive disorders, were also often lay healers and purveyors of amatory potions.[80]

Andean and African approaches to health and curative strategies were also incorporated into Iberian vernacular humoralism – although this syncretism is faintly adumbrated in the records because of its potential heretic nature.[81] We see only fleeting evidence of African or Andean ritual healing practices in the records, since buyers tried to prove their scrupulous adherence to humoralism by proffering the testimonies of doctors *(protomédicos)*. Some of the records mention that healers *(curanderas)* visited the patient, though the definitive opinion was deferentially left up to physicians' reports and diagnoses.[82] However, it would be incredulous to presume that buyers and slaves did not use local healing practices to treat illness.

A few buyers made vague claims to gynecological distress that hindered female slaves' ability to serve.[83] One owner sought to return a sixteen-year-old slave named Catalina Criolla because she had not as yet begun to menstruate.[84]

The buyer feared that this "imbalance" in Catalina would manifest itself in moodiness. We see in the witness testimonies that lay remedies were ineffective: the onset of Catalina's menstruation was impervious to teas, cleansing maize baths, and purgatives. The seller tried to protect himself by offering a doctor's testimony that young women's menstrual cycles could be delayed until their twenty-fourth birthday.

Only two of the men and women surveyed here were over fifty years old. They commanded a low purchase price.[85] At fifty-two years of age, Monica Ladina was sold for 150 pesos and returned because of illness of the womb (*mal de madre*) and excessive weepiness.[86] *Mal de madre* was a catchall term for gynecological distress and encompassed miscarriages, obstructions, and problems giving birth.[87] Cases of *mal de madre* were routine areas of intervention for lay healers and abortionists.

In a few cases, men and women were rendered mentally infirm as a result of high fevers or epileptic attacks. In the vivid descriptions offered by witnesses, the attacks simulated spirit possession. Others suffered from conditions associated with weak constitutions, feeble minds, and faulty bodies. María Feliciana was a convicted witch who appeared twice in the redhibition records, having been resold under false pretenses after her imprisonment in 1673 for engaging in witchcraft and idolatry.[88] Manuel Angola walked around stupefied, apparently besotted with love, and ran away to be with his lover. In his rebuttal, the seller claimed that Manuel's condition was provoked by the (effective) use of amatory magic by his lover, who was agitating for marriage.

There was only one woman among the eleven deaths reported. Bernarda Criolla ingested an abortifacient that provoked a lethal miscarriage.[89] Bernarda was purchased for 990 pesos – one of the highest prices paid for any of the slaves in this sample. Though we must read Bernarda's case with care, witnesses who knew her previously attested to her repeated attempts to end other pregnancies before ingesting the potion that killed her. As in Margarita de Torres's case, we know nothing of the relationships that preceded and gave rise to Bernarda's pregnancies. Even if we do not believe the witnesses who claimed that Bernarda had tried to end other pregnancies, she undoubtedly took decisive steps to terminate the pregnancy that ended her life.[90] Abortive practices, while not illegal at this time, were strongly discouraged. The *protomédico* prescribed an antidote for the abortifacient, but two days later when he went to check on Bernarda, he found her dead.

Antonio Mina, the lone suicide in this sample, was at risk of hanging himself long before he was sold.[91] Antonio's buyer brought a posthumous redhibitory action after he committed suicide by stabbing himself in the stomach. According to the buyer, Antonio had scars on his neck that corresponded to previous unsuccessful suicide attempts stemming from his insolent and irredeemable nature.[92] The seller's witnesses testified that the fatal wound came from the *alguaciles* who arrested Antonio as a fugitive, thereby rebutting the presumption that Antonio had killed himself.

Surprisingly, the seller prevailed in this case, despite the fact that the con-tract included his agreement to take Antonio back *in the event that he tried to hang himself* in the buyer's power. Alonso de Arcos (our busy, omnipres-ent procurator) pointed out that this kind of contingency was rare in the documents and asked the seller to explain it. The seller could not. Instead, the seller offered testimonies from Antonio's shipmates that the marks on Antonio's throat were scars from injuries he had sustained as a child in Africa.[93] Although we search diligently for vestiges of the African past in the documents, this version reads more like a rehearsed memory of a bucolic European boyhood than a genuine reminiscence. The only "truth" in this transcript is that Antonio was excessively punished for what seemed to be his insolence and insubordination under the buyer's power and his desperate attempt to leave his enslaved existence.

AT THE NEXUS BETWEEN PROPERTY AND PERSON

As abolitionism scholars have long noted, the slave *trade* prompted more moral outrage and anxiety than either the intergenerational transmission of slavery or its continued institutional existence. This perceived dichotomy between the slave block and the internal resale market both shaped and framed the double character of enslaved peoples.[94] Yet slave trading and slaveholding were part of the same transactional logic of labor acquisition and profit. Alongside and often in dialogue with studies of the international slave trade and abolition, scholars have increasingly focused on the relationship between the actuarial practices of slavery and racial capitalism.[95]

Studying defective slave sales in a single context gets around the dubious dichotomy between the slave block and the internal market. Internal mar-kets prompt questions of boundaries and scale. Was the trade "internal" as opposed to "transatlantic" when Ursula came from Panama City to Lima? Or when Margarita de Aguirre came to Lima from the north of Peru pawned (*en empeño*) to satisfy her owner's debt to someone else? How do we categorize the intergenerational transmission of wealth in the case of a slave like Margarita de Torres who did not enter the "market" but changed owners nonetheless?

Numerous scholars have used the redhibition context to juxtapose the relationship between the alienable (property) and the inalienable (self) as an inherent, built-in abstraction that emerged when people owned people. The neo-abolitionist inquiry into redhibition often unfolds in dialogue with writing about *marronage* as the ultimate rejection of the chattel principle and evidence of agency on the part of enslaved peoples. Because my argument throughout this book has been predicated on the existence of aggregate paths to freedom, I found it useful to think through temporary flight and *marronage* (*cimarronaje*) from a gendered perspective and compare these with the travails of remaining within the urban domestic household. In part, I privileged fractional freedoms as an analytical framework because the study of slave resistance was for so long focused on *marronage* that led to acts of rebellion as the sine qua non of resistance.[96] While *marronage* was undeniably a rejection of the slave owner's domination, women fit uneasily into the framework of resistance through flight. Stephanie Camp argues convincingly that enslaved women and men experienced space and movement differently.[97] Camp's observations about the disciplinary contours of the domestic environment, the perils of unfamiliar geographies, and the ways in which enslaved women sought temporary reprieve from intolerable situations through truancy resonates strongly with the experiences of many women in the redhibition cases I have examined.

At the extremities of the external market, the sources refer to pieces (*piezas*) transported from place to place. Rural entries show the acquisition of parcels (*parcelas*) of slaves for hacienda work. In the transactional parlance of freight and duty, a *pieza* was one whole product – the equivalent of an adult male slave. Half pieces could have been women, and quarter pieces children: traders paid customs and excise on one whole piece.[98] The administrative correspondence reveals constant haggling among the commercial trading house and its court and the Council of the Indies over revenue due the crown from the slave trade.[99] By the close of the sixteenth century, the dreams and speculations of the wealth potentially generated by the slave trade were less often couched in the erstwhile language of just war and conquest and increasingly harnessed to a discourse of revenue. As one influential Portuguese speculator contended to the Council of the Indies in 1589, "In Angola alone it was possible to take out eight thousand pieces annually, and in the process consolidate the conquest of the African coast."[100]

By the time slaves were resold on the internal market, they had acquired a property history, one that was both material and embodied. When buyers proffered evidence of unencumbered ownership, they pointed to decades of accumulated relationships, labor practices, and interwoven histories. Depending on the length of time the slave had been in Lima and the circumstances that prompted the slave's sale, we see property histories that are deeply intertwined. I have resisted writing in the vein of the external slave trade – even for someone new to Lima like Juliana Congo – by tracing the names, histories, and life stories of the slaves in these redhibitory cases. I did not adopt this approach because I find the alienation of the slave block a deliberately discomfiting and hence effective idiom. Rather, I did so because the neo-abolitionist language of market and capital falls short when I try to think about what liberty would look like to someone like Juliana and what "options" she may have had.

This is not a criticism of the powerful abolitionist rhetorical tradition. Even though I eschew the dispassionate economical language of the market and its transactions, I know that simply reverting to the methods of thick description does not displace its logics.[101] No amount of obsessive historiographical pointillism could obscure the fact that some of the men and women documented herein took extreme measures to end their lives. The people in this book were both property and persons, and more importantly, many owned fractions of themselves.[102] The market overlapped, traversed, and undergirded their personhood producing a friction between zones or border skirmishes that exposed just how intertwined these zones were – and perhaps laid bare the wholly fictive nature of the boundary itself.[103] In this chapter, I have tried to think through the chattel principle in a society in which slaves owned parts of themselves – that is, in a society where contingent liberty was aspirational and real for many people – and to imagine what redhibition looked like within those parameters.

Let me close on a case that touches on many themes raised throughout this chapter and the book in general. Enslaved women who married also posed difficulties for religious owners, as we have seen, as wives could become flight risks. In August 1655, don Diego Camaño de Figueroa purchased Catalina Criolla for 750 pesos.[104] Catalina was married to don Diego's slave Antonio Criollo. Don Diego was able to expedite the purchase because Catalina had run away to his house to be with her husband and refused to leave. Don Diego then approached Catalina's owner, proposing to purchase her. Catalina's owner grudgingly accepted the offer, complaining bitterly that it was nothing short of extortion because don Diego refused to release Catalina into her power. Moreover, as the reluctant seller maintained, she was obliged to sell Catalina at a huge loss, having purchased Catalina for 900 pesos in a previous transaction.

Was the redhibitory action a ploy on don Diego's part to acquire Catalina cheaply, motivated by opportunism in the couple's reproductive future? No doubt, some degree of opportunism prompted don Diego's offer. If we recall, Catalina and Antonio were María Albina's parents, whose baptismal manumission case is documented in Chapter 4. Catalina did not want to remain with her original owner in the cloister because she seemed reluctant to honor Catalina's conjugal rights. The redhibition case (which was based on Catalina's supposed flight) and its afterlife reveal the multiple layers of obligation that informed María Albina's parents' relationship with don Diego. Theirs was an insecure world that revolved around the orbit of one patron and his networks. Ironically, neither María Albina nor Catalina could avoid the Santísima Trinidad: the place from which Catalina fled exerted a centrifugal pull for the women in this family as María Albina was interned within it for nearly two decades.

María Albina's connection to this earlier redhibitory action is not merely a felicitous archival discovery (although it was indeed a happy moment in the archives for me). It also vividly illustrates the state of contingent liberty in which many enslaved peoples lived their lives, and it urges us to think more seriously about segmented freedom as the norm rather than as the exception. The generational connection also raises questions about how we think about "property" before the triumph of the market and the advent of commercialization that were hallmarks of nineteenth-century liberalism.[105]

I do not claim that there was no market in early modern Iberoamerica. Indeed, I have looked closely at the transactional logics and patterns of the sixteenth- and seventeenth-century slave trade that emerge from these disputed cases. Rather, I have suggested that a study of the internal slave trade benefits from treating property relations historically, a treatment inspired by the economic microhistories of individuals and their social networks.[106] Catalina's experience as a putatively defective slave two decades previously, and a valuable slave who relocated with the family to Lima later, is a striking example of how these cases wove together the life stages of property, debt, personhood, market, enslavement, marriage, and childbirth and how the law was fundamental to those configurations.[107]

Focusing on clerical transactions enables us to trace multigenerational relationships and reveals how deeply imbricated religious actors were in the slave trade. From their sedate position within their cloistered worlds, laywomen and mother abbesses were active participants in the exchange circuits in the interimperial slave trade.

In looking closely at the various stages of flight and *marronage* from a gendered perspective, we see that Juliana took a different path to seek her liberty from that of many others described in this book: she refused to negotiate with her owner and fled. We know nothing about Juliana. Yet as a runaway African slave, she resonates with a venerable historiographical legacy of rebellious actors. Here she joins Caetana, the Brazilian slave who resolutely said no to her owner's marriage plans, and Celie, who killed and burned her master after repeated sexual assault.[108] Though this book has largely discussed women who chose strategic negotiation and who experienced segmented freedom, Juliana's story (or lack of it) motivated my reading and writing of these cases.

NOTES

1 During the seventeenth century, buyers brought 129 redhibitory actions in the ecclesiastical court and 8 in the *Real Audiencia*. The epigraphs to this chapter are quoted from AAL, Causas de negros, leg. 15, exp. 17, año 1679, and leg. 1, exp. 23, año 1608, respectively.

2 Oppenheim, "The Law of Slaves." Oppenheim drew his observations regarding afflictions from Buckland's study, which classified theft, attempts at suicide, and escape as vices ("The Law of Slaves," 389 n. 32).

3 For the canonical case in property law regarding the rights of possession, see *Pierson v. Post*, 3 Cai. R. 175 2 Am. Dec. 264 (1805).

4 Daniel Murray's historical survey of implied warranty law ("Implied Warranty against Latent Defects") reviews Germanic, Egyptian, Semitic, Hindu, and Muslim (particularly the Hanífa school) laws, which all delimited the rights and responsibilities of buyers and sellers of enslaved persons. Although this was a cause of action based in the civil law, the rights of the buyer seem to originate from the universal distrust of unscrupulous slave sellers.

5 There were twenty-five final judgments in total: nineteen ruled for the buyer, four for the seller, and there were two in which the parties agreed to settle.

6 Gross, *Double Character*, 3.

7 See Schafer, "Guaranteed against the Vices and Maladies Prescribed by Law."

8   Johnson, *Soul by Soul.*

9   AAL, Causas de negros, leg. 1, exp. 23, año 1608, complaint of Bartolomé Ramírez regarding Juliana Conga.

10 AAL, Causas de negros, leg. 17, exp. 21, año 1674.

11 According to the Transatlantic Slave Trade Database, the *Santiago* arrived in Veracruz on April 26, 1607, under the direction of the Portuguese captain Diego Mendez with 269 captives aboard. The *Santiago* set sail with 379 captives. If this was the ship on which Juliana arrived, she was one of the survivors of that crossing. All we know about the outcome of that voyage was that slaves disembarked in the Americas after landing in Veracruz. See www.slavevoyages.org/tast/database/search.faces.

12 As the seller argued, "Yo vendí la dicha negra con las tachas que fueron las con que a mí me la vendieron."

13 David Barry Gaspar argues for a broader analysis of resistance and *marronage* in seventeenth-century Antigua. According to Gaspar, our notions of subversion have been broadened to include "behavior that [was unequable] with cooperation with slavery" ("From the Sense of their Slavery," 220). On subversive strategies within the antebellum plantation household, see Glymph, *Out of the House of Bondage.*

14 AAL, Causas de negros, leg. 3, exp. 13, año 1618.

15 AAL, Causas de negros, leg. 8, exp. 24, año 1642.

16 Refuting charges of Magdalena's runaway history, doña Francisca's procurator averred, "Todo el tiempo que la dicha mi parte se sirvió de la dicha esclava dentro del convento fue de las mejores que se a conocido y abiéndola salido del mismo convento andaba a ganar y aunque algunas veces los alguaciles la coxían por cimarrona, constándole desta verdad la soltaba sin llevar premio ni castigarla y así es evidente que nunca se huyó."

17 *Verdugos* were hired to torture criminal suspects and witnesses in the prisons, and allegedly in this case one was hired to discipline errant slaves.

18 At one point doña Catalina testified that she sent one of her slaves to tell doña Francisca about the exchange, but it was a very sunny day, and the slave sent her son instead, who was reputedly someone too irresponsible to have been entrusted with such an important missive: "Esta testigo enbió llamar a la dicha Francisca con una mulata esclava suya nombrada Ana la cual enbió a decir que por hacer mucho sol no venía y enbio a un hijo suyo que anda en avito de monigote."

19 The permit (*conque*) was an important document that specified the slave's owners and the owner's knowledge of the slave's whereabouts. They functioned in an equivalent manner to "pass laws" in the Anglo-American tradition. Slaves could be apprehended and impressed into hard labor without the requisite *conque*. A slave "between owners" also had to carry a *conque* to show that she was searching for a requisite master and to clarify that she was not yet a freed person. See Hünefeldt, *Paying the Price of Freedom*, 74–76.

20 See, for example, AAL, Causas de negros, leg. 14, exp. 2, año 1664. The buyer purchased fourteen-year-old Melchora for 730 pesos and left her in the Santísima Trinidad to learn basic laundering, cooking, and domestic skills. He was led to believe that Melchora was also pregnant at the time, and her internment was supposed to coincide with her training and safe parturition. However, Melchora was not pregnant. Instead, the swelling in her stomach appeared to be a uterine tumor (*un bulto en la bola matriz*).

21 The cases also reveal much about what attributes owners considered desirable in domestic slaves, as well as expressing preferences for *bozales* as opposed to criollas for certain kinds of work. Criollas were favored for domestic work, though they enjoyed a mixed reputation as wet nurses. Though tall and graceful, Minas were allegedly bad tempered and insolent. Jolofos and Congos were insubordinate (*castas de mal natural y soberbio*). Guineas, Angolas, and Brans were reputedly sought after for their "pleasant temperament." This racialized naturalization allows us to see how labor practices and regimes functioned and how new African arrivals were incorporated within the urban milieu. On the preference for *bozales* over criollos in rural environments, see Tardieu, "El esclavo como valor."

22 I presume that married couples arranged for conjugal visits in the husband's quarters or enjoyed relations with the tacit knowledge and consent of their owners inside the *celdas*. Nancy van Deusen writes that enslaved husbands made claims against the orders for denying their conjugal visits on designated days, which suggests that couples should have been permitted to maintain marital (and by extension, sexual) relationships. See van Deusen, "The 'Alienated' Body," 11. My reading of the redhibitory cases is that many cloistered owners either resisted the husbands' entries into their *celdas* or sold their slaves because of their marriages.

23 AAL, Causas de negros, leg. 15, exp. 21, año 1669. The buyer should have been suspicious in this case, given that María Victoria was purchased a few months previously for 1,000 pesos and had always lived within the convent. This case contains many half truths and misrepresentations. María Victoria's previous owner provided her with medical care after she gave birth to a baby daughter seven years earlier. It seemed she never recovered from the pelvic harm suffered in that pregnancy – she would only have been eleven years old when she first gave birth. When María Victoria had her second child, she suffered from dysentery, and the buyers proffered medical testimony that this sickness was aggravated by a preexisting condition. María Victoria's owner died almost immediately before her sale. It seems that the mother abbess did not want to continue caring for her and sold her – together with her daughter – at a considerable loss. Others testified that the abbess would have accepted the child as a *donada* but could not separate her from María Victoria – presumably because of the child's young age.

24 AAL, Causas de negros, leg. 23, exp. 28, año 1692. According to doña María, Polonia was "de tan mal natural que no atiende a socorrerme con la puntualidad que mi necesidad precisa."

25 Religious communities were the largest slave owners and purchased slaves for work on haciendas, in hospitals, or in other religious institutions directly from their own buyer (*asentista*) in Portobelo. Luis Martín estimates that at the time of the Jesuits' expulsion in 1767, the orders held at least 800 slaves (*Intellectual Conquest of Peru*, 71). For a discussion of the Jesuit haciendas in Peru, see Cushner, "Slave Mortality and Reproduction." Priests like Diego de Morales and Andrés Clavijo who resold slaves on a repeat basis, however, threatened to expose the mercantilist enterprise that underwrote slavery rather than its moral and theological legitimation.

26 In the entire corpus of redhibition cases, only two were directed at Lima's principal slave trader: Manuel Bautista Pérez. See AGN, Real Audiencia, Causas civiles, leg. 70, cuad. 263, año 1626, and AAL, Causas de negros, leg. 4, exp. 9, año 1620. Manuel Bautista Pérez was executed during the 1635 *complicidad grande*

that encircled prominent members of Lima's commercial community for suspected heresy as crypto-Jews. On the *complicidad grande* and Pérez's trial, see Silverblatt, *Modern Inquisitions*, 47–53. It is not clear why traders like Pérez who held the royal license (*asiento*) to import slaves were not implicated in more redhibition suits. On Pérez's global networks in the slave trade, see Newson and Minchin, *From Capture to Sale*.

27 Owners rebuffed the charges of dissatisfaction by pointing out that prospective buyers observed the slaves' performance in their homes that induced repeated offers of purchase. As Diego Morales averred in a subsequent suit regarding his reluctance to sell Guiomar Biafara, "Estaba tan buena y sana en mi poder y cuando se la vendí que aficionada de ella y de su talla y obras que la mujer de la parte contraria me enbio muchos recaudos y me pidió con instancia muchas veces le vendiese la dicha esclava" (AAL, Causas de negros, leg. 4, exp. 7, año 1619). Guiomar had her own version of Morales's treatment. According to Guiomar, she was healthy in her previous owner's employ, but he became angry at her for marrying her husband against his will. In a retaliatory rage, he sold her to Morales in whose household she fell ill. She never recovered, she alleged, because of Morales's neglect and his failure to summon a doctor to attend to her menstrual obstruction.

28 AAL, Causas de negros, leg. 6, exp. 1, año 1630.

29 Bowser, *The African Slave in Colonial Peru*, 192.

30 AAL, Causas de negros, leg. 7, exp. 34, año 1638.

31 Enslaved witnessess were referred to favorably as "personas de buena vida, costumbres y de confianza" or, conversely, as "vil, de mala lengua, desvergonzada y malas cristianas."

32 On family retainers, see Ray and Qayum, *Cultures of Servitude*, 67. Recall Margarita de Aguirre's case discussed in Chapter 1. Margarita cared for her former owners and nursed them during their illness for *decades* after she had purchased her liberty.

33 As Manuel Miño Grijalva notes for the *obrajes* of New Spain, "el obraje era también sinónimo de horror y cárcel" ("El obraje colonial," 4).

34 Rebecca Earle extensively traces the importance of bread in the Iberian diet. See *Body of the Conquistador*, ch. 2.

35 As Arrelucea Barrantes observes, "Nadie ignoraba que el pan era elaborado por esclavos y presos bajo condiciones deplorables, torturas, azotes, escasa luz, agotadoras jornadas, enfermedades endémicas e intenso calor" (*Replanteando la esclavitud*, 92).

36 Arrelucea Barrantes usefully sketches a continuum of domestic slavery that included the sexual partner and trusted housekeeper (*ama de llaves* like Joana de Loyola), the quasi-autonomous *jornalera* who lived in separate quarters and paid her owners a monthly quota, and those who were confined to the prison-like conditions of the *panaderías* (*Replanteando la esclavitud*, 37).

37 Flores Galindo, *Aristocracia y plebe*.

38 Leg restraints were located in the *amasijo* where the dough was kneaded, which was the most arduous and dreaded area of the bakery, operated almost exclusively by male "criminal" slaves.

39 AAL Causas de negros, leg. 10, exp. 33, año 1651.

40 Bryant, *Rivers of Gold, Lives of Bondage*, ch. 2; Johnson, *Soul by Soul*, ch. 6; Gross, *Double Character*, ch. 5.

41 For a study of a girl's correctional house in republican Buenos Aires, see Guy, "Girls in Prison."

42 For runaways from haciendas, see Cushner, "Slave Mortality and Reproduction," 188. For a lengthy treatise on conducting the *visita de cárcel*, see Castillo de Bobadilla, *Política para corregidores y señores de vasallos*, "De la visita de cárcel, y de lo criminal," cap. 15, 264–303. See also Martiré, "La visita de cárcel en Buenos Aires durante el virreinato."

43 Lima had limited cell space and could not accommodate a large prison population. In the early modern period, apprehension and imprisonment were no more than pretrial detention holdings. Prisoners were ideally supposed to come quickly before a magistrate for sentencing. See Langbein, *Torture and the Law of Proof*. On posting bonds and the responsibilities of jailers, see Atienza, *Reportorio de la nueua Recopilación de las leyes del reyno*, 39.

44 Arrelucea Barrantes, "Conducta y control social colonial." We see the following exchange in a sanctuary case, in which one enslaved fugitive (*retraído*) who had recently arrived at the Cathedral approached another asking him to rid him of his chains. "Vos sois de panadería, ven acá quitame estos grillos" (AAL, Causas de inmunidad eclesiástica, leg. 14, exp. 5, año 1676).

45 For a history of domestic theft in Spain, see Gil, "Hurtar a los de casa." As Gil points out, in the medieval and early modern worlds, domestic theft was both a sin and a betrayal of trust. As such, punishment was always privately arranged. However, judicial attention was increasingly paid to the value of the goods stolen, and the state intruded as the dispenser of punishment toward the end of the eighteenth century.

46 Arrelucea Barrantes, *Replanteando la esclavitud*, 112.

47 AAL, Causas de negros, leg. 10, exp. 32, año 1651.

48 Susana's case defied the pattern for "wayward" girls. In theory, Susana should have gone from religious confinement to a *panadería* instead of being sold as a household slave. Perhaps the mother abbess believed that Susana would reform her ways in domestic servitude, or she may have spared her sentence to the *panadería* because of her young age (Susana was only fourteen).

49 As Stephanie Smallwood observes in her study of thwarted slave sales, "The moments in which the agency and irrepressible humanity of the captives manifested themselves were more tragic than heroic: instances of illness and death, ... removal of slaves from the market by reason of 'madness' " (*Saltwater Slavery*, 34).

50 AAL, Causas de negros, leg. 8, exp. 5, año 1640.

51 Schafer writes that in the case of antebellum Louisiana, courts divided defects into body and character. Running away could not be detected from a visual inspection, and thus it became classified as a character defect ("Guaranteed Against the Vices and Maladies," 310–20). In her study of redhibition suits, Ariela Gross shows that slave flight was reclassified as a "medical condition" in later nineteenth-century cases (*Double Character*, 124).

52 An eighteenth-century notarial collection from la Villa de Neiva (Colombia) reveals a number of transactions of runaway slaves resold at fairs for 200 pesos (sometimes less), with full disclosure of their runaway histories. Many of the runaways bore the surname "de los Reyes," which I suspect was a shorthand way of referring to their provenance in Lima (Ciudad de los Reyes). I have not seen reference

to these resale fairs in connection with seventeenth-century Lima, although it is entirely possible that notarial records for Arica would document these kinds of resales. Plausibly, the low percentage of cases brought in the *Real Audiencia* corresponded to resale in other venues like Arica *ferias*.

53   Breast milk and wet-nursing were important subjects of domestic and imperial affairs. In the humoralist framework, breast milk – like semen – was "cooked blood." As Rebecca Earle notes, "To nurse from another's milk was essentially to imbibe their humours" (*Body of the Conquistador*, 50). Priests, physicians, chroniclers, and peninsular administrators continually admonished criollos for raising their children on the milk of black and Andean women. These anxieties had peninsular antecedents. Iberians also worried about the degenerative effects of using *morisca* and *conversa* wet nurses (*Body of the Conquistador*, 209). *Peninsulares* attributed the lack of virility and emotional propensities of criollos to their ingestion of Andean bodily fluids. In rebutting those claims, criollo men contended that their closeness to the Andean women (in particular) who suckled them made them suitable for governance and gave them familiarity with the customs and language of *naturales*. By implication, those who had not been raised in the Americas on Andean or black milk were unfit for high-ranking ecclesiastical or administrative positions. See Premo, "Misunderstood Love," and Brewer-Garcia, "Bodies, Texts, and Translators." This transmission of maternal fluids was contested (as it is today). On the conjoined fears of wet-nursing, child-rearing, and racial degeneration in other colonial contexts, see Stoler, *Carnal Knowledge and Imperial Power*.

54   AAL, Causas de negros, leg. 15 exp. 7, año 1668. The seller defended himself against the claim of ill health by saying that he inherited Feliciana six years previously and that she had given birth every year since: "Y también el que representa en decir que pare las criaturas muertas lo cierto es que de cuatro que a parido, dos están vivos, y los otros dos el aberlos parido muertos fue de no aber cumplido algunos antojos que tenía la dicha negra su marido."

55   The youngest runaways were twelve years old, and all four were boys. It is not clear from the complaints whether the boys were really runaways or whether they refused to settle down in their new owners' residences. One seller defended himself by saying that it was incumbent on the new owner to discipline the young boy, since he was used to coming and going at his leisure as a child (AAL, Causas de negros, leg. 2, exp. 8, año 1611). Juan was a twelve-year-old boy who wandered around unsupervised and aimless for months on end: "Juan de tierra mandinga, tiene costumbre de ausentarse muchas y diversas veces, yéndose de su casa a otras de donde lo sacaba." As discussed in Chapter 4, "childhood" was a liminal stage of life in which dependents were obliged to be under the tutelage of a social superior.

56   AAL, Causas de negros, leg. 13, exp 12, año 1658. According to the buyer, "Me ocultaron que la dicha negra era fugitiva, la dicha madre abadesa dixo que no tenía defecto alguno y que solo la vendían porque no quería asistir en el convento."

57   On northern *palenques* outside the town of Trujillo, see O'Toole, *Bound Lives*, 113–15.

58   See Bowser, *The African Slave in Colonial Peru*, 196–97, on the use of slaves and freed persons of African descent in capturing fugitive slaves. *Cuadrilleros* were not the only ones catching fugitive slaves for a fee. Indeed, many complaints cite rural laborers who returned slaves for a fraction of the price charged by the *cuadrilleros*.

59 The classic studies of *marronage* reveal a pattern of slaves running away in small numbers, joining a maroon community (known as a *palenque* or *quilombo*), and remaining there for as long as the community was able to avoid detection or pacification. Scholars have shown that the maroon communities were predominantly comprised of young men. For an early influential study, see Price, *Maroon Societies.*

60 Carlos Aguirre has shown that in the nineteenth century, urban runaway slaves fled to the haciendas or coastal *ingenios*, where they were assimilated into the labor force. Plantation owners, strapped for labor, turned a blind eye to the fugitives among their workers. See Aguirre, *Agentes de su propia libertad*, ch. 7.

61 The crown issued ten royal *cedulas* in the sixteenth century that prohibited the commingling of Andeans and blacks. The repeated proclamation raises the logical presumption that the laws were overlooked or unevenly enforced. See Konetzke, *Coleccion de documentos*, vol. 1.

62 See O'Toole, *Bound Lives*, 114. Historians who have looked at the sources for Ecuador and Nueva Granada have shown that there were more Afro-Andean and Afro-indigenous *palenques* there. In Nueva Granada, this admixture was sufficient to develop the term "zambaje," a neologist corollary of "mestizaje," along the Magdalena River. See McKnight, "En su tierra lo aprendió," 15.

63 See, for example, Newson and Minchin, *From Capture to Sale*, and Bowser, *The African Slave in Colonial Peru*, chs. 2 and 3.

64 As Wim Klooster notes, when we consider the volume of goods and people circulating in informal, poorly regulated commercial networks, "smuggling" as an economic term is rendered meaningless ("Inter-Imperial Smuggling in the Americas)" For smuggling into Quito and Guayaquil via the Río Magdalena and overland, see Bryant, *Rivers of Gold, Lives of Bondage*, 53–62.

65 In their most recent study, Borucki, Eltis, and Wheat document the arrival of over two million enslaved Africans in the Spanish Americas before 1810, decades before the era of large-scale sugar production in the Caribbean ("Atlantic History and the Slave Trade to Spanish America," 434).

66 Scholars have recently turned their attention to the mobility of the newly arrived slave population, especially when it was tied to the mobility of owners and speculators. On slave mobility that spanned the Yucatán, Belize, Cartagena, and Cuba, see Restall, "Manuel's Worlds," 147–74.

67 Morales was also sued in another redhibitory action. See AAL, Causas de negros, leg. 4, exp. 7, año 1619. Morales was a prospector who purchased slaves from incoming and departing clerics and then tried to turn them over to buyers for a profit.

68 Causas de negros, leg. 10, exp. 46, año 1652. According to doña Isabel, she sold María Angola because María had gotten married and did not want to remain in the cloisters. On African women's putative aptitude for physical strength, see Morgan, *Laboring Women*. On the Portobelo slave *ferias*, see Vila Vilar, "Las ferias de Portobelo."

69 Morgan, "'Some Could Suckle over Their Shoulder.'"

70 *Protomédicos* were doctors with university training who were licensed by a professional association. On *protomédicos* employed by slave traders, see Newson and Minchin, *From Capture to Sale*, ch. 7.

71 For a primary source, see, for example. Abreu, *Tratado de las siete enfermedades*. I thank Hugh Cagle for directing me to this source.

72 Abreu's *Tratado* has an entire section devoted to Guinea worms entitled, "el mal de Loanda del guzano, y de las fuentes y sedales."

73 My thanks to Pablo Gómez for his explanation of the Spanish medical terms.

74 See Earle, *Body of the Conquistador*, 26–53, for a complete discussion of early modern Iberian incorporations of humoralism.

75 See Earle's discussion of the curse of Ham from a humoralist perspective (*Body of the Conquistador*, ch. 6).

76 See McKnight, "En su tierra lo aprendió," for an in-depth reading of the Inquisition trial of Mateo Arará in Cartagena, an African enslaved healer accused of demonic pacts.

77 Cussen, "The Search for Idols and Saints," 430; Iwasaki Cauti, "Fray Martín de Porras."

78 Celia Cussen recounts an incident that occurred between Martín de Porras (before his beatification) and the newly nominated Archbishop Feliciano de Vega. In 1639, Feliciano de Vega became deathly ill. Bleedings and purgatives proved ineffective, and Vega prepared for his death. After last rites were administered, Vega's grief-stricken nephew suggested that they call for Martín de Porras in a desperate effort to heal his uncle. Martín's reputation for miraculous healing was well known in Lima's circles. Approaching Vega on his deathbed, Martín laid his hands on the Archbishop, who miraculously recovered. See Cussen ("The Search for Idols and Saints," 440–41). On the intercessory powers of the African-descent women Estefanía de San Joseph and Ursula de Jesús, see Brewer-García, "Sanctity, Slavery, and Legal Maneuvering in Colonial Peru," and van Deusen, *The Souls of Purgatory*.

79 On the growing popularity of amatory magic in Lima among Afro-Peruvian ritual specialists, see Garofalo, "Conjuring with the Coca," 61, and Osorio, *Inventing Lima*, ch. 5.

80 In his review of San Martín de Porras's apprenticeship as a lay healer, Fernando Iwasaki Cauti mentions the competition between licensed doctors and popular practitioners ("Fray Martín de Porras," 162–65). Though the records do not show this, it is plausible that *protomédicos* were also trying to establish their authority over lay healers and midwives – the majority of whom were poor women, slaves, Andeans, and *castas*. These were precisely the practitioners who were denounced for witchcraft and idolatry in front of the Inquisition and the extirpation tribunal. Granted, the practitioners were denounced by members of the community. I have not seen documentation about possible turf battles, as say in the English seventeenth-century cases where midwives were prevented from performing in extremis baptisms, largely because of the hostility toward their craft (and gender) on the part of the Royal College of Medicine. However, siphoning off the competition (and threatening the practitioners and believers) undoubtedly created professional opportunities for *protomédicos*. But how then could miraculous healing powers like those of the saintly Fray Martín be explained while maintaining the blurry terrain between magic and medicine? The *protomédicos* adroitly responded that doctors, like healers, were mere instruments of God's will (ibid., 165).

81 See von Germeten, *Violent Delights*, Earle, *Body of the Conquistador*, Garofalo, "Conjuring with the Coca," and McKnight, "En su tierra lo aprendió." For a

detailed study of healing practices from the African diasporic perspective, see Gómez, "The Circulation of Bodily Knowledge in the Seventeenth-Century Black Spanish Caribbean."

82 In the case in which the slave Guoimar testified, she mentioned that a black healer whose specialty was curing "mal de madre" told her owner, Diego de Morales, that her illness was a long-standing one. "Se le vino a pasar la madre y a derramársela para el cuerpo y fue de manera que estuvo muy peligrosa de la vida y le causó una purgación que después acá siempre a tenido y al presente la tiene y *visitándola una negra que cura de mal de madre* le dixo a esta testigo y a su amo Diego de Morales que no le servía dar remedio porque la madre se le había pasmado y derramado por el cuerpo" (my emphasis).

83 Earle, *Body of the Conquistador*.

84 AAL, Causas de negros, leg. 1, exp. 12, año 1606. This was one of the few cases in which the parties reached a settlement. The buyer paid 50 pesos for the time Catalina was in his power, and the seller accepted Catalina's return.

85 AAL Causas de negros, leg. 5, exp.19, año 1626. Luis Criollo was sold in his fifties for 180 pesos. Luis suffered from a stomach tumor and died four months after the sale.

86 AAL Causas de negros, leg. 1 exp. 11, año 1605. "Tiene muchas enfermedades especialmente dolor de madre que no se le quita y llorando día y noche lo cual hace desde el día que la compró nunca ha tenido della servicio."

87 Osorio, *Inventing Lima*, 126.

88 AAL, Causas de negros, leg. 17, exp. 2, año 1673. The case was relitigated in 1675, during which the buyer prevailed. Alejandra Osorio also details María Feliciana's case in her review of extirpation records. See *Inventing Lima*, 131.

89 AAL, Causas de negros, leg. 22, exp. 54, año 1690. According to Bernarda's new owner, she was not only an inveterate and depraved drunkard, but also a habitual runaway who never served in his house. The owner called a doctor to treat Bernarda for excessive bleeding and infection from her self-inflicted abortion, but to no avail. According to the doctor's testimony, "Dixo que el lunes que se contaron veintitrés del mes corriente fue llamado para ver la negra que se contiene en dicha petición y que aviendola reconosido la allo en la cama en urgentísimo peligro de la vida por aver abortado una criatura, la reconoció con una fiebre continua mui intensa, que como sabía doña Josepha de Cuenca, ama de la dicha negra le advirtió como sabía que en otra ocasión en poder de quien se la vendió abía mal parido y que para ello tomó bebida abortiva… Y que aviéndola mandado sangrar perseveraron los accidentes casi en un mismo tenor y que el miércoles por la mañana aviendo ydo a visitar la dicha negra enferma la alló ya difunta."

90 As Alejandra Osorio notes, we see evidence of women's abortion practices (and by inference their sexual histories) in these oppressive, inquisitorial circumstances. See *Inventing Lima*, 114.

91 AAL, Causas de negros, leg. 17, exp. 21, año 1674.

92 Alonso de Arcos, in the name of the buyer, drafted the following interrogatory: "Si saben que el dicho negro de casta mina era de condición soberbio y que desesperado que en diversas veces se quiso ahorcar y se dio una en la garganta de que se le veían las heridas y que estuvo en peligro de la vida." On suicide and murder in Lima's enslaved community, see McKinley, "Standing on Shaky Ground."

93 In his defense, the seller summoned two slaves, Antonio and Domingo Mina, who knew Antonio "por haberse criado juntos en Perú, y vio que en dicha su tierra siendo niño si hirió de la garganta y son carabales por haber venido juntos a esta ciudad." Both witnesses gave virtually the same testimony, raising the presumption that they were schooled in what to say. The third witness confirmed the story in much the same language: "Se crió junto con Antonio Mina en Guinea en una casa y vio de desde niño tuvo estos dos señales."

94 Johnson, *The Chattel Principle.*

95 For actuarial practices, see Baucom, *Specters of the Atlantic.* See also, Johnson, *The Chattel Principle.*

96 In Latin American historiography, the arguments regarding slave resistance treat runaway maroon communities separately from revolts. Stuart Schwartz's study of the 1814 Bahian Hausa rebellion brings together both strands and demonstrates how *quilombos* and revolts were mutually supportive rather than discrete strategies of resistance ("Cantos and Quilombos," 247–72).

97 "I Could Not Stay There." Tied to a place by family responsibilities – and subject to the opprobrium that abandoning children for one's freedom would occassion – women opted for temporary reprieves from the harsh labors of bonded life through truancy. Camp's argument is rooted firmly in the antebellum plantation south of the United States and so has only oblique relevance to Lima's enslaved women. We have discussed many cases of mothers who left their children in the households of others in order to earn enough to purchase the family's freedom. Nowhere in the prolific witness testimonies do we see recriminations of child abandonment. Moreover, the mobility of Lima's slaves was critical to their survival and livelihood: owners wanted slaves who moved in and out of circumscribed spaces to increase their productivity. Mobile slaves also reduced owners' expenses for their food and lodging.

98 See Newson and Minchin, *From Capture to Sale,* 64.

99 The *Consulado* was a commercial court in which merchants heard their cases. The *Casa de Contratación* was the royal House of Trade that bore responsibility for carrying out navigation and commerce in the name of the crown and for bringing in royal profit.

100 According to Vila Vilar, "Duarte López, viajero, cartógrafo y conocedor de Angola, donde había permanecido durante diez años, y que en el año 1589 llegó a España, [en un informe señala] que sólo de Angola se podrían sacar 8.000 anuales, sino también la única forma de consolidar la conquista de esta zona de la costa africana." Vila Vilar, "Los asientos Portugueses," 559–60.

101 Johnson, *Soul by Soul,* 14.

102 I take the term "historiographical pointillism" from Robin Blackburn's moving obituary for Raphael Samuel ("Raphael Samuel," 137). On slaves owning parts of themselves, see de la Fuente, "Coartación y papel."

103 I thank Kris Lane for pushing me to clarify these points in my thinking.

104 AAL, Causas de negros, leg. 12, exp. 13, año 1655.

105 As Sherwin Bryant has written in his study of slavery in early modern Quito, this time period "requires conceptualizations of slavery before and apart from

an economic rationale of governance – before the ascendancy of the plantation complex." See Bryant, *Rivers of Gold, Lives of Bondage* 147.

106 Thanks to Herman Bennett who shared his insights on the history of domesticity with me. On the microeconomics of individuals and social networks, see Rothschild, "Isolation and Economic Life in Eighteenth-Century France," 1056.

107 On the temporal force of law, see Mawani, "Law as Temporality."

108 See Lauderdale Graham, *Caetana Says No*, and Hartman, *Scenes of Subjection* for Celie's story.

Conclusion

On August 9, 1659, Ana María de Velasco and Juan González de Miranda appealed to the ecclesiastical court to resolve their respective predicaments. Ana wanted to get out of an iniquitous relationship with her owner; Juan wanted to leave an unhappy marriage with his enslaved wife. For purposes of symmetry, let us close this study in August – some 350 years later.

August is a busy time for historians. Archival researchers race against time to take notes (digital images nowadays) and tie up loose ends. We feverishly tabulate and count during the last remaining days of August, because we spent too long luxuriating in the rich narratives of our subjects during the previous months. We experience regret at leaving the site and our subjects and frustration about unanswered questions.

But rushed historians are not the only ones at the archives on a typical day in August. At Lima's Archbishopric archive, the doorbell and telephone ring incessantly. Anxious Limeños come to the archive to solicit parochial records to support their petitions for residency and study abroad, to fight for divorce, to settle disputes in probate, and to copy their birth certificates. Limeños still need their parochial documents to file the routine administrative paperwork required of modern citizens. While they wait in the anteroom with some trepidation to see whether their records exist, they must wonder who the people are in the quiet, chilly salon and what we do there.

In the National Archive, historians are neatly ensconced in a reading room within Lima's impressive architectural Plaza Mayor. Tourists wander in and stare desultorily at documents of great historical importance on display. Uniformed school children are brought to the Great Hall to see the independence proclamation of the liberators Simón Bolívar and José San Martín, the imperious royal seal of the City of Kings embossed with "Yo el Rey," and a barely discernible thumbprint of Francisco Pizarro. Casual observers do not see the link between the two institutional legacies of the Archbishopric and the National archives. I have tried to make that link visible in this book through excavating the life histories of women like Ana María de Velasco, María Josefa Martínez, Margarita de Torres, and Catalina Conde. I fervently hope that one day, we will see Catalina Conde's petition hanging in the Great Hall of the National Archives, where her rightful place as a freedom fighter and heroic historical subject would finally be acknowledged.

Why these women? Why this project? My analysis and thinking in this book owes much to intellectual debates within the fields of sociolegal studies, law and anthropology, and legal history, producing what I have dubbed "legal ethnohistory." But on a personal level, *Fractional Freedoms* is informed by my experience working as an anthropologist and as a lawyer in Latin America. My interest in this topic arose out of a long-standing study of legal consciousness among disenfranchised populations in Peru. In 2005, I completed a study of contemporary family violence laws in which I examined the ways that poor, urban women in Latin America began to adopt feminist human rights discourse to defend themselves against violent partners.[1] In that study, I tried to understand the translation of the abstract category of rights, which includes such prerogatives as autonomy and bodily integrity, by looking at family violence and divorce cases. After interviewing scores of women pursuing family violence complaints, I realized that Latin American women were articulating modern rights vernacular using language that was deeply embedded in a colonial discourse of female honor.

Initially, I turned to ecclesiastical archives in search of an explanation as to why a secular discourse of rights and, more broadly, of citizenship envisioned by the human rights corpus enjoyed such uneven success in Peru. For human rights to be effective, they must resonate within the public legal culture of a given society. My initial archival foray showed that women had been active litigants for centuries. Indeed, throughout the centuries, women appealed to the court to vindicate their rights. They used that public forum to call attention to their partner's transgressions from their socially determined roles as protector and provider. In so doing, women reclaimed their honor and integrity. Women sought judicial intervention, but they did not propose radical or alternative modes of domestic arrangements. Their petitions could only be successful if they appealed to the very codes of male and female honor that ultimately constrained them.

Though I was interested in the contemporary feminist movement, I could not help but be drawn in by the narratives I read. As Arlette Farge notes, "the judicial archives bring us inside a world fitful with passions and disorder."[2] My paleographic skills were then nonexistent, but the words engulfed me as I struggled to discern the letters recorded in the notaries' crabbed handwriting. As someone who drafted affidavits for relief for a living, I was familiar with the possibilities and limitations of the legal narrative form – the strategic decorum of the historical testimonies was obvious. I had been trained to treat legal documents with a healthy dose of skepticism and to appreciate silences, aporias, and lacunae. But I also recognized the importance of normative legal discourse and knew how good advocates could wield it strategically for a supplicant's purposes. Any immigration attorney worth her salt knows how to argue for relief for a client using the discourse of "e pluribus unum," how to appeal for family unification with the idioms of deservingness. Bankruptcy attorneys also know how to use the language of equity. Public defenders manipulate the norms of redemption, reintegration, mercy, and so forth.

As I became more engulfed in historical reading, I grafted a practitioner's sensibilities of normative legality and legal process onto the civil laws of slavery and manumission. In this early modern world, slavery was an unfortunate and unnatural condition, and to compensate for this misfortune, lawmakers created many legal avenues to liberty. Conditional liberty was the reality for a great many enslaved peoples, who either strove to achieve it or accommodated their lives around it. In general, people seemed to accept the contours of this system and played by its rules. They brought cases when their owners rejected those rules, reneged on private or unrecorded compacts, or foreclosed legal and extra-legal paths to liberty. It seemed entirely reasonable in a legal world that pivoted around the discourse of clemency and mercy that those who desired freedom for themselves and for loved ones would cast themselves in the position of deserving *miserables*. In this legal culture, people could adopt a stance of supplication by appealing to a remote and benevolent sovereign without imperiling their social identities as respectable, honorable, beatific, or industrious.

It also struck me that people went on with their lives as the legal process laboriously unfolded. Juan Arriola and María Albina grew old together over the course of their two-decade lawsuit. They raised children and grandchildren. All six of their children survived infancy in a world of precarious mortality. Juana de Loyola had a relationship for decades with Sebastián, during which the couple had at least four surviving children. They inhabited an interstitial space between slavery and freedom, established enduring relationships and social networks, and determined the course of their lives and that of their children. Whether these people were exceptional is (in my mind) beside the point.

I have made three main arguments throughout this book. First, law mattered. In the most obvious sense, law provided the basis for empire itself. Within the early modern Iberoamerican legocentric environment, the discourse of natural law provided a powerful framework for legal actors, supplicants, administrators, and colonial subjects. The reliance on lawyers and pervasive litigiousness – so reviled in the Old World – created vast bureaucracies and networks of practitioners, pettifoggers, and notaries who all administered "justice by paperwork." Drawing from the methods of sociolegal history and ethnography, I have given readers an overview of the social world of the court – particularly the ecclesiastical court – in order to portray the law "in action" as opposed to the law "on the books."

Many sociolegal scholars refer to "gap studies" to describe that fertile space between law on the books and the law in action.[3] Enterprising litigants like María de los Santos could exploit that gap or breach to protect her marital rights even though she was only recently betrothed.[4] If we remember, María requested an injunction to prevent the transfer and sale of her intended husband outside of Lima. María not only convinced the court to grant her an injunction but also arranged Josef's transfer out of prison from the port of Callao and found him a new buyer in record time. As I argue in discussing María's complaint, the fact that she was enslaved by the extremely powerful don Miguel Núñez de Sanabria undoubtedly empowered her to bring an action before the court. She did not bring her case because she had a blind faith in the law or because she was awestruck by the acumen of legal practitioners; rather she saw an opportunity to redress an injustice and acted on it.[5] Hers was something more contextual, result-oriented, and immediate. Legal mobilization was possible and effective because elites, highly ranked administrators, and ecclesiastical slaveholders responded to the institutional pressure exerted by the courts. Nevertheless, María's actions may have created precedents for other less-well situated couples to appeal for protection of their marital rights.

Those held in slavery by elite owners did not cower before their owner's prestige and position. Rather, litigants like Pascuala de Arias used their owner's vulnerability to public exposure to their advantage. Recall that Pascuala was the enslaved litigant who in 1674 asked for *censuras* to summon witnesses in her case against the heirs of the Archbishop Fernando Arias de Ugarte. Numerous enslaved litigants also used the *censura* as "spiritual subpoena" to compel their adversaries and social superiors to respond to their complaints. Elite and religious owners were extremely susceptible to exposure in front of the community of faith, which explains their compliance with the spiritual summons. However, even in cases of nonelite owners, we conclude that the intonation of *censuras* from the pulpit ensured that malfeasants would be more responsive to honor an unrecorded promise of liberty or comply with the letter of the law.[6]

In addition to providing a history of the lower branches of the legal profession, I have also closely examined the legal careers of two ecclesiastical provisors, Pedro de Villagómez and Feliciano de Vega. I chose these two provisors because of their lengthy tenure at the ecclesiastical court and because of the social environments and networks in which they were immersed. Don Feliciano de Vega was a distinguished criollo jurist who came into his position at a time when criollos and *benemeritos* had assumed a certain stature and proved their readiness for assuming judicial posts. Vega was a quintessential bureaucrat: efficient, professional, and ambitious. Don Pedro de Villagómez was a *peninsular* (Spaniard) and the nephew of the Archbishop of Lima. Villagómez was an evangelizer, whose fervent belief in the role of the church and its court in settling legal matters infused his rulings.[7] Villagómez rigidly defended marriage in tandem with criticizing his predecessors for having been too lax in dissolving marital ties.[8] I attribute the growing use of *censuras* during his tenure to his effort to streamline ecclesiastical legal procedure in the courts. As legal historians, we can get a sense of the law in action as opposed to law on the books by reviewing particular judges' rulings over time. More importantly, a focus on how "judges judge" is one of the few ways to isolate the elaboration of custom in a code-based regime.

In keeping with the importance of law and the monarchical function of law-giving, I have examined the administration of justice and the attendant jurisdictional tensions between church and crown in the baroque Spanish Empire and situated the protagonism of enslaved litigants within multiple orders of political dominance, racial hierarchy, and religious and cultural authority. As we have seen in the preceding chapters, enslaved litigants in Lima were most active in ecclesiastical courts. Given the premise of Christianization that legitimated slavery and conquest, Catholicism and slavery were profoundly entwined. Conversion and religious faith were intrinsically bound up with a slave's prospects for manumission. The African embrace of Catholicism no doubt helped soften the blow of uprooted lives, but it also strengthened the position of the church and its authority as a whole in the lives of enslaved and freed peoples.

Although I have posited that litigiousness in multiple forums was the product of a legal transplant from the Iberian Peninsula to the Americas, the legal activism of *bozales* challenges the transplant theory to a certain extent. African-born slaves assimilated Iberian litigious norms, but they had no experience on the peninsula. Diaspora and Atlantic history scholars have devoted significant attention to the syncretic processes inherent in African-descent peoples' embrace and adoption of Catholic idioms and beliefs in their studies of religious confraternities (*cofradías*). *Cofradías* offered critical material and spiritual support to recently arrived African slaves and those born in the New World. This syncretism can, I suggest, likewise explain the African enthusiasm for litigiousness. As Herman Bennett argues for Afro-Mexicans, "Christianity's regulatory impulse made possible a creolization process among persons of African descent that included the acquisition of a legal consciousness alongside Spanish and indigenous cultural practices."[9] Moreover, as contemporary studies of the indigenous embrace of Catholicism show more broadly, we do not have to equate the recourse to law with evidence of people's naive faith in its promises.[10]

African slaves quickly realized that the Catholic Church occupied a central place in the daily lives and ceremonial expressions of their owners and that clerics wielded considerable power in political battles among church, crown, and local magistrates.[11] Enslaved litigants' "forum shopping" enables us to invert the typical tale of unequal alliances by showing how frequently the interests of plebeians and legal dependents aligned with the goals of multiple social superiors who competed with each other to advance their respective jurisdictions.

My second claim in *Fractional Freedoms* is that manumission was a gendered and protracted process. The multiple paths to manumission within the civil law shaped people's short-term strategies and long-term hopes, especially for those who struggled to achieve lifetime liberty through self-purchase. In light of Tannenbaum's contested thesis, much comparative scholarship has highlighted the local context and the political or economic exigencies in which manumissions occurred.[12] Scholars have dismantled Tannenbaum's assertion that manumission was frequently granted in Spanish colonies, concluding on the basis of empirical research that manumission was a "happy incident, not a prospect."[13]

Studies disputing the weight of manumission on the basis of numbers inevitably differ from those like this one that emerge out of a close historical read of the sources. The insistence on numbers or frequency leads to an analytical tension between quantity and quality. It also raises the specter of exceptionalism. My approach has always been to think through the teleological place of contingent liberty in the lives of enslaved peoples and their owners. Enslaved peoples in seventeenth-century Lima would have had freed people as a frame of reference within their communities and relatives from the same "tierra y nación." Even the lowliest *jornalero*, runaway, apprentice, sanctuary seeker (*retraído*), or imprisoned slave shackled in a *panadería* would have known people who were on their way to self-purchase. In researching and thinking through these cases, I have tried to displace the scholarly notion of manumission as a "gift" with the more accurate account of it as a form of self-purchase achieved over a lifetime or at various life stages. Indeed, the subtitle of this book could easily have been "manumission," since most of its subjects were on a path to liberty through one or more myriad forms.

The prospect of eventual manumission, whether through testament, baptism, or self-purchase, profoundly structured the relationship between slave and slaveholder. Because the claims I have studied derived largely from unfulfilled promises to issue letters of freedom, people had tremendous incentives to appeal to the court to enforce those promises. Their appeals used the normative and contractual language of sacrifice, reliance, trust, promise, care, and price. The nature of the sources influenced my reading and interpretation of these cases.

Looking principally at domestic slavery, I have considered how men and women pursued divergent paths to liberty. Purchasing a child while remaining enslaved, freeing one's wife before a child was born, marrying after having been involved in a long-term relationship when one partner had accumulated enough *jornales* to purchase his or her freedom papers: these were strategies that made sense within an environment where lifetime manumission was legally possible and financially attractive for both owners and enslaved people. Yet the pervasive notion of manumission as a "gift," even when achieved through hard-earned sacrifice, permeated the bonds between owners and freed people.

Comparing testamentary and baptismal manumission reveals just how much the discourse of benevolence extracted surplus compliance from the indebted party. Recall the *censura* read at the behest of Margarita de Aguirre to compel a reluctant heir to honor his aunt's promise to free her daughter and granddaughter. Margarita's experience allows us to chart a negotiated exchange of care and inherited reward in the instance of childless families in a slaveholding society.[14] Customary norms delegated the care and responsibility for ailing parents to elder daughters or the wives of elder sons. In practice however, in slaveholding societies, it was enslaved women who bore the responsibility for the actual *care work*: washing and turning an ailing body, nursing a febrile brow, dealing with soiled sheets, and disposing of vomit and chamber pots.[15] Margarita continued to care for her former owners during their respective illnesses decades after earning her freedom. According to the numerous witness statements, she nursed the couple's adoptive child while they were alive. As a result of her devoted labor, Margarita expected to receive in exchange the freedom she sought for her descendants. We have seen repeatedly that neighbors, associates, parishioners, and friends of the deceased expressed support for the hard-earned freedom that enslaved litigants fought for in courts, especially in contexts of extended care work.

My third point follows from this: domestic slavery and care work created a sort of intimacy that fostered thick relationships with purchase in court and in the broader society.[16] However porous the boundary between property and person was, it was felt temporally. At times, enslaved people were property and treated as faulty or defective merchandise. At other times, enslaved people were confidantes, lovers, wet nurses, domestics, and childhood mates. In Chapter 2, I examine the chattel principle; in the cases I look at, family separation is not the salient issue that unmasks the transactional logic of paternalism. In Chapter 6, I think through the chattel principle in a society in which slaves owned parts of themselves – that is, in a society where contingent liberty was aspirational and real for many people – seeking to understand what redhibition looked like within those parameters.

Finally, as I delved into these relationships it became clear that people remained in each other's lives regardless of their legal status. Even as she sued Micaela's heirs for her liberty, Margarita de Torres returned to one of those heirs – Ynez– and eventually earned her freedom through Ynez's cession of her share in Margarita. Margarita de Aguirre spent years after paying her purchase price caring for her former owners. Juana de Tovar lived two doors away from doña Beatriz, and her daughters remained in Beatriz's house. And, of course, María Albina demonstrated unseverable ties to don Diego de Camaño that spanned two generations.

These were "thick," deeply intertwined relationships of dependency and bounded autonomy in an early modern world. They were bonds borne of care work and drudgery that inhered in the precarious nature of segmented freedom. They grew out of the politics of the domestic sphere. Single and childless owners like doña Beatriz availed themselves of the reproductive labor of their slaves by adopting their daughters as *criadas* (wards) to care for them in their old age. Cloistered owners clung to the daughters of their slaves as surrogate children and caretakers. Recall the words used in Graciela's baptismal letter of freedom: "Let it be known that while I am alive, Graciela must remain *by my side and in my company*. She cannot ever run away or leave the convent, even she comes of age, because if she does so, this letter of freedom will become null and void."[17] Conflicted mothers like Catalina Criolla and Juana de Tovar looked on as their owners raised their daughters, consoled only by the knowledge that the girls were being raised with virtue and *recogimiento*, ensuring their upward mobility in the next generation.

Clearly, domestic relations were highly unequal, though steeped in the idioms of loyalty, devotion, and protection. (When have they ever been equal?) The same logics of ownership that authorized doña Francisca to order Magdalena's whipping underscored doña Beatriz's power over María Josefa. Yet we have much more scholarship devoted to the power of whipping than we have on the subject of the complexities of the type of relationship embodied in the Beatriz-María Josefa-Juana matrix. We are left to examine the matrix with two unsatisfactory analytical frames: paternalism or exceptionalism. Neither frame is sufficient.

As I have demonstrated herein, domestic slavery does not map easily onto the conventional understandings of master-slave relationships. Formerly enslaved witnesses repeatedly revealed in their testimonies that they returned to the households where they were once enslaved on a regular basis. Many freedwomen assisted in their erstwhile households during peak production times with heavy domestic loads and prepared special desserts or dishes for *fiestas* and patronal processions. Freedwomen attended to their former owners during childbirth, prayed by their deathbeds, and were present during other life-stage events. Owners received their slaves' newborns "into their hands" ("nacida en mis manos") and held them "at their breasts" ("criadola en sus pechos"). In what I have called the emotional economy, it behooved freed people in unstable economic situations, living in a highly stratified society, to maintain a quasi-"retainer" relationship with the families within which they were once enslaved.[18]

RACE, RELIGION, AND ENGAGED CONVERSION

Fractional Freedoms has focused, where relevant and possible, on African *bozales* or first-generation criollos in the early modern period. The numerous lawsuits brought by Brans, Terranovas, Minas, and Angolas that comprise much of this study could have been recent arrivals who had little familiarity with the Spanish language or litigious customs and minimal exposure to the rites of the Catholic religion, or they could have been first-generation slaves who married and reproduced endogamously.[19]

In general, readers will identify *bozales* by their ethnonymic surnames that reflected the African port or place of origin where they were procured. Historians tend to agree that *bozal* identities quickly became creolized after a generation and the surnames slaves adopted (or had imposed on them) reflected a creole identity rather than an African one. Indeed, most first-generation slaves born in the Americas literally assumed "Criollo" as their surname. In a parallel

vein, colonial historians attribute racial differentiation with creolization, calling our attention to the ways in which African-descent peoples became classified as "morenas" and "pardas" especially after paying for their freedom.[20] It is widely contended that men and women preferred to identify as *morenas* and *pardas*, which demonstrated social mobility, rather than as *bozales*, which distinctly marked the proximity of their African past.[21] We do need more work to discern the subtleties of *bozal* identities, as diaspora scholars study what material and cultural resources peoples of African descent drew on to forge their lives in the Americas.[22]

Conversion was not altogether a one-sided battle for souls. Though Catholicism was promoted as the universal religion of Latin Christendom, we are mindful that Catholicism – wherever it was embraced – was profoundly localized. Indeed, as Joseph Miller insists, "Christianity does not 'spread'; *people* adopt and adapt elements [of it] for their own immediate purposes."[23] Scholars of colonial religiosity signal the popularity of nonwhite or *casta* (persons of mixed-race) saints as an innovative evangelizing strategy on the part of the clergy to indoctrinate Lima's urban population.[24] This partially explains the reverence paid to black saints and holy women like San Martín de Porras and Ursula de Jesús, which was so strikingly at variance with the negative association of blackness in the colonial milieu.[25] Though venerated black and *mestizo* holy women were found in other colonial sites over the centuries, these saints hailed from Lima as unassailable exemplars of New World Catholicism.[26]

Clearly, the processes of acculturation and creolization that we have attributed to life in the Americas began much earlier in Central and Upper West African communities. As James Sidbury and Jorge Cañizares-Esguerra argue, "the experience of captives disembedded from their natal communities and forced to adapt to new cultures was an endemic condition that created ongoing ethnogenesis in precolonial African polities."[27] In order to avoid the easy presumption that the advocacy of *bozales* was purely mimetic or derivative, I assume that similar legal and intercessory processes were a part of life in West and Central Africa and that they served as templates for African litigiousness.

The point here is not to fall into the morass of the debate between retentionists and creolization theorists.[28] Rather it is to posit litigiousness as evidence of processes of creolization and unfolding Catholicization and to recognize the thorny nature of these processes and the profound breaches traversed by both law and religion in the tumult and upheaval of life in the New World.[29]

NOTES

1 McKinley, "Emancipatory Practices and Rebellious Politics."
2 Farge, *The Allure of the Archives*, 42–43.
3 See, for example, Marshall and Barclay, "In Their Own Words." The equivalent Spanish translation also highlights the gap between text and deed: "entre el hecho y el derecho."

4   AAL, Causas de negros, leg. 24, exp. 65, año 1699.

5   In a recent review of the scholarship on indigenous people and legal culture, Yanna Yannakakis summarizes Woodrow Borah's legacy as the idea that indigenous peoples believed in Spanish law and its promises (as well as its compromises) of justice ("Indigenous People and Legal Culture in Spanish America").

6   Admittedly, legal action that unleashed ecclesiastical or institutional pressure may not have worked with all slaveholders. Poorer Spaniards, mobile sea captains, or rural owners may have been impervious to these pressures. Historians have often pointed out that rural slaves did not have access to courts on par with urban enslaved litigants. Nevertheless, in *Rivers of Gold, Lives of Bondage,* a study of legal actions brought by enslaved litigants in Popayán and Guayaquil, Sherwin Bryant has argued convincingly that legal mobilization was not solely a feature of urban slavery (149).

7   The church launched two extirpation campaigns to stamp out idolatrous practices in the seventeenth century: the first campaign lasted from 1609 to 1622, and a lengthier and more robust campaign occurred between 1649 and 1670 under the tenure of Archbishop Villagómez. See Mills, *Idolatry and Its Enemies.* It is therefore important to situate many of the complaints that came to Villagómez within the unfolding theological climate of the second extirpation campaign. We see this most sharply in the redhibition context, as it informed what the church, crown, inquisitors, and medical practitioners deemed acceptable or idolatrous healing practices in the seventeenth century.

8   As the viceroy Conde de Santisteban complained to the crown, "Las mujeres nobles divorziadas de sus maridos con informaciones falsas para amancebarse con libertad ellas y ellos" (Lavallé, "Divorcio y nulidad de matrimonio en Lima, 1650–1700," 24).

9   Bennett, *Africans in Colonial Mexico,* 10.

10 Yannakakis, "Indigenous People and Legal Culture in Spanish America."

11 Charles Beatty-Medina makes this point in his study of the evolution of the negotiations of maroon communities (*palenques*) with the church in Esmeraldas ("Between the Cross and the Sword," 100–101).

12 See, for example, Brana-Shute and Sparks, *Paths to Manumission.*

13 Klooster, "Manumission in an Entrepôt," 164.

14 See Hartog, *Someday This Will All Be Yours,* for a discussion of testator's promises, elder care, and the adult child.

15 As James Lockhart notes in his influential study on the early Peruvian colony, "No Spaniard felt happy until he owned a large house, land, livestock, and more to the point here – Negro servants. Most Spaniards could not hope to achieve this goal in its entirety, but they aimed at least for two essentials, a house (which could be rented) and Negroes" (*Spanish Peru,* 181).

16 See Hartog, *Someday This Will All Be Yours.*

17 AGN, Joseph Figueroa Dávila, Protocolo no. 570, año 1687, ff. 362–64v.

18 See Ray and Qayyum, *Cultures of Servitude,* 79.

19 Just how much exposure was enough to tip the scales toward an "Iberoamerican" embrace of litigiousness is the subject of much contemporary inquiry in new diaspora studies and Atlantic history.

20 See Graubart, "So color de una cofradía."

21 Twinam, "Purchasing Whiteness."

22 See, for instance, *Africans to Spanish America*, the excellent collection by Bryant, O'Toole, and Vinson representing the "fourth wave" of diaspora scholarship that "situates African descended peoples in their own narratives" through close reading of primary texts (9). As Rachel O'Toole points out in her study of diasporic Afro-Peruvian identity, some African place names were appropriated by freedwomen as markers of their elite status and prestige ("To Be Free and Lucumí").

23 Miller, "A Historical Appreciation of the Biographical Turn," 29.

24 *Vidas exemplares*, or hagiographies, were religious writings of the lives of saints or those thought worthy of beatification. See van Deusen, *The Souls of Purgatory*, and Greer, "Colonial Saints."

25 See Brewer-García, "Sanctity, Slavery and Legal Maneuvering in Colonial Peru."

26 For hagiographies of other Afro-descended saints, see Bristol, *Christians, Blasphemers, and Witches*.

27 Sidbury and Cañizares-Esguerra, "Mapping Ethnogenesis," 185.

28 For an excellent summary of the debates between proponents of creolization and its discontents, see ibid.

29 On the precarious identities of indigenous religious intermediaries, see Charles, *Allies at Odds*.

Note on References and Bibliography

The primary sources for *Fractional Freedoms* include fragments of lawsuits, as well as the complete court record. Given my interest in the relationships among owners and enslaved peoples, as well as the social constellations in which they circulated, I worked with a number of parochial sources and sacramental ledgers. These included marriage petitions and declarations of consent and baptism and marriage books for Spaniards and those for African-descent peoples. I also used numerous biographies and the voluminous records left by Lima's luminaries to glean clues about the intertwined lives of elite owners and slaves. To get a better sense of the directives and administrative priorities of the church and the court, I consulted the synods of the Lima Diocese (*concilios limenses*) and the town council books (*libros de cabildo*).

Perhaps unsurprisingly, religious orders had the best-kept local records and estate inventories, all of which were important sources for Chapter 4. I referenced diaries and journals of the period written by priests, viceregal legal advisers, bureaucrats, and scholars, sources that provide a vivid account of the daily rituals, processions, and ceremonial life of the baroque City of Kings. Writers of these accounts record when the city trembled (which it did with frequent earthquakes) and when the port of Callao came under siege by privateers. They note the death of a prominent Spaniard or the public execution of minor criminals. As agents of empire, these chroniclers reflect the staunch regalism, devout Catholicism, and gossipy proclivities of their social milieu. The accounts recorded by elite criollos exude a constant anxiety born of a desire to prove the city's grandeur, wealth, and nobility to their peninsular counterparts. In seeking to convince their rivals on the peninsula, their chronicles impart a sense of the elegance and joie de vivre of the baroque city.

I also used notarial records housed at the AGN under the Protocoles notariales series. Fredrick Bowser used the Protocoles and the town council records in his masterful *The African Slave in Colonial Peru*. Bowser left meticulous notes, and so it was possible to trace the afterlife of some of the individuals he studied for my own purposes. In that spirit, I have tried to include all the notarial and biographical details in the notes and text so that other researchers can pursue these leads in future studies.

I became aware of the *censuras* while I was on sabbatical in the final stages of writing. Although I badly wanted to finish writing the manuscript, I had three choices: write a huge footnote that alerted readers and researchers to their existence, save the discovery for a later project, or delve into the box. I chose the third option. In the interest of time, I deliberately chose to focus on the *censuras* that pertained to baptismal and childhood manumission. Nonetheless, these *censuras* represent an untapped source that demand further study, archival cataloguing, and digital preservation.

All materials were found in Lima's Archbishopric archive (AAL), Peru's National archive (AGN), and the Fondo Reservado (Special Collections) at the National Library (BNP). The Franciscan archive (Archivo Franciscano) also contains critical information about rural haciendas. When possible, I consulted primary sources at the Firestone Library, the Newberry Library, and the Library of Congress in the United States.

REFERENCES CITED

Abreu, Alexo, de. *Tratado de las siete enfermedades*. Lisboa: Casa de Pedro Craesbeeck, Impresor del Rey, 1623.

Abreu, Martha. "Slave Mothers and Freed Children: Emancipation and Female Space in Debates on the 'Free Womb' Law, Rio de Janeiro, 1871." *Journal of Latin American Studies* 28.3 (1996): 567–80.

Adorno, Rolena. *The Polemics of Possession in Spanish American Narrative*. New Haven: Yale University Press, 2008.

Aguirre, Carlos. *Agentes de su propia libertad: Los esclavos de Lima y la desintegración de la esclavitud, 1821–1854*. Lima: PUCP, 1995.

———. "Tinterillos, Indians, and the State: Towards a History of Legal Intermediaries in Post-Independence Peru." In *One Law for All? Western Models and Local Practices in (Post) Imperial Contexts*, ed. Stefan B. Kirmse, 119–51. Frankfurt: Campus, 2012.

———. "Working the System: Black Slaves and the Courts in Lima Peru, 1821–1854." In *Crossing Boundaries: Comparative History of Black People in Diaspora*, ed. Darlene Clark Hine and Jacqueline McLeod, 202–22. Bloomington: Indiana University Press; 1999.

Aguirre, Joaquin, and Juan Manuel Montalbán. *Tratado de procedimientos en negocios eclesiásticos*. Madrid: Imprenta y librería de D. Ignacio Boix, 1846.

Aguirre Beltrán, Gonzalo. *La población negra de México; estudio etnohistórico*. Mexico City: Fondo de Cultura Económica, 1972.

Albarrán, Nadia Carnero, and Miguel Pinto Huaracha. *Diezmos de Lima, 1592–1859*. Lima: Universidad Nacional Mayor de San Marcos, 1983.

Altamira, Rafael. *Técnica de investigación en la historia del derecho indiano*. Mexico City: José Porrua e hijos, 1939.

Altman, Ida. *Emigrants and Society: Extremadura and America in the Sixteenth Century*. Berkeley: University of California Press, 1989.

American Historical Review Forum. "The General Crisis of the Seventeenth Century Revisited." *American Historical Review* 113.4 (2008): 1029–99.

Andrien, Kenneth. *Crisis and Decline: The Viceroyalty of Peru in the Seventeenth Century*. Albuquerque: University of New Mexico Press, 1985.

Arrelucea Barrantes, Maribel. "Conducta y control social colonial: Estudio de las panaderías limeñas en el siglo XVIII." *Revista del Archivo General de la Nación* 13.2 (1996): 133–50.

Repleanteando la esclavitud: Estudios de etnicidad y género en Lima borbónica. Lima: CEDET, 2009.

Arrom, Silvia. *The Women of Mexico City, 1790–1857.* Stanford: Stanford University Press, 1985.

Atienza, Diego de. *Repertorio de la nueua Recopilación de las leyes del reyno.* Alcalá de Henares: En casa de Juan Iñiguez de Lequerica, 1598.

Avalos, Hector. "Pope Alexander VI, Slavery and Voluntary Subjection: 'Ineffabilis et Summi Patris' in Context." *Journal of Ecclesiastical History* 65.4 (2014): 738–60.

Ayliffe, John. *Paregon juris canonici anglicani.* London: D. Leach, 1726.

Bailyn, Bernard, and Patricia Denault, eds. *Soundings in Atlantic History: Latent Structures and Intellectual Currents, 1500–1830.* Cambridge, MA: Harvard University Press, 2009.

Baptist, Edward, and Stephanie Camp, eds. *New Studies in the History of American Slavery.* Athens: University of Georgia Press, 2006.

Barcia Paz, Manuel. "Fighting with the Enemy's Weapons: The Usage of the Colonial Legal Framework by Nineteenth-Century Cuban Slaves." *Atlantic Studies* 3.2 (2006): 159–81.

Barrientos Grandon, José. "Un canonista peruano del siglo XVII: Feliciano de Vega, 1580–1640." *Revista chilena de historia del derecho* 18 (1999–2000): 101–18.

Basadre Grohman, Jorge. *El conde de Lemos y su tiempo: Bosquejo de una evocación y una interpretación del Perú a fines del siglo XVII.* 2nd edn. Lima: Huascarán, 1948.

Baucom, Ian. *Specters of the Atlantic: Finance Capital, Slavery, and the Philosophy of History.* Durham: Duke University Press, 2005.

Benito, José Antonio. "Historia de la bula de la Cruzada en Indias." *Revista de estudios histórico-jurídicos* 18 (1996): 71–102.

Bennett, Herman. *Africans in Colonial Mexico: Absolutism, Christianity, and Afro-Creole Consciousness, 1570–1640.* Bloomington: Indiana University Press, 2003.
   Colonial Blackness: A History of Afro-Mexico. Bloomington: Indiana University Press, 2009.

Benton, Lauren, and Richard Ross, eds. *Legal Pluralism and Empires, 1500-1850.* New York: New York University Press, 2013.

Berlin, Ira. *Many Thousands Gone: The First Two Centuries of Slavery in North America.* Cambridge, MA: Harvard University Press, 1998.

Bermúdez, José Manuel. *Anales de la catedral de Lima, 1534–1824.* Lima: Imprenta del Estado, 1903.

Bermúdez Aznar, Agustín. "La abogacía de pobres in Indias." *Anuario de historia del derecho español* (1980): 1039–54.

Bernard, Carmen. *Negros esclavos y libres en las ciudades Hispanoamericanas.* Madrid: Fundación Histórica Tavera, 2001.

Blackburn, Robin. "Raphael Samuel: The Politics of Thick Description." *New Left Review* 221 (Jan. 1997): 133–39.

Black's Law Dictionary. Abridg. 5th edn. St. Paul: West Publishing, 1983.

Blanchard, Peter. *Under the Flags of Freedom: Slave Soldiers and the Wars of Independence in Spanish South America.* Pittsburgh: University of Pittsburgh Press, 2008.

Blumenthal, Debra. *Enemies and Familiars: Slavery and Mastery in Fifteenth-Century Valencia.* Ithaca: Cornell University Press, 2009.

"The Promise of Freedom in Late Medieval Valencia." In *Paths to Freedom: Manumission in the Atlantic World*, ed. Rosemary Brana-Shute and Randy Sparks, 51–68. Columbia: University of South Carolina Press, 2009.

Blumenthal, Susana. "The Deviance of the Will: Policing the Bounds of Testamentary Freedom in Nineteenth-Century America." *Harvard Law Review* 119.2 (2006): 959–1034.

Borah, Woodrow. *Justice by Insurance: The General Indian Court of Colonial Mexico and the Legal Aides of the Half-Real*. Berkeley: University of California Press, 1983.

Borchat de Moreno, Christiana. "El control de la moral pública como elemento de las reformas borbónicas en Quito." In *Mujeres, familia y sociedad en la historia de América Latina, siglos XVIII-XXI*, ed. Scarlett O'Phalen Godoy and Margarita Zegarra Flórez, 446–70. Lima: IFEA, 2006.

Borucki, Alex, David Eltis, and David Wheat. "Atlantic History and the Slave Trade to Spanish America." *American Historical Review* 120.2 (2015): 433–61.

Bowser, Frederick. *The African Slave in Colonial Peru, 1524–1650*. Stanford: Stanford University Press, 1974.

"Colonial Spanish America." In *Neither Slave nor Free: The Freedman of African Descent in the Slave Societies of the New World*, ed. David Cohen and Jack P. Greene, 19–58. Baltimore: Johns Hopkins University Press, 1972.

"The Free Person of Color in Mexico City and Lima: Manumission and Opportunity, 1580–1650." In *Race and Slavery in the Western Hemisphere, Quantitative Studies*, ed. Stanley Engerman and Eugene Genovese, 331–68. Princeton: Princeton University Press, 1975.

Boyer, Richard. "Honor among Plebeians." In *The Faces of Honor: Sex, Shame and Violence in Colonial Latin America*, ed. Lyman Johnson and Sonya Lipsett-Rivera, 152–78. Albuquerque: University of New Mexico Press, 1998.

Lives of the Bigamists: Marriage, Family, and Community in Colonial Mexico. Albuquerque: University of New Mexico Press, 2001.

Bradley, K. R. *Slaves and Masters in the Roman Empire: A Study in Social Control*. New York: Oxford University Press, 1987.

Brana-Shute, Rosemary. "Sex and Gender in Surinamese Manumissions." In *Paths to Freedom: Manumission in the Atlantic World*, ed. Rosemary Brana-Shute and Randy Sparks, 175–96. Columbia: University of South Carolina Press, 2009.

Brana-Shute, Rosemary, and Randy Sparks, eds. *Paths to Freedom: Manumission in the Atlantic World*. Columbia: University of South Carolina Press, 2009.

Brettel, Caroline. *Men Who Migrate, Women Who Wait*. Princeton: Princeton University Press, 1986.

Brewer, Holly. *By Birth or Consent: Children, Law, and the Anglo-American Revolution in Authority*. Chapel Hill: University of North Carolina Press, 2007.

Brewer-García, Larissa. "Bodies, Texts, and Translators: Indigenous Breast Milk and the Jesuit Exclusion of Mestizos in Late Sixteenth-Century Peru." *Colonial Latin American Review* 21.3 (2012): 365–90.

"Sanctity, Slavery, and Legal Maneuvering in Colonial Peru: Estephanía de San Joseph's Lives before the Law." Paper presented at "Histories on the Edge," Sixteenth Berkshire Conference on the History of Women, Toronto, May 22, 2014.

Bristol, Joan. *Christians, Blasphemers, and Witches: Afro-Mexican Ritual Practice in the Seventeenth Century*. Albuquerque: University of New Mexico Press, 2007.

Bromley, Juan, and José Barbagelata. *Evolución urbana de Lima*. Lima: Talleres gráficos de la Editorial Lumen S.A. 1945.

Brown, Kathleen. *Good Wives, Nasty Wenches, Anxious Patriarchs: Gender, Race, and Power in Colonial Virginia*. Chapel Hill: University of North Carolina Press, 1996.

Brundage, James. *Law, Sex, and Christian Society in Medieval Europe*. Chicago: University of Chicago Press, 1987.

Medieval Canon Law. New York: Longman, 1995.

The Medieval Origins of the Legal Profession: Canonists, Civilians, and Courts. Chicago: University of Chicago Press, 2008.

Bryant, Sherwin. "Enslaved Rebels, Fugitives, and Litigants: The Resistance Continuum in Colonial Quito." *Colonial Latin American Review* 13.1 (2004): 7–46.

Rivers of Gold, Lives of Bondage: Governing through Slavery in Colonial Quito. Chapel Hill: University of Chapel Hill Press, 2014.

Bryant, Sherwin, Rachel O'Toole, and Ben Vinson III, eds. *Africans to Spanish America: Expanding the Diaspora*. Urbana: University of Illinois Press, 2012.

Buckland, W. W. *The Roman Law of Slavery*. Cambridge: Cambridge University Press, 1970 [1908].

Bühnen, Stephan. "Ethnic Origins of Peruvian Slaves, 1548–1650: Figures for Upper Guinea." *Paideuma* 39 (1993): 55–110.

Burkholder, Mark. *Spaniards in the Colonial Empire: Creoles vs. Peninsulars?* Malden, MA: Wiley Blackwell, 2013.

Burkholder, Mark, and David Chandler. *Biographical Dictionary of Audiencia Ministers in the Americas, 1687–1821*. Westport, CT: Greenwood, 1982.

Burkholder, Mark, and Lyman L. Johnson, eds. *Colonial Latin America*. 5th edn. Oxford: Oxford University Press, 2004.

Burns, Kathryn. *Colonial Habits: Convents and the Spiritual Economy of Cuzco, Peru*. Durham: Duke University Press, 1999.

Into the Archive: Writing and Power in Colonial Peru. Durham: Duke University Press, 2010.

Burns, Robert. ed. *Las Siete Partidas*. 4 vols. Trans. Samuel Parsons Scott. Philadelphia: University of Pennsylvania Press, 2001.

Burton, Antoinette. *Dwelling in the Archive: Women Writing House, Home, and History in Late Colonial India*. New York: Oxford University Press, 2003.

Burton, Antoinette, ed. *Gender, Sexuality, and Colonial Modernities*. New York: Routledge 1999.

Cahill, David. "Colour by Numbers: Racial and Ethnic Categories in the Viceroyalty of Peru, 1532–1824." *Journal of Latin American Studies* 26.2 (1994): 325–46.

Camp, Stephanie. *Closer to Freedom: Enslaved Women and Everyday Resistance in the Plantation South*. Chapel Hill: University of North Carolina Press, 2004.

"'I Could Not Stay There': Enslaved Women, Truancy and the Geography of Everyday Forms of Resistance in the Antebellum Plantation South." *Slavery and Abolition: A Journal of Slave and Post-Slave Societies* 23.3 (2002): 1–20.

Cañeque, Alejandro. *The King's Living Image: The Culture and Politics of Viceregal Power in Colonial Mexico*. New York: Routledge, 2004.

Cañizares-Esguerra, Jorge, Matt Childs, and James Sidbury, eds. *The Black Urban Atlantic in the Age of the Slave Trade*. Philadelphia: University of Pennsylvania Press, 2013.

Cantuarias Acosta, Ricardo. "Las modas limeñas." In *Lima en el siglo XVI*, ed. Laura Gutiérrez Arbulú, 287–307. Lima: PUCP, Instituto Riva Agüero, 2005.

Castillo de Bobadilla, Jerónimo. *Política para corregidores y señores de vasallos en tiempo de paz y de guerra y para juezes eclesiásticos y seglares y de sacas, aduanas y de residencias y sus oficiales*. 2 vols. En Ambares: En casa de Juan Bautista Verdussen, 1704 [1640].

Caulfield, Sueann. "The History of Gender in the Historiography of Latin America." *Hispanic American Historical Review* 81.3 (2001): 449–90.

In Defense of Honor: Sexual Morality, Modernity, and Nation in Early Twentieth-Century Brazil. Durham: Duke University Press, 2002.

Charles, John. *Allies at Odds: The Andean Church and Its Indigenous Agents, 1583–1671*. Albuquerque: University of New Mexico Press, 2010.

Clark Hine, Darlene, ed. *Black Women in American History: From Colonial Times through the Nineteenth Century*. 4 vols. Brooklyn: Carlson, 1990.

Cline, Sarah. "Fray Alonso de Molina's Model Testament and Antecedents to Indigenous Wills in Spanish America." In *Dead Giveaways: Indigenous Testaments of Colonial Mesoamerica and the Andes*, ed. Susan Kellogg and Matthew Restall, 13–33. Salt Lake City: University of Utah Press, 1998.

Cobo, Bernabé. *Historia de la fundación de Lima*. Lima: Imprenta Liberal, 1882 [1639].

Comaroff, John. "Colonialism, Culture, and the Law: A Foreword." *Law and Social Inquiry* 26.2 (2001): 305–15.

Contreras, Miguel de. *Padrón de los indios de Lima en 1613*. Lima: Seminario de historia rural Andina, 1968 [1613].

Cope, R. Douglas. *The Limits of Racial Domination: Plebeian Society in Colonial Mexico City, 1660–1720*. Madison: University of Wisconsin Press, 1994.

Corbett, Percy. *The Roman Law of Marriage*. Oxford: Clarendon Press, 1979.

Córdoba y Salinas, Diego de. *Teatro de la santa iglesia metropolitana de los reyes: Anales de la Catedral de Lima*. Lima: Biblioteca Histórica Peruana, 1958 [1650].

Cosamalón Aguilar, Jesús. *Indios detrás de la muralla: Matrimonios indígenas y convivencia inter-racial en Santa Ana, Lima, 1795–1820*. Lima: PUCP, 1999.

Cott, Nancy. *Public Vows: A History of Marriage and the Nation*. Cambridge, MA: Harvard University Press, 2000.

Covarrubias de, Sebastián. *Tesoro de la lengua castellana o española*. Barcelona: S. A Horta, IE, 1943 [1611].

Cowling, Camillia. *Conceiving Freedom: Women of Color, Gender and the Abolition of Slavery in Havana and Rio de Janeiro*. Chapel Hill: University of North Carolina Press, 2013.

Cushner, Nicholas. "Slave Mortality and Reproduction on Jesuit Haciendas in Colonial Peru." *Hispanic American Historical Review* 55.2 (1975): 177–99.

Cussen, Celia. "The Search for Idols and Saints in Colonial Peru: Linking Extirpation and Beatification." *Hispanic American Historical Review* 85.3 (2005): 417–48.

Cutter, Charles. *The Legal Culture of Northern New Spain, 1700–1810*. Albuquerque: University of New Mexico Press, 1995.

Dainow, Joseph. "The Early Sources of Forced Heirship: Its History in Louisiana and Texas." *Louisiana Law Review* 4.1 (1941): 42–69.

Dammert, José. "Don Feliciano de Vega (1580–1639): Criollo, jurista, maestro y prelado." *Revista peruana de historia eclesiástica* 4 (1995): 21–53.

Dantas, Mariana. *Black Townsmen: Urban Slavery and Freedom in the Eighteenth-Century Americas.* New York: Palgrave Macmillan, 2008.

Davis, David Brion. *The Problem of Slavery in Western Culture.* New York: Oxford University Press, 1966.

Dawson, Kevin. "The Cultural Geography of Enslaved Ship Pilots." In *The Black Urban Atlantic in the Age of the Slave Trade*, ed. Jorge Cañizares-Esguerra, Matt Childs, and James Sidbury, 164–84. Philadelphia: University of Pennsylvania Press, 2013.

Deans-Smith, Susan. "Creating the Colonial Subject: Casta Paintings, Collectors, and Critics in Eighteenth-Century Mexico and Spain." *Colonial Latin American Review* 14.2 (2005): 169–204.

de la Fuente, Alejandro. "Slaves and the Creation of Legal Rights in Cuba: *Coartación* and Papel." *Hispanic American Historical Review* 87.4 (2007): 659–92.

"Slave Law and Claims-Making in Cuba: The Tannenbaum Debate Revisited." *Law and History Review* 22.2 (2004): 304–69.

de la Fuente, Alejandro, and Ariela Gross. "Comparative Studies of Law, Slavery, and Race in the Americas." *Annual Review of Law and Social Sciences* 6 (2010): 469–85.

de la Puente Brunke, José. "Codicia y bien público: Los ministros de la Audiencia en la Lima seiscentista." *Revista de Indias* 66.236 (2006): 133–48.

"Las estrellas solo lucen cuando en sol se pone: Los ministros de la Audiencia de Lima en el siglo XVII y sus expectativas." *Illes imperis* 14 (2011): 49–67.

"Los ministros de la Audiencia y la administración de justicia en Lima 1607–1615." *Revista de estudios histórico-jurídicos* 23 (2001): 1–7.

"Los oidores en la sociedad limeña: Notas para su estudio (siglo XVII)." *Temas americanistas* 7 (1990): 8–13.

de la Puente Luna, José Carlos. "The Many Tongues of the King: Indigenous Language Interpreters and the Making of the Spanish Empire." *Colonial Latin American Review* 23.2 (2014): 143–70.

de Penyafort, Raymond. *Summa on Marriage.* Trans. Pierre Payer. Toronto: Pontifical Institute of Mediaeval Studies, 2005.

Díaz, María Elena. "Beyond Tannenbaum." *Law and History Review* 22.2 (2004): 371–76.

The Virgin, the King, and the Royal Slaves of El Cobre: Negotiating Freedom in Colonial Cuba, 1670–1780. Stanford: Stanford University Press, 2000.

Díaz Soler, Luis. *Historia de la esclavitud negra en Puerto Rico.* San Juan: Editorial de la Universidad de Puerto Rico, 1970.

Din, Gilbert. *Spaniards, Planters, and Slaves: The Spanish Regulation of Slavery in Louisiana, 1763–1803.* College Station: Texas A&M University Press, 1999.

Domínguez Ortíz, Antonio. *La esclavitud en la edad moderna y otros estudios de marginados.* Granada: Comares, 2003.

Dore, Elizabeth, ed. *Gender Politics in Latin America: Debates in Theory and Practice.* New York: Monthly Review Press, 1997.

Draper, Lincoln. *Arzobispos, canónigos, y sacerdotes: Interacción entre valores religiosos y sociales del clero de Charcas del siglo XVII.* Sucre: Archivo-Biblioteca Arquidiocesanos Monseñor Taborga, 2000.

Dueñas, Alcira. *Indians and Mestizos in the "Lettered City": Reshaping Justice, Social Hierarchy, and Political Culture in Colonial Peru.* Boulder: University Press of Colorado, 2010.

Dueñas Vargas, Guiomar. *Los hijos del pecado: Ilegitimidad y vida familiar en la Santa Fe de Bogotá colonial*. Bogotá: Editorial Universidad Nacional, 1997.

Duran Montero, María. "Lima en 1613, aspectos urbanos." *Anuario de estudios Americanos* 49 (1992): 171–88.

Earle, Rebecca. *The Body of the Conquistador: Food, Race, and the Colonial Expansion in Spanish America, 1492–1700*. Cambridge: Cambridge University Press, 2013.

Edwards, Laura. "'The Marriage Covenant Is the Foundation of All Our Rights': The Politics of Slave Marriages in North Carolina after Emancipation." *Law and History Review* 14.1 (1996): 82–124.

Elliot, J. H. "A Europe of Composite Monarchies." *Past and Present* 137.1 (1992): 48–71.

"Revolution and Continuity in Early Modern Europe." *Past and Present* 42 (Feb. 1969): 35–56.

Spain, Europe and the Wider World, 1500–1800. New Haven: Yale University Press, 2009.

Eltis, David, and David Richardson. *Atlas of the Transatlantic Slave Trade*. New Haven: Yale University Press, 2010.

Erasmus, Desiderius. *Education of a Christian Prince*. Cambridge: Cambridge University Press, 1997 [1521].

Escobar, Arturo. "Latin America at a Crossroads: Alternative Modernizations, Post-Liberalism, or Post-Development?" *Cultural Studies* 24.1 (2010): 1–65.

Escobar Gamboa, Mauro. *Padrón de los Indios de Lima en 1613*. Lima: UNMSM, 1968.

Espelt-Bombín, Silvia. "Notaries of Color in Colonial Panama: *Limpieza de Sangre*, Legislation, and Imperial Practices in the Administration of the Spanish Empire." *The Americas* 71.1 (2014): 37–69.

Estenssoro Fuchs, Juan Carlos. "Los colores de la plebe: Razón y mestizaje en el Perú colonial." In *Los cuadros del mestizaje del Virrey Amat*, ed. Natalia Mahluf, 66–107. Lima: Museo de Arte de Lima, 2000.

Evans Grubbs, Judith. *Law and Family in Late Antiquity*. Oxford: Clarendon Press, 1995.

Falcão, Miguel. *Las prohibiciones matrimoniales de carácter social en el imperio Romano*. Pamplona: Ediciones Universidad de Navarra, 1973.

Falk Moore, Sally. *Social Facts and Fabrications: "Customary" Law on Kilimanjaro*. New York: Cambridge University Press, 1986.

Farge, Arlette. *The Allure of the Archives*. New Haven: Yale University Press, 2013.

Fenster, Thelma, and Daniel Lord Smail, eds. *Fama: The Politics of Talk and Reputation in Medieval Europe*. Ithaca: Cornell University Press, 2003.

Fields, Barbara Jeanne. *Slavery and Freedom on the Middle Ground: Maryland during the Nineteenth-Century*. New Haven: Yale University Press, 1985.

Fischer, Kirsten. *Suspect Relations: Sex, Race, and Resistance in Colonial North America*. Ithaca: Cornell University Press, 2002.

Fisher, Andrew, and Matthew O'Hara, eds. *Imperial Subjects: Race and Colonial Identity in Colonial Latin America*. Durham: Duke University Press, 2009.

Fix Zamudio, Hector. "The Writ of *Amparo* in Latin America." *Lawyer of the Americas* 13.3 (1981): 361–91.

Flores Galindo, Alberto. *Aristocracia y plebe: Lima, 1760–1830*. Lima: Mosca Azul, 1984.

Flores Galindo, Alberto, and Margarita Chocano. "Las cargas del sacramento." *Revista andina* 2.2 (1984): 401–23.

Ford, Lacy. "Reconsidering the Internal Slave Trade: Paternalism, Markets, and the Character of the Old South." In *The Chattel Principle*, 143–64.

Foster, W. H. "Women Slave Owners Face Their Historians: Versions of Maternalism in Atlantic World Slavery." *Patterns of Prejudice* 41.3–4 (2007): 303–20.

Fox-Genovese, Elizabeth. *Within the Plantation Household: Black and White Women of the Old South*. Chapel Hill: University of North Carolina Press, 1988.

Frank, Zephyr. *Dutra's World: Wealth and Family in Nineteenth-Century Rio de Janeiro*. Albuquerque: University of New Mexico Press, 2004.

Franke, Katherine. "Becoming a Citizen: Reconstruction Era Regulation of African American Marriages." *Yale Journal of Law and the Humanities* 11.2 (1999): 251–309.

Fredrickson, George. *Racism: A Short History*. Princeton: Princeton University Press, 2002.

Freyre, Giberto. *Casa grande y senzala: Formación de la familia brasileña bajo el régimen de la economía patriarcal*. Caracas: Biblioteca Ayacucho, 1977.

Galanter, Mark. "Why the Haves Come Out Ahead: Speculations on the Limits of Legal Change." *Law and Society Review* 9.1 (1974): 95–160.

Gálvez Peña, Carlos. "Obispo, financista y político: El doctor don Feliciano de Vega y Padilla (1580–1641)." *Histórica* 36.1 (2012): 97–133.

Ganster, Paul. "Miembros de los cabildos eclesiásticos y sus familias en Lima y la ciudad de México en el siglo XVIII." In *Familias novohispanas, siglos XVI al XIX*, ed. Pilar Gonzalbo Aizpuru, 150–62. Mexico City: El Colegio de México, 1993.

Garofalo, Leo. "Conjuring with Coca and the Inca: The Andeanization of Lima's Afro-Peruvian Ritual Specialists, 1580–1690." *The Americas* 63.1 (2006): 53–80.

Gaspar, David Barry. "From 'the Sense of their Slavery': Slave Women and Resistance in Antigua, 1632–1763." In *More than Chattel: Black Women and Slavery in the Americas*, ed. Darlene Clark Hine and David Barry Gaspar, 218–38. Bloomington: University of Indiana Press, 1996.

Genovese, Eugene. "Materialism and Idealism in the History of Negro Slavery in the Americas." In *Slavery in the New World*, ed. Laura Foner and Eugene Genovese, 238–55. Englewood Cliffs: Prentice Hall, 1969.

Roll Jordan Roll: The World the Slaves Made. New York: Vintage, 1974.

Gil, Pedro Ortega. "Hurtar a los de casa: Notas sobre hurtos domésticos." *Cuadernos de historia del derecho* 17 (2010): 449–70.

Glave, Luis Miguel. "Las redes de poder y la necesidad del saber: Cátedras y catedráticos en la Universidad de Lima (siglo XVII)." *Illes Imperis* 14 (2011): 69–86.

Glymph, Thavolia. *Out of the House of Bondage: The Transformation of the Plantation Household*. New York: Cambridge University Press, 2008.

Gómez, Pablo. "The Circulation of Bodily Knowledge in the Seventeenth-Century Black Spanish Caribbean." *Social History of Medicine* 26.3 (2013): 383–402.

Gonzalez, Ondina, and Bianca Premo, eds. *Raising an Empire: Children in Early Modern Iberia and Colonial Latin America*. Albuquerque: University of New Mexico Press, 2007.

Gordon-Reed, Annette. "Writing Early American Lives as Biography." *William and Mary Quarterly* 71.4 (2014): 491–516.

Graubart, Karen. "Hybrid Thinking: Bringing Postcolonial Theory to Colonial Latin American Economic History." In *Postcolonial Thought and Economics*, ed. S. Charusheela and Eiman Zein-Elabin, 215–34. New York: Routledge, 2003.

"Los lazos que unen: Dueñas negras de esclavos negros, Lima SS. XVI-XVII." *Nueva Corónica* 2 (Jul. 2013): 625–40.

"'So color de una cofradía': Catholic Confraternities and the Development of Afro-Peruvian Ethnicities in Early Colonial Peru." *Slavery and Abolition: A Journal of Slave and Post-Slave Societies* 33.1 (2012): 43–64.

Greer, Allan. "Colonial Saints: Gender, Race, and Hagiography in New France." *William and Mary Quarterly* 57.2 (2000): 323–48.

Gregory, Chris. "Economy's Tension: The Dialectics of Community and Market." Feature Review, *New Political Economy* 14.2 (2009): 303–09.

Grinberg, Keila. "Freedom Suits and Civil Law in Brazil and the United States." *Slavery and Abolition: A Journal of Slave and Post-Slave Societies* 22.3 (2001): 66–82.

Gross, Ariela. *Double Character: Slavery and Mastery in the Antebellum Courtroom.* Athens: University of Georgia Press, 2006.

What Blood Won't Tell: A History of Race on Trial in America. Cambridge, MA: Harvard University Press, 2008.

Grossberg, Michael. *Governing the Hearth: Law and the Family in Nineteenth-Century America.* Chapel Hill: University of North Carolina Press, 1985.

Gutman, Herbert. *The Black Family in Slavery and Freedom, 1750–1925.* New York: Vintage, 1976.

Guy, Donna. "Girls in Prison: The Role of the Buenos Aires *Casa Correcional de Mujeres* as an Institution for Child Rescue, 1890–1940." In *Crime and Punishment in Latin America: Law and Society Since Late Colonial Times*, ed. Ricardo Salvatore, Carlos Aguirre, and Gilbert Joseph, 369–90. Durham: Duke University Press.

Hall, Gwendolyn Mindlo. *Social Control in Slave Plantation Societies: A Comparison of Saint Domingue and Cuba.* Baltimore: Johns Hopkins University Press, 1971.

Hanke, Lewis. *The Spanish Struggle for Justice in the Conquest of America.* Philadelphia: University of Pennsylvania Press, 1949.

Harris, Marvin. *Patterns of Race in the Americas.* New York: Walker, 1964.

Harth-Terre, Emilio, and Alberto Marquez Abanto. "El negro artesano en la arquitectura virreinal limeña." *Revista del Archivo Nacional del Perú* 25 (1961): 3–73.

Hartman, Saidiya. *Scenes of Subjection: Terror, Slavery and Self-Making in Nineteenth-Century America.* New York: Oxford University Press, 1997.

Hartog, Hendrik. *Man and Wife in America: A History.* Cambridge: Cambridge University Press, 2000.

Someday This Will All Be Yours: A History of Inheritance and Old Age. Cambridge, MA: Harvard University Press, 2012.

Hayton, David, ed. *European Succession Laws.* Chichester: Chancery Law Publishing, 1992.

Hecht, Tobias, ed. *Minor Omissions: Children in Latin American History and Society.* Madison: University of Wisconsin Press, 2002.

Helmholz, Richard. "Baptism in the Medieval Canon Law." *Rechtsgeschichte Legal History* 21 (2013): 118–27.

Herzog, Tamar. *Defining Nations: Immigrants and Citizens in Early Modern Spain and Spanish America.* New Haven: Yale University Press, 2003.

Mediación, archivos y ejercicio: Los escribanos de Quito, siglo XVII. Frankfurt: Vittorio Klosk Mann, 1996.

Upholding Justice: Society, State, and the Penal System in Quito, 1650–1750. Ann Arbor: University of Michigan Press, 2004.

Hevia Bolaños, Juan de. *Curia philipica.* 2 vols. Valladolid: Lex Nova, 1989 [1615].

Higgins, Kathryn. *"Licentious Liberty" in a Brazilian Gold-Mining Region: Slavery, Gender and Social Control in Eighteenth-Century Sabará, Minas Gerais.* University Park: Pennsylvania State University Press, 1999.

Hodes, Martha. ed., *Sex, Love, Race: Crossing Boundaries in North American History.* New York: New York University Press, 1999.

Hünefeldt, Christine. *Lasmanuelos: Vida cotidiana de una familia negra en la Lima del siglo XIX; una reflexión histórica sobre la esclavitud urbana.* Lima: Instituto de Estudios Peruanos, 1992.

Liberalism in the Bedroom: Quarreling Spouses in Nineteenth-Century Lima. University Park: Pennsylvania State Press, 1999.

Paying the Price of Freedom: Family and Labor among Lima's Slaves, 1800–1854. Berkeley: University of California Press, 1994.

Ingersoll, Thomas. *Mammon and Manon in Early New Orleans: The First Slave Society in the Deep South, 1718–1819.* Knoxville: University of Tennessee Press, 1999.

Iwasaki Cauti, Fernando. "Fray Martín de Porras: Santo, ensalmador y sacamuelas." *Colonial Latin American Review* 3.1-2 (1994): 159–84.

Jennings, Evelyn. "In the Language of the Criminal: Slavery and Colonialism in Ibero-America." *Latin American Research Review* 49.2 (2014): 282–94.

Johnson, Lyman. "A Lack of Legitimate Obedience and Respect: Slaves and their Masters in the Courts of Late Colonial Buenos Aires." *Hispanic American Historical Review* 87.4 (2007): 631–57.

"Manumission in Colonial Buenos Aires, 1776–1810." *Hispanic American Historical Review* 59.2 (1979): 258–79.

Johnson, Lyman, and Sonya Lipsett-Rivera, eds. *The Faces of Honor: Sex, Shame and Violence in Colonial Latin America.* Albuquerque: University of New Mexico Press, 1998.

Johnson, Walter. "Resetting the Legal History of Slavery: Divination, Torture, Poisoning, Murder, Revolution, Emancipation, and Re-enslavement." *Law and History Review* 29.4 (2011): 1089–95.

Soul by Soul: Life inside the Antebellum Slave Market. Cambridge, MA: Harvard University Press, 1999.

Johnson, Walter, ed. *The Chattel Principle: Internal Slave Trades in the Americas.* New Haven: Yale University Press, 2004.

Jones, Catherine. "Ties That Bind, Bonds That Break: Children in the Reorganization of Households in Postemancipation Virginia." *Journal of Southern History* 76.1 (2010): 71–106.

Jones, Martha S. "Time, Space, and Jurisdiction in Atlantic World Slavery: The Volunbrun Household in Gradual Emancipation New York." *Law and History Review* 29.4 (2011): 1031–60.

Jouve Martín, José Ramón. "Death, Gender, and Writing." In *Afro-Latino Voices: Narratives from the Early Modern Ibero-Atlantic World, 1550–1812,* ed. Kathryn J. McKnight and Leo Garofalo, 105–25. Indianapolis: Hackett, 2009.

Esclavos de la ciudad letrada: Esclavitud, escritura y colonialismo en Lima (1650–1700). Lima: Instituto de Estudios Peruanos, 2005.

Kagan, Richard. *Lawsuits and Litigants in Castile: 1500–1700*. Chapel Hill: University of North Carolina Press, 1981.

Students and Society in Early Modern Spain. Baltimore: Johns Hopkins University Press, 1974.

Karasch, Mary. *Slave Life in Rio de Janeiro, 1808–1850*. Princeton: Princeton University Press, 1987.

Kellogg, Susan. *Law and the Transformation of Aztec Culture, 1500–1700*. Norman: University of Oklahoma Press, 1995.

Kellogg, Susan, and Matthew Restall, eds. *Dead Giveaways: Indigenous Testaments of Colonial Mesoamerica and the Andes*. Salt Lake City: University of Utah Press, 1998.

Kennedy, Duncan. "Distributive and Paternalist Moves in Contract and Tort Law with Special Reference to Compulsory Terms and Unequal Bargaining Power." *Maryland Law Review* 41 (1981–82): 563–600.

Klein, Herbert. "Anglicism, Catholicism and the Negro Slave." *Comparative Studies in Society and History* 8.3 (1966): 295–327.

Klein, Herbert, and Francisco Vidal Luna. *Slavery in Brazil*. Cambridge: Cambridge University Press, 2010.

Klooster, Wim. "Inter-Imperial Smuggling in the Americas, 1600–1800." In *Soundings in Atlantic History: Latent Structures and Intellectual Currents, 1500–1830*, ed. Bernard Bailyn and Patricia Denault, 141–80. Cambridge, MA: Harvard University Press, 2009.

"Manumission in an Entrepôt: The Case of Curaçao." In *Paths to Freedom: Manumission in the Atlantic World*, ed. Rosemary Brana-Shute and Randy Sparks, 161–74. Columbia: University of South Carolina Press, 2009.

Konetzke, Richard. *Colección de documentos para la historia de la formación social de Hispanoamérica, 1493.1810*. 3 vols. Madrid: Consejo Superior de Investigaciones Científicas, 1958.

Knight, Franklin. *Slave Society in Cuba during the Nineteenth Century*. Madison: University of Wisconsin Press, 1970.

Kuehn, Thomas. *Heirs, Kin, and Creditors in Renaissance Florence*. Cambridge: Cambridge University Press, 2011.

"Reading Microhistory: The Example of Giovanni and Lusanna." *Journal of Modern History* 61.3 (1989): 512–34.

Kuznesof, Elizabeth. "Ethnic and Gender Influences on 'Spanish' Creole Society." *Colonial Latin American Review* 4.1 (1995): 1530–76.

"The House, the Street, Global Society: Latin American Families and Childhood in the Twenty-First Century." *Journal of Social History* 38.4 (2005): 859–72.

Household Economy and Urban Development: São Paulo, 1765 to 1836. Boulder: Westview Press, 1986.

"Sexual Politics, Race and Bastard-Bearing in Nineteenth Century Brazil: A Question of Culture of Power?." *Journal of Family History* 16.3 (1991): 241–60.

Landers, Jane. *Black Society in Spanish Florida*. Urbana: University of Illinois Press, 1999.

"Cartagena." In *The Black Urban Atlantic in the Age of the Slave Trade*, ed. Jorge Cañizares-Esguerra, Matt Childs, and James Sidbury, 147–62. Philadelphia: University of Pennsylvania Press, 2013.

Lane, Kris. "Captivity and Redemption: Aspects of Slave Life in Early Colonial Quito and Popayán." *The Americas* 57.2 (2000): 225–46.

Latasa Vassallo, Pilar. *Administración virreinal en el Perú: Gobierno del Marqués de Montesclaros, 1607–1615*. Madrid: Editorial Centro de estudios Ramón Areces, 1997.

"La celebración del matrimonio en el virreinato peruano: Disposiciones sinodales en las archidiócesis de Charcas y Lima (1570–1613)." In *El matrimonio en Europa y el mundo Hispánico, siglos XVI y XVII*, ed. Ignacio Arellano y Jesús and María Usunáriz, 237–56. Madrid: Visor Libros.

Lauderdale Graham, Saundra. *Caetana Says No: Women's Stories from a Brazilian Slave Society*. Cambridge: Cambridge University Press, 2002.

House and Street: The Domestic World of Servants and Masters in Nineteenth-Century Rio de Janeiro. Austin: University of Texas Press, 1988.

Lavallé, Bernard. *Amor y opresión en los Andes coloniales*. Lima: IFEA and IEP, 2001.

Lavrin, Asunción, ed. *Sexuality and Marriage in Colonial Latin America*. Lincoln: University of Nebraska Press, 1989.

Lazarus-Black, Mindie, and Susan Hirsch, eds. *Contested States: Law, Hegemony and Resistance*. New York: Routledge, 1994.

Lepore, Jill. "Historians Who Love Too Much: Reflections on Microhistory and Biography." *Journal of American History* 88.1 (2001): 129–44.

Lewin, Linda. *Surprise Heirs: Illegitimacy, Patrimonial Rights and Legal Nationalism in Luso-Brazilian Inheritance, 1750–1820*. 2 vols. Stanford: Stanford University Press, 2003.

Libby, Douglas Cole, and Alfonso de Alecanstro Graça Filho. "Notarized and Baptismal Manumissions in the Parish of São José do Rio das Mortes, Minas Gerais (c. 1750–1850)." *The Americas* 66.2 (2009): 211–40.

Libby, Douglas Cole, and Clotilde Andrade Paiva. "Manumission Practices in a Late Eighteenth-Century Brazilian Slave Parish: São José d'El Rey in 1795." *Slavery and Abolition: A Journal of Slave and Post-Slave Societies* 21.1 (2012): 96–127.

Lira González, Andrés. *El amparo colonial y el juicio de amparo mexicano: Antecedentes novohispanos del juicio de amparo*. Mexico City: Fondo de Cultura Económica, 1972.

Lockhart, James. *Spanish Peru, 1532–1560*. Madison: University of Wisconsin Press, 1968.

Lohmann Villena, Guillermo. *Los americanos en las órdenes nobiliarias, 1529–1900*. Madrid: Consejo Superior de Investigaciones Científicas, 1993.

El corregidor de indios en el Perú bajo los Austrias. Lima: PUCP, 2001.

Los regidores perpetuos del Cabildo de Lima (1535–1821): Crónica y estudio de un grupo de gestión. 2 vols. Seville: Artes Gráficas Padura, 1983.

Lombardi, John. *The Decline and Abolition of Negro Slavery in Venezuela, 1820–1854*. Westport: Greenwood, 1971.

Lucena Samoral, Manuel. *Leyes para esclavos: El ordenamiento jurídico sobre la condición, tratamiento, defensa y represión de los esclavos en las colonias de la América española*. Madrid: Fundación Ignacio Larramendi, 2011.

Macera, Pedro. *Instrucciones para el manejo de las haciendas Jesuitas del Perú (ss. XVII–XVIII)*. Lima: Universidad Nacional Mayor de San Marcos, 1966.

Macauley, Melissa. *Social Power and Legal Culture: Litigation Masters in Late Imperial China*. Stanford: Stanford University Press, 1998.

MacLachan, Colin. *Spain's Empire in the New World: The Role of Ideas in Institutional and Social Change.* Berkeley: University of California Press, 1988.

Mahluf, Natalia, ed. *Los cuadros del mestizaje del Virrey Amat.* Lima: Museo de Arte de Lima, 2000.

Maine, Henry. *Ancient Law.* New York: Cosimo Books, 2005 [1861].

Malagón Barceló, Javier. *Código negro carolino (1784).* Santo Domingo: Taller, 1974.

Mallon, Florencia. "The Promise and Dilemma of Subaltern Studies: Perspectives from Latin American History." *American Historical Review* 99.5 (1994): 1491–515.

Mangan, Jane. *Trading Roles: Gender, Ethnicity, and the Urban Economy in Colonial Potosí.* Durham: Duke University Press, 2005.

Mannarelli, María Emma. "Inquisición y mujeres: Las hechiceras en el Perú durante el siglo XVII." *Revista andina* 3.1 (1985): 141–55.

——— *Pecados públicos: La ilegitimidad en Lima, siglo XVII.* Lima: Flora Tristán Centro de la mujer peruana, 1993.

——— "Sobre la historia de lo público y lo privado en el Perú desde una perspectiva feminista." *Revista Iberoamericana* 70.206 (2004): 141–56.

Marshall, Anna-Maria, and Scott Barclay. "In Their Own Words: How Ordinary People Construct the Legal World." *Law and Social Inquiry* 28.3 (2003): 617–28.

Martin, Joan. "Plaçage and the Louisiana *Gens de Coleur Libre*: How Race and Sex Defined the Lifestyles of Free Women of Color." In *Creole: The History and Legacy of Louisiana's Free People,* ed. Sybil Klein, 57–70. Baton Rouge: Louisiana State University Press, 2000.

Martín, Luis. *Intellectual Conquest of Peru: The Jesuit College of San Pablo, 1568–1767.* New York: Fordham University Press, 1968.

Martínez, María Elena. "The Black Blood of New Spain: *Limpieza de Sangre*, Racial Violence, and Gendered Power in Early Colonial Mexico." *William and Mary Quarterly* 61.3 (2004): 479–520.

——— *Genealogical Fictions: Limpieza de Sangre, Religion, and Gender in Colonial Mexico.* Stanford: Stanford University Press, 2008.

Martinez-Alier, Verena. "Elopement and Seduction in Nineteenth-Century Cuba." *Past and Present* 55 (May 1972): 91–129.

——— *Marriage, Class, and Colour in Nineteenth-Century Cuba: A Study of Racial Attitudes and Sexual Values in a Slave Society.* Cambridge: Cambridge University Press, 1974.

Martínez-Serna, J. Gabriel. "Procurators and the Making of the Jesuits' Atlantic Network." In *Soundings in Atlantic History: Latent Structures and Intellectual Currents, 1500–1830,* ed. Bernard Bailyn and Patricia Denault, 181–209. Cambridge, MA: Harvard University Press, 2009.

Martiré, Eduardo. "La visita de cárcel en Buenos Aires durante el virreinato." *Revista Chilena de historia del derecho* 13 (1987): 39–59.

Mawani, Renisa. "Law as Temporality: Colonial Politics and Indian Settlers." *University of California-Irvine Law Review* 4.1 (2014): 65–95.

Mazín, Oscar. *Gestores de la Real Justicia: Procuradores y agentes de las catedrales hispanas nuevas en la corte de Madrid.* Mexico City: El Colegio de México, Centro de estudios históricos, 2007.

McKinley, Michelle. "Emancipatory Politics and Rebellious Practices: Incorporating Global Human Rights in Family Violence Laws in Peru." *New York University Journal of International Law and Politics* 39.1 (2006): 75–139.

"Illicit Intimacies: Virtuous Concubinage in Colonial Lima." *Journal of Family History* 39.3 (2014): 204–21.

"Standing on Shaky Ground: Criminal Jurisdiction and Ecclesiastical Immunity in Seventeenth-Century Lima: 1600–1700." *University of California-Irvine Law Review* 5.3 (2014): 101–34.

"The Unbearable Lightness of Being (Black): Racial Constructions of Culture and Cultural Constructions of Race in Latin America." In *Racial Formations in the 21st Century*, ed. Daniel Martinez-Hosang, Oneka LaBennett, and Laura Pulido, 116–42. University of California Press, 2012.

McKnight, Joseph. "Spanish *Legitim* in the United States: Its Survival and Decline." *American Journal of Comparative Law* 44.1 (1996): 75–107.

McKnight, Kathryn Joy. "*En su tierra lo aprendió*: An African *Curandero's* Defense before the Cartagena Inquisition." *Colonial Latin American Review* 12.1 (2003): 63–84.

Meiklejohn, Norman. "The Implementation of Slave Legislation in Eighteenth-Century Nueva Granada." In *Slavery and Race Relations in Latin America*, ed. Robert Brent Toplin, 176–203. Westport, CT: Greenwood, 1974.

Mendiburu, Manuel de. *Diccionario histórico-biográfico del Perú.* 8 vols. Lima: J. Francisco Solís, 1874–90.

Merry, Sally Engle. *Getting Justice and Getting Even: Legal Consciousness among Working-Class Americans.* Chicago: University of Chicago Press, 1990.

Metcalf, Alida. "Searching for the Slave Family in Colonial Brazil." *Journal of Family History* 16.3 (1991): 283–97.

Mommsen, Theodor, Paul Kruger, and Alan Watson, eds. *The Digest of Justinian.* 4 vols. Philadelphia: University of Pennsylvania Press, 1985.

Morgan, Jennifer. *Laboring Women: Reproduction and Gender in New World Slavery.* Philadelphia: University of Pennsylvania Press, 2004.

"'Some Could Suckle over Their Shoulder': Male Travelers, Female Bodies, and the Gendering of Racial Ideology, 1500–1770." *William and Mary Quarterly* 54.1 (1997): 167–92.

Mörner, Magnus. *Race Mixture in the History of Latin America.* Boston: Little, Brown, 1967.

Morris, Christopher. "The Master-Slave Relationship Reconsidered." *Journal of American History* 85.3 (1998): 982–1007.

Mignolo, Walter. "Afterword: Human Understanding and (Latin) American Interests – The Politics and Sensibilities of Geocultural Locations." *Poetics Today* 16.1 (1995): 171–214.

Milanich, Nara. "Degrees of Bondage: Children's Tutelary Servitude in Modern Latin America." In *Child Slaves in the Modern World*, ed. Gwynn Campbell, Suzanne Miers, and Joseph C. Miller, 104–23. Athens: Ohio University Press, 2011.

"Whither Family History: A Road Map from Latin America." *American Historical Review* 112.2 (2007): 439–58.

Miller, Joseph C. "A Historical Appreciation of the Biographical Turn." In *Biography and the Black Atlantic*, ed. Lisa Lindsay and John Wood Sweet, 19–47. Philadelphia: University of Pennsylvania Press, 2014.

Mills, Kenneth. *Idolatry and Its Enemies: Colonial Andean Religion and Extirpation, 1640–1750.* Princeton: Princeton University Press, 1997.

Milner, Neal. "The Intrigue of Rights, Resistance, and Accommodation." *Law and Social Inquiry* 17.2 (1992): 313–33.

Miño Grijalva, Manuel. "El obraje colonial." *European Review of Latin American and Caribbean Studies* 47 (1989): 3–19.

Mitchell, Mary Niall. *Raising Freedom's Child: Black Children and the Visions of the Future after Slavery*. New York: New York University Press, 2008.

Moscoso y Peralta, Juan Manuel. *Aranzel de derechos eclesiásticos parroquiales, de hospitales, curia eclesiástica, y Secretaría de Cámara del Obispado del Cuzco*. Lima: Imprenta Real, 1782.

Mugaburu, Josephe de. *Chronicle of Colonial Lima: The Diary of Josephe and Francisco Mugaburu, 1640–1697*. Trans. Robert Ryal Miller. Norman: University of Oklahoma Press, 1975.

Muldoon, James. *The Americas in the Spanish World Order: Justification for Conquest in the Seventeenth Century*. Philadelphia: University of Pennsylvania Press, 1994.

Muñoz, Juan. *Práctica de procuradores para seguir pleytos civiles, y criminales*. Charleston: Nabu Press, 2011 [1659].

Murray, Daniel. "Implied Warranty against Latent Defects: A Historical Comparative Study." *Louisiana Law Review* 21.3 (1960): 586–605.

Nader, Laura. *Law in Culture and Society*. Berkeley: University of California Press, 1997.

Nazzari, Muriel. "Jose Antonio da Silva: Marriage and Concubinage in Colonial Brazil." In *The Human Tradition in Colonial Latin America*, ed. Kenneth Andrien, 229–40. Lanham, MD: Rowman and Littlefield, 2002.

Nessler, Graham. "'They Always Knew Her to Be Free': Emancipation and Re-enslavement in French Santo Domingo, 1804–1809." *Slavery and Abolition: A Journal of Slave and Post-Slave Studies* 33.1 (2012): 87–103.

Newson, Linda, and Susie Minchin. *From Capture to Sale: The Portuguese Slave Trade to Spanish South America in the Early Seventeenth Century*. Leiden: Brill, 2007.

Nishida, Mieko. *Slavery and Identity: Ethnicity, Gender, and Race in Salvador Brazil, 1808–1888*. Bloomington: University of Indiana Press, 2003.

Noonan, John. *Power to Dissolve: Lawyers and Marriages in the Courts of the Roman Curia*. Cambridge, MA: Harvard University Press, 1972.

Oppenheim, Leonard. "The Law of Slaves – A Comparative Study of the Roman and Louisiana Systems." *Tulane Law Review* 14.3 (1939): 384–406.

Osorio, Alejandra. *Inventing Lima: Baroque Modernity in Peru's South Sea Metropolis*. New York: Palgrave Macmillan, 2008.

"The King in Lima: Simulacra, Ritual, and Rule in Seventeenth-Century Peru." *Hispanic American Historical Review* 84.3 (2004): 447–74.

O'Toole, Rachel Sarah. "As Historical Subjects: The African Diaspora in Colonial Latin American History." *History Compass* 11.12 (2013): 1094–110.

Bound Lives: Africans, Indians, and the Making of Race in Colonial Peru. Pittsburgh: University of Pittsburgh Press, 2012.

"Manumitted but Not Free: Women Working to Freedom in Colonial Peru." Paper presented at *Dangerous Dependencies* symposium, University of Oregon, May 4, 2012.

"To Be Free and Lucumí: Ana de la Calle and Making African Diaspora Identities in Colonial Peru." In *Africans to Spanish America Africans to Spanish*

America: Expanding the Diaspora, ed. Sherwin Bryant, Rachel O'Toole, and Ben Vinson III, 73–92. Urbana: University of Illinois Press, 2012.

Ots Capdequí, José María. *Estudios de historia del derecho español en las Indias.* Bogotá: Minerva, 1940.

Owens, J. B. *By My Absolute Royal Authority: Justice and the Castilian Commonwealth at the Beginning of the First Global Age.* Rochester: University of Rochester Press, 2005.

Owensby, Brian. "Between Justice and Economics: 'Indians' and Reformism in Eighteenth-Century Spanish Imperial Thought." In *Legal Pluralism and Empires, 1500–1850*, ed. Lauren Benton and Richard Ross, 143–69. New York: New York University Press, 2013.

——— *Empire of Law and Indian Justice in Colonial Mexico.* Stanford: Stanford University Press, 2008.

——— "How Juan and Leonor Won Their Freedom: Litigation and Liberty in Seventeenth-Century Mexico." *Hispanic American Historical Review* 73.3 (2005): 361–91.

Painter, Nell. *Southern History across the Color Line.* Chapel Hill: University of North Carolina Press, 2002.

Palmer, Colin. *Slaves of the White God: Blacks in Mexico 1570–1650.* Cambridge, MA: Harvard University Press, 1976.

Panfichi, Aldo. "Urbanización temprana de Lima, 1535–1900." In *Mundos interiores: Lima 1850–1950*, ed. Aldo Panfichi and Felipe Portocarrero, 15–42. Lima: Centro de Investigación de la Universidad del Pacifico, 2004.

Panzer, Joel. *The Popes and Slavery.* New York: Alba House, 1996.

Parker, Kunal. "Making Blacks Foreigners: The Legal Construction of Former Slaves in Post-Revolutionary Massachusetts." *Utah Law Review* 75.1 (2001): 75–124.

Parry, J. H. *The Sale of Public Office in the Spanish Indies under the Hapsburgs.* Berkeley: University of California Press, 1953.

Pascoe, Peggy. *What Comes Naturally: Miscegenation Law and the Making of Race in America.* New York: Oxford University Press, 2009.

Patterson, Orlando. "Three Notes of Freedom: The Nature and Consequences of Manumission." In *Paths to Freedom: Manumission in the Atlantic World*, ed. Rosemary Brana-Shute and Randy Sparks, 16–29. Columbia: University of South Carolina Press, 2009.

Peabody, Sue. *There Are No Slaves in France: The Political Culture of Race and Slavery in the Ancien Régime.* New York: Oxford University Press, 1996.

Peabody, Sue, and Keila Grinberg. "Free Soil: The Generation and Circulation of an Atlantic Legal Principle." *Slavery and Abolition: A Journal of Slave and Post-Slave Studies* 32.3 (2011): 331–39.

Pedersen, Susan. "The Maternalist Moment in British Colonial Policy: The Controversy over 'Child Slavery' in Hong Kong, 1917–1941." *Past and Present* 161.1 (2001): 161–202.

Pelletier, George, and Michael Sonnenreich. "A Comparative Analysis of Civil Law Succession." *Villanova Law Review* 11.2 (1966): 323–56.

Pérez Cantó, Pilar. *Lima en el siglo XVIII: Estudio socioeconómico.* Madrid: Instituto de Cooperación Iberoamericana, 1985.

Pérez Perdomo, Rogelio. *Latin American Lawyers.* Stanford: Stanford University Press, 2006.

Perry, Mary Elizabeth. "Finding Fatima, a Slave Woman in Early Modern Spain." *Journal of Women's History* 20.1 (2008): 151–67.

Phillips, William D. "Manumission in Metropolitan Spain and the Canaries." In *Paths to Freedom: Manumission in the Atlantic World*, ed. Rosemary Brana-Shute and Randy Sparks, 31–50. Columbia: University of South Carolina Press, 2009.

Slavery in Medieval and Early Modern Iberia. Philadelphia: University of Pennsylvania Press, 2014.

Pike, Ruth. *Aristocrats and Traders: Sevillan Society in the Sixteenth Century*. Ithaca: Cornell University Press, 1972.

Porcari Coloma, César. *'Lima Antigua' por Carlos Prince [1890]*. Lima: Instituto Latinoamericano de Cultura y Desarrollo, 1992.

Premo, Bianca. "Before the Law: Women's Petitions in the Eighteenth-Century Spanish Empire." *Comparative Studies in Society and History* 53.2 (2011): 261–89.

Children of the Father King: Youth, Authority, and Legal Minority in Colonial Lima. Chapel Hill: University of North Carolina Press, 2005.

"Misunderstood Love: Children and Wet Nurses, Creoles and Kings in Lima's Enlightenment." *Colonial Latin American Review* 14.2 (2005): 231–61.

Price, Richard. *Maroon Societies: Rebel Slave Communities in the Americas*. New York: Anchor, 1973.

Proctor, Frank T. *"Damned Notions of Liberty:" Slavery, Culture, and Power in Colonial Mexico, 1640–1769*. Albuquerque: University of New Mexico Press, 2010.

"Gender and the Manumission of Slaves in New Spain." *Hispanic American Historical Review* 86.2 (2005): 309–36.

"An 'Imponderable Servitude': Slave versus Master Litigation for Cruelty (*Maltratamiento* or *Sevicia*) in Late Eighteenth-Century Lima, Peru." *Journal of Social History* 48.3 (2015): 662–84.

Quiroz, Francisco. *Artesanos y manufactureros en Lima colonial*. Lima: Instituto de Estudios Peruanos, 2008.

Ramos, Donald. "From Minho to Minas: The Portuguese Roots of the Minheiro Family." *Hispanic American Historical Review* 73.4 (1993): 639–62.

"Gossip, Scandal, and Popular Culture in Golden Age Brazil." *Journal of Social History* 33.4 (2000): 887–912.

Ramos, Gabriela. *Muerte y conversión en los Andes: Lima y Cuzco, 1532–1670*. Lima: Instituto de Estudios Peruanos, 2010.

Rankin, David. "The Tannenbaum Thesis Reconsidered: Slavery and Race Relations in Antebellum Louisiana." *Southern Studies* 18.1 (1979): 5–31.

Rappaport, Joanne. "Asi lo paresçe por su aspeto: Physiognomy and the Construction of Racial Difference in Colonial Bogotá." *Hispanic American Historical Review* 91.4 (2011): 601–31.

Ratto, Cristina. "La ciudad dentro de la gran ciudad: Las imágenes del convento de monjas en los virreinatos de Nueva España y Perú." *Anales del Instituto de investigaciones estéticas* 94 (2009): 59–92.

Ray, Raka, and Seemin Qayum. *Cultures of Servitude: Modernity, Domesticity, and Class in India*. Stanford: Stanford University Press, 2009.

Riall, Lucy. "The Shallow End of History: The Substance and Future of Political Biography." *Journal of Interdisciplinary History* 40.3 (2010): 375–97.

Ribera, Diego de, and Bernardo de Olmedilla. *Primera [segunda y tercera] parte de escrituras, y orden de partición y cuenta, y de residencia judicial, ciuil, y criminal, con una instrucción a los escriuanos del Reyno al principio, y aranzel*. Madrid: Viuda de Alonso Martín de Balboa [1605].

Rípodas, Daisy. *El matrimonio en Indias: Realidad social y regulación jurídica.* Buenos Aires: Fundación para la Educación, la Ciencia y la Cultura, 1977.

Rodríguez Jímenez, Pablo. *Seducción, amancebamiento y abandono en la colonia.* Bogotá: Fundación Símon y Lola Guberek, 1991.

Rosenn, Keith. "Judicial Review in Latin America." *Ohio State Law Journal* 35.4 (1974): 785–819.

Rosenwein, Barbara. "Worrying about Emotions in History." *American Historical Review* 107.3 (2002): 821–45.

Ross, Richard, and Philip Stern. "Reconstructing Early Modern Notions of Legal Pluralism." In *Legal Pluralism and Empires, 1500–1850,* ed. Lauren Benton and Richard Ross, 109–41. New York: New York University Press, 2013.

Rothschild, Emma. "Isolation and Economic Life in Eighteenth-Century France." *American Historical Review* 119.4 (2014): 1055–82.

Rupert, Linda. "Seeking the Waters of Baptism: Fugitive Slaves and Imperial Jurisdiction in the Early Modern Caribbean." In *Legal Pluralism and Empires, 1500–1850,* ed. Lauren Benton and Richard Ross, 199–231. New York: New York University Press, 2013.

Saguier, Eduardo. "Church and State in Buenos Aires in the Seventeenth Century." *Journal of Church and State* 26.3 (1984): 491–514.

"The Social Impact of a Middleman Minority in a Divided Host Society: The Case of the Portuguese in Early Seventeenth-Century Buenos Aires." *Hispanic American Historical Review* 65.3 (1985): 467–91.

Sánchez, Ana. *Amancebados, hechiceros y rebeldes: Chancay, siglo XVII.* Cusco: Centro de estudios regionales Andinos, Bartolomé de las Casas, 1991.

Sánchez, Tomás. *Sancto matrimonii sacramento disputationum.* 3 vols. Lyon: Sumptibus Societatis Typographorum, 1625.

Sandoval, Alonso de. *De instauranda Aethiopum salute, el mundo de la esclavitud negra en América.* Bogotá: Empresa Nacional de Publicaciones, 1956 [1627].

Sarat, Austin, and Thomas Kearns, eds. *Law in Everyday Life.* Ann Arbor: University of Michigan Press, 1995.

Scardaville, Michael. "Justice by Paperwork: A Day in the Life of a Court Scribe in Bourbon Mexico City." *Journal of Social History* 36.4 (2003): 979–1007.

Schäfer, Ernesto. *El consejo real y supremo de las Indias: Su historia, organización y labor administrativa hasta la terminación de la Casa de Austria.* 2 vols. Castilla y León: Marcial Pons Historia, 2003.

Schafer, Judith Kelleher. "'Guaranteed against the Vices and Maladies Prescribed by Law:' Consumer Protection, the Law of Slave Sales, and the Supreme Court in Antebellum Louisiana." *American Journal of Legal History* 31.4 (1987): 306–21.

Slavery, the Civil Law, and the Supreme Court of Louisiana. Baton Rouge: Louisiana State University Press, 1994.

Schwartz, Stuart. "Cantos and Quilombos: The Hausa Rebellion in Bahia, 1814." In *Slaves, Subjects, and Subversives: Blacks in Colonial Latin America,* ed. Jane Landers and Barry Robinson, 247–72. Albuquerque: University of New Mexico Press, 2006.

"The Manumission of Slaves in Colonial Brazil: Bahia, 1684–1745." *Hispanic American Historical Review* 54.4 (1974): 603–35.

"Resistance and Accommodation in Eighteenth-Century Brazil: The Slaves' View of Slavery." *Hispanic American Historical Review* 57.1 (1977): 69–81.

Scott, Rebecca. "Paper Thin: Freedom and Re-enslavement in the Diaspora of the Haitian Revolution." *Law and History Review* 29.4 (2011): 101–87.

Scott, Rebecca, and Jean Hébrard. *Freedom Papers: An Atlantic Odyssey in the Age of Emancipation*. Cambridge, MA: Harvard University Press, 2012.

Scully, Pamela, and Diana Paton, eds. *Gender and Slave Emancipation in the Atlantic World*. Durham: Duke University Press, 2005.

Seed, Patricia. *To Love, Honor, and Obey in Colonial Mexico: Conflicts over Marriage Choice, 1574–1821*. Stanford: Stanford University Press, 1988.

Seed, Patricia, and Philip F. Rust. "Estate and Class in Colonial Oaxaca Revisited." *Comparative Studies in Society and History* 25.4 (1993): 703–10.

Sensbach, Jon. "Black Pearls: Writing Black Atlantic Women's Biography." In *Biography and the Black Atlantic*, ed. Lisa Lindsay and John Wood Sweet, 93–107. Philadelphia: University of Pennsylvania Press, 2014.

Serra Silva, Pablo. "María de Terranova: A West African Woman and the Quest for Freedom in Colonial Mexico." *Journal of Pan African Studies* 6.1 (2013): 45–62.

Sharp, William. *Slavery on the Spanish Frontier: The Colombian Chocó, 1680–1810*. Norman: University of Oklahoma Press, 1976.

Sidbury, James, and Jorge Cañizares-Esguerra. "Mapping Ethnogenesis in the Early Modern Atlantic." *William and Mary Quarterly* 68.2 (2011): 181–208.

Silverblatt, Irene. *Modern Inquisitions: Peru and the Colonial Origins of the Civilized World*. Durham: Duke University Press, 2004.

Sio, Arnold. "Interpretations of Slavery: The Slave Status in the Americas." *Comparative Studies in Society and History* 7.3 (1965): 289–308.

Smail, Daniel Lord. *The Consumption of Justice: Emotions, Publicity, and Legal Culture in Marseille, 1264–1423*. Ithaca: Cornell University Press, 2003.

Smallwood, Stephanie. *Saltwater Slavery: A Middle Passage from Africa to American Diaspora*. Cambridge, MA: Harvard University Press, 2007.

Socolow, Susan. "Acceptable Partners: Marriage Choice in Colonial Argentina, 1778–1810." In *Sexuality and Marriage in Colonial Latin America*, ed. Asunción Lavrin, 209–51. Lincoln: University of Nebraska Press, 1989.

Solórzano Pereira, Juan de. *Política indiana*. Madrid: Atlas, 1972 [1648].

Souloudre-La France, Renee. "Esclavos de su magestad." In *Slaves, Subjects and Subversives: Blacks in Colonial Latin America*, ed. Jane Landers and Barry M. Robinson, 175–208. Albuquerque: University of New Mexico Press, 2006.

"Socially Not So Dead! Slave Identities in Bourbon Nueva Granada." *Colonial Latin American Review* 10.1 (2001): 87–103.

Spalding, Karen. *Huarochirí: An Andean Society under Inca and Spanish Rule*. Stanford: Stanford University Press, 1984.

Stampp, Kenneth. *The Peculiar Institution: Slavery in the Ante-Bellum South*. New York: Vintage, 1956.

Starr, June, and Joan Collier, eds. *History and Power in the Study of Law: New Directions in Legal Anthropology*. Ithaca: Cornell University Press, 1989.

State of New Jersey. *Laws of the State of New-Jersey*. Trenton: State of New Jersey, 1821.

Steedman, Carolyn. "Intimacy in Research: Accounting for It." *History of the Human Sciences* 21.4 (2008): 17–33.

Master and Servant: Love and Labor in the English Industrial Age. Cambridge: Cambridge University Press, 2007.

Stern, Steve. *The Secret History of Gender: Women, Men, and Power in Late Colonial Mexico.* Chapel Hill: University of North Carolina Press, 1995.

Stoler, Ann. *Carnal Knowledge and Imperial Power: Race and the Intimate in Colonial Rule.* Berkeley: University of California Press, 2002.

Suardo, Juan Antonio. *Diario de Lima de Juan Antonio Suardo (1629–1639).* Vols. 1 and 2. Lima: PUCP, 1936 [1639].

Tannenbaum, Frank. *Slave and Citizen: The Negro in the Americas.* New York: Vintage, 1946.

Tardieu, Jean-Pierre. "El esclavo como valor en las Américas españolas." *Iberoamericana, Nueva época* 2.7 (2002): 59–71.

Telles, Edward. *Race in Another America: The Significance of Skin Color in Brazil.* Princeton: Princeton University Press, 2006.

Tomás y Valiente, Francisco. *La venta de oficios en Indias. 1492–1606.* Madrid: Instituto Nacional de Administración Pública, 1972.

Tomlins, Christopher. *Freedom Bound: Labor, Law, and Civic Identity in Colonizing English America, 1580–1865.* Cambridge: Cambridge University Press, 2010.

"Transplants and Timing: Passages in the Creation of an Anglo-American Law of Slavery, Histories of Legal Transplantations." *Theoretical Inquiries in Law* 10.3 (2009): 389–421.

Torres Arancivia, Eduardo. *Corte de virreyes: El entorno del poder en el Perú del siglo XVII.* Lima: PUCP, 2006.

Treggiari, Susan. *Roman Marriage.* Oxford: Clarendon Press, 1991.

Twinam, Ann. "The Church, the State, and the Abandoned: *Expósitos* in Late Eighteenth-Century Havana." In *Raising an Empire: Children in Early Modern Iberia and Colonial Latin America,* ed. Ondina Gonzalez and Bianca Premo, 163–86. Albuquerque: University of New Mexico Press, 2007.

Public Lives, Private Secrets: Gender, Honor, Sexuality, and Illegitimacy in Colonial Spanish America. Stanford: Stanford University Press, 1999.

"Purchasing Whiteness: Conversations on the Essence of Pardo-ness and Mulatto-ness at the End of Empire." In *Imperial Subjects,* 141–66.

Purchasing Whiteness: Pardos, Mulattos, and the Quest for Social Mobility in the Spanish Indies. Stanford: Stanford University Press, 2015.

Vallejo, Jesús. "Power Hierarchies in Medieval Juridical Thought: An Essay in Reinterpretation." *Ius Commune* 19 (1992): 1–29.

van Deusen, Nancy. "The 'Alienated' Body: Slaves and Castas in the Hospital de San Bartolomé in Lima, 1680–1700." *The Americas* 56.1 (1999): 1–30.

Between the Sacred and the Worldly: The Institutional and Cultural Practice of Recogimiento in Colonial Lima. Stanford: Stanford University Press, 2001.

"Determining the Boundaries of Virtue: The Discourse of Recogimiento among Women in Seventeenth-Century Lima." *Journal of Family History* 22.4 (1997): 373–89.

"The Intimacies of Bondage: Female Indigenous Servants and Slaves and their Spanish Masters." *Journal of Women's History* 24.1 (2012): 13–43.

"The Lord Walks among the Pots and Pans: Religious Servants of Colonial Lima." In *Africans to Spanish America: Expanding the Diaspora,* ed. Sherwin Bryant, Rachel O'Toole, and Ben Vinson III, 136–60. Urbana: University of Illinois Press, 2012.

The Souls of Purgatory: The Spiritual Diary of a Seventeenth-Century Afro-Peruvian Mystic, Ursula de Jesús. Albuquerque: University of New Mexico Press, 2004.

Van Kleffens, E. F. *Hispanic Law until the End of the Middle Ages.* Ann Arbor: University of Michigan Press, 1968.

Vargas Ugarte, Rubén. *Concilios limenses (1551–1772).* Vols. 1 and 2. Lima: Carolus Gómez Martinho, SJ. 1951 [1590].

Historia de la iglesia en el Perú. Vols. 1–4. Burgos: Imprenta de Aldecoa, 1963.

Historia del Perú, Virreinato siglo XVII. Buenos Aires: Librería Studium, 1954.

Vega Franco, Marisa. *El tráfico de esclavos: Asientos de Grillo y Lomelín, 1663–1674.* Seville: Escuela de Estudios Hispanoamericanos de Sevilla, 1984.

Vergara, Teresa. "Growing Up Indian: Migration, Labor, and Life in Lima (1570–1640)." In *Raising an Empire: Children in Early Modern Iberia and Colonial Latin America,* ed. Ondina Gonzalez and Bianca Premo, 75–106. Albuquerque: University of New Mexico Press, 2007.

Verlinden, Charles. *The Beginnings of Modern Colonization.* Ithaca: Cornell University Press, 1970.

Vieira Powers, Karen. *Women in the Crucible of Conquest: The Gendered Genesis of Spanish American Society, 1500–1600.* Albuquerque: University of New Mexico Press, 2005.

Vila Vilar, Enriqueta. "Los asientos Portugueses y el contrabando de negros." *Anuario de estudios americanos* 30 (Jan. 1973): 557–609.

Hispanoamérica y el comercio de esclavos. Seville: Publicaciones de la Escuela de estudios Hispano-Americanos de Sevilla, 1977.

Villegas, Juan, SJ. *Aplicación del concilio de Trento en Hispanoamérica, 1564–1600, provincia eclesiástica del Perú.* Montevideo: Instituto Teológico del Uruguay, 1972.

Von Germeten, Nicole. *Violent Delights, Violent Ends: Sex, Race, and Honor in Colonial Cartagena de Indias.* Albuquerque: University of New Mexico Press, 2013.

Walker, Tamara. "'He Outfitted His Family in Notable Decency': Slavery, Honour, and Dress in Eighteenth-Century Lima, Peru." *Slavery and Abolition: A Journal of Slave and Post-Slave Societies* 30.3 (2009): 383–402.

Watson, Alan. *Legal Transplants: An Approach to Comparative Law.* Edinburgh: Scottish Academic Press, 1974.

Slave Law in the Americas. Athens: University of Georgia Press, 1989.

Welch, Pedro. *Slave Society in the City: Bridgetown, Barbados, 1680–1834.* Oxford: James Carrey, 2003.

Wertheimer, John. "Gloria's Story: Adulterous Concubinage and the Law in Twentieth-Century Guatemala." *Law and History Review* 24.2 (2006): 375–421.

Wheat, David. "The First Great Waves: African Provenance Zones for the Transatlantic Slave Trade to Cartagena de Indias, 1570–1640." *Journal of African History* 52.1 (2011): 1–22.

Wickham, Chris. "Gossip and Resistance among the Medieval Peasantry." *Past and Present* 160 (Aug. 1998): 3–24.

Williams, Patrick. *The Great Favourite: The Duke of Lerma and the Court and Government of Philip III of Spain, 1598–1621.* Manchester, UK: University of Manchester Press, 2006.

Wisnoski, Alexander. "'It Is Unjust for the Law of Marriage to Be Broken by the Law of Slavery': Married Slaves and Their Masters in Early Colonial Lima." *Slavery and Abolition: A Journal of Slave and Post-Slave Societies* 35.2 (2014): 234–52.

Wong, Edlie. *Neither Fugitive nor Free: Atlantic Slavery, Freedom Suits, and the Legal Culture of Travel.* New York: New York University Press, 2009.

Yamin, Priscilla. *American Marriage: A Political Institution.* Philadelphia: University of Pennsylvania Press, 2012.

Yannakakis, Yanna. "Indigenous People and Legal Culture in Spanish America." *History Compass* 11.11 (2013): 931–47.

Zavala, Silvio. *Las instituciones jurídicas en la conquista de América.* 3rd edn. Mexico City: Editorial Porrúa, 1988.

Index